The Fragmentation of Being

The Fragmentation of Being

Kris McDaniel

OXFORD
UNIVERSITY PRESS

OXFORD
UNIVERSITY PRESS

Great Clarendon Street, Oxford, OX2 6DP,
United Kingdom

Oxford University Press is a department of the University of Oxford.
It furthers the University's objective of excellence in research, scholarship,
and education by publishing worldwide. Oxford is a registered trade mark of
Oxford University Press in the UK and in certain other countries

First Edition published in 2017

Impression: 2

Published in the United States of America by Oxford University Press
198 Madison Avenue, New York, NY 10016, United States of America

British Library Cataloguing in Publication Data
Data available

Library of Congress Control Number: 2017935791

ISBN 978-0-19-871965-6

Printed and bound by
CPI Group (UK) Ltd, Croydon, CR0 4YY

Dedicated to Leneah, Nina, Ranger, and Safira

Contents

Acknowledgments

I have been working on the issues discussed in this book for over a decade, and as a consequence I have many, many people to thank for their helpful comments and incisive criticisms, each of which has helped me in ways that are difficult to enumerate. Philosophy is never conducted in a vacuum. I know that I have been fortunate to benefit from the advice of so many people, and I am grateful for that.

The seeds of this project began in 2002, when Gary Matthews led a reading group on Heidegger's *Being and Time*. I was a graduate student at UMass Amherst at the time; it was an excellent place for both contemporary metaphysics and the history of philosophy but not a place where Heidegger's texts could find much sympathy. But Gary had an expansive view of philosophy, and he thought that it was an important text, and that we would benefit from our exposure to it. I don't remember who all participated in the group. Jason Raibley, Marcy Lascano, Jack Hanson, myself, and maybe a few others. (My first copy of *Being and Time* was given to me by Jason and Marcy, with the inscription, "In hopes that your future inquiries into Being will be truly ontological.") In order to make headway on the text, I wrote down about thirty questions that I would ask Heidegger to answer, and discussed them with Gary. What a gentle, patient, and wise man Gary was. He is still sorely missed.

In the spring of 2006, I was tasked with teaching early twentieth-century philosophy to a group of graduate and undergraduate students at Syracuse University. With Gary's example in mind, I decided to cover as many different figures as I could cram in the semester and to use only primary texts, including selections from *Being and Time*. Most of the undergraduates dropped the class quickly. But the graduate students were great! One of the pedagogical issues I faced was how to make Heidegger's question of the meaning of being feel like a genuine issue to a class of analytic philosophers. My mostly successful attempt spurred me to write up several of the disconnected notes I had amassed on Heidegger into something presentable. By the summer of 2006, I produced a manuscript consisting of about 40,000 words on the metaphysics of *Being and Time*. A significant portion of this manuscript was a version of chapter 1 of this book. (Two other chunks of this manuscript have since been published as independent articles. I hope to return to this project sometime in the future.) Thankfully, I was able to talk about my Heidegger manuscript with Gary. Later, Jonathan Schaffer provided me with detailed written feedback and encouragement. I also benefited from discussions of the Heidegger manuscript with Jason Turner and Ted Sider.

There have been many times when I feared I would never finish *this* manuscript. (As I type these very words, I have this fear!) Joshua Spencer provided much needed moral support, as well as amazingly detailed comments on drafts of every single chapter. Thank you, Joshua. Peter Finocchiaro and Byron Simmons also gave me excellent comments on each chapter. Thank you, Peter. Thank you, Byron.

I received excellent feedback from the anonymous referees at Oxford University Press. I've refereed books myself. I know it can be a lot of work, and there is very little professional reward for doing it. The main reward is the knowledge that you have helped improve someone's work and hopefully have his or her gratitude as a consequence. You did, and you do. I don't know who you were, but thank you!

Thank you Mark Barber, Elizabeth Barnes, Donald Baxter, Karen Bennett, William Blattner, Ricki Bliss, Philipp Blum, Ben Bradley, Jeff Brower, Ross Cameron, Ben Caplan, Taylor Carman, Paek Chae-Young, David Chalmers, Heeyoon Choi, Phil Corkum, Sam Cowling, Andy Cullison, Shamik Dasgupta, Louis deRosset, Imogen Dickie, Jordan Dodd, Matti Eklund, Neil Feit, Kit Fine, Daniel Fogal, André Gallois, Tyron Goldschmidt, Sungil Han, James Harrington, John Hawthorne, Mark Heller, Benj Hellie, Thomas Hofweber, Hud Hudson, Kim Jeong Hyeon, Jennan Ismael, Mark Johnston, Li Kang, William Killborn, Hyosung Kim, Jiwon Kim, Sol Kim, Yewon Kim, Kathrin Koslicki, Marcy Lascano, Chan-Woo Lee, James Lee, Sarah-Jane Leslie, Sam Levey, Michaela McSweeney, Ofra Magidor, Trenton Merricks, Kevin Mulligan, Bence Nanay, Alyssa Ney, Daniel Nolan, Josh Parsons, Robert Pasnau, Laurie Paul, Nikolaj Jang Lee Linding Pedersen, David Plunkett, Graham Priest, Jason Raibley, Gurpreet Rattan, Mike Rea, Gabriela Reason, Roth Reason, Kara Richardson, Gideon Rosen, Raul Saucedo, Jonathan Schaffer, Joshua Schechter, Eric Schliesser, Jisoo Seo, Ted Sider, Peters Simons, Alex Skiles, Brad Skow, Olla Solomyak, Roy Sorensen, Nick Stang, Steve Steward, Meghan Sullivan, Amie Thomasson, Kelly Trogdon, Jason Turner, William Vallicella, Christina van Dyke, Peter van Inwagen, Ryan Wasserman, Robert Williams, Jessica Wilson, Jeremy Wyatt, Takashi Yagisawa, and Dean Zimmerman. My apologies to anyone I have forgotten.

Almost all of the chapters were presented in various conferences, talks, and workshops. Philosophy is a collaborative enterprise and the opportunity to present my work and receive valuable feedback from this wide variety of audiences helped me immensely. I am very grateful to have had these opportunities, and I thank once again the various venues that invited me to present my work. Earlier versions of chapter 1 were presented at the University of Leeds conference on Structure in Metaphysics (2007), the Inland Northwest Philosophy Conference (2007), and at the University of Rochester. Earlier versions of chapter 2 were presented at the Inland Northwest Philosophy Conference (2008) and Williams College. Earlier versions of chapter 3 were presented at the University of Toronto, the Central Division of the APA (2008), the Arizona Ontology Conference (2009), Metaphysical Mayhem (2010), and at the University of Iowa at Ames. Earlier versions of chapter 4 were presented at Duke University, the Princeton Conference on Philosophical Logic (2009), LOGOS Conference on Fundamentality

(2010), and The Relationship Between Metaphysics and Logic Conference at the University of Southern California (2015). Earlier versions of chapter 6 were presented at a conference on Persistence at the University of Southern California (2012), the University of Kentucky-Lexington, Johns Hopkins University, the University of Ottawa, Boston University, the University of Alberta, a conference titled "Themes from Baxter II" at Ligerz, Switzerland (2013), and at the University of Iowa at Ames. Earlier versions of chapter 7 were presented at SUNY-Fredonia, the Mellon Metaphysics Workshop at Cornell University (2009), Metaphysical Mayhem (2010), the Australian National University Conference on Fundamentality (2010), the University of Birmingham, the University of Nottingham, and NYU. Earlier versions of chapter 9 were presented at the Pacific Division of the American Philosophical Association (2014), the University of Vermont, Conference on Intensional/Hyper-Intensional Metaphysics at the National Autonomous University of Mexico (2014), Georgetown Conference on the Philosophy of Religion (2014), Brown University, Eidos Conference on Existence, Non-Existence, and Intentionality at the University of Geneva, Switzerland (2015), Hamburg University, MIT, and Kyoto University.

After a full version of the manuscript was completed and refereed, I gave five lectures based on it at the Seoul National University at the invitation of the Pluralisms Global Research Network organized by Nikolaj Jang Lee Linding Pedersen and Sungil Han. I was also invited by Timothy O'Connor to the University of Indiana at Bloomington to discuss the entire manuscript over several days with him and his metaphysics graduate students, Dave Fisher, Hao Hong, Tim Leisz, Nick Montgomery, and Tim Perrine. Their helpful comments improved the manuscript before it was sent off in its final version.

Material from the following articles has been incorporated into this book:

2009. "Ways of Being" originally appeared in David Chalmers, David Manley, and Ryan Wasserman (eds.), *Metametaphysics: New Essays on the Foundations of Ontology*, Oxford University Press.

2010. "A Return to the Analogy of Being," *Philosophy and Phenomenological Research* 81.3: 688–717.

2010. "Being and Almost Nothingness," *Noûs* 44.4: 628–49.

2013. "Degrees of Being," *Philosophers' Imprint* 13.19: 1–19.

2013. "Pasnau on Category Realism: Author Meets Critics, Robert Pasnau, *Metaphysical Themes 1274–1671*," *Philosophical Studies* 171.1: 17–25.

I thank the respective publishers for permission to use this material, and for publishing these articles in the first place. Let me also thank again the anonymous referees of the original articles for their feedback.

I gratefully acknowledge the two non-concurrent semesters of research leave granted by Syracuse University to work on this book manuscript as well as other projects.

Peter Momtchiloff was an ideal editor, and helped steer this project to completion. Thank you, Peter. Neil Morris helped edit the book, and made many valuable suggestions. Thank you, Neil. Byron Simmons also helped edit the book and prepared the index. Thank you again, Byron.

Finally, let me thank Nina Stoeckel. It's very hard to find the words that aptly express the gratitude I feel for you. Thank you for all that you do and are.

Introduction

One of the oldest questions in metaphysics concerns not the various natures of beings but rather the nature of being itself: is being *unitary* or does being *fragment*? The primary aims of this book are to explicate the idea that being fragments, to show how the fragmentation of being impacts various other extant philosophical disputes, and to defend the tenability and fruitfulness of the idea that being fragments.

These aims are interdependent. An inexplicable idea is neither tenable nor fruitful. And an idea is fruitful only if it sheds light on extant disputes or provides new paths for interesting research. If the claim that being fragments has no philosophical payoff elsewhere, one must forgive those who neglect or dismiss the question of the fragmentation of being. My hope is that I will convince you of the importance of the claim that being fragments by extensively exploring the connections between the various ways being might fragment and philosophical issues pertaining to metaphysical fundamentality, substances and accidents, time, modality, ontological categories, absences and presences, persons, value, ground, and essence. This book is devoted to these explorations.

The question of whether being is unitary or fragments is a complex question whose answer turns on the answers to (at least) the following questions. There are many kinds of beings—stones, persons, artifacts, and perhaps numbers, abstract propositions, and maybe even God—*but are there also many kinds of being*? For anything such that there is such a thing, *does that thing also exist*? The world contains a variety of objects, each of which, let us provisionally assume, exists—*but do some objects exist in different ways*? Some objects, let us assume, exist as a matter of necessity while others exist merely contingently; some objects are atemporal whereas others are bound by time (and space); some (but perhaps not all) objects are modally dependent on others, where an object *x* is modally dependent on another object *y* just in case, necessarily, *x* exists only if *y* exists. But do some objects *enjoy more being or existence than other objects*? Are there different ways in which one object might enjoy more being than another?

If being is unitary rather than fragmentary, then there is only one way to be; there are no modes of being. If being is unitary rather than fragmentary, then being is coextensive, and in fact identical with existence, for if being and existence were not one, existence would be a way of being. If being is unitary rather than fragmentary, then everything that there is *is to the same extent or degree*.

In contemporary analytic metaphysics, the by far dominant view is that being is unitary. But in the philosophical tradition that stems from Plato—the tradition of so-called "Western" philosophy—there have been few, if any, proponents of the view that being is unitary. As we will see later, even by my lights the paradigmatic medieval champion of the "univocity" of being, Duns Scotus, endorsed some fragmentation of being by virtue of holding that some things enjoy more being than others; being, on his view, at least embraces an "analogy of inequality," to use the medieval terminology. Things bear an analogy of inequality with respect to an attribute, roughly, just in case one thing enjoys more of that common attribute than another thing, or one thing is a more perfect instance of that attribute than another. Although *being is univocal,* on Scotus's view, *being still comes in degrees,* and so different entities can stand in an analogy of inequality with respect to being.[1]

The view that existence comes in many flavors is suggested by the Aristotelian slogan "being is said in many ways," and according to some interpretations is Aristotle's view.[2] Variants of this slogan were championed by various medieval philosophers, such as Aquinas, who worried that God cannot be said to exist in the same sense (or in the same way) as created things.[3] In the early modern period, we find Descartes alluding to the medievals' worry, but extensive discussion of the problem of being disappeared from the central stage by the time of the modern period.[4] However, although the view itself receded into the background, it never really disappeared. In the later philosophy of Leibniz, we find a distinction between well-founded phenomena, which enjoy some sort of attenuated existence, and the monads, which enjoy a genuine or absolute kind of reality.[5] In Kant's critical philosophy, he famously distinguishes between two kinds of reality, empirical reality and transcendental reality.[6] In the late nineteenth century, we find Lotze (1884: 438–40) distinguishing between several different kinds of being: among them are

---

[1]   See Hochschild (2010: ch. 6) for a discussion of the analogy of inequality, and especially pp. 101–3 for a discussion of Scotus.

[2]   For a defense of the claim that Aristotle believed that there are ways of existence, see M. Frede (1987: 84–6). Barnes (1995b) and the first two chapters of Witt (1989) provide a good introduction to Aristotle and the question of the meaning of "being." Brentano discusses Aristotle's views extensively in Brentano (1981a); for a much shorter and somewhat different treatment, see Brentano (1978: 20–2). For criticism of Aristotle on ways of being, see Shields (1999: 236–40).

[3]   Aquinas claims that "being is said in many ways" in many places; see, for example, Aquinas (1993: 92–3) and Aquinas (1961: 216–20). See also Ashworth (2013a) and Cross (1999: 31–9) for a clear and accessible account of medieval theories concerning kinds of existence and senses of "being." I take Aquinas to be an ontological pluralist in my sense. For a defense of the claim that Aquinas believes in ways of being, see McCabe (1969: 90–1) and, more recently, Brower (2014).

[4]   See, for example, Descartes' 51st principle in the *Principles of Philosophy* (1992: 210).

[5]   There are many places in which Leibniz downgrades the ontological status of well-founded phenomena by saying that they are not "real things"; see, e.g., Leibniz (1989: 181, 185 fn. 239). Further, in this period, Leibniz (1989: 189) holds that, "speaking with metaphysical rigor . . . at bottom there should only be these intelligible substances, and that sensible things should only be appearances. However, our lack of attention lets us take sensible things for the only true things."

[6]   This distinction is appealed to in many places in Kant, but see (1999a: 425–31/A367–80) for a particularly intriguing occasion. We'll revisit this distinction in section 6.2.

that which belongs to things, that which belongs to events, and that which belongs to ideal laws. And even in the early twentieth century, we find many friends of ways of being, including such important figures as Alexius Meinong (1983: 49–62), G.E. Moore (1993: 161–3), Bertrand Russell (1997: 91–100), L. Susan Stebbing (1917), Edmund Husserl (2005a: 249–50; 2005b: 17), Edith Stein (2002, 2009), and Martin Heidegger (1962). Recall that it was common in the days before Quine for philosophers to distinguish between the way in which an abstract object is—it *subsists*—and the way in which a concrete object is—it *exists*. We find variants of this distinction in the early works of Moore, Russell, Stebbing, Meinong, and Husserl.[7]

The ideas we are considering and the terminology I used earlier to convey them could use some clearing up. And it would be nice if the various ways in which being might fragment could be systematically accounted for. Both of these jobs are important preparatory tasks for the more important projects of determining whether being does in fact fragment, and if it does fragment, determining how it fragments. For this reason, chapter 1 is devoted to explicating the idea that there are modes of being, and to developing a catalogue of ways in which being might fragment.

There is only one way for being to be unitary, but being might fragment in many different ways, some of which are more extreme than others. One of the milder ways in which being might fragment is one in which, although there are different modes of being enjoyed by different objects, there is a maximally general mode of being that everything enjoys as well. A red sphere and a blue sphere enjoy different ways of being colored but they still share a common property, the determinable of being colored. Similarly, the various ways of being might be something like determinates of a common determinable, being itself.

There are other interesting relations between what can be called in a broad sense "features" besides the relation that determinates bear to determinables. Perhaps the various modes of being are related to an overarching mode of being by being *species* of that overarching mode, which in turn we construe as a *genus*. On this view, the overarching mode of being is a universal genus, and the particular modes of being are derived by conjoining that genus with various differentiating characteristics. It is this sort of view that Aristotle rejects by claiming that being is not a genus.[8] But it is also in the spirit of the Aristotelian position to reject the claim that there is a common determinable, being, of which the other modes are determinates.

A more radical way in which being might fragment is one in which there is no most general mode of being, and so the way in which the number two exists and the way in which a stone exists are not unified by an overarching determinable or genus and instead are, at most, unified by some more tenuous relation. This is a historically popular view: the various ways of being are related only *analogically*. In chapter 2, I provide a contemporary spin on the old idea that being is unified only analogically.

---

[7] See also Marvin (1912: 106–8), Moore (1927: 102–5), and Ryle (1971: 16–22).
[8] Aristotle says this in many places, such as *Metaphysics* III.3, 998b21 (Aristotle 1984b: 1577).

There I explicate the more general idea of a feature's being analogous and then apply this account to the case of being.

Red flags might have been raised when I compared being with attributes or properties such as color. This comparison suggests that being, and the various modes of being, are themselves properties, but there are reasons to be cautious about suggesting such things. First, there might not be any properties, but we might still want to distinguish between different ways things might exist. Relatedly, we might not want to think of being as being itself a being, and similarly for modes of being, even if in general we believe that properties are entities. Moreover, even if we are comfortable with believing in properties, we might worry that we shouldn't think of being or existence as properties of things such as stones or numbers. For example, we might be attracted to a view often attributed to Frege and Russell, and sometimes even Kant, according to which, if being or existence are features, they are features of "higher-order" entities.[9] On this view, it is not Sam the Stone that has the property of existence, but rather the property of being Sam the Stone, or the concept of Sam the Stone, or some such. We'll revisit these worries in more depth in chapters 1 and 2, as well as in chapter 4.

For the sake of brevity, call the view that there are ways of being *ontological pluralism*.[10] The bulk of the first half of this book consists in the exploration of various arguments for ontological pluralism.

But in addition to considering whether there are distinct modes of being, we'll also explore whether being comes in amounts or degrees. Are some things greater in being than others? As I hope will be apparent later in the book, three different conceptions of ontological superiority should be carefully distinguished. But these three conceptions are not necessarily competitors. Rather, in my view, they simply have different fields of application.

Consider the following putative pairs of entities, each of which contains an element ontologically superior to its complement: a substance and one of its modes, an existing object and a Meinongian object that fails to exist or subsist, and a donut and the hole in the donut. In each case, the *kind* of ontological superiority is different. Clarifying these different kinds of ontological superiority goes hand and hand with regimenting the terminology used to label them. To anticipate later chapters, substances enjoy a *better order* of being than modes, existing objects enjoy a *higher level* of being than non-existent objects, and presences enjoy a *greater degree* of being than absences. There are actually two tasks here: to clarify and

---

[9] See Frege (1980a: 64–5; 1980b: 38) and Russell (1968: 232–3) for representative articulations of the view. See McDaniel (2013a) for critical discussion of one of the main arguments for this view. Bennett (1974: 62–3) attributes this to Kant; the text in Kant that inspires this interpretation is Kant (1999a: 567, A599/B627). Remarks in Heidegger (1988: 41, 55) suggest that he also attributes this view to Kant.

[10] When I first began my examinations of the doctrine that there are modes of being, I did not use "ontological pluralism" as its name. Sadly, I gave it no name. Jason Turner (2010) later suggested this name for the doctrine I defended. Since the name is both apt and evocative, I have since adopted it.

distinguish these distinctive kinds of ontological superiority, but also to show why they are properly thought of as distinctively *ontological* kinds of superiority. Orders of being are discussed in chapter 2; levels of being are discussed in chapter 3; and chapters 5 and 7 focus on degrees of being. For now, we'll focus on ontological pluralism.

Broadly speaking, there have been (at least) three dominant historical motivations for ontological pluralism. We can call these motivations the *theological, phenomenological,* and *logical* motivations.

The theological motivation for ontological pluralism stems from many considerations about the nature of God, but we'll focus here on two of the more prominent ones. First, there is the consideration that God is so radically different from any created thing that no literal ascription of a feature could be true of them both.[11] But some literal ascriptions must be true of both God and finite creatures: it is obvious that "is a God or is a finite creature" truly and literally applies to both God and finite creatures. Similarly, it is obviously true that "is not a convection oven" is literally true of both God and myself. So the claim that no literal ascription of a feature could be true of both a created being and the divine being must not be taken in complete generality. Rather, there is some special subset of ascriptions of features that cannot be literally and truly applied to both God and created beings.

What is this special subset of features? It appears to consist of those features that are neither mere disjunctions nor mere negations of other features. The concepts of a merely disjunctive feature and a merely negative feature are in need of clarification, but I assume that we have enough of a grasp of them to provisionally proceed. An example of a merely disjunctive feature is *being an electron or being a donkey.* Let's provisionally call such features that are neither mere disjunctions nor mere negations of other features *fundamental* features.

Instead of saying that no literal ascription of any feature to both God and finite beings is true, a better way of formulating the doctrine that God is radically other than His creatures is that there is no literal predication of a fundamental feature which is true of both God and finite creatures; God and His creatures have no fundamental properties in common.[12] Merely disjunctive or negative predicates can be truthfully predicated of both, but these predicates never designate fundamental features, and so in some sense do not ascribe *features* to God and creatures. It follows from the assumption that "is an existent" is predicated both of God and creaturely things, that "is an existent" is not a predicate whose sole semantic value is fundamental. Perhaps it stands for a non-fundamental feature; or perhaps it is ambiguous, and it stands for two different fundamental features. But either way,

---

[11] See, for example, Aquinas's *Summa Theologica* I, q. 13, article 5 (Aquinas 1948: 63–4).
[12] I suggested this way of understanding one kind of "negative theology" in McDaniel (2010a). A similar view has since been developed by Jacobs 2015. See also Davies (2006a: 141–2).

the way in which God exists and the way in which creatures exist are metaphysically more fundamental than existence simpliciter.

A related theological worry stems from the doctrine of divine simplicity.[13] The classical doctrine of divine simplicity encompasses more than the claim that God is without proper parts. Rather, on the classical doctrine of divine simplicity, there are no metaphysical distinctions to be found in God. And so there is no distinction to be drawn between God and his attributes. If God is absolutely simple, then there is no real distinction between God's essence and God's existence, i.e., the way in which God exists. Both God's essence and God's existence are numerically identical with God himself. But in creaturely things there is a real distinction between essence and existence. Moreover, although creaturely things instantiate existence, they do not instantiate God. So the existence instantiated by creaturely things cannot be identical with the existence that is numerically identical with God. So the way in which creaturely things exist must be different than the way in which God exists.[14]

A second historical motivation for ontological pluralism is *phenomenological*. On an interpretation I favor, Heidegger claimed that different ways of being are *given to us* in experience. Heidegger embraced the Husserlian doctrine that the job of phenomenology is to describe what is given as it is given. The phenomenologist holds that more is given in experience than objects having various "sensory" qualities such as redness, hardness, or shape. In addition, *essences* are given, and can be consciously attended to. For example, in Husserl's *Logical Investigations*, it is suggested that the necessary connections between having a color and having a shape, and having an audible pitch and having an audible volume, can be given in experience.[15] Husserl also held that we have intuitions of the "categorial" aspects of states of affairs. For example, the state of affairs in which *everything in the room is red* might be given, along with the quantificational aspect of this state of affairs, its *allness*, as it were.[16] As I understand the Husserl of the *Logical Investigations*, various logical concepts, such as the concept of *something, conjunction*, or *negation*, arise from these original experiences of aspects of states of affairs. As originally conceived by Husserl, the job of the phenomenology of logic is to show which original experiences of states of affairs give rise to the various logical concepts.

Heidegger seems to agree with Husserl that aspects of various states of affairs are given, but he holds that among those aspects that are given are the *specific ways of*

[13] See Klima (2013: 157).

[14] See, for example, Aquinas's *Summa Theologica* I, q. 3 (Aquinas 1948: 14–19). See Stump (1999) for a brief overview and Hughes (1989) for extensive discussion. Michael Rea has pointed out to me that a contemporary way of formulating the doctrine of divine simplicity is as the conjunction of the claims that (i) some kind of nominalism is true and (ii) the truth-maker for predications of God is always God. On this contemporary view, the doctrine of divine simplicity might not motivate ontological pluralism. For further discussion of divine simplicity, see Brower (2008, 2009, 2014: 190–6).

[15] See, for example, Husserl (2005a: 175–6).

[16] See the discussion of categorial intuition in Husserl's sixth logical investigation; this appears in volume II of the *Logical Investigations* (Husserl 2005b).

being. Among the ways of being that are given are *Existenz* (the kind of being enjoyed by creatures like ourselves), readiness-to-hand (the kind of being enjoyed by equipment), presentness-at-hand (the kind of being enjoyed by bits of matter), and subsistence (the kind of being enjoyed by abstract objects).[17] Somehow from these original experiences of these modes of being we have constructed the general concept of being that applies to everything there is regardless of its mode of being.[18] It is hard to see how this construction was created and therein stems the motivation for the fundamental ontological project of *Being and Time*. We'll return to Heidegger's ontological investigations in chapter 1.

In a similar vein, Meinong held that the distinction between *subsistence* and *existence* is given and apprehended immediately.[19] On this view, modes of being are *presented to us*; those who cannot see the distinction between subsistence and existence suffer from a kind of blindness. A proper phenomenological description of our experience will encode information about the modes of being of those entities presented to us. If you don't notice that there are modes of being, you need to more carefully attend to what is given. Back to the things themselves, and to how those things themselves are!

Finally, some historically prominent champions of ontological pluralism have had what can be broadly construed as *logical* motivations for the doctrine as well. Consider, for example, Aristotle's argument that being is not a genus, which turns on complicated logical and metaphysical issues.[20] According to Aristotle, species of the same genera are differentiated from the genera and one another by characteristic features appropriately named "differentiating characteristics". For example, the species human is of the genus animal with the differentiating characteristic being rationality. Also according to Aristotle, a differentiating characteristic cannot fall under the genera that it differentiates. It follows from these two claims that being cannot be a genus. For, if it were a genus, it would be differentiated from its species by some characteristic. But this characteristic would itself be a being, and hence would fall under the genus that it differentiates.

Why did Aristotle accept that no differentiating characteristic can fall under the genus that it differentiates? W.D. Ross's (1924: 235–7) diagnosis is that, if genera can be predicated of their differentiating characteristics, then we could predicate *animal* of rationality. (Recall that the species of humanity is defined via the genus of animal and the differentiating characteristic of rationality.) But it makes no sense to say that rationality is an animal. Agreed. But what this shows us is merely that we cannot always predicate a genus of a differentiating characteristic, not that we never can. Aquinas, who seems (in some places) to endorse Aristotle's argument, suggests

---

[17] See Heidegger's *Being and Time* (1962: 67, 97–8, 121, 258–9, 285, and 382).
[18] I thank Peter Simons for helpful comments here.
[19] See Meinong (1983: 58) and Findlay (1933: 74) for discussion.
[20] See Aristotle's *Metaphysics* III.3, 998b21 (Aristotle 1984b: 1577).

the following line of reasoning, which is both different from Ross's and by my lights somewhat more compelling.[21] What defines the species in question are the differentiating characteristic and the genus. In turn, what defines the differentiating characteristic is whatever kinds it falls under as well as whatever features distinguish those kinds from others in their genus. If the differentiating characteristic were to fall under the genus *being*, then *being* would enter into the definition of the species of the genus *being* twice: once by virtue of it being the genus that the species falls under, and a second time by virtue of being part of what defines the differentiating characteristic that is itself part of the definition of the species. But things can't enter the same definition twice over in this way.

These motivations potentially connect in interesting ways. For example, Aquinas endorses Aristotle's argument that being is not a genus, and uses that argument as the basis for the claim that God falls under no genus. And the claim that God falls under no genus is relevant to the question of whether there is any composition in God.[22] If there is no composition in God, then God is maximally simple—and hence we have a route to a theological motivation for ontological pluralism that is partially driven by logical motivations.

The theological, phenomenological, and logical motivations for ontological pluralism are interesting and worthy of study. But none of these motivations fully explain my attraction to ontological pluralism. My motivations are secular rather than theological, more theoretical than phenomenological, and metaphysical rather than logical (unless logic is conceived very broadly indeed). Ontological pluralism promises to be a fruitful doctrine, potentially solving or at least ameliorating various puzzles and problems that concern material objects, time, actuality and possibility, the nature of ontological categories, ontological dependence and necessary connections more generally, the status of "negative entities" such as holes and shadows, grounding, and essence.

I am interested in whether the fragmentation of being makes being a metaphysician a little bit easier. It might be that some kinds of ontological pluralism do while others do not, and for this reason I consider many versions of ontological pluralism in the pages to come. I do not determine the final, best version of ontological pluralism in the pages that follow; I fear that this task was too large for a single book, or at least it proved to be too large for me to accomplish in a single book. The reader should therefore be prepared for some unresolved tensions between the theories that will be explored. My view is that we must approach metaphysics with great humility. The questions are large and the considerations that might favor

---

[21] Aquinas, *Summa Contra Gentiles*, book 1, chapter 25, section 6 (Aquinas 1991: 127). For further commentary, see Alexander of Aphrodisias (1992: 142–6). See Aristotle's *Topics* VI.6, 144a27–b11 (Aristotle 1984a: 243) for Aristotle's account of why, in general, differentiating characteristics can't fall under the genera they differentiate.

[22] Aquinas, *Summa Contra Gentiles*, book 1, chapter 25, section 6 (Aquinas 1991: 127).

answers to them are highly complex. I have done my best to show this, at least with respect to the question of whether being fragments.

Here is the plan for the rest of the book. In chapter 1, I carefully explicate ontological pluralism, the doctrine that there are ways of being. In this chapter, I aim to get clearer on what one is committed to when one believes in modes of being instead of presenting my preferred metaphysical system. It is hard to assess this question in the abstract, so I begin with a lengthy discussion of a particular philosopher's system, namely Heidegger's (around the time of *Being and Time*). In chapter 2, I address some popular arguments against ontological pluralism, as well as discuss some plausible versions of ontological pluralism. In chapter 3, I turn to the philosophy of time. In this chapter, I explore a version of ontological pluralism according to which present entities (such as you and I) and past entities (such as Abe Lincoln and dinosaurs) enjoy different ways of existing. Levels of being are discussed in chapter 3, in the context of exploring in what ways present existence might be ontologically superior to past existence. The phenomenological motivation for a kind of ontological pluralism is discussed as well. In chapter 4, I address the questions of whether and in what ways the notion of a way of being connects up with the notion of an ontological category. In chapter 5, the status of various "absences," such as holes, cracks, and shadows is investigated. There, the notion of a degree of being is explored, and a distinction is drawn between existing to the fullest extent and existing in a merely degenerate way. In chapter 6, the question of whether persons exist to the fullest extent is investigated. In chapter 7, the notion of a degree of existence, which played a prominent role in the previous two chapters, receives an in-depth examination of its own. There it is argued that the notion of a degree of being is a crucial metaphysical notion, one that metaphysicians ought to employ in their theorizing, but also one that might already be employed in contemporary metaphysical debates, albeit under a different guise. I'll also investigate whether degrees of being can be used to characterize modes of being, orders of being, and levels of being. In chapter 8, I explore whether we can understand some notion of grounding in terms of some ontological notion, such as degree of being. Finally, in chapter 9, I assay the connections between being, essence, and ground.

Although the question of whether being is unitary or fragmentary is an ancient question, and a very important one in the history of philosophy, this is a book whose genre, if I may use that term, is contemporary analytic metaphysics. So permit me a brief digression about the role that the history of philosophy plays in what follows. My primary interest is in discovering the ways in which ontological pluralism has ramifications for metaphysical issues that I find fascinating, rather than tracing out the ramifications the doctrine was taken to have for various issues of importance to historical figures long dead. However, in the course of this book, the views and arguments of various long-dead historical figures will be critically discussed, and the fact that the focus of this book is on contemporary issues should not serve as an excuse for misrepresenting their views and arguments. Moreover, insofar as the intuitions of various thinkers long dead are cited as evidence in favor of various positions defended in this book, it is of paramount importance that those intuitions are accurately represented.

That said, I am not an expert in the history of philosophy and won't pretend to be one. I've tried to do the best I can do given my background, training, and philosophical abilities. I read my philosophical predecessors sympathetically, with a view towards finding points of contact between their concerns and my own. But although I have found the history of philosophy to be a source of inspiration, I have tried to acknowledge that inspiration without engaging in undue anachronistic ascriptions.[23] And I have, when possible, consulted some of the (enormously large) relevant secondary literature on the figures cited, as well as discussed my interpretations with living authorities on these figures. I hope this book will provide an illustration of the possibility of a productive engagement of both contemporary concerns and the history of metaphysics.[24]

Similar remarks apply to the infrequent discussions of figures from Eastern philosophy in the pages that follow. The questions I address here were addressed not only in the history of Western philosophy, but were pressing in the history of Eastern philosophy as well.[25] To me, this became most apparent when thinking through the issues in chapters 5 and 6. But the discussion of figures from the history of Western philosophy occupies more of the book than that of their counterparts in the history of Eastern philosophy, largely because I don't know enough about those traditions to do more. I hope in future research to rectify this. In general, we do ourselves as philosophers and philosophy itself a disservice by continuing to dichotomize philosophy in this way. But I can do now only what I can do now, and this book is long enough as it is.

Finally, let me say one last bit about methodology. Like most philosophers, I am puzzled and troubled by the question of what method or methods we ought to pursue in order to acquire knowledge of the answers to philosophical questions. But I am relatively confident of one thing: insofar as we take intuitions (whatever these might turn out to be) to be evidence for our theories, we ought to take into account as many

---

[23] Sleigh (1990: 2–4) distinguishes two ways of doing history of philosophy: exegetical history of philosophy and philosophical history of philosophy. Exegetical history focuses on what a philosophical text actually means, and why the philosopher actually said what he or she said. There are two ways of doing philosophical history of philosophy. The first way is to set out a philosophical theory inspired by some historical doctrine and then correct it insofar as it is deemed to be in error; the second way is to treat the historical figure as someone akin to a colleague to converse with. I suppose that insofar as I am doing history of philosophy in this book, I am doing philosophical history of philosophy—but I am doing so only in the hope that the historical claims made could stand up to scrutiny from an exegetical historian of philosophy.

[24] See Nolan (2007) for interesting reflections on the usefulness of the history of philosophy for contemporary theorizing.

[25] See Mou (2013) for an interesting comparison of Quine, Heidegger, and Lao-Zhuang Zi (among many others!) on whether being fragments. For another example of an interesting parallel, Potter (1977: 134–5) claims that, according to the Nyāya-Vaiscśika philosophy, being is a genus.

intuitions relevant to the issue at hand when assessing a given theory. The history of philosophy as well as comparative contemporary philosophy can help here.[26] But so could the use of the theoretical tools and methods characteristic of the social sciences. It is here that there is room for a kind of "experimental philosophy" to play a role even in fundamental ontological investigations.[27]

Let me illustrate with an example. Many of us have had the following experience. You are teaching an undergraduate philosophy class—perhaps it is an introductory class—and for some reason the topic of the existence of abstract objects has come up. Some student—often many students!—resists the claim that the number two exists in the same way that tables exist. The student is happy to say that there are numbers, and is happy to say that there are tables. But the student hesitates to say that they enjoy the same kind of existence. You are convinced that the student must be confused—everything that there is exists in the same way, after all, so either the student really wants to say that the number two does not exist, or the student mistakenly thinks that "to exist" really means something like "to exist and to be spatiotemporal". You experience frustration as you try to get the student to grasp the concept of a generic unrestricted quantifier. The student experiences frustration as well.

On the position that I endorse, the metaphysical mistake is yours, not the student's. The student presumably has two non-overlapping existence-concepts, one of which ranges over concrete objects, while the other ranges over abstract objects. Each of the student's concepts latches on to something ontologically import-ant. The unrestricted quantifier that you are desperately trying to foist on the student is less fundamental than the restricted quantifiers your student currently (and successfully) employs. By my lights, you do the student a disservice by leading her to trade her concepts for yours.

Regardless of whether you share my evaluation of the student's ontological scheme, many of us have had this sort of classroom experience. It would be worth doing some experimental philosophy to assess the extent that the folk accept some sort of frag-mentation of being. I have not done so here in this book. I hope that in the future I can enlist some experimental philosophers to work with me or at least inspire them to investigate on their own. Philosophy is never finished. There is always more work to be done.

---

[26] See McDaniel (2014b) for further methodological explorations.

[27] There is also a role for collaborative work of the sort envisioned by Paul (2010a) between philo-sophers, cognitive scientists, and psychologists on how these intuitions are brought about.

1

Ways of Being

1.1 Introduction

This chapter will first be devoted to developing a meta-ontological theory based on the work of Martin Heidegger circa 1927. I focus on Heidegger's work partly because of the historical importance of Heidegger's philosophy, and partly because Heidegger provides a particularly clear statement of the doctrine that there are many ways to be. Heidegger's views are also philosophically interesting in their own right, and by reflecting on them we can draw some general lessons about the myriad ways in which one can believe in ways of being.

So I'll begin by carefully discussing and then formulating the relevant aspects of Heidegger's meta-ontological theory. This takes place in section 1.2. After this is done, I will move beyond the particulars of Heidegger's philosophy and develop a more general framework for thinking about modes of being.

I understand the discipline of meta-ontology (and meta-metaphysics more generally) as standing in the same sort of relation to ontology proper as the discipline of meta-ethics stands to ethics proper.[1] We can ask a variety of first-order ethical questions, such as: what are the necessary and sufficient conditions for right action; which character traits are worthy of admiration and which are worthy of contempt; and what kinds of things have intrinsic value? But reflection on the practice of raising, contemplating, arguing over, and answering these questions itself generates further questions. Some of them are epistemological, such as: what are our sources of evidence for claims about which actions are right? Some of them are semantical, such as: what do the expressions "worthy of admiration" and "worthy of contempt" mean? And some of them are metaphysical, such as: what must the world be like in order for anything to have intrinsic value? In addition, there are also logical, methodological, and even ethical and political questions raised by the practice of doing first-order ethics.

The same is true of ontology. But though Heidegger has interesting things to say about the methodology and epistemology of ontology, and deplorable things to say about the ethics and politics of ontology, an in-depth discussion of these topics would take us too far afield. Our discussion of Heidegger's meta-ontological views will focus

---

[1] We can thank van Inwagen (2001b) for stressing the importance of this discipline.

on his answers to (broadly construed) semantical and metaphysical questions concerning expressions like "being," "existence," and "there is."

Heidegger claims both that the word "being" has many meanings and that there are different ways in which things exist. Section 1.2 explicates the former thesis, as well as elucidates the connection between senses of "being" and quantification. In what follows, I do not distinguish between the notions of existence, and being, and what there is. On the view I will articulate, everything that there is exists or has being, but existing things can exist in different ways or enjoy different modes of being. I claim that any distinction lost by this terminological convenience can be recaptured in the framework defended in section 1.5. We will see if I am correct![2]

Some contemporary philosophers mistakenly believe that the idea that different kinds of beings can enjoy different ways of being is metaphysically bankrupt, and probably even meaningless.[3] In section 1.3, I discuss the doctrine that there are ways of being, and show how we can understand this doctrine in terms of the meta-ontological framework recently defended by Theodore Sider (2009, 2011), who in turn draws heavily on the work of David Lewis (1983a, 1984, 1986), who in turn draws on the work of Merrill (1980). I then contrast Sider's views on existence with the Heideggerian position developed here, thus establishing a point of contact between the ancient concern of whether being fragments and more contemporary issues.

In section 1.4, I compare and contrast this Heideggerian meta-ontological position with *quantifier variance*, a view inspired by Carnap (1956) and recently defended by Eli Hirsch (2002a). Very roughly, quantifier variance is the view that there are many possible senses of expressions such as "there are," "exist," and so forth, which are just as good as each other and whatever senses we have actually given to these expressions. Because of this parity of possible meanings, the quantifier variantist concludes that many (and even perhaps all) ontological disputes—disputes over what there is, what exists, and so forth—are ultimately trivial. And perhaps each disputant utters truths by virtue of selecting different meanings for their respective ontological expressions. In section 1.5, I argue that quantifier variantism is a form of ontological pluralism.

More generally, in section 1.5, I will abstract away from the particulars of Heidegger's theory and provide a more general understanding of what belief in different ways of existing amounts to. Unsurprisingly, there are many ways to believe in ways of being. In section 1.5, I discuss worries about the impossibility of unrestricted quantification, plural and singular quantification, the distinction between specific and individual existence, and Fine's (2001) notion of truth in reality, all with an eye to implications for how to understand the claim that there are ways of being.

---

[2] Do not think that, by using these expressions as more or less interchangeable, I thereby attribute to any of the thinkers discussed here (e.g., Heidegger) the view that these expressions (or the natural language correlates of them in the native tongues of these speakers) are interchangeable.

[3] See Quine (1969b: 242). Van Inwagen (2001b) is a prominent neo-Quinean.

1.2 Senses of "Being," Ways of Being

Heidegger is famous for raising anew the question of the meaning of "being." Heidegger (1962: 31) believed that one cannot successfully engage in first-order ontological inquiry unless one also engages in meta-ontological inquiry, and determines the meaning of "being":

Basically, all ontology, no matter how rich and firmly compacted a system of categories it has at its disposal, remains blind and perverted from its ownmost aim, if it has not first adequately clarified the meaning of Being, and conceived this clarification as its fundamental task.

Determining the meaning of "being" is the ultimate goal of *Being and Time*. I understand the project of determining the meaning of "being" as being a (broadly construed) semantic project that is both motivated and founded on deeper meta-physical concerns about the plurality of different ways to be.[4] In this respect, I concur with Mark Okrent (1988: 6–7), who writes, "[Heidegger] hoped to arrive at conclusions about what it means for an entity to be (that is, a statement of necessary conditions for being an entity), as well as conclusions concerning the ontological sorts of entities there are...." On my view, Heidegger wants an account of "being" which will yield necessary *and sufficient* conditions for being an entity. Okrent (1988: 205) also notes that, "The entire program of *Being in Time* is designed to explicate the meaning, or signification, of 'being.'" Okrent (1988: 67-68), tells us that *meaning* is to be understood as "meaning in the more philosophically familiar intentional or linguistic sense of the semantic content of a mental act or assertion...."[5]

Although a fully adequate answer to the question of the meaning of "being" will provide informative necessary and sufficient conditions for being an entity, the form of the answer will not consist in a mere itemized list of what there is, or even a list of ontological categories. In general, simply providing a list of things that satisfy a concept does not suffice as a clarification or an analysis of that concept. Nor does providing a list of kinds of thing whose members satisfy the concept. An answer to the question of being will tell us what it is *to be*, rather than merely tell us what there is.

This straightforward reading is strongly supported by the following passages:

The question posed by Plato in the *Sophist*..."What then do you mean when you use (the word) 'being'?" In short, what does "being" mean?—this question is so vigorously posed, so full of life. But ever since Aristotle it has grown mute, so mute in fact that we are no longer aware that it is muted.... [Heidegger 1992: 129]

---

[4] Philipse (1998) defends the view that Heidegger's question of the meaning of "being" does not have a unique answer because there is not a unique question posed. Instead, there are a plurality of meanings to Heidegger's question of the meaning of "being," one of which is the question that I am interested in. I should note, however, that Philipse (1998: 35) appears to grant that Heidegger did believe in ways of being.

[5] See also Kisiel (1993: 306–7), McInerney (1991: 118), and Witherspoon (2002: 91).

The question asks about being. What does being mean? Formally, the answer is Being means this and that. The question seeks an answer which is already given in the very questioning. The question is what is called a *question of definition*. It does not ask whether there is anything like being at all but rather what is meant by it, what is understood under it, under "being." ... We ("Anyone") do not know what "being" means, and yet the expression is in some sense understandable to each of us.... There is an understanding of the expression "being," even if it borders on a mere understanding of the word. The question is asked on the basis of this indeterminate preunderstanding of the expression "being." What is meant by "being"?   [Heidegger 1992: 143]

Heidegger's interest in the question of being was stimulated by reading Franz Brentano's (1981a) *On the Several Senses of Being in Aristotle*, which contains an explication of Aristotle's doctrine that "being is said in many ways."[6] In *Being and Time*, Heidegger endorses the Aristotelian slogan:

There are many things which we designate as "being," and we do so in various senses.

[Heidegger 1962: 26]

The "universality" of Being "*transcends*" any universality of genus. In medieval ontology "Being" is designated as a "*transcendens.*" Aristotle himself knew the unity of this transcendental "universal" as a *unity of analogy* in contrast to the multiplicity of the highest generic concepts applicable to things.   [Heidegger 1962: 22]

In order to help us understand the claim that "being is said in many ways," Aristotle brought our attention to expressions like "health" and "is healthy."[7] Many things can be truly said to be healthy. Phil Bricker, a marathon runner, is healthy. His circulatory system is healthy. Tofu is healthy. My relationship with my wife is healthy. However, it seems that the meaning of "is healthy" as used in these sentences differs in each instance. But the various senses of "is healthy" are not merely accidentally related to each other. Rather, they are *systematically* related to each other.

   In the literature on Aristotle, an expression whose meanings are related in this way is called "*pros hen* equivocal" or one that has *focal meaning*.[8] Something has focal meaning just in case it has several senses, each of which is to be understood in terms of some central meaning of that expression. The central sense of "is healthy" is the sense that applies to living organisms when they are flourishing. Phil Bricker is healthy in this sense, as is your pet turtle. But there are other senses of "is healthy." Food can be said to be healthy when its consumption contributes to the flourishing of its consumer. A proper part of an organism can be said to be healthy when it is properly functioning. If "is healthy" has focal meaning, then either there is no sense of "is healthy" such that one can truthfully say that Phil Bricker and tofu are healthy,

---

[6] See D. Frede (1993), Philipse (1998: 78–98), and Safranski (1998: 24–5) for a discussion of the influence of Brentano's work on Heidegger's thought, as well as for interesting discussion of how Heidegger's project relates to Aristotle's. Mulhall (1996: 9–10) is also interesting and helpful.

[7] See, for example, Aristotle's *Metaphysics* IV.2, 1003a33–b19 (Aristotle 1984b: 1584–5). For helpful commentary, see also Barnes (1995b: 76–7) and Witt (1989: 45).

[8] See, for example, Owen (1986), Burrell (1973: 83–6), and Wedin (2009: 128–31).

or such utterances are semantically defective. (Well, this isn't quite right—for it might be that eating Phil Bricker will contribute to the flourishing of the organism that eats him in much the same way that eating tofu will. But set this disturbing culinary possibility aside.)

It isn't obvious that "is healthy" is *pros hen* equivocal. Perhaps there is a generic sense of "is healthy" according to which each of the items mentioned above counts as healthy. (By "generic," I do not mean a sense that corresponds to a *genus*, but merely mean a highly general sense.) If so, the predicate "is healthy" when used in this way is univocal, and "both tofu and Phil Bricker are healthy" is true and in good shape semantically. However, although each of these entities is healthy, the reason that they are each healthy differs from case to case. Each is healthy *simpliciter* in virtue of being healthy in the way that is appropriate for the kind of entity it is. Tofu is not healthy in the *way* that Phil Bricker is healthy.

If there is a generic sense of "is healthy," it is unified by virtue of a complex web of relationships obtaining between the various kinds of healthiness. An exhaustive list of actual and possible healthy things would provide necessary and sufficient conditions for being healthy. But this list would not constitute a proper *definition* of healthiness. A proper definition of "is healthy" must illuminate the relations between these different kinds of healthiness.

On this way of understanding "healthiness is said in many ways," what this sentence expresses is true if and only if there are many different ways to be healthy. To put the point in Platonic terms, if a predicate F is "said in many ways," then there is no single Platonic Form of the F: there are many ways for a thing to be F.[9]

Brentano (1981a: 65) provides a second example of an expression "said in many ways":

Language does not always proceed with...precision. She finds it sufficient that everything which belongs together and which is grouped around one is called by the same family name, regardless of *how* each belongs in this assembly. Thus we call royal not only the royal sovereign who bears the royal power, but we also speak of a royal scepter and a royal dress, of royal honor, of a royal order, of royal blood....

Brentano appears to recognize a generic sense of "is royal." The phrase "is royal" applies to each of the objects Brentano lists: "each belongs in this assembly." But the reason why each belongs differs from case to case.

Many medieval philosophers called such expressions *analogical*. As far as I can tell, Aquinas holds that many analogical phrases are *pros hen* equivocal; specifically, those that are unified by what he calls an analogy of attribution.[10] Aquinas also

---

[9] Barnes (1995b: 73) states the following formula: "In general, Fs are so-called in several ways if what it is for x to be F is different from what it is for y to be F." See, for example, Aristotle's rejection of a Platonic form of the Good in his *Nicomachean Ethics* I.6, 1096a11–b25 (Aristotle 1984b: 1732–3).

[10] See Ashworth (2005: 85–9) for discussion of the medieval semantics of analogous terms. See Alston (1993: 148–53) and McInerny (1996) for a discussion of Aquinas and analogy. As Shields (1999: 107,

distinguishes several other ways in which the meaning of phrases might be unified by analogy, and in the next chapter we will briefly discuss some of these.

I will borrow "analogical" from the medievals, but I won't use "analogical expression" to refer to expressions with focal meaning. Rather, I will call an expression *analogical* just in case it has a generic sense, which, roughly, applies to objects of different sorts in virtue of those objects exemplifying different features. As I am using the terms, no expression is both *pros hen* equivocal and analogical. An expression might be analogical and polysemous: in addition to having a generic sense it might also have several restricted senses. Alternatively, an expression might be analogical but have only one sense. But, for the sake of clarity, I will stipulate that an expression is *pros hen* equivocal *only if* it fails to have a generic sense. On this way of regimenting terminology, all *pros hen* equivocal expressions are expressions with focal meaning, but the converse might not hold.

For the sake of clarity, let's further regiment our terminology. An expression is *ambiguous* if it has many meanings, but these meanings may or may not be closely related. An expression is *polysemous* if it has many meanings that are closely related, but these meanings need not be related by way of a central sense or focal meaning. Accordingly, an expression is *pros hen* equivocal only if it is polysemous only if it is ambiguous, but none of the converses necessarily holds.

Consider "is a part of." Many things are said to be parts: this hand is a part of that man, the class of women is a part of the class of human beings, this subregion is a part of space, this minute is a part of this hour, this premise is a part of this argument, and so forth. Some philosophers, such as David Lewis (1991: 75–82), believe that "is part of" is used univocally in these contexts, and that one fundamental relation is appealed to. On this view, "is a part of" is importantly like what many philosophers believe about "is identical with." Everything that there is, is identical with something (namely itself). Propositions are self-identical, as are mountains and moles. The identity predicate is used univocally in these contexts, and the identity relation invoked is the same in each case. Things are self-identical in the same way; identity is not "said in many ways."[11]

I think that "is a part of" is analogical. I am a compositional pluralist: there is more than one fundamental relation of part to whole. The fundamental parthood relation that your hand bears to your body is not the fundamental parthood relation that this region of space–time bears to the whole of space–time.[12] The ordinary word "part" is used univocally in sentences ascribing parts to material objects and to regions of space–time; I don't see much evidence for positing extra semantic meanings. But

---

fn. 4) notes, Aquinas's notion of analogical predication is not the same notion as what Aristotle calls "analogy."

[11] I am granting this claim about identity for the sake of argument. We will see some cause for caution about it in chapter 5.

[12] I defend compositional pluralism in McDaniel (2004, 2009a, and 2014a).

ultimately I am indifferent whether "part" is polysemous. What matters is that there is a generic sense of "part" which is in play (or can be in play) in both of these kinds of ascriptions. This generic sense corresponds to a non-fundamental parthood relation exemplified by objects of both sorts. (I'll have more to say about the analogy between compositional pluralism and ontological pluralism in section 2.3, where the varieties of analogy will also be revisited.)

According to Heidegger, expressions like "being," "existence," "exists," "is an entity," "some," and "there are" are analogical. There is a multiplicity of modes of being.[13] Heidegger (1962: 67) reserves the term "Existenz" for the kind of being had by entities like you and me, whom Heidegger calls "Dasein." Other ways of existing include *readiness-to-hand*, the kind of existence had by (roughly) tools (Heidegger 1962: 97–8; 1988: 304); *presence-at-hand* or *extantness*, the kind of existence had by objects primarily characterized by spatiotemporal features (Heidegger 1962: 121; 1988: 28); *life*, the kind of existence had by living things (Heidegger 1962: 285); and *subsistence*, the kind of existence enjoyed by abstract objects such as numbers and propositions (Heidegger 1962: 258–9).

However, there is also a concept of being that covers every entity that there is. Let us call this concept the *general concept of being*. Heidegger (1988: 28) employs this concept in many places, such as the *Basic Problems of Phenomenology*:

For us...the word "Dasein"...does not designate a way of being at all, but rather a specific being which we ourselves are, the *human Dasein*. We are at every moment a Dasein. This being, this Dasein, like every other being, has a specific way of being. To this way of being we assign the term "*Existenz.*".... Therefore, we might, for example, say "A body does not exist; it is, rather, extant." In contrast, Daseins, we ourselves, are not extant; Dasein exists. But the Dasein and bodies as respectively existent or extant at each time *are*.

The general concept of being appears early in *Being and Time*:

But there are many things which we designate as "being," and we do so in various senses. Everything we talk about, everything we have in view, everything towards which we comport ourselves in any way, is [a] being.   [Heidegger 1962: 26][14]

If we have a Dasein and a table before us, we have two beings before us. Both Daseins and bodies are, although each of them *is* in a different way from the other. *The Metaphysical Foundations of Logic* contains an explicit discussion of the function of the general concept of being:

---

[13] See Caputo (1982: 41, 80) and Inwood (1999: 26–8, 128–30) for discussion. Gibson (1998: 12–13) notes that Heidegger both accepts that there are ways of existence and that the concept of existence is not elementary.

[14] An anonymous referee has called to my attention an interesting parallel between this passage in Heidegger and a passage in Russell's (1964: 43–4) *Philosophy of Mathematics* in which Russell claims that anything that can be mentioned or thought is a *term*.

There is a multiplicity of modi existendi, and each of these is a mode belonging to a being with a specific content, a definite quiddity. The term "being" is meant to include the span of all possible regions. But the problem of the regional multiplicities of being, if posed universally, includes an investigation into the unity of this general term "being," into the way in which the general term "being" varies with different regional meanings. This is the problem of the *unity of the idea of being and its regional variants*. Does the unity of being mean generality in some other form and intention? In any case, the problem is the unity and generality of being as such. It was this problem that Aristotle posed, though he did not solve it.   [Heidegger 1984: 151]

The function of the general concept of being is to cover all that there is: no matter what kind of being something is, no matter what its essential nature, and no matter how it exists, it is a being. This is why Heidegger says that the term "being" includes the span of all possible regions.

Finally, the general concept of being is systematically related to the general concept of an entity, which is also recognized in *Being and Time*. The same notion also makes a cameo in Heidegger's essay, "The Origin of the Work of Art," where it appears under the label "thing":

On the whole the word "thing" here designates whatever is not simply nothing. In this sense the work of art is also a thing, so far as it is some sort of being.   [Heidegger 1993: 147]

This general concept of being is indispensable, at least to creatures such as ourselves. One might be very confident that something is, but be highly uncertain about which mode of being it enjoys. Consider biological species. We can be reasonably confident that they exist. But it is controversial whether biological species are *kinds* of individuals or *sums* of individuals.[15] So what kind of being do species have? If they are kinds—which I take to be abstract objects—then they *subsist*. If they are mereological sums of living things, then they enjoy either *life* or *extantness*; I'm not sure how Heidegger would decide between these options. But we can be confident that species *are* even though we can't say *how* they are.

Similarly, does a virus have the same kind of being as a rock or as a plant or as something else entirely? Do chimpanzees exist in the same way we do?[16] These are tough questions for someone who believes in Heidegger's modes of being. Yet whether there are viruses or chimpanzees is easy to determine. We can be confident that some things *are* even when we are unsure *how* they are.[17]

---

[15] See Hull (1999) for a discussion of some of the issues involved in determining whether species are individuals or kinds.

[16] Okrent (1988: 18) raises this question.

[17] This sort of argument was employed by Duns Scotus to show that "being" is not equivocal. See Scotus (1962: 6, 23–4) as well as Ashworth (2013a: 6), Kenny (2005b: 139–42), and Marrone (1988: 50) for discussion. Marrone (1988: 26) suggests a second motivation for Scotus: we need a univocal concept of being in order to explain how creatures can think of God via a concept accessible to them without the aid of divine illumination.

Heidegger (1988: 18) wants to know what unifies the general concept of being:

How can we speak at all of a unitary concept of being despite the variety of ways-of-being? These questions can be consolidated into *the problem of the possible modifications of being and the unity of being's variety*. Every being with which we have any dealings can be addressed and spoken of by saying "*it is*" thus and so, regardless of its specific mode of being.

As Heidegger notes, the question of the unity of being was also wrestled with by medieval philosophers. Heidegger (1992: 173–4) even employs some of their terminology:

When I say, for example, "God is" and "the world is," I certainly assert being in both cases but I intend something different thereby and cannot intend the term "is" in the same sense, univocally.... I can only speak of both God and the world as entities analogously. In other words, the concept of being, insofar as it is generally applied to the entire manifold of all possible entities, as such has the character of an analogous concept.

The last passage is excerpted from a discussion of medieval doctrines concerning the disparity between God's way of existing and the way in which creaturely things exist. Heidegger wants us to see that his concerns about the meaning of "being" are similar to the preoccupations of the medievals, as these passages from *Being and Time* and *Basic Problems of Phenomenology* indicate:

Here Descartes touches upon a problem with which medieval ontology was often busied—the question of how the signification of "Being" signifies any entity which one may on occasion be considering. In the assertions "God is" and "the world is," we assert Being. The word "is," however, cannot be meant to apply to these entities in the same sense, when between them there is an *infinite* difference of Being; if the signification of "is" were univocal, then what is created would be viewed as if it were uncreated, or the uncreated would be reduced to the status of something created. But neither does "Being" function as a mere name which is the same in both cases: in both cases "Being" is understood. This positive sense in which the Schoolman took as a signification "by analogy," as distinguished from one which is univocal or merely homonymous.   [Heidegger 1962: 126]

The ontological difference between the constitution of Dasein's being and that of nature proves to be so disparate that it seems at first as though the two ways of being are incomparable and cannot be determined by way of a uniform concept of being in general. *Existence* and *extantness* are more disparate than say, the determinations of God's being and man's being in traditional ontology.... Given this radical distinction of ways of being in general, can there still be found any single unifying concept that would justify calling these different ways of being ways of *being*?   [Heidegger 1988: 176]

A proper definition of the meaning of "being" should provide necessary and sufficient conditions for being an entity that will illuminate whether and how the different ways of being are systematically related to each other.

The careful reader will note that Heidegger sometimes slides from talking about ways of being to senses of the word "being." This might lead one to worry that

Heidegger commits what Gareth Matthews (1972) has called *the Sense-Kind Confusion*. Consider the following pair of sentences:

(S1): There are entities x and y such that x exists in one way, whereas y enjoys a distinct kind of being.

(S2): There are several senses of the words "being," "there are," etc., each of which corresponds to some way of existing, some distinct kind of being. None of these modes is enjoyed by all things. There is no other sense of "being," "there are," etc. besides these.

Note that, if (S2) is true, then (on the assumption that (S1) is a sentence in our language) (S1) is both equivocal and *false on every disambiguation*. For there is no sense of "there is" available to us on which (S1) comes out true. The Sense-Kind Confusion is the mistaken belief that (S1) and (S2) are jointly assertible and perhaps even ways of saying the same thing.[18]

Here is a useful analogy to bring home the point that one will assert both (S1) and (S2) only if one is confused. Suppose someone asserts the following claims:

(S3): There are exactly two kinds of banks: those that are made of sand and are near water, and those that are made of bricks and are filled with money.

(S4): There are exactly two senses of the word "bank." One sense of the word "bank" is "sandy area near water"; the other sense is "brick building filled with money."

Given that (S4) is true of the language in which (S3) is asserted, (S3) has two readings, which are:

(S3.1): There are exactly two kinds of sandy areas near water: those that are made of sand and are near water, and those that are made of bricks and are filled with money.

(S3.2): There are exactly two kinds of brick buildings filled with money: those that are made of sand and are near water, and those that are made of bricks and filled with money.

It is clear that both (S3.1) and (S3.2) are false. (S3) and (S4) are not jointly assertible.

Heidegger does not succumb to the Sense-Kind Confusion. Since Heidegger recognizes a generic sense of "there is," he can easily claim that there are different kinds of being enjoyed by different kinds of entities.[19] In short, Heidegger rejects (S2). (If there were a sense of "bank" that covered both sandy beaches and brick buildings

---

[18] Actually, things are even more problematic than that. It is hard to see how (S2) can even be asserted if the expressions constituting (S2) are in the same language as those existential expressions that (S2) is about.

[19] Matthews (1972: 151) recognizes that, if one has at one's disposal a generic concept of existence, no problem arises. See also Matthews (1971: 91–3). Loux (2012: 25) worries about whether Aristotle recognizes a generic sense of being. Normore (2012: 81) claims that, although for Ockham "being" is equivocal, he nonetheless recognizes a universal sense that applies to everything.

filled with money, there would be no problem with asserting (S3). But, if this were the case, (S4) would be false.) For Heidegger, "being" and its ilk are analogical terms in the technical sense defined earlier, not *pros hen* equivocal.

Heidegger's position is also not threatened by a recent challenge of Peter van Inwagen (2001b: 17):

No one would be inclined to suppose that number-words like "six" or "forty-three" mean different things when they are used to count different sorts of object. The very essence of the applicability of arithmetic is that numbers may count anything: if you have written thirteen epics and I own thirteen cats, then the number of your epics *is* the number of my cats. But existence is closely tied to number. To say that unicorns do not exist is to say something very much like saying that the number of unicorns is 0; to say that horses exist is to say that the number of horses is 1 or more. And to say that angels or ideas or prime numbers exist is to say that the number of angels, or of ideas, or of prime numbers is greater than 0. The univocity of number and the intimate connection between number and existence should convince us that there is at least very good reason to think that existence is univocal.[20]

As van Inwagen points out, there is some connection between being and number: claims of the form "there are n Fs (where n is a natural number)" can be represented by sentences that use only quantifiers, negation, identity, and F.[21]

One might respond to van Inwagen by arguing that numerals are also not univocal. Among van Inwagen's targets is the view defended by Gilbert Ryle (1945:15–16), according to which it is nonsense to say in one breath that the Pope and the number two exist, and are two things.[22] But one who is willing to claim that "being is said in many ways" is probably also willing to say that "oneness is said in many ways" as well as twoness, threeness, etc. And in fact Aristotle even tells us that "oneness is said in many ways."[23]

Heidegger need not fear van Inwagen's argument, regardless of how effective it is against Ryle. Since Heidegger recognizes this general concept of existence, he is willing to say (and capable of saying) of two things that enjoy different kinds of being that they are two. Consider a human being, whose way of being is *Existenz*, and $\sqrt{-1}$, whose way of being is *subsistence*. There is a sense of "being" according to which these two entities are *two* entities.[24] Just as there is a generic sense of "there is

---

[20]   See also van Inwagen (2014: 41–2, 61–5).

[21]   However, as Kathrin Koslicki has pointed out to me, mass-quantification does not seem closely related to number in the same way. We say, for example, that there is water on Mars or that gold exists in the hills, but it is hard to see how to associate these claims with a number.

[22]   See also Ryle (1949). Matthews (1971: 93) attributes this view to Ryle. Ryle avoids the Sense-Kind Confusion by refusing to assert (S1). According to Ryle, (S1) is not even meaningful. We'll have more to say about Ryle in section 4.5.

[23]   See Aristotle's *Metaphysics* X.1, 1052b (Aristotle 1984b: 1662). See also Berti (2001: 192–193). Brentano (1981a: 59–60) claims that "the identical, the different, and the opposite" are also said "in many ways" for each category, which suggests a kind of identity pluralism that would also make numerals non-univocal.

[24]   On this view there is also a sense of "being" and its ilk according to which one cannot say that these are two. This does not seem to me to be problematic.

at least one *x* such that . . . ," for each number *n*, there is a generic sense of "there are exactly *n* *x*s such that. . . ."[25]

But now one might worry that there isn't a real issue here, and that Heidegger's position is devoid of interest. Heidegger claims that being comes in many flavors, but recognizes a generic sense of "being." Someone like van Inwagen holds that "being" is univocal, but can account for the senses of "being" that Heidegger believes in. To resolve the puzzle we need a metaphysically serious account of talk about ways of being.

The general concept of being is represented in formal logic by the unrestricted existential quantifier.[26] This quantifier ranges over whatever there is, regardless of which kind of being the thing enjoys. For absolutely everything that there is, i.e., for all *x*, we can say truly that $\exists y \, (y = x)$. We can adequately represent the generic sense of "being" with the unrestricted quantifier of formal logic.

What is the best way to formally represent Heidegger's restricted senses of "being"? Not via constant symbols, e.g., proper names, to stand for the various kinds of being countenanced by Heidegger. This way of articulating Heidegger's position definitely won't do, since this procedure seems to identify ways of being with *beings*. In standard first-order logic, constant symbols—informally, these can be thought of as names—are employed to refer to entities within the domain of the quantifier.[27] Since the constant symbols can be replaced by first-order variables, we can derive from the claim that Dasein has Existenz the claim that there is an *entity* such that Dasein has *it*. However, Heidegger holds that this is an illicit inference. Heidegger warns us that being is not *a* being, and that the various ways of existing are not themselves entities.[28]

Should we introduce special predicates that mark the relevant distinctions that Heidegger wants to make? This seems inappropriate, since this procedure assimilates attributing a way of being to a thing to predicating a property of that thing. *Being* is not a kind of overarching property, exemplified by everything. Nor is *being*, on Heidegger's view, a determinable property of which the various kinds of being, such as *Existenz*, are determinates in the way that *being red* is a determinate of *being colored*. Ways of being are not merely special properties that some entities have

---

[25] For further discussion of ways in which the ontological pluralist can respond to van Inwagen, see Turner (2010).

[26] I focus on standard first-order logic, since many ontologists (such as Quine) take the language of first-order logic as the canonical language for formulating ontological disputes. We'll have more to say about other logics in sections 1.5.2 and 2.5.

[27] Although this is not the case in so-called free logic, which will briefly be the discussed in section 1.5.2.

[28] See, for example, Heidegger (1962: 26). Carman (2003: 200–1) contains a nice discussion of Heidegger's claim that *being* is not a being. Things are tricky, though, in that Heidegger also seems to recognize some attenuated sense in which modes of being and being itself are available to be quantified over. See Carman (2013), McDaniel (forthcoming-b), and Tepley (2014) for a discussion of the complications.

and that other entities lack, and so are not most perspicuously represented by predicates.[29]

The generic sense of "being" is represented formally by the "∃" of mathematical logic, not by a special constant symbol or a special existence predicate. A natural thought then is that the specific senses of "being" also are best represented by quantifiers. The notion of a *restricted quantifier*—one that ranges over only some proper subset of that which the unrestricted quantifier ranges—is perfectly intelligible. Heidegger's senses of "being" are properly represented in a formal system by special restricted quantifiers.

Just as being is not a being—and in fact talk about being or existence can be represented by way of the unrestricted existential quantifier—so too no kind of being is a being, and so too talk about kinds of being is best represented by special restricted existential quantifiers, not by special names or predicates. Note that Heidegger accepts that claims of the form "An F exists" are most perspicuously represented as "Something is an F."[30] Note also that Heidegger recognizes no way of being such that entities that have that way of being cannot be said to be in the generic sense of "to be." So for every special kind of being recognized by Heidegger, there corresponds a restricted quantifier whose domain is a proper subclass of the domain of the unrestricted quantifier, and that ranges over all and only those things that have that kind of being. So representing Heidegger's ways of being by restricted quantifiers—quantifiers that by virtue of their meaning range over only some proper subset of what the unrestricted existential quantifier ranges over—seems like an excellent way to proceed. These restricted quantifiers each correspond to some sense of "being" recognized by Heidegger.

For example, consider the *existenzial* quantifier, which in virtue of its meaning ranges over all and only those entities that have *Existenz* as their kind of being, and a *subsistential* quantifier, which in virtue of its meaning ranges over all and only those entities that have subsistence as their kind of being. We can represent these quantifiers with the following notation: "$\exists_{existenz}$" for the existenzial quantifier, and "$\exists_{subsistence}$" for the subsistential quantifier.

From a Heideggerian perspective, the existenzial quantifier and the subsistential quantifier are *prior in meaning* to the generic unrestricted existential quantifier. The unrestricted quantifier is in some way to be understood in terms of these restricted quantifiers (as well as others corresponding to readiness-to-hand, extantness, and

---

[29] See Philipse (1998: 41). That said, it might be that claims about existence are perspicuously represented not by predicates that apply to first-order individuals, but by predicates that apply to properties. For a contrary view, see Tepley (2014), who argues that modes of being are actually first-order properties.

[30] See Heidegger's discussion of this issue in Heidegger (1988: 41), where he seems to agree with Kant that "God exists" is more precisely expressed as "something is God." Heidegger (1988: 55) calls this "Kant's negative thesis," says that it cannot be impugned, and says that by this thesis Kant wishes to express the claim that being is not a being.

life), not the other way around. Recall that Heidegger holds that an adequate account of the generic sense of "being" will explain how the various specific senses of "being" are unified.

If the restricted quantifiers are prior in meaning to the unrestricted quantifier, then they must be *semantically primitive*. A semantically primitive restricted quantifier is not a complex phrase that "breaks up" into an unrestricted quantifier and a restricting predicate. I borrow the idea of a semantically primitive restricted quantifier from Eli Hirsch (2005: 76):

> It seems perfectly intelligible to suppose that there can also be *semantically restricted quantifiers*, that is, quantifiers that, because of the semantic rules implicit in a language, are restricted in their range in certain specific ways. If the quantifiers in a language are semantically restricted, they are always limited in their range, regardless of the conversational context.

The phrase "semantically primitive restricted quantifier" is not one with which I am entirely happy. There is a sense in which any semantically primitive quantifier is an *unrestricted* quantifier. If a speaker had grasped and internalized the meaning of *exactly* one of these semantically primitive quantifiers (and had no other quantifier in her language), this speaker would not be in a position to say or even to believe that there is anything more than what is ranged over by that quantifier. (Keep in mind that the meanings for the semantically primitive restricted quantifiers Hirsch introduces are taken by him to be possible meanings for the unrestricted quantifier.) Consider, for example, the subsistential quantifier, which ranges over all and only abstract entities such as numbers or propositions. A language equipped with only the subsistential quantifier is a language that is not only unable to express facts about material objects, but is also unable to express the fact that it is unable to express facts about material objects. From the perspective of someone who speaks only this language, it will seem as though the subsistential quantifier is unrestricted.

Moreover, we can envision that these restricted quantifiers are equipped with a character that allows them to be tacitly restricted by contexts, so that, for example, one could say truthfully while using the subsistential quantifier that everything is divisible by one, but nothing is divisible by zero. (The tacit restriction in play in this context is that the subsistential quantifier has been restricted to numbers, which form only a subset of that which subsists.) This fact seems to help bring home the thought that these quantifiers are, in an important sense, "unrestricted." They are not to be understood as expressions that are either explicitly or implicitly "defined up" from a more general quantifier and special predicates or special operators.

Heidegger recognizes van Inwagen's genuinely unrestricted quantifier as a legitimate philosophical notion. However, Heidegger holds that the generic unrestricted quantifier is somehow to be defined in terms of the semantically primitive restricted quantifiers. How it is to be defined is not at all obvious, given that Heidegger does not seem to think that the generic sense of "being" is merely the disjunction of the various specific senses of "being." Recall that "being" is instead, on his view, "unified by analogy."

The difficulty in seeing what the proper definition of "being" is given that "being" is "unified by analogy" is what motivates the philosophical project of *Being and Time*. That it is not at all obvious how to "define up" the generic sense of "being" doesn't show that "being" is semantically primitive. No one knows what the correct definition of "S knows that P" is, and few infer from this sad state of affairs that either "S knows that P" is in fact semantically primitive, or that we do not in fact have the concept of knowledge.[31] "S knows that *P*" is not semantically primitive—it is somehow "defined up" out of the notions of belief, truth, evidence, and who knows what else, although it should be clear by now that the project of "defining up" this expression is no walk in the park.

It is an interesting question why, despite his numerous disagreements with Aristotle about the question of being, Heidegger nonetheless follows Aristotle in taking being to have a central mode in terms of which the others are to be understood. For Aristotle, the central mode is the mode of being enjoyed by substances, whereas for Heidegger, it is *Existenz*, the mode of being enjoyed by Daseins. Perhaps Heidegger follows Aristotle here in this assumption about how modes of being are related to one another because it is harder to see how one can answer the question of the meaning of "being" at all without it.[32] And the mode of being of Dasein is a good choice for a focal mode since Dasein is that entity for whom its own being is an issue—and so in a sense Dasein's mode of being has being built into it![33]

(In chapter 5, I will discuss an answer to the question of the meaning of "being" that is neutral on whether there is a central mode of being.)

Van Inwagen should be willing to concede the intelligibility of a language that contains semantically primitive restricted quantifiers. But he will resist the notion that English is such a language. From van Inwagen's perspective, Heidegger's putatively primitive restricted quantifiers can be shown to be equivalent to *defined* restricted quantifiers in a perfectly obvious way:

x has *Existenz*, i.e., $\exists_{existenz} y\ (x = y)$ = df. $\exists y\ (x = y$ and x is a Dasein.)[34]

x has *subsistence*, i.e., $\exists_{subsistence} y\ (x = y)$ = df. $\exists y\ (x = y$ and x is a number or some other abstracta.)

On van Inwagen's view, the unrestricted quantifier is prior in meaning to the restricted ones.

---

[31] If Williamson (2001) is correct, "knows" is semantically primitive.

[32] My remarks here are profitably contrasted with McNamus (2013: 559–60). Note that I do not think Heidegger thought that the relations between Dasein's mode of being and the other modes of being are to be understood in terms of Aristotle's four causes. Perhaps Aristotle thought this about how the mode of being of substances relates to the modes of being of accidents; see Shields (1999) and Ward (2008: ch. 3) for discussion of this hypothesis.

[33] See Heidegger (1962: 32–5).

[34] I'm tabling the question of whether Heidegger thinks that other entities besides Dasein have *Existenz* as their way of being.

Given that both sides can in some way recognize the senses of "being" postulated, is there anything here worth worrying about? The question of the meaning of "being" might be interesting to a linguist, but why should a metaphysician care about it? The job of the unrestricted quantifier is to range over everything there is. As long as it does this, why care about the question of the meaning of "being"?

1.3 Theodore Sider meets Martin Heidegger

Even though Heidegger recognizes van Inwagen's general concept of being, and van Inwagen could in principle recognize Heidegger's various senses of "being," there is still a question about which is more *metaphysically fundamental*. In what follows, I discuss how one can make sense of the notion that one quantifier is more fundamental than another.

It is one thing to recognize an aspect of an object, and another thing to hold that the aspect is *basic*, or *fundamental*, or—to use the terminology of David Lewis (1983a and 1986)—*perfectly natural*.[35] Consider the property of having a charge of −1 and the property of either being loved by Sarah Jessica Parker or having a charge of −1. Eddie the electron exemplifies both features. −1 *charge* is a real respect of similarity between electrons, but it is bizarre to think that Matthew Broderick and Eddie are similar in virtue of both of them enjoying either being loved by Sarah Jessica Parker or having a charge of −1. There is a metaphysical distinction between these two features: the former property *carves nature at the joints*, while the latter is a *mere disjunction*.

Embracing a notion of naturalness does not require embracing a robust ontology of properties.[36] Regardless of whether there "really are" properties, there is an important metaphysical difference between predicates like "is an electron" and predicates like "is an electron if discovered before 2024 or is a positron". Sider (2009) discusses several nominalistic accounts of naturalness. One account takes the notion of naturalness to apply to languages rather than properties. Informally, a language is more natural than another language to the degree that its primitive (i.e., undefined) locutions match the joints of reality. Formally, the notion of one language being more natural than another is simply taken as primitive by the nominalist. A second account introduces a primitive sentence-operator **N** that can be prefixed to pairs of open sentences. Sentences of the form "**N** (x is an F, x is a G)" are ascriptions of comparative naturalness: informally, they tell us that to be an F is more natural than to be a G.[37] Presumably there are other ways in which a clever nominalist could

---

[35] See also Merrill (1980).

[36] Lewis (1983a) discusses ways in which the nominalist could account for naturalness without properties.

[37] Perhaps it would be better to informally understand **N** as "at least as natural as," but nothing turns on this in what follows. Note that Sider (2011) now prefers to use an "**S**" operator instead, which is monadic rather than binary. As far as I can tell, nothing of substance here hangs on which locution to prefer, though in chapter 7 we will return to the question of which notion of naturalness or structure is better to employ.

accommodate the notion of naturalness. The important thing is to account for the distinguished structure of the world. (This will be important later because Heidegger holds that neither *being* nor *kinds of being* are to be reified.)

Accordingly, in what follows, I will talk about natural *predicates* instead of natural properties. If there are natural *properties,* no harm is done: natural predicates are those that designate natural properties.

The notion of a natural predicate appealed to here is not conceptually equivalent to the notion of a *physical predicate*, where (roughly) a physical predicate is true of only physical objects. For this reason, I will use the expressions "basic" and "fundamental" as well as "perfectly natural."

Does the notion of fundamentality apply to other grammatical categories? Can we distinguish natural from unnatural *names*? Do some quantifiers carve reality closer to the joints than others?

Heidegger recognizes a generic sense of "being" that covers every entity that there is, but holds that it is not metaphysically fundamental: this generic sense represents something *akin to* a *mere disjunction* of the *metaphysically basic ways of being*. We need to determine the meaning of "being" in order to determine what unifies *being simpliciter*. Recall the earlier discussion concerning "is healthy." Although "is healthy" is true of both Phil Bricker and tofu, the kind of healthiness exemplified by Phil Bricker and the (distinct) kind of healthiness exemplified by tofu are both less "disjunctive" or "gerrymandered" than *healthiness simpliciter*. (Healthiness simpliciter is not as unnatural as a *mere* disjunction, since it is unified in some way.)

The same holds for more philosophically interesting notions, such as parthood. The compositional pluralist admits that there is a generic parthood relation that encompasses every specific parthood relation, but holds that the specific parthood relations are more fundamental.

If "being" is unified only by analogy, the kind of being had by Dasein and the kind of being had by a number are metaphysically prior to *being simpliciter*. The unrestricted quantifier is *metaphysically posterior* to the restricted quantifiers corresponding to the kinds of being recognized by Heidegger.

Just as mere disjunctions are less metaphysically basic than that which they disjoin, so too *mere restrictions* are metaphysically posterior to that for which they are restrictions. Consider *being an electron near a bachelor*. This is a mere restriction of being an electron because being an electron near a bachelor partitions the class of electrons into gerrymandered, arbitrary, or merely disjunctively unified subclasses.

Although this is not explicitly stated, van Inwagen (2001b) seems to be committed to the claim that the ways of being that Heidegger favors are *mere restrictions* of the *metaphysically basic* notion of existence, the one expressed by the unrestricted existential quantifier. Regardless of whether van Inwagen is committed to this view, other metaphysicians certainly are. For example, Theodore Sider (2001: xxi–xxiv; 2009; 2011) explicitly defends this position, which Sider calls *ontological realism*.

Ontological realism is abhorrent to Heidegger. Not because all quantificational expressions are metaphysically on a par: the true logical joints—it would be better to say the true *ontological* joints—do not correspond to the unrestricted existential quantifier, but rather to semantically primitive restricted quantifiers. They are the fundamental quantifiers.

Heidegger does not view his list of the various flavors of being as arbitrary. He intends his list to capture the real *ontological* structure of the world. There is not a way of being for *every* way of demarcating the domain of the unrestricted existential quantifier. There is not a way of being had by all and only those things that are either ugly or a prime number. There is not a way of being had by all and only those things that are either under three feet tall or believe in the existence of aliens from outer space. Heidegger thinks that the ways of being he calls our attention to are metaphysically special: the restricted quantifiers that represent them enjoy a status unshared by most of their brethren. There are only a few, proud restricted quantifiers that are metaphysically basic.

Recall the worry mentioned at the end of section 1.2. To keep things simple, consider a meta-ontological theory that recognizes two ways in which entities can exist: the way in which abstract objects exist and the way in which concrete objects exist. According to the account offered here, there are two fundamental semantically primitive restricted quantifiers, represented symbolically as "$\exists_a x$" and "$\exists_c x$". Consider the domain of "$\exists_a x$." We can introduce a special predicate, "Ax," that objects satisfy if and only if they are members of this domain. Let "Dx" be a fundamental predicate that applies to some but not all entities within the domain of "$\exists_a x$". Now consider the following two sentences:

(1) $\exists_a x\ Dx.$
(2) $\exists x\ (Ax\ \&\ Dx).$

The worry is that (1) and (2) are necessarily equivalent, and consequently seem to be equally good ways of expressing exactly the same facts about the world. In what respect is (1) a better sentence to assert than (2)? If there is no metaphysical difference between these two ways of speaking, then the hypothesis that there are ways of being is idle.[38]

Let's examine a parallel case.[39] Recall the following definitions introduced to us by Nelson Goodman (1955):

x is *grue* = df. *x* is green and is examined before the year AD 3000, or is blue and is not examined before AD 3000.

x is *bleen* = df. *x* is blue and is examined before the year AD 3000, or is green and is not examined before AD 3000.

---

[38] I thank Josh Parsons for pressing me on this worry.
[39] I thank Jason Turner for suggesting the analogy employed here.

Although "is grue" and "is bleen" are intelligible, they are highly unnatural, whereas "is green" and "is blue" are in far better shape. Now consider a culture that speaks a language much like ours, except that this language lacks the color-vocabulary we have in our language. Let's call this language *the Gruesome Tongue* (GT). GT has two semantically primitive predicates, "is grue*" and "is bleen*," which are necessarily equivalent to "is grue" and "is bleen." When speakers of GT first encounter us, they are bewildered by assertions that employ color-predicates.[40] They ask us to define "is blue" and "is green," but since these terms are semantically primitive in our language, we can't do this. We point at things that are green or blue and hope that they will catch on, but they just don't get it.

Eventually, a clever linguist from their culture introduces terms in their language that allow them to state the truth-conditions for sentences in our language that employ color-predicates:

> *x is green** = df. *x* is grue* and is examined before the year AD 3000, or is bleen* and is not examined before the year AD 3000.
>
> *x is blue** = df. *x* is bleen* and is examined before the year AD 3000, or is grue* and is not examined before the year AD 3000.

"Is green" does not have the same meaning as "is green*," since "is green" is semantically primitive while "is green*" is capable of explicit definition. Nonetheless, "is green" and "is green*" are necessarily coextensive. So the defectiveness of GT does not simply consist in its inability to describe possibilities that we can describe. But GT is defective nonetheless.

A language is defective if its primitive predicates are not fundamental. It is certainly a mistake to think that language *must* mirror reality in the sense that one is guaranteed that there will be a correspondence between our words and the world. However, it is no mistake to think that language is in one respect *defective* to the extent that there is no such correspondence between word and world. Having primitive but non-fundamental predicates is one metaphysically bad feature of a language. We can generalize. Call a language *metaphysically ideal* just in case every primitive expression in that language has a perfectly natural meaning.[41]

Heidegger holds that there are several senses of the word "being," each of which corresponds to a way of existing, as well as the generic sense of "being." In this respect, Heidegger's position appears closer to the position of Aristotle than the position of Gilbert Ryle (1949), who emphatically rejects the existence of a generic sense of "being." Owen (1986: 181) attributes to Aristotle the thesis that the word "being" is ambiguous between the various kinds of being, and his remarks suggest that the early Aristotle did not recognize a generic sense of "being." However,

---

[40] I assume that *grue* and *bleen* also correspond to conceptual primitives in the mental lives of the speakers of GT. Thanks to Peter Finocchiaro for noting this.

[41] I defend the appropriateness of these evaluative judgments in chapter 6.

Aristotle's argument for the conclusion that *being* is not a genus seems to presuppose that there is a general concept of being, since one of the premises is that everything whatsoever (including differentiating characteristics) is a being.[42] It is hard to see how this argument can even be stated without employing a generic sense.

Regardless, Heidegger seems less committed to the linguistic thesis that "being" is polysemous than he is to the claim that "being" is analogical. This is important, because even if there aren't several senses of "being" in ordinary language, we can still make good sense of the claim that "being" is analogical. To claim that a univocal phrase is analogical is to claim that it *should not* be semantically primitive: in a metaphysically ideal language it would not be. According to the position explicated here, a language in which the generic quantifier is semantically primitive is not a metaphysically ideal language. A language is metaphysically better, at least with respect to its apparatus of quantification, if its generic quantifier is "defined up" out of those semantically primitive restricted quantifiers that do correspond to the logical joints.

Even those analytic metaphysicians suspicious about the notion of metaphysical fundamentality and its partners in crime *being a mere disjunction* and *being an arbitrary restriction* should realize that their own view is a substantive metaphysical (or meta-ontological) claim, to which Heidegger's position poses a serious challenge. These metaphysicians hold that *no* quantifier expression is metaphysically special. Sider claims that exactly *one* (existential) quantifier expression is privileged. Heidegger holds that *many* but not all are equally metaphysically basic. Heidegger was right: we must theorize about the meaning of "being" in order to have a complete ontological theory.

The debate between Heidegger and Sider is not trivial or senseless. There is a *metaphysical* reason to care about the question of the meaning of "being." If "being" is analogical, then Sider's formulation of ontological realism is false.[43]

1.4 Heidegger and the Ontological Deflationist

Recent meta-ontological inquiry has been motivated by worries that certain first-order ontological debates are merely verbal. Consider the debate over when some entities compose a whole. *Universalists* hold that composition always occurs: whenever there are some *x*s, those *x*s compose a *y*. *Nihilists* hold that composition *never* occurs. And there are many moderate positions between universalism and nihilism. It seems like these views genuinely conflict.

According to the *ontological deflationalist*, there is no genuine disagreement here.[44] What the universalist means by "there is" is not what the nihilist means by "there is."

---

[42] See *Metaphysics* III.3, 998b1–20 (Aristotle 1984b: 1577); see also Barnes (1995b: 73).

[43] Vallicella (2014: 47) claims that every quantificational account of "being" is a "thin" account. The reflections here show that this is not so.

[44] The foundations for a defense of deflationalism can be found in Hirsch (2002a, 2002b, 2005). Hirsch's own view is subtler. On his view, (i) there could be a linguistic community in which something like universalism is true because of the meaning of the quantifier expressions in that language, (ii) there could

Here is a speech that the deflationalist might make: what the nihilist means by "there is" is determined by how the nihilist uses "there is": a meaning of a term fits use best when it makes more sentences using that term come out true than alternative candidate meanings. There is a candidate meaning for the quantifier that best fits the nihilist's use: call this meaning *nihilist-quantification*. Similarly, call the candidate meaning for the quantifier that best fits the universalist's use *universalist-quantification*. Since no single candidate meaning for "there is" can maximize fit with how the nihilist and the universalist use quantificational expressions, *nihilist-quantification* and *universalist-quantification* must be distinct. So the nihilist and the universalist must be talking past each other; they are not really disagreeing. Moreover, the language spoken by the nihilist is just as a good as the language spoken by the universalist: there are no facts expressible in one of the languages not expressible by the other. So the nihilist and the universalist do not disagree, and moreover, there are no facts for them to disagree over.

The deflationalist's speech is too quick. Fit with use is not the only factor in determining what our words mean. A second factor is how natural the candidate meanings are.[45] This second factor can trump fit with use. That said, the deflationalist could concede this point, but insist that nihilist-quantification is as natural a meaning for the quantifier as universalist-quantification. This view is *quantifier variance.*

Sider is no friend of quantifier variance. According to Sider's ontological realism, there is a perfectly natural candidate meaning for the unrestricted quantifier that fits how the universalist and the nihilist use it well enough to ensure that the universalist's and the nihilist's quantifiers have this candidate meaning.[46]

What if the degree to which naturalness helps to determine meaning is not significant enough to trump our use of "being," "existence," and "there is"? If this scenario obtains, Sider (2009) recommends abandoning ordinary language, and then reframing the debate between the nihilist and the universalist in a language that Sider dubs "Ontologese." Roughly, Ontologese is a language in which "∃" is *stipulated* to stand for *the* fundamental quantifier meaning.

Note that the fan of genuine disagreement can make similar responses without assuming that any candidate meaning for the unrestricted quantifier is fundamental. What matters is that there be a unique candidate meaning that is more natural than the others and natural enough to trump use. Even given the Heideggerian meta-ontology sketched here, there might be some candidate meaning for the unrestricted quantifier that is far more natural than alternatives to it. (How natural? We'll discuss this in chapters 4 and 5.)

---

be a distinct linguistic community in which something like nihilism is true for similar reasons, and (iii) there is no respect in which one language is more metaphysically privileged than the other.

[45] See Lewis (1983a, 1984) and Merrill (1980) for the inspirations for this claim. I believe that causation plays a role in determining reference as well.

[46] See Sider (2001: xvi–xxiv; 2004; 2009; 2011) for discussion and defense of ontological realism.

Keep in mind that, according to the friend of quantifier variance, there are many equally fundamental meanings for the *unrestricted* existential quantifier. This is why the variantist concludes that there is no uniquely privileged meaning for the unrestricted quantifier. The fundamental quantifier-meanings postulated by Heidegger are meanings for *restricted* quantifiers. There is still room for a privileged meaning for the unrestricted quantifier, one that ensures that the quantifier encompasses the domains of each of the privileged restricted quantifiers and adds nothing extra.[47] On such a view, this meaning for the unrestricted quantifier will not be perfectly natural, but it will be more natural than its competitors, and natural enough to serve as a "reference magnet."

Another option is for the Heideggerian to frame ontological disagreements in something like Sider's Ontologese. But according to the Heideggerian, in the fundamental language all quantificational expressions are semantically primitive restricted quantifiers. The appropriate language for doing metaphysics must have *each* of these quantifiers in order to mirror the ontological joints of the world.

Arguably, this is in fact what Heidegger does: abandon ordinary language, and create and then employ a new language in which new primitive terms are introduced along with accompanying remarks to aid the reader in grasping these terms. The accompanying remarks constitute a minimal use of the terms, but one that is sufficient for these terms to latch on to any ontological joints that might be in the neighborhood. This technical language might be initially unfamiliar to us and perhaps even off-putting, but by immersing ourselves in it—by *using it*—we can grasp the fundamental meanings that are there to be meant. And it is in this novel language that ontological assertions are to be made and evaluated. Readers of Heidegger might be frustrated by the novel and apparently under-explained terminology that he confronts them with, but if Heidegger is trying to construct a metaphysically better language for communicating ontological results, this is unavoidable.

One can formulate interesting ontological debates using Heideggerian Ontologese. Consider the kind of being had by those entities that Heidegger calls *merely-present-at-hand*. The merely-present-at-hand are, roughly, the objects studied by the physical sciences: elementary particles or aggregates of matter. We can represent the kind of being had by these entities with the "presence-at-hand quantifier", which, in symbols, looks like this: "$\exists_{pah}$." We can now ask interesting metaphysical questions about the entities within the range of this quantifier. For example, we can ask whether Q is true:

(Q):   If $\exists_{pah} x: x = a$ and $\exists_{pah} y: y = b$, then $\exists_{pah} z: z$ such that z is composed of a and b.

And the compositional nihilist will say that Q is false—the only present-at-hand entities are mereological simples—while the compositional universalist will say that Q is true.

---

[47] Whether this is the meaning of the ordinary English "being" and its buddies will be the topic of chapter 5.

1.5 Ways of Believing in Ways of Being

Let's now abstract away from the particulars of Heidegger's theory in order to discern some general lessons. There are different kinds of existence *if* there are possible meanings for semantically primitive restricted quantifiers such that (i) each restricted quantifier has a non-empty domain that is properly included in the domain of the unrestricted quantifier, (ii) none of these domains overlap, and (iii) each meaning is at least as natural as the meaning of the unrestricted quantifier. On the Heideggerian view, there are restricted quantifiers that are even more natural than the unrestricted quantifier. (In order to state this thesis, I used the unrestricted quantifier of ordinary English, which might not have a perfectly natural meaning; we will return to the question of whether it does, and the consequences for ontology if it does not, in later chapters.)

One way to hold (i)–(iii) is by reifying quantifier-meanings. Suppose that *existence* is a second-order property: a property of properties, or propositional functions.[48] Now consider someone who holds that this second-order property is akin to a *mere disjunction* of a finite list of fundamental second-order properties. One might hold that this property is less natural than the modes of being but is more natural than a mere disjunction—one might hold that this property is "unified by analogy"; we'll discuss this idea more in the next chapter. Regardless, it seems to me that (i)–(iii) also follow from this person's beliefs, since these properties are well-suited to serve as the meanings of semantically primitive restricted quantifiers. However, we have also seen that one can make sense of (i)–(iii) without reifying meanings: one can believe that things exist in different ways without believing in entities that are ways in which things exist.

Belief in the conjunction of (i)–(iii) suffices for belief in ways of being. But it is not necessary. I will now discuss views that seem committed to ways of being without implying (i)–(iii). In section 1.5.1, we'll talk a bit more about quantifiers; in section 1.5.2, we'll discuss worries about quantifying over everything and plural quantification; in section 1.5.3, we'll discuss worries arising from the alleged distinction between specific existence and individual existence; and, in section 1.5.4, we'll discuss whether we'd be better served by using Fine's (2001) notion of *truth in reality* rather than naturalness when formulating ontological pluralism.

1.5.1 Quantifiers: Some Accounts

I have helped myself to the notion of a quantifier. But what makes an expression a quantifier expression?

One way to characterize quantifiers is via an account of the kinds of entities that are their semantic values. One popular view is that the semantic value of quantifiers are relations between properties.[49] Sometimes these relations are easy to describe but

---

[48] See, for example, Russell (1971: 232–3).
[49] See Westerståhl (2011) for discussion of quantifiers more generally.

only if we use the quantifier itself in the description. For example, "some" is a relation that obtains between F and G just in case there is something that is both F and G, and "most" is a relation that obtains between F and G (in that order) just in case most Fs are Gs. But many of these relations will be such that there are no natural language expressions that have them as their semantic values. Perhaps some of these relations are among those perfectly natural meanings for an existential quantifier.[50]

It is acceptable for natural language semanticists to talk as if there are such relations when providing models for the ways in which meaningful expressions in natural language combine with each other to form larger meaningful units. We shouldn't begrudge these incursions into metaphysics any more than we should complain when a physicist talks as though she were a Platonist when providing a mathematical model of reality. But we are doing metaphysics now, and among our metaphysical interlocutors are those who do not think that there are entities that correspond to quantifier-expressions. So let's consider a more neutral characterization of what it is to be a quantifier in order to accommodate them.

Certain kinds of quantifiers, such as the quantifier "some," can be characterized by their inferential role. From the truth of "Ranger is a dog," one may infer that "something is a dog" is also a truth. And from the truth of "something is a dog" one may infer that "not everything is not a dog" is also a truth. To be an existential quantifier is to be a kind of expression that permits a certain range of inferences.

1.5.2 More on Quantification

Here we will discuss what to say if unrestricted quantification is impossible and if either plural quantification or higher-order quantification is fundamental.

First, someone could believe that unrestricted quantification is impossible but also hold that there are ways of being, perhaps for entirely independent reasons. There are interesting worries about the coherence of quantifying over absolutely everything.[51] Suppose you believe in sets. Suppose you hold that whenever there are some things, there is a set of those things, that is, if some things are in the domain of quantification, there is a set of those things. You will be led to a contradiction if you assume then that you can quantify over all the sets there are, for on these hypotheses one can quantify over all of the sets that there are only if there is a set of all the sets that there are; and there are proofs that there can be no such set on pain of contradiction.[52] You might hold instead that, for every quantifier Q1, there is a more inclusive quantifier Q2 that ranges over everything Q1 ranges over but not vice versa. On this view, every quantifier is a restricted quantifier. And so any natural quantifier will be a restricted

---

[50] I have been told that many linguists deny that "there is" is a quantifier. I am largely indifferent to whether this is the case: although I will sometimes speak as if "there is" is a quantifier, I am happy to replace sentences in which "there is" is discussed with ones in which "some" is the object of focus.

[51] See the papers in Rayo and Uzquiano (2007) for a discussion of the relevant issues.

[52] Perhaps the thing to do is embrace a paraconsistent logic. See Priest (2006) for further motivation. Paraconsistent logic will be discussed very briefly in chapter 2.

quantifier. But since there is no unrestricted quantifier, it is hard to say that some semantically primitive restricted quantifier is at least as natural as the unrestricted quantifier.

In order to keep things simple, consider a view that holds that sets enjoy one way of being whereas concrete entities enjoy another. Consider now an infinite sequence of quantifiers, indexed to the ordinals, such that the first member, Q0, ranges over all and only concrete objects, Q1 ranges over all and only concrete objects and sets of concrete objects, Q2 ranges over everything Q1 ranges over as well as sets of things within Q1's range, etc. Consider a second infinite sequence of quantifiers, also indexed to the ordinals, Q0,..., Qn-, which is such that Q0 ranges over all and only concrete objects, while each of Q1-,..., Qn- range over all and only the sets ranged over by Q1...Qn. (In short, none of the domains of Q1-...Qn- include concrete objects.) Basically, the first sequence is a sequence of increasingly expansive quantifiers that have both individuals and sets within their domains, whereas the second sequence is a sequence of increasingly expansive quantifiers that have only sets within their domains (save Q0). Someone who wants to distinguish the mode of being of a set from the mode of being of an individual while still denying the possibility of unrestricted quantification can claim that the perfectly natural quantifiers are Q0 along with Q1-,..., Qn- rather than Q1,..., Qn. So we can make sense of the view that there are modes of being without believing in the possibility of absolutely unrestricted quantification.

There is still the worry that, in describing this view, I am quantifying over everything. This is a real worry, but it is an instance of a more general worry: how can the denier of absolute quantification state her view without quantifying over everything? I don't know how this question is to be answered, but I believe that the friend of ways of being who is also a foe of unrestricted quantification can follow suit, provided that it can be answered at all. But exploring this further would take us very far afield indeed.

Another view worth considering holds that the domains of the fundamental quantifiers overlap. This view is interesting, for according to it, there is an x such that x exists in more than one way. For historical antecedents, consider that Aristotle (1984a: 17) discusses the possibility that some qualities might also be "relatives" in the *Categories* at 11a37. Brower (2014: 53) notes a suggestion of Aristotle in *Physics* III.3 that every entity that falls under the category of *passion* also falls under the category of *action*.[53] Furthermore, Brower (2014: 206–10) argues that this is Aquinas's view as well. More recently, Bertrand Russell (1964) distinguished between *being* and *existence* but held that everything that exists has being but not vice versa.[54] And regardless of its historical antecedents, we can envision how such a view could be motivated: consider the view that (i) particulars and universals exist in different ways, (ii) the actual and the possible also exist in different ways, and (iii) these divisions cross-cut.

---

[53] See Aristotle's *Physics* III.3 (1984a: 344–5); 202b1–10 seem especially relevant.
[54] See Caplan (2011) for further discussion of Russell's ontological pluralism.

On this view, one thing can enjoy two ways of being. Another possibility is to hold that there are four modes of being, none of which overlap, but we shouldn't be forced by the framework here to conflate this possibility with the possibility of four overlapping categories.[55]

So I offer up the following more general sufficient condition: one believes in ways of being if one believes that there is more than one *relatively fundamental* meaning for an existential quantifier. An existential quantifier meaning is *relatively fundamental* just in case no other quantifier meaning is more fundamental than it. This is what all the views that have been elucidated so far have in common. I'll now consider two worries about this sufficient condition. The first concerns quantifier variance; the second concerns Meinong's meta-ontology.

First, one interesting upshot of this proposal is that it classifies the quantifier variantist as a friend of ways of being. Recall that the quantifier variantist believes that there are multiple possible primitive meanings for the quantifier that are equally good from a metaphysical perspective, and each of which is as good as the meaning we actually use in ordinary language. Debates between, for example, the compositional universalist and the nihilist are at rock bottom pointless, because there are (at least two) available senses of "there is" available for use, and among them is one that legitimates the universalist's claims, while the other legitimates the nihilist's claims. And there is no better sense of "there is" available that would delegitimize their respective claims. So each of the quantifier variantist's potential meanings is relatively fundamental—and there are more than one of them!

Perhaps it's surprising that quantifier variantism is properly classified in this way, since quantifier variantism is supposed to be a "deflationary" or "anti-metaphysical" view, while the view that there are modes of being is a paradigmatically inflationary metaphysical view. But we should get over our surprise. Those who oppose metaphysics are brother and sister metaphysicians with a metaphysics of their own.[56]

Second, how should we understand the Meinongian view? Meinong (1904) accepted modes of being: he distinguished between existence, the mode of being enjoyed by concreta, and subsistence, the mode of being enjoyed by objectives. (Objectives are complexes that have the structure of propositions and facts, but which of these they should be identified with is a tricky issue I ignore here.) But in addition to the things enjoying either mode of existence, there are further things which, according to Meinong, enjoy no mode of being at all. And it is the outermost quantifier, the one that ranges over all the objects that Meinong countenances, that is troublesome.[57] Meinong takes this outer quantifier, which ranges

---

[55] In chapters 3 and 4, we will discuss additional views in which something can enjoy more than one mode of being.

[56] Compare with Bradley's (1930: 1) famous introduction to *Appearance and Reality*.

[57] See Simons (2012a: 245). Van Inwagen (2014: 95–8) also ascribes to Meinong the view that there is an outer quantifier and at least one inner quantifier; he is also concerned about the status of the outer quantifier. See also von Solodkoff and Woodward (2013) for a profitable discussion of Meinongianism.

over not only the existent and the subsistent but many other things as well (including things such that it is impossible that they exist or subsist), to be of crucial importance to philosophical theorizing: we ignore it at our peril. Corresponding to this outer quantifier is a possible science (dubbed the "Theory of Objects") whose doctrine is focused on the fundamental principles governing the objects it ranges over. Moreover, pure mathematics should be understood as an actually developed branch of this science. What this suggests is that the outer quantifier has as much right to be regarded as a fundamental expression as the two inner ones countenanced by Meinong. But then, contrary to Meinong's claim, things ranged over by the outer quantifier do enjoy a mode of being, which we could call *Quasisein*.[58] It also turns out that everything ranged over by the two "inner" quantifiers enjoys two modes of being, Quasisein and either existence or subsistence.

A similar worry arises for Bolzano's (2014a: 59, 173) view, according to which there are entities such as abstract propositions and ideal meanings that lack being. Nonetheless, it is crucial that philosophers recognize these beingless entities. Bolzano freely quantifies over the very entities to which he denies being, but because he stresses the fundamental importance of quantifying over them, I worry that, if he is correct, some highly natural quantifier ranges over them and hence, by the criterion suggested here, they enjoy a mode of being. The worry is compounded when we note that Bolzano (2014b: 44–6) also treats *being* as a first-order property.

How problematic is this? Strictly, what I have offered so far is only a criterion of what it is to believe in modes of being rather than a criterion of what it is to be a mode of being. But it is obvious that the criterion trades on the idea that perfectly natural quantifiers and modes of being go hand in hand, and the criterion is unmotivated unless this is true. So it would be good to have a response to the puzzle raised by the real historical Meinong; we can hope that contemporary Meinongians will find it sensible as well. Similar remarks apply to the historical Bolzano and any of his contemporary followers; accordingly, I will focus on Meinong.

I think the real Meinong should have just accepted Quasisein as a genuine mode of being: as noted earlier, the generic concept of an entity is bound up with the general concept of being, and all of Meinong's objects fall under the generic concept of an entity (or "object," to use his terminology). That said, there are things that a neo-Meinongian could say, which the real Meinong did not say, to distance themselves from endorsing Quasisein as a genuine mode of being. First, they could say that the outer quantifier is not a perfectly natural quantifier: although there is a sense of "being" available for us to use, and perhaps even sometimes actually in use, according to which there are objects that neither exist nor subsist, this sense of "being" is not perfectly natural. If the neo-Meinongian goes this route, she should probably also abandon the idea that this sense is crucially philosophically important in the way that

---

[58] For a discussion of Meinong's initial embrace and then rejection of *Quasisein*, see Jacquette (2001). See also Perszyk (1993: 54–67) and Vallicella (2002: 38–9).

Meinong thought. (Perhaps it is merely a quirk of our language or a consequence of our finite cognitive abilities that we have latched on to this less natural sense of "being." We'll revisit this question later in chapter 5.)

A second, more complicated move available to the Meinongian is to embrace a view like the following. In a metaphysically ideal language—one in which every expression is a natural expression (and every natural expression appears in the language)—there are quantifiers, one that ranges over existent objects, and one that ranges over subsistent objects. But there is no generic quantifier that has in its domain more objects than are ranged over by the existential and subsistential quantifiers. However, there are *terms* in this language that play the same syntactic roll as names, and some of these terms are such that there is no object ranged over by either the existential quantifier or the subsistential quantifier that is a referent for that term. In short, there are natural names in the metaphysically ideal language that cannot be substitution instances for variables bound by any of the quantifiers in the ideal language. Call such terms *metaphysically empty names.* In the ideal language, one can state truths using metaphysically empty names in subject-predicate sentences. And these truths might form interesting patterns or laws which *we* can articulate only by using a less-than-perfectly natural generic quantifier expression. And this is why, when we try to articulate such laws, we are inevitably led to such expressions as "there are things such that it is true that there are no such things."

On this picture, the logic of such a metaphysically ideal language is something like a *free* logic.[59] This view seems difficult to motivate, but it is one that the Meinongian who hates Quasisein but believes in the fundamental metaphysical importance of Meinongian objects ought to consider.

Let's confront other tricky questions. First, what should we say about *plural* quantification? In addition to phrases such as "there is," there is "there are." The position that plural quantifiers are really disguised singular quantifiers that range over objects other than those they appear to range over used to be (and perhaps still is) popular. On this view, when one says "there are some apples on the fridge" what one says is something like "there is a set of apples on the fridge" or "there is something made out of apples on the fridge." I think the case for the semantic reduction of plural quantifiers in English to singular quantifiers in English is weak, and moreover the case against such a reduction is strong.[60] However, the case for treating singular quantification as a special case of plural quantification (and more generally singular predication as a special case of plural predication) is much more straightforward.[61]

It might be then that, in English, the only semantically primitive quantifiers are plural quantifiers. It is still possible that in a metaphysically ideal language the only primitive quantifiers are singular quantifiers. (This seems to be the position Sider (2011) favors.) For our purposes, the sticky question is what to say if both primitive

[59] On free logics, see Nolt (2014).   [60] See McKay (2006) for more on plural quantification.
[61] See McKay (2006: 58–60, 120–1) for discussion.

plural and primitive singular quantifiers appear in the metaphysically ideal language. If the metaphysically ideal language has both plural and singular quantifiers with non-identical domains, then there is no especially tricky issue: we can straightfor-wardly say that there are at least two different modes of being. But suppose the metaphysically ideal language has exactly one singular quantifier and exactly one plural quantifier, and that the domains of the two kinds of fundamental quantifiers are the same. Then should we say that there are two modes of being, and that everything enjoys the same modes of being?

In such a case, I think this is what we should say.[62] Modes of being correspond with fundamental quantifier expressions, and such expressions may be plural or singular. The result generated in this case is surely odd, but I think that we are in the kind of situation in which a sensible criterion yields a silly result when applied to something that is in itself silly. I can't see what might justify claiming that the metaphysically ideal language is like this. Either the ideal language has a plural quantifier ranging over a given domain, or a singular quantifier, but not both. And though I actually incline towards the idea that the fundamental quantifiers are plural, in what follows here and in the successive chapters I will speak as though they are singular. By and large, my doing so will make it easier for me to state and argue for various positions and nothing in what follows will turn on my talking this way for reasons of convenience.

More interesting is what one should say about higher-order quantification. First-order quantifiers and names, broadly construed, are connected in the following way. Given a sentence of the form "a is F," in which "a" is a name and "F" is the predicate, one can replace the name with a variable, such as "x", and then bind that variable with a first-order quantifier, such as "some." This procedure yields the quantified sentence "some x is F." One kind of second-order quantifier, which I'll call a predicate-quantifier, is connected with predicates in an analogous way: one can replace the predicate with a different kind of variable, such as "$\dot{f}$", and bind that variable with a predicate-quantifier, also called "some." This procedure yields the sentence "a is some $\dot{f}$," which could be taken to say that a is some way or other.

Some philosophers have argued that higher-order quantification is really singular quantification over "higher-order entities," such as sets or properties.[63] A natural extension of such a view is that, although in the metaphysical ideal language all quantifiers are first-order quantifiers, the domain of some of those quantifiers includes sets or properties. On the other hand, some philosophers have argued that some (and perhaps all?) higher-order quantifiers can be treated as special plural quantifiers over "first-order" individuals such as tables and chairs.[64] Obvious cases are easy: "there is some way that all tables and chairs are" can be understood as "there

---

[62] One lesson of Caplan (2011: 97–100) is that it would be very hard for me to not say this without also ruling out other versions of ontological pluralism that I would prefer not to rule out.

[63] Most famously, Quine (1970).   [64] Most famously, Boolos (1984, 1985).

are some things such that all tables and chairs are among those things." Cases involving predications of relations are much trickier.[65]

For our purposes here, the interesting question is what to say if the metaphysically ideal language contains both first-order and second-order quantifiers. Suppose it has one of each: should we say that there are two distinct modes of being, or is that somehow inappropriate? Consider the following line of reasoning for holding that claims about beings and modes of being can come apart. The substitution instances of the variables of second-order quantifiers are predicates rather than (broadly speaking) names, and it is names that denote beings, and it is beings that have modes of being.

I'm not sure what to say about this line of reasoning. Such a metaphysical system is interesting regardless of whether it is classified as a system in which there are modes of being. The various metaphysical views we will consider are all ones in which there are multiple first-order quantifiers in the metaphysically ideal language. So perhaps we can postpone taking a stand on this thorny issue.[66]

1.5.3 Specific and Individual Existence

More troublesome to my classificatory scheme than the distinction between singular and plural quantifiers, or between first-order and second-order quantifiers, is the alleged distinction between specific and individual existence. "Specific" in this context does not mean "particular" but rather means something like "pertains to species." "General" is an equally apt term. Consider the difference between the claim that dogs exist and the claim that Ranger (an individual dog) exists. The former is arguably to be understood in terms of quantifiers, and as semantically equivalent to "There are dogs."[67] The latter is allegedly to be understood as an attribution of a property to an individual.

There is a tradition of understanding individual existence in terms of specific existence. Earlier in this chapter, I suggested that x exists if and only if there is some y such that $y = x$. Different modes of individual existence can be straightforwardly understood in terms of different modes of specific existence. But what should we say of those who (i) do not wish to analyze individual existence in terms of specific existence but (ii) commit themselves to different ways of (individually) existing? Such individuals might even go further by saying that there is only one metaphysically fundamental sense of the quantifier. On such a view, naturalness of quantificational phrases seems to come apart from the multiplicity of modes of existence. One could resist this position by claiming that whenever there is a natural property had by

---

[65] See the appendix of Lewis (1991) for discussion.

[66] Insofar as we want to understand the kind of ontological pluralism Frege seemed to endorse, we should find this matter a little troubling. See Caplan (2011: 81–3) for discussion of Frege's ontological pluralism.

[67] See, e.g., Kenny (2005a: 42).

all and only some things, there is a natural semantically primitive restricted quantifier that ranges over all and only those things. But this is both strained and not independently plausible.

Belief in many relatively fundamental existential quantifier expressions was offered as a sufficient condition for belief in ways of being, and not as a necessary condition, and a hard distinction between specific and individual existence does not falsify it. But such a distinction does make it difficult to see how one can offer a more general account of belief in modes of being that both covers views that embody this hard distinction and generates the sufficiency condition just mentioned. In itself, the fact that it is hard to come up with a fully general classification of ways of believing in modes of being doesn't matter much. There are many other philosophical views that are really better thought of as families of views, some more loosely unified than others.[68] Consider, for example, the dispute between endurantism and perdurantism in the literature on persistence through time. It is an exaggeration to say that there are hundreds of different formulations of "the endurantist view of persistence over time," but it feels sometimes like it is barely an exaggeration. I doubt that there is a criterion of what it is to believe in endurantism that can be stated in terms of necessary and sufficient conditions that can cover all these formulations. What seems to be the case is this: there is a core intuition (or a small set of core intuitions) and there are many possible ways to crystallize it (or them) in a formal statement of a view. And there is some set of arguments that favor some form or other of endurantism without clearly favoring any particular form. But when there are arguments that favor some particular version of endurantism over other formulations, the details of the particular formulations matter. (Similar remarks apply to arguments against endurantism.)

The same is probably true of the doctrine that there are modes of being. For example, the theological motivation for belief in modes of being that stems from the claim that we cannot speak univocally of God and creatures doesn't seem to favor versions in which individual existence is analyzed in terms of specific existence over versions in which they are both taken as given, or vice versa. Whether this is true with respect to the other motivations is less clear. For example, it is an interesting question whether the consideration from divine simplicity favors versions in which such a distinction is drawn; but the answer to this question, as we will see, is that it does not.

According to Aquinas, in God there is no composition, and so in God, unlike in creatures, there is no distinction between existence and essence. God *is* (this is the "is" of identity) his existence. Does it follow that his existence must be his *individual* existence, and so we must draw a distinction between specific and individual

---

[68] Spencer (2012) seems sympathetic with this line of thought. Caplan (2011) argues that attempts to come up with a unified criterion for being a version of ontological pluralism are unlikely to succeed; instead, probably "ontological pluralism" is itself a somewhat disjunctive notion. I'm comfortable with this conclusion, as will become clear in the final section of this chapter.

existence? There is an argument, inspired by remarks by Peter Geach (1969) and Anthony Kenny (2005a), for the conclusion that we cannot understand Aquinas as talking about specific existence. Consider the following passage by Kenny (2005a: 43–4):

Now let us ask whether, when it is said that God's essence is existence, it is specific or individual existence that is in question. The fact that the doctrine is supported by the phoenix argument suggests that Aquinas had specific existence in mind; but as Peter Geach has shown, if interpreted as referring to specific existence, the thesis is an absurdity. Statements of specific existence can be paraphrased in terms of the quantifier: so if God is pure existence, then "God" must be equivalent to "For some x, x.... "—a quantifier with a bound variable attached to no predicate. So understood, the thesis reduces the divine name to an ill-formed formula.[69]

This is a weak argument. First, if it were sound, a similar argument would suffice to show that God cannot be identical with His goodness: statements about the goodness of something can be understood as subject-predicate sentences in which the predicate "is good" appears, as in "pleasure is good." So if God is His goodness, then "God" must be equivalent to "is good," an unsaturated predicate. But pseudo-sentences like "Is good loves us" and "I pray to is good" are ill-formed, nonsensical constructions. So understood, the thesis that God is His goodness reduces the divine name to an ill-formed formula.

Perhaps Kenny would also welcome this conclusion, but he shouldn't. It's a bad argument too, but it is easier to see why it is a bad argument. Suppose there are properties, such as the property of being good. Perhaps there is even more than one property of being good: perhaps there is the property of being good in the way that God can be good, and there is the property of being good in the way that a creaturely thing can be good, and perhaps these properties are only analogously related. Set this aside for now—let's assume that "is good" can be used to ascribe a single property of goodness to both God and creatures. That's the function of the predicate "is good," and its semantic content is the property of being good. We can if we like introduce a name for the property as well—we've already been referring to it with the term "the property of being good" but let's give it a proper name too. We'll call it "Bob." The semantic content of this name is the same as the semantic content of the predicate "is good." But it in no way follows from this that the sentence "Bob is identical with is good" is a well-formed sentence. Although the semantic content of "Bob" is identical with the semantic content of "is good"—put less blandly, the thing denoted by "Bob" is the property expressed by "is good"—the way in which that content is attached to its different linguistic representations is correlated directly with the different ways in which it can occur in propositions about it.[70]

---

[69] See also Klima (2013: 160) for a similar complaint.
[70] Aquinas thought that one and the same thing can appear in the subject position of a judgment and the predicate position, but when it does, it does so under different guises. See, for example, *Summa Theologia* I, question 13, 12th article (Aquinas 1948: 71). This is in fact noted by Kenny (2005a: 156–8), so it is surprising that he does not allow for a similar move for quantification phrases.

The same is true of whatever is the semantic content of quantificational phrases. Set aside considerations having to do with divine simplicity or modes of being for now. Suppose that the semantic content of the existential quantifier simply is a higher-order property, perhaps a property of properties. Let's assume that it is simply the property of having at least one instance. Let's also give it a name. Call it "Sartre." The following sentences are each OK:

1. Sartre is a property had by the property of being a cat.
2. The property of being a cat has at least one instance.
3. There is at least one cat.

One and the same semantic content enjoys three different representational vehicles: name, predicate, and quantifier. In English, we can name whatever entity is expressed by other linguistic vehicles. It doesn't follow from this that "Sartre is identical with there is" is an acceptable sentence.

Similarly, even if God is identical with the kind of specific existence had by divine beings, or even if God is identical with the kind of existence had by every being (which is a claim that Aquinas definitely rejects), it does not follow that it makes sense to write "God is identical with there is" or that the divine name simply has the same meaning as "some." The absurd consequence that Kenny draws does not follow from the doctrine of divine simplicity. Kenny's argument that Aquinas must have in mind what Kenny calls "specific" existence is unsuccessful. The conclusion of it might still be correct, but Kenny has not established it.[71]

And one can use the framework here to explicate a clear sense in which God is identical with his existence while no creaturely thing is identical with her existence. There is a special mode of existence had by God which is representable by a special semantically primitive restricted quantifier; it is also denoted by the name "God," because it is identical with God. There is a distinct kind of existence had by creaturely things, or perhaps only by created substances, which is also representable by a special semantically primitive restricted quantifier. But no created substance is identical with the special mode of existence had by created substances.[72]

In general, many of the motivations for ontological pluralism previously discussed do not require taking a stand on whether there is a fundamental difference between specific and individual existence; in fact, in the next chapter, I'll speak mainly in terms

---

[71] Nor has Kenny (2005a: 43, fn. 26) demonstrated that questions concerning the priority of essence over existence are vitiated by the failure to distinguish between specific and individual existence. These questions will be the focus of chapter 9.

[72] This is not to say that Aquinas definitely thought about God's mode of being in terms of perfectly natural quantifiers. As Brower (2014: 54) points out, this interpretation would be anachronistic. And yet, as Brower (2014: 51–4) nicely argues, the model described here is still a very useful model for understanding Aquinas's thoughts on being. See McDaniel (forthcoming-a) for a discussion of philosophical models in the history of philosophy.

of individual existence since that will make the exposition a bit easier, but all of what I say can be recaptured in terms of specific existence. My own preferred metaphysics does not appeal to any fundamental kinds of existence that can be expressed only via predicates. D. C. Williams (1962: 763) "dispensed" with existence in favor of the prior notion of something. I am happy to follow suit, provided that we accommodate ways of being something. Perhaps in natural language, modes of being are expressed via predicates rather than perfectly natural semantically restricted quantifiers. But from a metaphysical perspective, the better language is one in which they are expressed via the latter rather than the former—or so I will argue in the chapters to come!

1.5.4 Metaphysical Naturalness and Truth in Reality

Although I have formulated ontological pluralism by appealing to a primitive notion of naturalness that applies to sub-sentential expressions, one can formulate a similar view by appealing to an alternative metaphysical framework. I have in mind the framework of Kit Fine (2001, 2006), which draws a metaphysical distinction between what is true and what is *really* true. Fine's framework is motivated by the observation that frequently philosophers want to deny the reality of some domain of entities, such as moral properties or mathematical objects, while upholding the literal truth of existential claims about these entities. In order to do this consistently, we must be able to

consistently . . . affirm that something is the case and yet deny that it is really the case. [We require] a *metaphysical* conception of reality, one that enables us to distinguish, within the sphere of what is the case, between what is really the case and what is only apparently the case.
[Fine 2001: 2–3]

In order to make the distinction he cares about, Fine postulates a special operator, *it is really the case that* ("R"). R is not extensional, that is, for some true statements P and Q, $R(P)$ is true whereas $R(Q)$ is false. It might be that, for example, it is true that properties exist without it being really true that they exist. On Fine's view, not all truths are *really* true.

Consider a meta-ontology that recognizes two modes of being that correspond to the semantically primitive quantifiers "$\exists_1$" and "$\exists_2$". Suppose further that this meta-ontology denies that the unrestricted existential quantifier is perfectly natural. How can these facts be expressed in Fine's system? Since "R" applies only to whole sentences, we can't simply preface these quantifiers with "R" to get the desired result.[73] But we can get a desirable result in the following way: state that, for all Φ, it's false that $R(\exists x \, \Phi)$, but there is a Φ and there is a Ψ such that it is true that $R(\exists_1 x \, \Phi)$

---

[73] Recall that Sider's naturalness operator operates at the sub-sentential level.

and it is true that $R(\exists_2 x\ \Psi)$. "$\exists_1$"and "$\exists_2$" figure in statements that are true in reality, whereas "$\exists$" does not. Perhaps other, more sophisticated meta-ontologies could be treated in a similar fashion.[74]

A different, and perhaps more radical way, to think of ontological pluralism in this context is as the view that there is more than one "true in reality" operator: each mode of being corresponds to a different way of being "true in reality"; better put, each mode of being corresponds to a different kind of reality in which something might be true.

In the chapters that follow, I will continue to make use of naturalness rather than Kit Fine's notion of truth in reality, or some variant of it.[75] But that is not because I think that this is ultimately the best way to understand modes of being. My preferred view identifies naturalness with a distinctively ontological phenomenon: a property is natural to the extent that it exists. The relation between naturalness and existence is the focus of chapter 7. For now, though, I will continue to speak in terms of naturalness.

The upshot of these reflections is that it is highly unlikely that we can give necessary and sufficient conditions for a theory to count as an instance of ontological pluralism. But really, would that make the doctrine any different than any other interesting philosophical doctrine? Since all of the versions of ontological pluralism that I will discuss in the successive chapters are clear cases of ontological pluralism, I am untroubled by the fact that I have not yet provided necessary and sufficient conditions that a view must meet in order to be a version of ontological pluralism.

So in some sense, I accept what Caplan (2011) calls "ontological superpluralism," at least to this extent: the various versions of ontological pluralism are more interesting than the question of what they each have in common, and we are more likely to make philosophical progress by examining the merits and demerits of individual versions of ontological pluralism rather than ontological pluralism in general. This is why in the succeeding chapters we will examine various applications or instances of ontological pluralism rather than attempt further to answer the question of what it is to be a version of ontological pluralism.

1.6 Chapter Summary

In this chapter, I developed a version of ontological pluralism that appealed to semantically primitive restricted quantification and naturalness. I also articulated

---

[74] Note that this way of construing modes of being seems to rule out a maximally general mode of being, but strictly what it rules out is that the quantifier of ordinary language corresponds to one. I'm OK with this result (as will be discussed in chapters 4 and 5).

[75] We'll discuss truth in reality a bit more in section 5.4.

different ways of formulating versions of ontological pluralism. Although I defended ontological pluralism from some objections, the main goals of this chapter were to get some versions of ontological pluralism on the table, show that they are intelligible and worthy of consideration, and show how concerns about ontological pluralism connect up with historical and contemporary meta-metaphysical issues.

2

A Return to the Analogy of Being

2.1 Introduction

In the history of philosophy, the question of whether there are ways of being has been closely related to a seemingly more general question: when should one think that some philosophically interesting expression is *analogous*? This is because on many of the historically interesting ways of implementing ontological pluralism, ontological expressions such as "being," "there is," and "exists" are analogous in one or many of the varied technical senses given to the term "analogy."

In this chapter, the primary focus will be on explicating a contemporary and metaphysical notion of analogy, and then providing ontologies on which ontological expressions such as "being," "existence," and so on, are analogous. In what follows, I will articulate two distinct tests for being an analogous expression, and then illustrate how, on many ways of implementing ontological pluralism, "being" is analogous. Along the way, I will present a series of ontological schemes, each of which meets at least one of the tests. If you are attracted to one of these ontologies, you have some reason to believe in ways of being.

In general, I see the goal of making a case for ways of being to contemporary metaphysicians as being challenging enough that a book-length defense is required. I do not believe that one could ever be rationally *required* to believe in ways of being. Still, a metaphysic is a live option if it is rationally permissible to believe. In recent decades, the dominant view among analytic metaphysicians was that ontological pluralism is silly or confused, so establishing the rational permissibility of belief in ways of being is an important task. We made good progress on this task in the previous chapter, but there is still more work to do. Let's proceed.

2.2 Varieties of Analogy

My focus will be on exploring a notion of analogy that is metaphysical in nature and applies primarily to entities such as properties and relations. My preferred view is that an analogous term is one that expresses an analogous property or relation. The phenomenon of analogy then is primarily metaphysical rather than semantical, and an analogous term might be univocal in ordinary language.

This way of thinking presupposes a kind of realism about properties and relations. (How strong is this realism? We'll return to that question in section 7.3.) But we might wish for some flexibility and try to carve out a distinctively metaphysical notion of analogy that applies to terms directly and independently of the semantic relations that terms in a given language bear to each other. (Recall the machinery introduced by Sider that we discussed in the previous chapter, which allows one to state comparative naturalness claims without ontologically committing oneself to objects such as properties.)

These remarks are at this stage highly abstract, and perhaps it's useful to discuss some of the historical accounts of analogy in order to contrast those accounts with the one to be explored here. In the medieval tradition, a variety of kinds of analogy were catalogued and explored. We'll look at some of them in order to draw out the desired comparisons and contrasts.

One kind of analogy is the *analogy of inequality*, sometimes also called the *analogy of priority and posterity*. With respect to this kind of analogy, "F" is said analogously of x and y whenever x and y are both F but one of them is a more perfect F than the other. One way to be a more perfect F is to be more of an F.[1] This way of thinking of the analogy of being naturally leads to considering whether being is gradable, so that one thing can be more of a being than another. Since this will be the focus of chapters 5, 6, and 7, and our focus here is on modes of being rather than grades of being, in a moment we will set this kind of analogy aside. However, before we move on, first note that this kind of analogy is primarily metaphysical rather than semantic. It might be no part of the *meaning* of the term "F" or the concept of F that F comes in grades, or that instances of F can be more perfect Fs than others. That "F" is analogous might have more to do with the nature of F than with the meaning of "F."

A second kind of analogy is the analogy exemplified by "healthy," which was briefly discussed in section 1.2. Often this kind of analogy was called *an analogy of attribution*.[2] As noted there, in contemporary parlance a term that is analogous in this respect exhibits *focal meaning*. A term with focal meaning is polysemous but the polysemy is structured in an orderly way. There is a primary meaning of the term "health," and the other meanings of the term are definable in terms of this primary meaning. This kind of analogy is primarily semantic rather than metaphysical. For example, it might be that all of the meanings of a given term with focal meaning correspond to properties or relations that are roughly on a par with each other with respect to how natural or fundamental they are.

That said, there is an analogous metaphysical kind of analogy, one that is exhibited by *being* according to the Aristotelian tradition, of which I take Heidegger to tenuously belong. On this metaphysical analogue of focal meaning, an analogous property is akin to a determinable property in that it has specifications that bear

---

[1] See Hochschild (2010: 101–3) for discussion.
[2] See Coffey (1938: 36), Ashworth (1995: 56–9; 2013a), and Ward (2008: 2).

structural relations to each other.[3] These specifications are such that, among them, one is the central specification and the others are to be understood via how they are related to that central specification.[4] With respect to this kind of analogy, one specification of an analogous property enjoys more naturalness or fundamentality than the other specifications, since the central specification is more intrinsic than the remaining specifications in the following sense: the remaining specifications are both extrinsic features (while the central specification *might* be an intrinsic feature, but it needn't be) and they are instantiated because of a relation that their exemplifiers bear to an exemplifier of the central specification. For this reason, I say that the central specification is *more* intrinsic than the remaining ones, and hence is more natural or fundamental than the remainders.

A third kind of analogy is an attenuated version of the second metaphysical kind, or at least a more general version that encompasses the second kind. With respect to this kind of analogy, the specifications are both different from each other and alike, but there might not be a central or focal feature to unify the specifications. Let's try to get a bit clearer about this kind of analogy.

Let us say that a possibly instantiated feature is *topic-neutral* if it can apply to objects from any ontological category. For now, I'll remain neutral on what it is to be an ontological category and simply help myself to the idea that things belong to different ontological categories. In chapter 4, we will examine more critically what it is to be an ontological category.

A plausible candidate of a topic-neutral feature is self-identity: propositions are self-identical, properties are self-identical, concrete objects are self-identical, and so forth. Let us say that a possibly instantiated feature is *topic-specific* just in case there is some ontological category such that the feature cannot apply to entities in that category. Being spatially located is a topic-specific feature, since no proposition is or could be spatially located.

It will be helpful to have the following notion of relative topic-neutrality. Let F1 and F2 be possibly instantiated features and say that F1 is *more* topic-neutral than F2 if the class of kinds of things that F2 can apply to is a proper subclass of the class of kinds of things that F1 can apply to. (A feature F *applies* to a class of things K just in case a possible member of K is F.) This account here is not fully general, since it does not allow us to compare the relative topic-neutrality of properties whose possible extensions are completely disjoint. Moreover, this account of topic-neutrality pre-supposes some background assumptions about what the ontological categories are and how they relate to each other in order to yield the right results in some cases.

---

[3] Similarly, Shields (1999: 59) distinguishes between *focal meaning*, which is a semantic phenomenon, and *focal connection*, which is an object-level phenomenon.

[4] As Shields (1999: 59) notes, it is very tricky to determine which relations are relevant to determining focal connections. Shields (1999: 110–24) adopts the view that what determines focal connections are the various Aristotelian forms of causation. Ward (2008: 80–1) criticizes Shields's account.

For example, if necessarily everything were located in space–time, then being spatiotemporally located would be classified as a topic-neutral property, contrary to what was said in the previous paragraph. So this characterization of topic-neutrality is rough. However, it will suffice for our purposes here.

Whenever we have a feature that applies to many different ontological categories (or kinds of things more generally), there is an interesting metaphysical question: is this relatively topic-neutral feature perfectly natural (or at least highly natural) or is it akin to a mere disjunction of more natural, more topic-specific features?

Consider again *being healthy*. I am healthy, my circulatory system is healthy, and broccoli is healthy. Let us suppose that there is a common property that we all share. On many theories of properties, such as Lewis's (1986) theory according to which any set of possible individuals is a property, there definitely is a property we exemplify. Even so, that in virtue of which we exemplify this common property differs from case to case. I am healthy in virtue of being a flourishing organism, my circulatory system is healthy in virtue of functioning properly, and broccoli is healthy in virtue of its contributing to the flourishing of organisms like me. Being healthy is something like a mere disjunction whose disjuncts include *being a flourishing organism*, *being a properly functioning part of an organism*, and *being something that contributes to the flourishing of an organism*. Each of these properties is more natural than being healthy. Being healthy is an *analogous* feature: each of the specifications of being healthy just listed are more natural than the "generic" feature of being healthy. But being healthy is not a mere disjunction: the various specifications of being healthy are related in such a way to ensure some kind of unity. (Unlike, say, *being an electron or a female sibling*.) The kinds of healthiness are unified via how they relate to a single specification.

It is good to have a rich diet of examples. Consider *being flexible*. My aunt is flexible, my rubber chicken is flexible, my thinking on these matters is flexible, and my schedule is flexible. My inclination is to distinguish ways of being flexible and to hold the generic property of being flexible is analogous. Consider *being elegant*. The swan is elegant, Obama's speech was elegant, and the theory of general relativity is elegant. Finally, I suspect that *x is a cause of y*, *x is an explanation for y*, and *x is a consequence of y* are all analogous relations, but I won't argue for this here. I merely suggest these relations for further consideration.

Analogous features are something akin to disjunctive properties, but they aren't merely disjunctive. Analogous features enjoy a kind of unity that merely disjunctive features lack: their specifications are, to put it in medieval terms, *unified by analogy*.

We've discussed some examples of analogous properties. For a putatively contrasting example, consider the identity relation. The dominant view about the identity relation is that it is topic-neutral but neither merely disjunctive nor analogous. Instead, it is a good candidate for being a perfectly natural logical relation. I say that identity is a "good candidate" because I don't want to dogmatically reject a kind of identity pluralism according to which identity is analogous. For example, such a view might be defended by appealing to considerations about the different ways in which objects and events have parts or persist through time.[5]

Let us call the specific properties from which an analogous property is derived the *analogue instances* of that property. (Analogue instances of a common analogous property are *analogates* of each other.) The relation between an analogous property and its analogue instances is similar to the relation between a determinable property and its determinates in that analogue instances and determinates are both "specifications" of a "broader property." However, there is one key difference: on my view, all determinates of a determinable are equally natural, and any determinate of a determinable is as natural as the determinable.[6] But neither need be true of analogous properties and their analogue instances.

An example of a property that is not analogous is *being a bank**. Something is a bank* just in case it is either a riverbank or a financial institution. Clearly there is a difference between *being a bank** and *being healthy*, even though it is very hard to precisely state in what this difference consists. *Being a bank** is a mere disjunction, while *being healthy* is analogous. The individual ways of being healthy (the analogue instances of *being healthy*) have something importantly in common with each other that is not captured by treating *being healthy* as a mere disjunction.[7]

Similarly, even if God's way of existing and the way of existing of created things are numerically distinct, these two ways of existing are similar enough to ensure that *existence simpliciter* is *not* a mere disjunction of the two. If God's way of existing and creaturely ways of existing were radically unalike, it would be hard to see what would make these features ways of *existing* as opposed to just two totally different features. There is a serious issue here: what, if anything, accounts for the *unity* of analogous properties? Can anything explain why analogue instances form an analogous property rather than a mere disjunction?

Suppose analogous properties always enjoyed focal specifications. That is, each analogous property is such that among its analogue instances one is the most natural and the others derive their degree of naturalness by virtue of how they are related to this most natural analogue instance. This more or less is the picture of health and being depicted in the previous chapter. Then we would be able to make some headway at answering these questions.

Unfortunately, however, I think there is good reason to doubt that all analogous properties have this feature. In a few moments, I'll explain why I think that parthood

---

[5] See McDaniel (2014a) for a discussion of the motivations for this kind of identity pluralism. We'll have more to say about the status of identity in section 5.7.

[6] This is a controversial view, to be sure. Armstrong (1997: 50) advocates a reductionist view about determinable properties, and Rosen (2010: 128–9) is sympathetic to treating determinables as mere disjunctions of their determinates. By contrast, Wilson (2012) is a full-fledged defender of some fundamental determinable properties. I side with Wilson here.

[7] The boundary between mere disjunctiveness and analogicity is vague, because some properties are more disjunctive than others. Conversely, some analogous properties might enjoy more unity than others. This will be further discussed shortly.

is an analogous feature, but the explanation of why parthood is analogous will leave open whether the more natural (and more topic-restricted) parthood relations are each as natural as each other, with none of them being the "central kind" of parthood.

Sometimes this unity of analogy is via relations to a single specification. But I believe in other cases it is not, but rather it is simply a fact that a set of specifications have a kind of internal unity, even though we cannot explicate in what this unity consists.[8] In those cases, I can't give a criterion for when a feature is an analogous feature as opposed to a merely disjunctive feature. It might be that in this sort of case there is little more that we can do than take the difference between analogous and disjunctive properties as a brute difference in how natural the properties in question are.

The following remarks give barely more than the appearance of precision, but might still be of some use. Consider two functions on sets of properties. The first function takes a set of properties to the mere disjunction of the members of that set. The second function takes a set of properties to an analogous property "derived from" the members of that set. Mere disjunctions and analogous properties are always less natural than their disjuncts or analogue instances. But disjunctive properties are far less natural than their disjuncts, whereas analogous properties can be almost as natural as their analogue instances. This gives some content to the idea that some properties are "unified by analogy" whereas others are unified by nothing more than a mere list of the actual or possible things that have them.

This way of talking suggests that properties can be necessarily coextensive yet non-identical. I am inclined to think that properties are individuated more finely than necessary coextension, but a more cautious statement is this: some "disjunctive" properties are less "disjunctive" than others. There are equinumerous sets of properties H and P such that there is a 1–1 correspondence between H and P that preserves degree of naturalness, and yet the analogous property consisting of the members of H is more natural than the disjunctive property consisting of the members of P. And even this way of speaking might be more committal than we want, since it requires *degrees* of naturalness. An even more cautious statement, which I owe to Joshua Spencer, is this: there are two sets of properties, H and P, and a 1–1 correspondence, f, between the members of H and the members of P such that for each x of H, x is as natural as $f(x)$ and yet the "disjunction" of the properties in H is more natural than the disjunction of the properties in P.

My conception of an analogous property is in many ways less sophisticated than the conceptions of analogy of my medieval predecessors from whom I have appropriated the term. There are many ways in which the analogue instances of an analogous property could be related to each other in such a way that the analogous property enjoys more unity—that is, a higher degree of naturalness—than a mere

---

[8] Pasnau and Shields (2004: 116–19) discuss what they call "analogical predication," a species of which is ordered analogical predication. This suggests that they recognize other species of analogical predication.

disjunction of these analogue instances would. For example, consider that the salient relation between the kind of healthiness enjoyed by an animal and the kind of healthiness enjoyed by that animal's heart is not identical with the salient relation between the kind of healthiness enjoyed by an animal and the kind of healthiness enjoyed by that animal's urine. Menn (2005: 165–6), from whom these examples are drawn, follows Suárez in calling the former relation "an analogy of intrinsic denomination" and the latter relation "an analogy of extrinsic denomination." Perhaps analogous properties whose analogue instances are related wholly via analogies of intrinsic denomination enjoy more naturalness than properties whose analogue instances are related via both analogies of intrinsic and extrinsic denomination, at least on the assumption that there is a one–one function between the analogue instances of each analogous property that preserves degrees of naturalness. This is a hypothesis I am open to since the former properties are plausibly more unified than the latter. In general, it would be profitable to recapitulate the various forms of analogy recognized in the medieval tradition in terms of the naturalness framework articulated here.

My notion of an analogous property is metaphysical rather than semantic. A property can be analogous and yet be the sole semantic value of a predicate— and so in no semantic sense is that predicate less than univocal. Moreover, an analogous property might be the sole semantic value of a predicate in a language in which no terms have as their semantic values the analogue instances of this property.[9] The relation between an analogous property and its analogue instances is not mediated by semantic considerations. Similarly, there needn't be any articulate structure in a mental state that represents an analogous property. From the perspective of the cognitive economy of the agent, a concept standing for an analogous property could be a conceptual primitive. Even if there is only one concept of being, rather than many closely related concepts, that which the concept is about might be analogical.[10]

For this reason, the friend of modes of being has nothing to fear from what we can call *the neo-Quinean thesis*, according to which (i) the meaning of "existence" in ordinary English is fully captured by the existential quantifier of first-order formal logic and (ii) this meaning can be completely specified by saying which inferences containing the quantifier are valid. Those inferences are the ones validated by

---

[9] Compare with Vallicella (2002: 19–22), who also carefully distinguishes the metaphysical thesis that there are modes of being from any semantic thesis about the linguistic vehicles that represent (or fail to represent) them.

[10] According to Amerini (2014: 328), Alexander of Alessandria held that that the concept of being functions as a univocal concept although being is analogous, and that, although there are different ways of existing, this doesn't mean that there are different senses of "existing." Schwartz (2012b: 8–9) notes that Suárez distinguishes between a "formal concept" of being that is a unity from the "objective concept of being," which is that which the formal concept is about, and this objective concept is analogical; see also Pereira (2007: 73–7, 118).

first-order logic. On this thesis, if you want to know what "existence" means, you need to study the logic of quantification.[11]

Recall that in the previous chapter we discussed how to accommodate ontological pluralists such as Heidegger by taking on board the Lewisian–Siderian notion of naturalness, and holding that there are possible semantically primitive restricted quantifiers that are at least as natural as the unrestricted quantifier of ordinary English. For the Heideggerian, these quantifiers are *more* natural than the existential quantifier. On this view, it would be *metaphysically better* to speak one of those languages than the languages we actually speak. Modes of being are *ontological joints*, and a language is metaphysically better to the extent that its primitive notions correspond to real distinctions. But note that one could hold this view without holding that the ordinary English word "existence" is ambiguous or that its meaning is not captured by the existential quantifier of formal logic. The possible semantically primitive quantifiers might be *merely* possible rather than actually realized in a natural language.[12] So the doctrine that things exist in different ways is compatible with the neo-Quinean thesis, although one could hold that things exist in different ways while rejecting the neo-Quinean thesis. Accordingly, the claim that there are modes of being is not refuted by the view that the meaning of "existence" or "being" is fully captured by the role of the existential quantifier of formal logic.[13]

This way of characterizing ontological pluralism plausibly implies that whether ontological pluralism is true can't be contingent.[14] This consequence is acceptable to me. However, there might still be a kind of contingency in the neighborhood: it might be that, in some worlds, only one of the many perfectly natural quantifiers has a non-empty domain. In that sense, ontological pluralism might be contingently true.

Finally, in what follows I talk as if existence is a first-order property, though not much turns on this. First, I am happy to formulate the views that follow in accordance with what we can call *the Kant-Frege thesis*, according to which existence is a property, but not of individuals. Rather, existence is a second-order property of concepts, propositional functions, or properties.[15] Because nothing in what follows

---

[11] For an apparent expression of this thesis, see Quine (1969b). I doubt that Quine ever held the neo-Quinean thesis, since the thesis is true only if a term in one language—English—is synonymous with a term in a distinct language, the language of formal logic. But many contemporary philosophers do endorse this thesis. Peter van Inwagen (2001b) is one prominent example among many.

[12] There are some tricky issues about what it means for a possible language to realize a quantifier. I assume that the English expression "there is" is synonymous with the German expression "es gibt." Each of these expressions is a quantifier-expression, but I would prefer to say that there is just one quantifier that each expresses. It is not obvious that saying this requires reifying quantifier meanings as abstract objects over and above the particular quantifier-expressions. See Sider (2011: ch. 10.2) for a more extensive discussion.

[13] Szabó (2003) suggests that something like this view about the meaning of "being" is what led many contemporary philosophers to reject modes of being.

[14] Thanks to an anonymous referee for discussion here.

[15] Whether Kant himself endorsed the Kant-Frege thesis is controversial. See Kant (1999a: 567, A600/B628) for texts that have inspired some to attribute this thesis to him. Bennett (1966: 199) claims that Kant

turns on whatever differences there might be between concepts, propositional functions, or properties, let's focus on the view that existence is a property of properties.
Although the doctrine that there are ways of being is consistent with the Kant–Frege
thesis, it is not committed to it. As noted in section 1.5.3, the friend of ways of being
might hold instead that existence is a first-order property of individuals. Moreover,
existence might not be a perfectly natural property but instead might be similar to
a mere disjunction of more natural first-order properties, the ways of being.
However, as also noted in section 1.5, one could believe that things exist in different
ways without believing that there are ways in which things exist. There are (at least)
two ways to coherently formulate the doctrine that things exist in different ways:
one that takes the notion of ways of existence ontologically seriously, and one that
does not. It will be occasionally convenient to focus on the ontologically serious
formulation, but most of what matters in what follows could be recast in terms
acceptable to the nominalist. Similarly, the friend of ways of being might agree with
the Kant–Frege thesis that *existence* and *modes of existence* are second-order
properties, or she might hold instead that they are first-order properties.[16] It will
occasionally be convenient to focus on the version of the view that existence is a
first-order property, but the arguments to come could be recast so as to be in line
with the Kant–Frege thesis.

2.3 Two Tests for Metaphysical Analogy

On many versions of ontological pluralism, *existence* or *being* is an analogous
feature.[17] Accordingly, if we first determine the conditions in which we should
think that a philosophically interesting feature is an analogous feature (or even
merely disjunctive), we should then be able to determine whether *existence* or
being satisfies these conditions. The key thing is that, if a property F is analogous,
then F is not a perfectly natural property and there are properties, the Gs, such that
(i) each of the Gs is more natural than F and (ii) necessarily, anything that exemplifies one of the Gs is F. Paradigm examples of analogous properties also satisfy a third

---

anticipates Frege. See van Cleve (1999: 187–91) for discussion. Heathwood (2011) is also relevant,
and contains further references. Frege's (1980b: 48–50) allegiance to the Kant–Frege thesis is substantially
clearer.

[16] For a defense of the view that existence is a first-order property, see Miller (2002).

[17] Hence the name: "the analogy of being." Some ontological pluralists, especially those who distinguish
between *existence* (roughly, the way in which concrete things are) and *subsistence* (roughly, the way in
which abstract things are), do not explicitly endorse the view that *being* is analogous. Some of these
philosophers speak as if they do not recognize a fully topic-neutral sense of "existence" or "being."
Nonetheless, the view that *being simpliciter* is analogous is a natural accompaniment to such views. For
a contrary take, see Moore (1969: 372–3), who is willing to grant that particulars enjoy a mode of being not
enjoyed by universals, but holds that nonetheless the mode of being enjoyed by both particulars and
universals is metaphysically more fundamental. Thanks to an anonymous referee for directing me to this
reference.

condition: (iii) each of the Gs applies to fewer kinds of things than F.[18] The putatively analogous features of interest to ontologists will be more topic-neutral than their topic-specific analogue instances.

As a test case, let us consider once more the *parthood* relation. The parthood relation might not be strictly topic-neutral, but it at least enjoys a relatively high degree of topic-neutrality.[19] Spatiotemporal regions, material objects, immaterial souls, propositions, sets, properties, and facts have all been thought of as having part–whole structure.

On my view, parthood is analogous. I accept compositional pluralism: there is more than one fundamental parthood relation. Consider an ontological scheme that includes spatiotemporal regions, enduring material occupants of spatiotemporal regions, properties, and facts understood not as true propositions but rather as entities capable of making true propositions true. Let's suppose this ontological scheme is true. This ontological scheme motivates compositional pluralism in two ways.[20]

First, focus on material occupants and regions of space–time. Since material objects persist by enduring, they successively occupy distinct regions of space–time. Since a material object can gain or lose parts, material objects have parts relative to regions of space–time. But regions do not have parts relative to regions; they have parts simpliciter.

Now one *could* say that there is one perfectly natural relation that is exemplified by both regions and occupants. However, if one does say this, one must hold that this perfectly natural relation is *variably polyadic*—it is sometimes fully saturated by exactly two entities, and it is sometimes fully saturated by exactly three entities. Moreover, this variably polyadic relation is *systematically* variably polyadic: necessarily, parthood is fully saturated by two regions, or by two material objects and one region. Let us say that a feature F is systematically variably polyadic just in case there are ontological categories O1 and O2 such that whenever some things in O1 participate in F, exactly n things are necessary to fully saturate F, whereas whenever only things in O2 participate in F, exactly m things are necessary to fully saturate F (where n is not the same number as m). Being systematically variably polyadic is an ugly way for a putatively perfectly natural relation to behave.

I am not suspicious of variably polyadic natural relations in general.[21] Rather, the thought is this: when you have a highly topic-neutral feature that behaves in a fundamentally different way when applied to objects from different ontological categories, but behaves uniformly within single ontological categories, it is reasonable

---

[18] For example, this is true of being healthy. The specifications of being healthy (its analogue instances) apply to fewer kinds of things than being healthy simpliciter.

[19] See McDaniel (2010c) for a discussion of whether parthood is topic-neutral.

[20] For further discussion of compositional pluralism, see McDaniel (2004, 2009a, and 2014a).

[21] This is not to say that there are no arguments against taking multigrade relations to be perfectly natural. D. H. Mellor (1995: 207–28) argues that multigrade relations are not "genuine universals." See also Armstrong (1997: 85).

to suspect that the more natural features are the topic-specific features defined on individual categories. Change of *adicity* constitutes a fundamental difference of behavior! Moreover, the behavior is "disjunctive" in character: it is either one way or the other, but in a systematic way. So I say that, other things being equal, if a feature is systematically variably polyadic, do not believe that it is a perfectly natural feature.

Parthood is systematically variably polyadic. The specific parthood relations are more fundamental than the generic relation of parthood. But note that it is clear to us that the various kinds of parthood relations are all kinds of parthood relations! It is not that we have simply decided to label each of the respective specific parthood relations with a common term, but rather there is something that they all have in common that makes it appropriate to introduce a common term to cover them all. Parthood is not a merely disjunctive relation. However, we cannot account for its non-disjunctive nature by articulating a common feature that makes each specification of parthood appropriately lumped together. (What would that feature be?) And none of the specifications of parthood seems clearly to be the central specification in terms of which the others are defined. (Which one of the specifications is even a good candidate for being *the* central kind of parthood?) Rather, in some way that we cannot explicate, the specifications are analogues of each other. In short, this is a case of the third kind of metaphysical analogy: analogy without a focal point.

Let us now explore the other route to compositional pluralism. Let us say that the "logic" of a feature consists in those necessary truths stateable using only some term, such as a predicate or a name, standing for the feature along with purely logical vocabulary. The principles constituting the logic of a feature are principles that *govern* that feature: they apply to all possible situations in which that feature is exemplified, but explicitly mention no other qualitative features obtaining in that situation. Let us say that a feature is *systematically variably axiomatic* just in case the principles governing that feature differ systematically from one ontological category to the next. If a feature is systematically variably polyadic, it will follow that the feature is also systematically variably axiomatic. However, the converse need not hold.

Focus now on regions of space–time and facts. Both the parthood relation defined on regions and the relation defined on facts is two-placed. One *could* say that there is one perfectly natural relation that is exemplified by both regions and facts. However, note that the logic of this relation is ugly. The principles of classical mereology govern how parthood applies to regions: (i) whenever there are some regions, there is a region composed of them (unrestricted composition); (ii) whenever region $r1$ and region $r2$ are composed of the same regions, then $r1$ and $r2$ are identical (extensionality); and (iii) if $r1$ is a part of $r2$, and $r2$ is a part of $r3$, then $r1$ is a part of $r3$ (transitivity).[22] However, the principles of classical mereology do not govern how

---

[22] Unrestricted composition, extensionality, and transitivity are taken as the three axioms of classical mereology in its formulation in Lewis (1991).

parthood applies to facts: neither universal composition nor extensionality hold.[23] So the "logic" of the topic-neutral parthood relation is ugly, but systematically ugly: when applied to objects of one ontological category, it behaves in one way, but when applied to objects of another ontological category, it behaves in a radically different way. The "logic" of parthood is most naturally expressed as a disjunctive list of two (or more!) disjoint axiom systems, each such that the variables are restricted to objects of the relevant kinds.[24] Parthood is systematically variably axiomatic. This is a bad way for a perfectly natural relation to behave: its behavior looks *disjunctive* at worst, less than uniform at best.

A more natural response is to deny that the topic-neutral parthood relation is perfectly natural. Instead, there are three perfectly natural topic-specific parthood relations, one for regions, one for material objects, and one for facts.[25] Each topic-specific parthood relation behaves uniformly across its field. The topic-neutral relation isn't a mere disjunction of these three topic-specific relations: instead, it is an analogous relation, one less natural than its analogue instances but still enjoying some kind of unity. (The various topic-specific parthood relations seem to be more like each other than, for example, spatiotemporal distance and *being the same color as*.)

The driving intuition is that highly natural features enjoy a kind of unity across their instances. When that unity is lacking in a feature, and lacking in a systematic way, while the related topic-specific features display such a unity, one is warranted in holding that the topic-specific features are more natural than the topic-neutral one. Insofar as we think that there is *some* unity to the parthood relation, we will be inclined to think that parthood is an analogous relation rather than a mere disjunction. If we accept an ontology of regions, enduring objects, and facts, we aren't *forced* to say that parthood is analogous. The intuitions elicited here do not constitute a deductive *proof* that parthood is analogous. However, they do make the claim reasonable, and they generate significant pressure to hold that parthood is analogous.[26]

There is a twofold lesson to be drawn. First: if a relatively topic-neutral feature is systematically variably polyadic, then that feature is probably not perfectly natural. Second: if the principles governing a topic-neutral feature differ systematically from one ontological category to the next, then that feature is probably not perfectly

---

[23] If universal summation held, the mere existence of a property and an object would ensure the existence of a fact that the object has that property. If extensionality held, the fact that I love you would be identical with the fact that you love me. Neither of these results is acceptable to the friend of facts. See McDaniel (2009a) for further discussion.

[24] As an anonymous referee has pointed out to me, though, it can be a non-trivial task to determine what the relevant kinds are.

[25] This is the view discussed in McDaniel (2004, 2009a)

[26] In McDaniel (2009a), I provide a stronger argument for compositional pluralism. Briefly, I argue that, given Armstrong's ontology of fact and object, the topic-neutral parthood relation is either non-transitive or lacks an irreflexive proper parthood relation. I then argue that either feature disqualifies it from being a perfectly natural parthood relation.

natural. In either case, insofar as we hold that there is any unity to the feature at all, we will be under pressure to hold that the feature is analogous.

Can we apply these lessons to the case of *existence*?

2.4 The Analogy of Being

A reasonable ontological scheme is one that could be reasonably believed. We will address two questions. First, are there reasonable ontological schemes in which existence is systematically variably polyadic? Second, are there reasonable ontological schemes in which existence is systematically variably axiomatic? If the answer to either question is "yes," then there are reasonable ontological schemes on which it would be reasonable to hold that *existence* is analogous. Accordingly, it would be reasonable to believe in ways of being.

Here, in section 2.4, I discuss reasonable ontological schemes according to which existence is systematically variably polyadic. In section 2.5, I discuss reasonable ontological schemes according to which existence is systematically variably axiomatic.

2.4.1 Temporally Relativized Existence and Atemporal Existence

Sometimes we discover that what we previously thought was an *n*-place property or relation is really an 1+*n*-place property or relation. We thought that simultaneity was absolute, but then we did some physics and learned that simultaneity is always relative to a reference frame. We didn't learn from physics that there are no simultaneous events; we learned that simultaneity doesn't have the logical form we thought it had. Note that we learned something about the property that is the semantic value of "simultaneous"; I don't think we learned that the predicate "simultaneous" requires at least three terms to complement it in a complete sentence.[27] We do sometimes discover hidden complexities in our expressions, but when we do, it is via linguistics rather than physics.

Consider *endurantism*, the view that objects persist through time by being wholly present at each moment they exist. Enduring objects frequently undergo change over time, as when the leaves of a tree change color from green to red. One way endurantism accommodates change over time is via claiming that many of what people took to be properties are really relations to regions of time or space–time.[28] For example, the shape of a material object is really a relation to a region of time or space–time, not a 1-place property, as one might have pre-theoretically thought.

---

[27] That said, in what follows, I will temporarily speak as though simultaneity is absolute.

[28] This is the so-called *relationalist* strategy for dealing with the so-called Problem of Temporary Intrinsics. See Haslanger (1989), Lewis (1986: 202–5), McDaniel (2004), and Wasserman (2003) for discussion.

Could we learn something similar about *existence*? We can wrap our heads around the idea that existence is a property (either first- or second-order), but could existence be a *relation*? And, if so, what could the relata possibly be?

The material objects with which we are most familiar exist at some times rather than others. The abstract objects that populate Plato's heaven—such as *mathematica* and their ilk—do not exist at any time at all, but rather exist atemporally. Let us explore a view that takes these statements at face value, one according to which the kind of existence enjoyed by material things is literally *relative to a time* whereas the kind of existence enjoyed by abstract objects is not. On such a view, *existence* is a systematically variably polyadic feature: when restricted to one category, it is a relation to a time, when restricted to another, it is a monadic property.

On this view, for a material object to be at a time is for it to literally exist at that time. For a material object *to be* it must *be at some time or other*. The kind of existence enjoyed by a material being is existence relative to a time.

One frequently sees the phrase "exists at a time" in the literature on persistence through time. This expression is extremely common. To see this, simply search, via an Internet search engine, "exists at a time". (Note that I used it myself in the second paragraph of this subsection. Did you even bat an eye?) Now one could hold that the phrase is extremely misleading, and that it would be better to say that an object is *located* at a time rather than that it *exists* at a time. But one is not required to say this. The fact that "exists at a time" and similar locutions have enjoyed such currency among metaphysicians and ordinary people suggests that they are perspicuous. The view described here takes them at face value.

This view also receives support from metaphysical considerations. Material objects are necessarily temporal. It is hard to see what could ground this necessity if the *location* relation is metaphysically distinct from *existence*. On this alternative hypothesis, there are material objects and there are times, and there is a metaphysically primitive relation linking the two.[29] On this hypothesis, it is not at all clear why any material object must bear this relation to some time or other. I suspect that it is this view of the relation of material objects to times that has led some philosophers to take seriously the claim that material objects could exist in worlds without time. For example, Sider (2001: 99–101) presents an argument that takes this putative possibility as a premise and has as its conclusion the view that material objects cannot persist through time via enduring. However, there is no mystery if what it is for a material object to be is for it to be at some time. It is part of the very being of a material being that it is in time, and hence timeless worlds of the sort Sider envisions are impossible. This response to Sider does presuppose that objects necessarily enjoy the mode of being they actually enjoy provided that they enjoy any mode of being at all. We'll subject this presupposition to greater scrutiny in chapters 3 and 9, but for

---

[29] See Gilmore (2007), Hudson (2005), and McDaniel (2006a, 2007) for explications of this picture.

now it suffices to note that at the very least it is open to the endurantist to say that material objects endure in any world in which they exist in the way that they actually exist, and that this is all the necessity that their metaphysical view demands.

Jonathan Barnes (1972) flirts with an analogous view to the one described here, according to which the primary sense of "exists"—the sense that applies to material objects—is the sense of "is somewhere."[30] If to be simply is to be somewhere or other, the primary notion must be *existence at a place*.

Barnes discusses many considerations in favor of this view; I will briefly mention two of them.[31] First, Barnes (1972: 64) notes that in many languages, "the phrases used to express existential propositions are locative in character." Second, Barnes discusses the hypothesis that there is a single lexeme common to "exists," "happens," and "occurs" (among others). According to this hypothesis, how this lexeme appears is determined by the kind of thing referred to by the subject term to which the lexeme is appended. This hypothesis explains why it is natural to say that an event *occurs* but unnatural to say that an event *exists*, while it is natural to say that a material object exists but unnatural to say that a material object occurs.[32] Since *happenings* are always *happenings at places*, it would, on this hypothesis, be natural to say the same about *existings*.

An obvious way to blend these views is to hold that existence is relative to a spatiotemporal region: to be is to be some-where-when. This sort of view nicely incorporates the advantages of its predecessors. Given that we can define the notions of existence at a time (relative to a frame of reference) and existence at a place (relative to a frame of reference) in terms of existence at a space–time, it seems that we can still explain the linguistic phenomena alluded to earlier.[33] Much more importantly, we can explain why material objects are necessarily spatiotemporal beings: their very being is enjoyed only relative to some part of space–time, and so a possible world without space–time is a world that lacks material objects.

Although for a material object to be is for it to be at some region or other, this is not true of other entities. Unless a spatiotemporal region exists at itself, we should not say the same thing about them. And more clearly, numbers, propositions, and Platonic universals exist but lack location. A natural thing to say then is that *existence is systematically variably polyadic. existence* as applied to concrete material objects is two-placed; *existence* as applied to abstract objects is one-placed. (This doesn't necessarily commit us to understanding modes of existence as primarily being

---

[30] This view is discussed in ch. 3 of Barnes (1972); see especially pp. 63–5.

[31] Miller (2002: 48) briefly discusses Barnes's view.

[32] Recall that Lotze (1884: 438–40) insists that events do not exist, but rather occur. Occurrence, for Lotze, is a mode of being.

[33] Let us say that *t* is a *time at reference frame F* just in case *t* is the fusion of all space–time points simultaneous at F. We now define existence at a time at a frame in terms of the primitive *exists at region R*: *x exists at t at F* just in case there is some space–time region R such that x exists at R, R is a part of *t*, and *t* is a time at F.

first-order properties of individuals. More on this momentarily.) Since *existence* on this view is systematically variably polyadic, prima facie *existence* is analogous. The mode of being had by material objects—call it *being-there*—and the mode of being had by abstract objects—call it *subsistence*—are more natural than *existence*.

Subsistent objects are necessarily outside of space–time. This too might seem mysterious. If *location* is metaphysically fundamental, why can't a number have a location? However, on the view we have just explored, to be located at a place is literally to exist at that place. The very being of a number or other abstract object is not relative to a place, and so, given our analysis of *location* in terms of existence at a space–time region, no abstract object *can* have a location.

Finally, there has long been thought to be a close connection between *being* and *space and time*. Many have taken being outside of time and space to suffice to enjoy a different mode of being than those things within time or space. See, for example, Lotze (1884: 438–40), who distinguishes that which exists and that which occurs from that which has atemporal validity; Husserl (2005a, 2005b), who holds that only objects in time are real, whereas abstracta enjoy a mode of being called ideality; Meinong (1983: 52), who holds that numbers and other atemporal abstracta do not exist but rather subsist; and Russell (1997), who adopts the Meinongian terminology in this work, and then argues that relations subsist rather than exist. Reinach (1982) also distinguishes between existence and subsistence; I take him to be following Husserl and Meinong as well.[34] This sort of view has many precedents, most famously Plato, who in his *Timaeus* (27d5–28a1; Plato (1978: 1161–2) famously states the doctrine of being versus becoming. This intuitive connection is theoretically explained by the view explored here, according to which *existence at a space–time region* is both a locative relation and a mode of being.

The ontological scheme elucidated here is Platonic in spirit.[35] Insofar as we are inclined to hold that it is better that one's mode of being be non-relative than relative, we will be inclined to prize the realm of subsistence (Plato's realm of *Being*) over the realm of *being-there* (Plato's realm of *Becoming*). If having a relative mode of being induces a kind of dependence on that to which that mode is relative, and dependence is an imperfection, then non-relative modes of being are, in this respect, more perfect than relative ones. To use the terminology introduced in the introduction, non-relative modes of being are of a *higher order* than relative modes of being. That said, insofar as we are inclined to value malleability, causal interaction, and progression towards perfection, we might favor *being-there* over subsistence. As Russell (1997: 100) pointed out, our differences in temperament and outlook will determine which realm we concentrate our attention on.

---

[34] See also Stebbing (1917), Moore (1927: 102–5), and Stein (2009: 10–11).

[35] Interestingly, Ward (2008: 31–41) argues that Plato needs a notion of systematic homonymy to explain how the way in which the form of F is F differs from the way in which something that partakes in this form is F. She also suggests that Aristotle was probably influenced by this aspect of Plato's metaphysics.

Does talk of relative and non-relative modes of being commit us to thinking of modes as first-order properties? No. Talk of one-place and two-place existence can be understood in terms of second-order features. If we think of existence as a second-order relation, as many semanticists do, then we could say instead that the second-order feature defined on properties of material objects is the three-placed relation having a common instance at a region. This relation is what is expressed by "some ... is ... (at R)." And we should also say that the second-order feature defined on properties of abstracta is the two-placed relation having a common instance. Even on this scheme, existence is systematically variably polyadic. We can then introduce in the standard way first-order properties of objects via appealing to the relation of identity, thus enabling us to define first-order properties of spatiotemporally relative existence and absolute existence. The fundamental existential notions are still primary from the metaphysical perspective. But since it makes exposition easier to speak in terms of the first-order notions, this is what I will do in the remainder of this chapter.

We have now explored a view according to which existence is a systematically variable feature. Given such a view, there is considerable pressure to hold that existence is an analogous feature, since prima facie, systematically variable features are at best analogous. (I presume there is no temptation to think of the generic form of existence as a *mere* disjunction of being and being-there.) Let us now explore a second view with the same implication.

2.4.2 Being and Being-in

The previous ontological scheme was inspired by Plato. It is now appropriate that we turn to one inspired by Aristotle. According to one of philosophy's founding myths, Aristotle brought Plato's forms down to earth, reversing the previous ontological order.[36] On the ontological scheme thereby birthed, *substances* enjoy ontological priority whereas *attributes* enjoy a second-class kind of being. I'll cash out this ontological reversal via a description of a view in which substances enjoy a higher order of being than attributes.

On this view, attributes are not "self-standing" entities. Rather, they *exist in* substances. Let us explore a view that takes the expression "exists in" as maximally perspicuous. According to this view, there are two ways to exist. The kind of existence had by an attribute is *being-in*: the existence of an attribute is strictly and literally relative to something else, a substance. The logical form of the mode of existence of attributes is two-placed: *x exists in y*, where any such *y* is always a substance in which *x* inheres. On this view, *inherence* need not be taken as a fundamental notion: inherence reduces to *being-in*; *x inheres* in *y* if and only if *x exists in y*.[37]

---

[36] See Matthews (2009: 154).

[37] Lowe (2004) distinguishes *characterization*, the fundamental tie between an accident (what he calls a "mode") and its bearer, from *ontological dependence*, which a mode bears to its bearer. He also claims that a fact that a given mode depends on a given bearer is constituted by the obtaining of the characterization

The second mode of existence recognized by this view is *absolute being*, the kind enjoyed by substances. The logical form of this mode of existence is one-placed: *x* exists *simpliciter*. The mode of being of substances is prior to the mode of being of attributes: to grasp fully the mode of being of an attribute one must be acquainted with the mode of being of substances, and understand that what it is for an attribute to be is for it to be in a substance.

Many friends of modes of being have held that the mode of being of a substance is distinct from the mode of being of an attribute. According to the view articulated here, they were right to do so. For on this view, *being* is a systematically variably polyadic feature: when restricted to substances it is one-placed, but when restricted to adjectival entities it is two-placed. Systematically variably polyadic features are not good candidates for being perfectly natural: better to hold that *being* is *analogous* and that the modes of being of substances and adjectival entities are prior to *being* simpliciter.

This view captures the intuitions had by a wide variety of philosophical greats. Its source, as suggested earlier, is Aristotle, who in the *Categories* discussed what is *in* a substance but not as a part of that substance.[38] But many Aristotelians and non-Aristotelians have embraced it as well. Unsurprisingly, on the side of Aristotle, we find Averroes (1984: 69–70), who holds that only substances exist absolutely while items from the other categories exist relatively, and Aquinas (1961 218-19; 1993: 92–3), who distinguishes that which exists in itself from that which exists in some-thing.[39] Many other medieval philosophers held a similar view.[40] But even Descartes (1991a: 31) continued to accept a distinction between substance and mode, with the latter existing in the former.[41] Still much later, the German metaphysician Baumgarten (2014: 136–8) distinguishes between the mode of being of substances, which is *subsistence*, from that of accidents, which is *inherence*, while also noting that accidents *exist in* substances. And Kant (1999a: 302–3, A186/B230–A188/B231) follows Baumgarten in maintaining both this terminology and the underlying

relation. However, on my view, characterization simply reduces to the mode of being of accidents. Ward (2008: 131) notes that, for Aristotle, the existence of non-substances presupposes the existence of substance; the account of inherence developed here explains what this presupposition consists in. See also Galluzzo (2013: 24–5).

[38] See Aristotle, *Categories* 1a20–25, 3a30–35 (1984a: 3, 6). For commentary, see Galluzzo (2013: 21–6, 36). See also Coffey (1938: 46, 59). Corkum (2009) presents several interpretations of what Aristotle means by "in," but the "existential" approach suggested here is not one of them.

[39] For commentary on Averroes on the being of accidents, see Galluzzo (2013: 171–5) and Gilson (1952: 42). Aquinas's commitment to understanding the mode of being of accidents as relative was not firm, however. See Donati (2014: 155–6). For more on Aquinas, see Galluzzo (2014: 218–23).

[40] Conti (2014a: 262) reports that Giles of Rome distinguished between the mode of being of substances and accidents, and held that the latter kind of being was "feebler" and dependent. Conti (2014b: 557–8) attributes a similar view to Paul of Venice. See also Pini (2005: 68, 71–2) for discussion of some medieval philosophers on the mode of being of accidents.

[41] Perhaps this indicates a remainder of Aristotelian philosophy within the Cartesian system? See Chappell (2011) for a discussion of Descartes and Aristotle on substance and mode.

distinction in modes of being it serves to mark. The terminology continued to be in currency even in the twentieth century, in which we find Bosanquet engaged in a dispute over whether finite existents all have the mode of being of "adjectival entities"; in this dispute, Bosanquet endorsed an affirmative answer and argued that only the absolute is a true substance.[42] Finally, Perszyk (1993: 108–10) suggests that Meinong had some use for this mode of being as well: some of Meinong's incomplete objects enjoy "implexive being," a mode of being analogous to Aristotle's exists-in. (For example, the triangle, an incomplete object, has implexive being in actual triangles.)

The view also explains why attributes are necessarily dependent on the existence of substances. The very being of an attribute encodes the information that some substance exists and exemplifies it: for an attribute to be just is for that attribute to be exemplified.[43] In the previous section, we looked at a view that grounded the necessity of a material object's being spatiotemporally located in the mode of being of material objects. In this context, it is natural to think of substances as being the locations of attributes: they are the *nexus* of inherence.[44] And so by similar reasoning, the way in which an attribute exists provides the ground for the necessary truth that modes are always "located" in substances.[45] (This explanation is subject to similar conditions as the explanation presented in section 2.4.1 of why material things are necessarily spatiotemporal: it presupposes that entities have their mode of being essentially.)

Suppose that a necessary condition of being a substance is enjoying an absolute form of existence. Is it also a necessary condition of being a substance that such entities do *not* enjoy a relative form of existence as well? If so, substances cannot persist via *existing at times*. Given that there are substances, this suggests that time must be understood either adjectivally or relationally, rather than as consisting of entities at which objects exist, or the relation between objects and time must not be an ontological one. However, if substances can enjoy two modes of being,

---

[42] Bosanquet et al. (1917–18). See also Mander (2011: 382–91) for further context. Note then that Bosanquet is not merely a "priority" monist who holds that the One grounds its parts; hence, the notion of ground does not suffice by itself to fully characterize the dispute between a monist of Bosanquet's stripe and his opponents. We'll have far more to say about ground in chapter 8. On priority monism, see Schaffer (2007b, 2010).

[43] Vallicella (2002: 21) holds that substances and attributes exist in different ways, and the ontological dependence of attributes on substances is grounded in the mode of being of the attribute. But the key next step is to provide an explanation of why and how this dependence is grounded in the mode of being of attributes. The view that attributes have a relative mode of being is the bedrock for the explanation offered here.

[44] See Hawthorne and Sider (2002) for a full-blooded defense of this analogy.

[45] Knuuttila (2012: 71) notes that, for Scotus, the being of an accident is not *being in*, and this is why Scotus recognizes the need to postulate a new kind of entity called "inherences" in order to link accidents to substances. Kok (2014: 528–32) describes Buridan as being in a similar position, and positing a new kind of entity called "added dispositions" as well. See also Amerini and Galluzzo (2014b: 11). Similarly, Oderberg (2007: 155–6) holds that accidents merely naturally inhere in substances, but not as a matter of metaphysical necessity, but he is silent on whether this position requires adding to the ontology.

existence-full-stop and existence-at-a-time, then we should ask ourselves whether there are worlds in which substances enjoy merely one of these. I set these questions aside for future consideration.

2.4.3 Absolute and Conceptually Relative Existence

Consider the view that claims, in a vaguely neo-Kantian spirit, that some things exist relative to one *conceptual scheme* but not relative to another. This view is suggested by the following remarks made by Ernest Sosa (1998: 409):

> Conceptual relativism can be viewed as a doctrine rather like the relativism involved in the truth of indexical sentences or thoughts. In effect, "existence claims" can be viewed as implicitly indexical, and this is what my conceptual relativist in ontology is suggesting. So when someone says that Os exist, this is to be evaluated relative to the position of the speaker or thinker in "conceptual space" (in a special sense). Relative to the thus distinguished conceptual scheme, it might be that Os do exist, although relative to many other conceptual schemes it might rather be true to say that "Os do not exist."

One might read this passage as advocating *quantifier variance.* Recall that quantifier variance (discussed in sections 1.4 and 1.5.2) is the doctrine that there are many equally good meanings for the existential quantifier; in this context, we can assimilate quantifier variance to the doctrine that there are many perfectly natural properties equally deserving of the name "existence," one of which might be employed by one speaker in one context, while a different speaker might employ a different property in a different context.

But there is another way in which the ontological pluralist can capture the intuitions expressed in the passage above: *existence* is not a one-place property, but is rather two-place, with a hidden parameter for conceptual schemes. The way of explicating conceptual relativism that most naturally captures the intuition in play here is as a genuine relativism: *existence* itself is relative to a scheme.[46]

However, this kind of existence-relativism seems unstable. A natural worry is that, in addition to relative existence, there must be absolute existence. For mustn't, at the very least, conceptual schemes exist absolutely? Perhaps conceptual schemes are Fregean senses or something similar, as suggested in Brueckner (1998), and if so they exist both atemporally and absolutely. And if they don't, then mustn't there at least be some other fundamental substratum, some concrete domain of *things-in-themselves*, that enjoy absolute reality? Perhaps what exists absolutely are persons and material simples, whereas apersonal composite material objects exist merely relatively.[47] If any of these thoughts is right, then there are two ways to exist: to exist

---

[46] This might be the view of Susanne Langer (1930: 135–9; 1933). See McDaniel (ms-2) for further discussion of Langer's meta-ontology.

[47] There are passages in Husserl's (1983: 109–12) post-*Logical Investigations* work that suggest an even more radical kind of idealism in which all of spatiotemporal reality enjoys merely a form of relative

absolutely and to exist relative to a scheme. Conceptual relativism of this vaguely neo-Kantian variety seems most at home with ontological pluralism.

We have explored three views that imply that existence is a systematically variable feature, and hence arguably an analogous feature. Although each of these ways is distinct from the others, I see no immediate problems with a theory that combines them. Consider a view that holds that mathematical objects enjoy absolute existence, mereological simples enjoy temporally relativized existence, composite objects exist relative to conceptual schemes, and accidents exist in simples or composites. Insofar as each part of the package can be motivated, the whole might be as well. That certain modes of being are relational also suggests the possibility of a "ladder of being"; consider, for example, a view in which space–times are substances, material objects have being-there, and accidents have being-in. On this view, accidents occupy the lowest rung on the ladder.

Views that imply that existence is systematically variably polyadic are well worth pursuing. However, it is now time to pursue a different approach: let us examine views that imply that existence is systematically variably axiomatic.

2.5 The Logic of Being

The second approach to motivating modes of being is to determine whether *being* or *existence* is systematically variably axiomatic. In order to determine this, we first need to address which principles govern existence.

Comparing existence and parthood has served us well so far, so we will continue to pursue relevant similarities. Mereology is the "logic" of parthood. Mereology is the study of part and whole; mereological principles are just those principles that govern the parthood relation. However, if compositional pluralism is true, there is more than one fundamental parthood relation, and hence, strictly speaking, there are many mereologies, not one.

What is the "logic" of being? One plausible answer is that the "logic" of being is the logic of quantification. Earlier, we said that a principle governs a certain feature if it is a necessary truth that can be stated using only logical vocabulary and some term that represents the feature.[48] The term in question might be a name or a predicate. In the case we are now considering, the bit of logical vocabulary that represents *existence* is the existential quantifier.

If the logic of quantification were to work one way when applied to objects of one kind, and another way when applied to objects of a different kind, then logic itself would display variable systematicity. Accordingly, *existence* would be systematically

---

existence whereas *consciousness* enjoys a form of absolute existence. See Smith (1995: 375–6) for a discussion.

[48] This is a sufficient condition, but it is not necessarily a necessary condition. We will discuss the possibility of "substantive" non-logical governing principles in section 2.7.

variably axiomatic. And, if this were the case, we would have a reason to be ontological pluralists.

The views that will be discussed fly in the face of Frege's (1980a: iii) dictum that "Thought is in essentials the same everywhere: it is not true that there are different kinds of laws of thought to suit the different kinds of objects thought about." However, although Frege's dictum is plausible, obeying it is not mandatory. Frege's dictum is a substantive thesis about logic, not a thesis that we are forced to endorse on pain of being illogical or unreasonable. On the view explored here, entities that exist in different ways can be subject to different laws of logic, just as entities with different fundamental properties can be subject to different laws of nature.[49]

In what follows, I will discuss four ontologies that each imply that existence is systematically variably axiomatic: an ontology of intentional objects, an ontology of things and stuff, an ontology of necessary and contingent beings, and finally an ontology of actual objects and mere possibilia.

2.5.1 Intentionalia and the Logic of Being

Consider an ontology that includes *mere intentionalia* in addition to actual concrete objects. To be a merely intentional object is to be an object of a possible thought, but it is not necessarily to be a possible object. For among the mere intentionalia are *incomplete objects* and *inconsistent objects*. Incomplete objects are such that, for some property, they neither have it nor have its negation. Inconsistent objects are such that, for some property, they have both it and some property incompatible with it (perhaps its negation).

Don't think that this view must be unmotivated! It is a familiar point in modal metaphysics that possibilia—possible worlds and the possible objects residing within them—have a number of important roles to play in the semantics and metaphysics of modality and intentionality.[50] But perhaps impossibilia—impossible worlds and the objects residing with them—are needed as well.[51] If a modal realist view of possibilia is the best contender for the field, it might be as well that a realist view about *impossibilia* deserves a serious look.

One of the niftier developments in contemporary logic is paraconsistent logic. A logic is *paraconsistent* just in case it does not license the derivation of every proposition from a contradiction.[52] The existence of paraconsistent logic shows that one can reason sensibly about inconsistent objects, and that one can posit them without being committed to the claim that *every* object is an inconsistent object.[53]

---

[49] The views discussed here are instances of *local logical pluralism* in the sense of Haack (1978: 223).

[50] See, for example, Lewis (1986), especially chapter 1.

[51] This point is stressed in Yagisawa (1988) and Lycan (1994: 38–40), although Lycan would be unhappy with the realism about impossibilia suggested here. See also Perszyk (1993: 266–78).

[52] See Priest (2004b) for a concise introduction to paraconsistent logic.

[53] For discussions of the connections and interplays between Meinongian theories of inconsistent objects and paraconsistent logic, see the interesting essays in Priest, Routley, and Norman (1989).

Any ontology that includes contradictory impossibilia must hold that the topic-neutral logic is paraconsistent. But if we restrict our attention to a particular topic, specifically, the category of actual concrete objects, we can get by with classical logic, for actual objects are both complete and consistent.[54] Restricting the scope of the law of non-contradiction to actual objects is not a new move; it was flirted with by Meinong, here paraphrased by Russell (1973: 92):

> Impossible objects, it is admitted, do not obey the law of contradiction; but why should they? For after all, this law has never been explicitly asserted except of the actual and the possible, and there is no reason for assuming that it holds also of the impossible.[55]

It is natural to think that natural properties ground the laws of nature: the causal profile of objects is fixed by the natural properties they exemplify. When objects exemplify fundamentally different kinds of features, they participate in different fundamental laws. On the view described here, the fundamental laws of logic are grounded in the modes of being of the entities they govern. The logic of existence is the logic of quantification: on views in which there are different ways of existing, it is not as surprising that there can be different laws of logic governing them.

Could an ontology like this be *reasonable*? According to this ontology, there are true contradictions. One might worry that, even if true contradictions are possible, they cannot be rationally believed. And so this ontology could not be reasonable.

However, perhaps this worry is too quick. There are many epistemic values, that is, features of theories that make them worthy of belief. Consistency is one of them. But it is not the only one. In addition to consistency, Graham Priest (2004a: 32) cites simplicity, problem-solving ability, non-ad-hocness, and fruitfulness. Epistemic values are plural and competing. A theory that lacks some of these values might nonetheless be worthy of belief by virtue of the presence of a high degree of the others. It is not at all obvious that any of these values always trumps the others. An inconsistent theory that enjoys a high degree of simplicity, problem-solving ability, non-ad-hocness, and fruitfulness might well be worthy of belief.[56]

An ontology that includes impossibilia implies that existence is systematically variably axiomatic. And we have seen that if a feature is systematically variably axiomatic, there is a prima facie case that it is an analogous feature. This ontology is not *mandatory*—it is not unreasonable to reject it. But it might also be reasonable to embrace it, and with it the modes of being that naturally accompany it.

We have said that a principle governs a feature just in case that principle can be stated using only logical vocabulary and a term standing for that feature. In what preceded, we implicitly limited the whole of logic to a mere proper part, namely, extensional first-order predicate logic. If there is more to logic, then there might be

---

[54] I ignore here worries about the completeness of actual objects stemming from vagueness.
[55] See also Berto (2013: 104–5) for further discussion.
[56] For further discussion, see Priest (2004a).

further ways for *existence* to show itself as a systematically variably axiomatic feature. We will now look at ontologies that, in conjunction with a more capacious view of logic, yield further modes of being.

2.5.2 *The Logic of Things and the Logic of Stuff*

Some philosophers have thought that the most fundamental ontological difference is the difference between *things* and *stuff*. On their view, reality divides into entities and non-individuated matter or stuff. *Things* can be counted: whenever there are some things, it always makes sense to ask how *many* of them there are. *Stuff* cannot be counted, but it can be measured: whenever there is some stuff, it always makes sense to ask how *much* of it there is.

Why believe in irreducible stuff in addition to things? Laycock (2006) cites apparent reference to stuffs in ordinary speech and thought. Zimmerman (1997) and Kleinschmidt (2007) discuss the alleged usefulness of positing stuff in solving the puzzle of material constitution, and Kleinschmidt explicitly states that stuff and things belong to different ontological categories. Finally, Markosian (2004a) argues that things and stuff have different persistence conditions, and argues that positing stuff is necessary for dealing with puzzles facing certain views of the nature of material simples.

Markosian (2004a: 413) defends what he calls a "mixed ontology," the official formulation of which is as follows:

The Mixed Ontology: (i) The physical world is fundamentally a world of both things and stuff. (ii) Among the most basic facts about the physical world are facts about things and also facts about stuff. (iii) The most accurate description of the physical world must be in terms of both things and stuff. (iv) Thing talk and quantification over things, as well as stuff talk and quantification over stuff, are both ineliminable.

What does it mean to say that quantification over things and quantification over stuff are both ineliminable? It is clear that Markosian does not mean by this claim only that sentences in which a mass-quantifier appears cannot be systematically para-phrased via sentences in which no mass-quantifier appears. This is probably true, but this fact alone is not clearly of ontological significance. Sentences in which *plural quantifiers*—quantifiers such as *some Fs are G*—cannot be systematically para-phrased via sentences in which no plural quantifier appears. However, it would be rash to conclude that sentences containing plural quantifiers are *about different entities* than sentences containing singular quantifiers. Arguably, even if plural quantifiers cannot be semantically reduced to singular quantifiers, the *plural and singular quantifiers range over exactly the same things.*[57]

---

[57] This is the view forcefully defended in McKay (2006). Note that one could still hold that plural and singular quantifiers correspond to distinct modes of being enjoyed by the same things, although I think this view is unmotivated. Thanks to Peter Finocchiaro for discussion here.

However, on Markosian's view, stuff quantification is not an irreducibly different way of talking about the same things quantified over via a thing quantifier. Rather, Markosian is explicit that these domains do not even overlap. Mass-quantification is as fundamental as thing-quantification: on his view, the fundamental language must include both. Markosian's (1998, 2004a) primary motivation is to account for the possibility of objects that lack proper parts but are nonetheless qualitatively heterogeneous across an extended region of space. On his view, a sphere might be half red and half blue despite having no parts that are its red half and its blue half. Markosian explains this apparent possibility by claiming that such an object is constituted by a portion of stuff that itself contains two portions of stuff, one of which is red and the other of which is blue. If "portions of stuff" are just things in disguise, then Markosian's story is unsuccessful.[58]

Recall that one way of formulating the doctrine that there are ways of being is as the doctrine that there is more than one fundamental quantifier expression. Mixed ontologies are committed to there being more than one fundamental quantifier expression, and hence are committed to *ways of being*. On this view, stuff and things enjoy equally primordial but disparate modes of existing.

2.5.3 Modal Logic I: Necessity and Contingency as Modes of Being

Consider *modal logic*, the "logic" of possibility and necessity. If modal logic is properly considered as a part of logic, then "necessarily" and "possibly" are among the logical vocabulary. On this view, there are logically valid formulae that cannot be expressed using only the resources of first-order logic.

Consider now an ontological scheme that consists of necessarily existing abstract objects and contingently existing concrete objects. On this scheme, existence is a systematically variably axiomatic feature, since "Everything that exists, exists contingently" is stateable using only logical vocabulary and is necessarily true when the quantifier is restricted to one ontological category but necessarily false when restricted to the other. The hypothesis that contingently existing things and necessarily existing things exist in different ways is especially compelling in this case, since on this hypothesis that a thing is contingent rather than necessary is grounded in that thing's mode of being.[59]

Similarly, if *tense logic* is properly considered as a part of logic, then "it is always the case" and "it is sometimes the case" are among the logical vocabulary. Presumably, if something is an abstract object, it is necessarily true that it always exists,

---

[58] This is the principal complaint of McDaniel (2003). See Markosian (2004a) for a rejoinder. In McDaniel (2009c), I present my preferred solution to the problem of heterogeneity.

[59] See, for example, Vallicella (2002: 23; 2014: 67). One might hold instead that it is grounded in a difference in essence, but, in chapter 9, I will suggest a way in which essences can be grounded in modes of being.

whereas there is no concrete object (save, perhaps, a divine concrete object, if such a being exists) such that it is necessarily true that it always exists.

These arguments go through only if (i) there are real differences between genuinely logical vocabulary and other expressions and (ii) modal or tense vocabulary is genuinely logical. Both issues are thorny and difficult, and can't be addressed here. For instance, the claim that *tense logic* is a part of logic seems to me especially precarious.[60] However, inasmuch as these claims are defensible, the view defended in this section can be motivated.

2.5.4 Modal Logic II: Actuality and Possibility as Modes of Being

Let's examine a second attempt at using considerations of modal logic to buttress a modes of being ontology. In this case, we will consider the difference between the actual and the merely possible.

Possibilism is the view that there are objects that are *merely* possible. Possibilism has enjoyed a recent resurgence thanks to the work of David Lewis (1986), who famously holds that the merely possible are ontologically on a par with the actual. Possible worlds, on Lewis's view, are spatiotemporally isolated physical universes, many of which contain human beings differing from you and me only in that they are much harder to visit. To be actual, on Lewis's (1986: 92–6) view, is merely to be spatiotemporally related to me: *actuality* is on this picture merely indexical, just like *being here*.[61]

Despite modal realism's incredible ontology, there are impressive arguments for it. But no impressive argument suffices to overcome the following worry, succinctly stated by Phillip Bricker (2001: 29):

The alternative [to Lewis's view] for the realist is to hold that actuality is absolute, and that there is an ontological distinction in kind between the actual and the merely possible. In my opinion, this is the only viable option for the realist. Our conceptual scheme demands that actuality be *categorical*: whatever is of the same ontological kind as something actual is itself actual. To hold then, as Lewis does, that the actual world and the possible worlds do not differ in kind is simply incoherent.

Bricker accordingly holds that there is a primitive fact about which things in modal reality are the actual things. But Bricker (2001: 30) also correctly notes that this fact cannot consist in some things having a *quality* that others lack.[62] In what then does this primitive fact consist? The obvious answer is that the merely possible exist in a fundamentally different way than the actual. There are merely possible things and there are actual things but the ways in which there are these things differ.

---

[60] But for a defense of tense logic as logic, see Geach (1980: 312–18.)

[61] Lewis's version of possibilism is the most well known, but there are many ways to be a possibilist. See Bricker (2001, 2006) and McDaniel (2004, 2006b) for other versions of possibilism.

[62] Bricker (2006) sort of takes this back by appealing to "non-qualitative" properties.

In contemporary circles, a common complaint against possibilism is that actuality and existence are coextensive as a matter of conceptual necessity.[63] Is this correct? Ontologies that recognize the existence of merely possible objects existed well before the birth of David Lewis. The question of the reality of the merely possible has been a thorny one for many centuries, and philosophers such as Scotus, Suárez, and Descartes are each plausibly interpreted as recognizing an ontology that includes merely possible beings as well as actual ones.[64] But none held that the way in which the possibles are real is the same as the way in which actual objects are real.[65] By the time the twentieth century is well on its way, we find the metaphysician Jared Sparks Moore (1927: 94–5) confidently claiming that to assert that something is actual is *certainly* more than to assert that something is real or that it is. Perhaps each of these philosophers is conceptually confused. But I think not.

Let's examine some ways for a possibilist to be an ontological pluralist. There are at least two different possibilist views on which existence is systematically variably axiomatic, at least given one further assumption. This assumption is that there can be a second-order logic that permits quantification into the predicate position, and this second-order logic is properly thought of as *logic*. Perhaps this assumption is ultimately dispensable to the arguments we'll soon explore—I suspect that it is—but it is certainly convenient to make when stating the views in question. Let's now turn to the views.

The first view is a Bricker-style possibilism according to which possible objects can have exactly the same properties as actual objects, and moreover have them in exactly the same way as actual objects. On Bricker's (2001) view, every actual object has at least one merely possible duplicate. For example, there is a merely possible individual who is a duplicate of me, and hence is a person, is made of flesh and blood, and has sorrows and joys. (I hope his book is finished on time!)

There are two ways to develop a Bricker-inspired possibilist version of ontological pluralism.[66] The choice point is whether to take one mode of being to encompass both the possible and the actual whilst a second encompasses merely the actual, or rather to plump for a view on which these two modes of being do not overlap at all.[67] Let's consider a version that takes the first option: there is an outer-domain quantifier that includes the merely possible as well as the actual, and an inner-domain quantifier that includes only the actual. On this kind of possibilism, existence is systematically

---

[63] Lewis (1986: 97–101) eloquently states and responds to this complaint. Gibson (1998: 2) and Miller (2002: 82) claim that "actual" and "exists" are synonyms. They are not.

[64] On Scotus, see King (2001); on Suárez, see Coffey (1938: 44) and Doyle (1967); on Descartes, see Brown (2011) and Cunning (2014). Additionally, McDermott (1969: 6–10) reconstructs the logical system of the Buddhist philosopher Ratnakīrti as one employing quantification over possible individuals.

[65] Gilson (1952: 3) says that the first division of being is between the actual and the merely possible.

[66] Also worth considering is the view defended by Solomyak (2013), according to which the two modes of being correspond to two different ways of bearing properties or saturating facts. I'll have more to say about this sort of view in section 3.7.

[67] Bricker (2001, 2006) unsurprisingly faces a similar choice.

variably axiomatic. If the existential quantifier in play corresponds to the possibilist mode of being, the following principle is necessarily true: for any F, if it is possible for something to be F, then there is something that is F. However, if the quantifiers are restricted to actual objects, this principle is not clearly true; it's probably false, and if it is true, it is merely contingently true.

The second version of possibilism is one inspired by (but not equivalent to or a consequence of) necessitarianism, according to which everything necessarily exists, and on which the Barcan formulas are accepted at face value.[68] The conjunction of the two Barcan formulas is this: every x is necessarily Fx if and only, necessarily, every x is Fx.[69]

On this kind of necessitarianism, although there is no actual entity that is my brother, there is an entity that possibly is my brother. This is not a view I find particularly attractive, and in fact a parallel view about tense will be critically discussed in section 3.6. But the point here is not to assess which views are the most attractive, but rather merely to present defensible views according to which existence is systematically variably axiomatic. So let us consider a view according to which the Barcan formulas are satisfied by entities enjoying one mode of being—the mode of mere possibility—but not by entities enjoying actual existence.[70] On this sort of view, which modal logic is appropriate to use depends on the kind of existence in play, and hence existence is systematically variably axiomatic.

2.6 Mixed Views

Trivially, any feature that is systematically variably polyadic will be systematically variably axiomatic. But there might also be more interesting connections between doctrines that imply that existence is systematically variably polyadic and doctrines that imply that existence is systematically variably axiomatic.

Consider, for example, the views defended in sections 2.4.1 and 2.4.2, and the views defended in 2.5.2. (There we talked about existence at a time vs. absolute existence, substantial existence vs. inherence, and necessary existence vs. contingent existence respectively.) I'm inclined to hold that a substance is a necessary being only if its mode of being is non-relative. Given this principle, it will follow that no material substance is a necessary being if we accept the ontology explored in section 2.4.1, according to which the being of a material substance is existence at a time. So if there are any necessarily existing substances, we have a reason for holding that the mode of being of such a substance differs from the mode of being of contingent material

---

[68] This is the sort of view recently defended by Williamson (2013).

[69] The Barcan formulas are named after Ruth Barcan Marcus, who first formulated them and first defended their importance. Barcan Marcus (1995) is a collection of some of her famous papers, many of which discuss the formulae named after her.

[70] This sort of view was independently suggested to me by Maeghan Fairchild and Phil Corkum. I do not know whether either has pursued such a view in writing as of yet.

substances, and we also must think that any necessarily existing substance is an atemporal being.

On the other hand, if we wish to hold fast that material objects can be substances, then we must claim that location cannot be understood existentially. Either *location* is a primitive relation, or we should be a relationalist about space–time. Probably for the Aristotelian the latter is the more attractive option.

There are surely other interesting ways in which one could formulate complicated ontologies drawing from the preceding subsections.

2.7 Non-Logical Governing Principles

I have argued that systematically variably polyadic features and systematically variably axiomatic features are prima facie less than perfectly natural features. I then presented ontological schemes according to which *existence* is either a systematically variably axiomatic feature or a systematically variably polyadic feature, thus establishing the prima facie case that existence is analogous. Although these arguments do not *conclusively show* that we must accommodate modes of being in our ontology, they suffice to show that modes of being deserve to be taken seriously.

In section 2.5, I focused on principles governing existence, that is, principles stateable using only purely logical vocabulary along with some sort of expression whose semantic value is existence. The idea was that this would force us to focus as much as possible on the status of existence itself rather than on putatively extraneous concerns about the natures of existents. (If, however, it turns out that what we think of as logic is itself not topic-neutral, it might be that a crisp contrast of this sort cannot be drawn.) In the remainder of this chapter, I will look at principles that are not principles of any logic, since they contain non-logical vocabulary by pretty much everyone's lights. But those principles also suggest that there are different modes of being.

As a way of entry into this discussion, let's reconsider two of the varieties of possibilism discussed in section 2.5.4, specifically David Lewis's version of possibilism, and a view just like Lewis's except that actuality is taken to be an absolute status and a mode of being that only some of what there is enjoys. To many of us, the second view is far more plausible. However, on the face of it, it also seems that we should judge that it is the worse view: the second view has all of the same ontological and ideological commitments as Lewis's view but also makes an additional metaphysical distinction that Lewis's view does not make. Why would adding a commitment improve a view rather than make it worse?

Part of the explanation that I favor is that there are *epistemological* principles governing actuality that are obliterated if actuality is a merely indexical status. The epistemology of the possible and the actual is fundamentally different: for example, we can know a priori that there is a merely possible talking donkey, but we cannot know a priori that there is an actual talking donkey. If something exists in exactly the same way as an actual donkey exists, then any knowledge of its existence must be via the ways in which we know actual donkeys exist.[71] I suspect that there are also different normative and evaluative principles governing these two modes of existence. For example, how we should feel about the pleasures and pains of possible people and how we should feel about the pleasures and pains of actual people are very different. Like many, I also don't see how the Lewisian view can make sense of this difference.[72]

More generally, different modes of being might ground differences in our routes to having knowledge of or evidence about the entities that enjoy those modes. In the introduction, I discussed what I called the *phenomenological motivation* for ontological pluralism, which makes much use of this idea. In line with this motivation, one might hold that things enjoying actual concrete existence are knowable only empirically, that abstracta are known via intuition, that possibilia are known via imagination, and that ethical realities are known via emotion. In each case, the mode of access to entities enjoying a certain mode of being is ultimately grounded in the mode of being itself.

Our discussion of a wide variety of different ontological schemes in this chapter has moved rapidly. In the chapters that follow, we will slow things down considerably when assessing whether there are further reasons to think that being fragments.

2.8 Chapter Summary

In this chapter, I explored the metaphysics of what I called "analogous properties." An analogous property is a non-specific property that is less natural than its specifications (which I called "analogue instances") but is not as unnatural as a merely disjunctive property. I discussed and then applied two tests for being an analogous property: a property is analogous provided that it has more unity than a mere disjunction but yet systematically varies with respect to either its logical form or the axioms that govern its behavior. I used the notion of an analogous property to formulate several more versions of ontological pluralism. One kind of ontological pluralism appealed to a distinction between absolute and relative modes of existence. This distinction between modes of being was then used to articulate one kind of ontological superiority, which I called "orders of being."

---

[71] Compare with Skyrms (1976: 326).
[72] Lewis (1986: 123–8) attempts to address this sort of worry, unsuccessfully in my view.

3

Ways of Being and Time

3.1 Introduction

In this chapter, we will determine how thinking in terms of modes of being is helpful in the philosophy of time. Several "tensed" versions of ontological pluralism will be developed and assessed.

Say that an entity is *present* just in case some moment in its lifetime is present; an entity is *past* just in case every moment in its lifetime is prior to the present moment; an entity is *future* just in case every moment in its lifetime is posterior to the present moment. According to *presentism*, there are present things, but past and future things do not exist. According to *eternalism*, in addition to present things, there are also past and future objects, such as dinosaurs and manned moon bases.[1] According to the *growing block theory*, both present and past objects exist, whereas the merely future is unreal.[2] These views appear to be mutually exclusive and exhaustive: you can't endorse more than one of them and it seems that you must endorse at least one of them.[3] But each of these views presupposes that things in time all exist in the same way. If we drop this presumption, new positions become apparent. One such view—*presentist existential pluralism* (PEP)—will be defended in this chapter.

Presentist existential pluralism distinguishes between two modes of existence: *past existence*, which is the way that past things exist, and *present existence*, which is the way that present things exist. In this chapter, I will set aside the questions of whether there are any future existents, and if there are, in what way they are. By the end of this chapter, it will be clear how one might formulate variants of PEP that take stands on these issues.

---

[1] See Markosian (2002) for a nice discussion of presentism and eternalism, as well as related views. Markosian (2004b) defends presentism.

[2] Tooley (1997) defends the growing block view.

[3] Provided that you believe that anything is in time at all. I suppose there are other options in logical space, such as the *shrinking block view*, according to which the future and the present (but not the past) are real, and the *no-present view*, according to which only the future and the past are real. These views are non-starters. Another stance towards this debate is to hold that it is a pseudo-debate because it is terminologically defective, or because each view is an "equally good way of talking about time." This latter position will be revisited in section 3.2.

PEP has a novel name, but it is not a novel view. In an interesting paper on presentism, Simon Keller (2004) alleges that Augustine, despite his strong presentist inclinations, didn't fully give up the idea that past things are in some way real. Quite appropriately! Similar remarks are made by Moore (1927: 88–9), who distinguishes between past, present, and future modes of being. Later in the twentieth century, Nino Cocchiarella (1969) embraces the view that past and present objects enjoy different modes of being. According to T. L. S. Sprigge (1992: 1), the ordinary person's view is "that the present is fully real, that the past has a kind of secondary reality, and that the future is hardly real at all." If this is right, then PEP is the view most supported by pre-theoretic intuition.[4]

A theory of time is worthy of belief to the extent that it is supported by intuition, solves or dissolves philosophical problems facing rival theories, doesn't suffer from serious difficulties of its own, and is consonant with the findings of the natural sciences. That PEP comports nicely with pre-theoretic intuition is one of its positive features. That said, consonance with the natural sciences trumps the others. Unfortunately, the question of whether a view that holds that the present is in some way metaphysically distinguished can be consonant with physics is too large to address here.[5]

Accordingly, I have modest aims for this chapter. First, I want to show that PEP does at least as well with respect to the remaining factors as other theories in which the present is in some way metaphysically distinguished. Call a theory according to which the present is in some way metaphysically distinguished an *A-theory*. For this reason, I will contrast PEP with those A-theories that are well discussed in the literature. Second, I want to show that the best versions of the A-theory are versions that embrace ontological pluralism. For this reason, I will sometimes contrast PEP with other A-theories that either make use of the notion of modes of being or ought to make use of this notion. So-called *B-theories* deny that the present is in any way metaphysically privileged. I have nothing new to say about the B-theory here, and hence it will rarely be mentioned in what follows.[6] Even though my aims here are limited, if I can show that PEP is a strong contender in the philosophy of time, I will have gone some way towards showing that ontological pluralism is a fruitful thesis.

My plan is as follows. In section 3.2, I further contrast PEP with presentism, eternalism, and the growing block theory. In section 3.3, I contrast PEP with Meinongian presentism, the view that there are things (past things in particular) that do not exist. I discuss Meinongian presentism because it is the extant view in the literature that is most similar to PEP. Moreover, I argue, the best version of Meinongian presentism is an ontologically pluralist view that is minimally different from PEP.

---

[4] Note that the ordinary person's view is not Sprigge's: his paper is titled "The Unreality of Time." Gibson (1998: 12–20) notes the appeal of such a view, but rejects it; see also Gibson (1998: ch. 7).

[5] See Balashov and Janssen (2003) for a discussion of some of the difficulties.

[6] For a defense of the B-theory, see Mellor (1981, 1998).

In section 3.4, I contrast PEP with *Degrees Presentism*, which is the doctrine that existence comes in degrees, and that past objects are less real to the extent that they are temporally distant from the present. Although I argue (in chapters 5 and 7) that existence comes in degrees, here I argue that PEP is a better view than Degrees Presentism.

By the end of sections 3.2–3.4, I will have contrasted PEP with a number of standard and non-standard views in the literature. Moreover, I will have argued that PEP is preferable to the non-standard views I discuss. In section 3.5, I return to a discussion of one of the standard views, specifically presentism. I argue that PEP satisfies many of the intuitions that motivate presentism while avoiding an objection that appears to refute presentism, namely, the so-called truth-making objection.

In section 3.6, I contrast PEP with a view defended by Timothy Williamson (2002), according to which material objects are only contingently and temporarily concrete. I argue that Williamson's view is also problematized by the truth-making objection.

The final sections are devoted to issues raised by PEP. Section 3.7 discusses how the friend of PEP should account for the fact that objects change properties over time. Section 3.8 focuses on how we know we are present.

3.2 Formulating Presentist Existential Pluralism (PEP)

PEP is a version of *ontological pluralism*, the doctrine that there are modes of being or different ways to exist. The particular version of PEP that I will focus on agrees with the neo-Quinean orthodoxy that there is a deep connection between quantification and existence: since there are fundamentally different ways to exist, there are corresponding to them metaphysically important quantifiers. The different modes of existence correspond to different highly natural quantifier expressions.

Interestingly, many participants in the current debate between the growing block theory, presentism, and eternalism appeal to logical joints in order to ensure that their debate is substantial.[7] Metaphysicians purport to substantially dispute with each other over the nature of reality, but perhaps the disputes in the philosophy of time are merely apparent disputes. The presentist grants that, although there are no dinosaurs, there *were* dinosaurs, and although there are no manned moon bases, there *will be*. The eternalist claims that, tenselessly speaking, there are all of these things. But one might worry that what the eternalist means by "$\exists x \, \Phi$" is simply what the presentist means by "it was the case that $\exists x \, \Phi$ or it is now that case that $\exists x \, \Phi$ or it will be the case that $\exists x \, \Phi$." And the presentist thinks that, in this sense of "$\exists$," the claim that there are dinosaurs is true! And so the apparent disagreement between the presentist and the eternalist over what exists is merely verbal: the presentist and the

---

[7] See Sider (2011, chs. 4 and 11) for discussions of naturalness and substantivity, and related issues in the philosophy of time.

eternalist mean different things by "∃," but it is possible to translate claims made by the presentist into claims acceptable to the eternalist, and vice versa.

In order for presentists and eternalists to substantially disagree about what there is, they need to mean the same thing by "there is." But if meaning is determined by *use* and the use of a term consists of dispositions to assert certain sentences employing the term, then it initially looks like the presentist and the eternalist must mean different things by "there is." But the alleged "translatability" of claims made by the presentist into claims made by the eternalist (and vice versa) shows that there is some phrase employed by the presentist that has the same use as "there is" when employed by the eternalist. This helps cement the idea that the presentist and the eternalist are "speaking past each other," that their "dispute" is not substantive.[8]

One could argue that the presentist's "there will be, there is now, or there was an F" does not have the same use as the eternalist's "there (tenselessly) is an F," since the two expressions have different properties.[9] But, as noted in section 1.4, an independent (and more general) rejoinder is that meaning is not determined by use alone. A second factor is *naturalness*: natural meanings are more eligible to be meant, other things being equal. Recall that, according to Sider (2001, 2009, 2011), there is a metaphysically fundamental meaning for "∃" that both the presentist and the eternalist employ when they argue about what exists, and this is why their debate is genuine.[10]

With this in mind, let's re-characterize presentism, eternalism, and the growing block theory so that each explicitly appeals to metaphysical fundamentality:

Presentism* = the view that there is a metaphysically fundamental sense of "∃" such that "∼∃x (x is a past or future object)" is true.
Growing block theory* = the view that there is a metaphysically fundamental sense of "∃" such that each of the following is true: "∃x (x is a past object)," "∃x (x is a present object)," and "∼∃x (x is a future object)."
Eternalism* = the view that there is a metaphysically fundamental sense of "∃" such that each of the following is true: "∃x (x is a past object)," "∃x (x is a present object)," and "∃x (x is a future object)."

---

[8] Strictly, meanings are determined by the use of all the members of the linguistic community rather than merely by the individual uses of individual speakers. Let's set this aside though, since it might not make the philosopher of time happy to learn that the way to assess which view here is correct is via analysis of her community's use of ontological expressions.

[9] This line is pursued in Sider (2006). Sider (2001: 15–16) points out that there are sentences that are true according to the eternalist, but false according to the presentist. For example, consider: "There is a set that contains a dinosaur and a computer." The eternalist believes this sentence is true, but the presentist doesn't think there was such a set, is such a set, or will be such a set, and so will deny it. In a similar vein, Cocchiarella (1969: 37) suggests that past existence cannot simply be understood in terms of present existence and tense operators.

[10] Or, at least, there is a metaphysically fundamental meaning that both *could* employ in order to ensure a substantive debate.

In each case, the senses I am talking about needn't be actually realized in ordinary language; they might be merely possible senses. But from a metaphysical perspective, a language that housed them would be a better one to speak.

Let's contrast these views with PEP, which we can provisionally formulate as:

PEP = the view that there are two semantically primitive restricted quantifiers, "$\exists_p$" and "$\exists_c$," the first of which ranges over all and only past objects whereas the second of which ranges over all and only present objects. Both quantifiers are metaphysically fundamental. There is no fundamental quantifier that ranges over both past and present objects.

PEP distinguishes between two kinds of existence: the way that past things exist, represented by "$\exists_p$," and the way that present things exist, represented by "$\exists_c$." According to PEP, there is a sense in which both present and past things exist: this is represented by the generic quantifier "$\exists$," the domain of which is the disjunction of the domains of these two quantifiers. But this generic quantifier is not a perfectly natural expression, but rather is analogous.

There is a second way of understanding PEP and other ontologically pluralist views. In section 1.2, I called the fundamental quantifiers *restricted* because each individually does not range over all that is ranged over by the "some" of ordinary English, even though none of them is defined in terms of the ordinary English "some" and restricting predicates. This is a legitimate use of "restricted quantifier." However, it's also legitimate to say that a quantifier is restricted if and only if its domain is a proper subset of the domain of a *fundamental* quantifier. On the view defended here, the ordinary English "some" is not metaphysically fundamental. Neither "$\exists_p$" nor "$\exists_c$" is restricted in this second sense. This suggests that a second way of understanding ontological pluralism is as the doctrine that there is *more than one* metaphysically fundamental meaning available for the unrestricted "$\exists$."[11] Accordingly, a second way of understanding PEP is as:

PEP* = the view that there are two metaphysically fundamental (possible) meanings for the unrestricted quantifier "$\exists$": "$\exists_p$" ranges over all and only past objects, whereas "$\exists_c$" ranges over all and only present objects. There is no fundamental quantifier that ranges over objects in both domains.[12]

As before, each meaning might be merely possible rather than actually possessed by expressions in ordinary language.

---

[11] See Turner (2010) for further discussion of these issues. Views that allow for nesting of fundamental quantifiers (such as the version of Meinongian presentism discussed in section 3.3) raise additional thorny questions. Such views will have fundamental quantifiers that are restricted both in the sense of not ranging over everything ranged over by the "there is" of ordinary English and in the sense of ranging over only some of what a fundamental quantifier ranges over.

[12] I'm not sure whether the quantifiers embraced by PEP* are appropriately titled "primitive tensed quantifiers" in the sense of Lewis (2004: 11–12). Note that the friend of PEP* does not deny that these quantifiers have domains.

Let's adopt PEP* as our canonical formulation of PEP. (After this section, I will drop the asterisk and simply understand PEP as PEP*.) According to PEP*, there is a perfectly natural sense of the quantifier according to which only presently existing things exist. The friend of PEP* can say that in a very strict and metaphysical sense, there are no non-present objects. If we understand presentism as presentism*, then PEP* is a version of presentism. In fact, PEP* entails presentism*. Moreover, PEP* is inconsistent with the growing block theory* and eternalism*.

However, according to PEP*, there is also a perfectly natural sense of "∃" according to which there are non-present things. Few presentists would approve. Perhaps then we should understand presentism not as presentism*, but rather as:

*Presentism*** = the view that there is *exactly one* metaphysically fundamental sense of "∃," and this sense is such that "~∃x (x is a past or future object)" is true.

Presentism understood as presentism** *is* inconsistent with PEP*.

"∃$_p$" and "∃$_c$" obey different fundamental principles. A statement making use of one of the quantifiers might state something necessarily true, while a statement differing from the first only in that it employs the other quantifier might say something that is at best contingently true. For example, (a) is necessarily true whereas (b) is contingently false:

(a)   ∀$_c$x ∀$_c$y (x and y are simultaneous).
(b)   ∀$_p$x ∀$_p$y (x and y are simultaneous).

(a) is necessarily true, since all things that exist as present things occupy the present moment, and hence are simultaneous, whereas (b) is contingently false since not all past things overlap temporally: no human person is simultaneous with a dinosaur.

Different tense logics govern these quantifiers. Let "W" be the *it was the case that* sentential operator; let "N" be the *it is now the case that* sentential operator; let "F" be the *it will be the case that* sentential operator. Suppose you hold the Lockean view that nothing can enjoy two beginnings.[13] Then you will hold that every statement that results from uniformly substituting for the free variable in (c) is necessarily true, whereas (d) is necessarily true of few or no values of the free variable:

(c)   ∃$_p$x x = y → F(∃$_p$x x = y)
(d)   ∃$_c$x x = y → F(∃$_c$x x = y)

Moreover, you will hold that all instances of (e) are necessarily true, whereas some ways of uniformly substituting for the free variable in (f) yield contingent falsehoods:

(e)   ∃$_p$x x = y → ~F(∃$_c$x x = y)
(f)   ∃$_c$x x = y → ~F(∃$_c$x x = y)

---

[13] See Locke (1979: 328).

Informally, (e) says that if something becomes past, it will never again be present, whereas (f) says that if something is present, it will never again be present. The only time (f) is true of some object is when that object is enjoying the last instance of its (present) existence.

Regardless of whether one accepts the Lockean view, one should hold that all ways of substituting for the free variable in (g) yield necessary truths, whereas not all instances of (h) are necessarily true:

(g) $\exists_p x \; x = y \rightarrow \mathbf{W}(\exists_c x \; x = y)$
(h) $\exists_c x \; x = y \rightarrow \mathbf{W}(\exists_c x \; x = y)$

Informally, (g) says that all past things once were present, which is necessarily true, whereas (h) is false of some entity at the time at which it first comes into being.

If PEP* is true and tense logic is logic, existence is systematically variably axiomatic.[14]

3.3 PEP and Meinongian Presentism

Meinongian presentism is the view that, although non-present things do not exist, nonetheless *there are* non-present things. The real Meinong rejected Meinongian presentism for most of his career. See, for example, Meinong (1983: 60), in which he defends the view that all things in time share the same mode of being, namely, existence. According to J. N. Findlay (1933: 79–80), late in his life Meinong changed his mind and endorsed something like Meinongian presentism. But regardless of whether Meinong endorsed Meinongian presentism, the view has current defenders, and its interest is independent of the psychological fact that it has been believed.[15]

There are commonalities between Meinongian presentism and PEP. Allow me to highlight some differences. First, the friend of PEP need make no dealings with non-existent entities per se: she can hold that, although there are different ways to exist, everything that there is exists in some way or other. Second, the friend of PEP can insist that it is metaphysically mistaken to assimilate dinosaurs to elves: past things have ontological status, whereas there simply are no fictional, imaginary, in short, non-real entities.[16] A view that treats past entities as fundamentally on a par with "creatures of fiction," mere *possibilia*, or even *impossibilia*, as standard Meinongian-ism does, fails to respect the ontological facts.[17]

---

[14] Recall section 2.5.

[15] See Keller (2004) and Markosian (2004b) for critical discussion. Defenders of Meinongian presentism include Gallois (2004), Hinchliff (1988), and Yourgrau (1993). Berto (2013: 98–101) and von Solodkoff and Woodward (2013: 573–4) also discuss versions of Meinongian presentism.

[16] My own view is that there are fictional entities, but they do not enjoy a fundamental mode of being, unlike some past entities. Fictional entities will be briefly discussed in section 5.5.

[17] As Yourgrau (1993: 140) writes, "Talk of the dead is of an entirely different order from, say, talk of the tooth fairy, which cries out for paraphrase." Note, however, that Yourgrau is himself a friend of non-existent past and future objects, non-existent possible worlds, and babies that are never born. Given this, it

The Meinongian presentist could minimize these differences by holding that the only non-existent objects are past objects. Call this view *minimal Meinongian presentism* (MMP). MMP and PEP are not merely notational variants. As discussed in section 1.5.2, I understand Meinongianism as the view that there are (at least) two fundamental quantifier locutions, which we can neutrally call the (or an) *inner quantifier* and the *outer quantifier*.[18] According to contemporary Meinongians, the outer quantifier—henceforth "$\exists_o$"—corresponds to the unrestricted "some" of ordinary English, whereas the inner quantifier—henceforth "$\exists_i$"—corresponds to "there exists." Table for a moment this linguistic thesis, and focus on this key feature of Meinongianism: everything within the domain of the inner quantifier is within the domain of the outer quantifier, but the converse does not hold. In short, the two fundamental quantifiers are nested.[19] (This is why a Meinongian says that there are some things that do not exist, but doesn't say that there are some existents that nonetheless aren't.)

By contrast, the fundamental quantifiers recognized by PEP have disjoint domains. So, according to PEP, there is no fundamental sense of "some" whereby "some entities are both past and present" is a truth. Note that, although both PEP and MMP are inconsistent with presentism**, MMP unlike PEP entails *both* the growing block theory* *and* presentism*. These facts ensure that PEP and MMP are not mere notational variants.

However, I grant that both views might receive support from some of the same considerations. They might also face some of the same objections. For example, Simon Keller (2004) claims that it is very hard to see how one knows that one is present given Meinongian presentism. A similar worry can be raised about PEP. I take this worry very seriously, and will discuss it in section 3.8.

3.4 PEP and Degrees Presentism

PEP is in some respects like the view defended by Quentin Smith (2002), Degrees Presentism. According to Degrees Presentism,

Being temporally present is the highest degree of existence. Being past and being future *by a merely infinitesimal amount* is the second highest degree of existence. Being past *by one hour* and being future *by one hour* are lower degrees of existence, and being past *by 5 billion years* and being future *by 5 billion years* are still lower degrees of existence. The degree to which an item exists is proportional to its temporal distance from the present; the present, which has

---

is unclear what he has against the tooth fairy. That said, Joshua Spencer has pointed out to me that one might think that fictional objects cannot actually exist. McGinn (2000: 38–9) holds this view.

[18] See Perszyk (1993: 7–9, 16) and van Inwagen (2006: 122–5) for discussion of Meinongianism that also appeals to an inner and outer quantifier.

[19] We could also consider a third view in which there are three nested fundamental quantifiers: one for everything that there is, one for everything spatiotemporal, and one for everything present.

zero-temporal distance from the present, has the highest (logically) possible degree of existence.... There is a difference of degree and not of kind between the present and what is no
longer present or not yet present.   [Smith 2002: 119–20]

While PEP says that past existence and present existence are different kinds
of existence, Degrees Presentism claims that they are merely different degrees of
existence. Overall, I think PEP is the better theory, and in what follows I will
explain why.

We have seen how one can make sense of *ways of being*, but how should one make
sense of *degrees* of existence? There are two options: define the notion or take it as
primitive. One might try to define *degrees of existence* directly in terms of concepts
other than *being* or *mode of being*. For example, one might define *x has more
existence than y* as *y modally depends on x but x does not modally depend on y*.[20]
Or one might define *x has more existence than y* as *x has more causal power than y*.
(More sophisticated definitions could be offered.) Note that neither definition is
promising for the temporal case. Defining degrees of reality in terms of modal
dependence gets things backwards: I am modally dependent on my parents, and
they are dependent on my grandparents, and so on. But my great-grandparents are
not modally dependent on my grandparents, nor are my grandparents dependent on
my parents, and so on. So, on this way of defining degrees of reality, my great-
grandparents enjoy a higher degree of existence than I enjoy, even though I am
present and they are past. Similarly for definitions that appeal to causal power. The
Big Bang that began the universe had more causal potency than I ever will, and yet it
is past and I am present. One way of defining the notion of degrees of reality gets the
right result but at the cost of utterly trivializing Smith's view: *x* exists to a greater
degree than *y* = df. *x* is closer to the present moment than *y*. (The B-theorist could
accept this definition and then say that the past is less real than the present!) It seems
to me that none of these ways of thinking of degrees of existence is really about
existence; rather, they are about different subjects that are discussed in old but inapt
terminology.

This is not to say that these are the only plausible ways of understanding "degree of
existence." In chapter 5, I will define a notion of degree of existence in terms of
relative naturalness of quantifiers. And in chapter 7, I will discuss whether this notion
of degree of existence should rather be taken as primitive and used to define up a
notion of naturalness instead![21] But for Smith's purposes, the notion of degree of
existence that I will discuss in chapters 5 and 7 is inadequate, since the nature and
existence of the things that are fully existent fix the nature and existence of the things

---

[20] *x* modally depends on *y* just in case any possible world in which *x* exists is one in which *y* exists.

[21] These are not the only proposals, either. Tim Perrine has suggested to me a proposal on which
existence is a first-order property and instantiation comes in degrees. I'm not opposed to degrees (or
modes) of instantiation, but I hope to explore in future work how these could be captured using degrees
(and modes) of being, and so will not pursue this interesting suggestion further here.

that are not. If we understand "degree of existence" in my way and Smith's degree presentism is true, it follows that all facts about past and present objects are fixed by facts about the present. Whether this is the case though is highly controversial, and is a large part of what lies behind the truth-maker objection to presentism, which I discuss in section 3.5.

So let's see whether some other notion in the neighborhood of what I call degrees of existence can be understood in terms of *modes of existence* and (perhaps) other concepts. Smith (2002) seems to take his notion of degrees of existence as a primitive. I have no objection to this, provided that we can characterize (not define!) this primitive in such a way as to distinguish it from other notions in its neighborhood with which it might be confused. In the introduction, I distinguished between what I called orders of being, levels of being, and degrees of being. For me, each of these notions is important, and importantly different.

We've already encountered orders of being in sections 2.4–2.4.3. There is something to be said for the idea that substances enjoy *more* reality than attributes. In general, it seems right to say that things that exist *absolutely* have in some sense more being than those that exist *relatively*: x has a higher order of being than y = df. The logical form of the kind of existence enjoyed by x is *less polyadic* than the kind of existence enjoyed by y.

The notion does have an interesting possible application to the philosophy of time. Consider the view that present existence is the only kind of absolute existence, whereas things that exist in the past enjoy only a kind of relative existence, specifically existence relative to a time. This view implies that past existence is a deficient mode of existence: past existence is a lower order of being. However, on this view, past existence is still a fundamental (yet relative) mode of being, and hence there is no expectation that all facts about past existents must be fixed by facts about the present.

That said, orders of being do not seem to be what Smith has in mind. For on the view I've just described, it doesn't follow that, as you recede further into the past, your mode of being proportionately deteriorates. There is no obvious way of appealing to orders of being to achieve the result Smith wants.

From the perspective of Degrees Presentism, PEP itself is a kind of "degrees presentism," albeit one that recognizes only two "degrees" of being and that does not explicitly state that *presently existing* is a greater degree. Similar remarks apply to Meinongian presentism, although since for the Meinongian presentist present objects enjoy two modes of being, perhaps it is clearer how present existence is superior to past existence. This suggests that one way of modeling Degrees Presentism is to hold that, for each time, there is a unique way of being corresponding to that time. One could then claim that there is a primitive relation ordering the ways of being, which is formally analogous to the *greater than relation* and which has the way of being corresponding to the present moment at its apex. But it is hard to see why this relation, despite its formal character, really correlates with "amounts of being."

Here is a suggestion that seems to do the trick.[22] Corresponding to the present moment is a unique way of being. Additionally, corresponding to every temporal interval centered on the present moment is a unique way of being. (So there is a way of being corresponding to the interval beginning one second before the present moment and ending one second after the present moment, there is a way of being corresponding to the interval beginning one hour before the present moment and ending one hour after the present moment, and so forth.) On this suggestion, things enjoy more than one way of existing. We now define *x has a higher level of being than y* as: the set of ways of being enjoyed by *y* is a *proper* subset of the set of ways of being enjoyed by *x*.[23] On this account, things that presently exist have "more being" than things that do not, and the further an existent is from the present, the "less being" it has: a thing that exists *in more ways* than others has a richer *existential profile* and hence *enjoys*, in this sense, *more being*.[24] In order to keep the terminology consistent, I will henceforth use only "level of being" when describing this sort of ontological difference between entities.

We've described a version of Degrees Presentism in which the "degrees" are understood in terms of levels of being. It is hard to see what theoretical advantages it has over PEP. And there are theoretical costs: Degrees Presentism, as understood above, posits literally infinitely many modes of existence: in effect, it is Meinongian presentism with infinitely many fundamental inner quantifiers.[25] Standard Meinongian presentism and PEP posit only two fundamental quantifiers.

Smith's (2002: 119–20) main motivation for Degrees Presentism is *phenomeno-logical*: he holds that what he calls degrees of existence are given in experience, and that it is obvious that Degrees Presentism is true. I am not unsympathetic to the phenomenological motivation for ontological pluralism. However, in this case, I don't think that Smith has correctly described the phenomenology. It doesn't seem to me that it is given in experience that Socrates is less real than Aristotle. Which experiences did I have in which this fact was given? What does seem true is that, as events recede in time, our memories of them often become less vivid and vivacious. But this is not always the case: my memories of the births of my daughters are more vivid and vivacious than my memories of what I did two days ago. Both kids

---

[22] Thanks to Jason Turner for the suggestion.

[23] An even more general proposal but in the same spirit is to define "*x* has a higher level* of being than *y*" as "let C*x* be the class of ways in which *x* exists; let C*y* be the class of ways in which *y* exists; then: the cardinality of C*x* is greater than the cardinality of C*y*." However, given standard assumptions about the continuity of time, the cardinality of many of these sets will be the same even when some of them are proper subsets of others of them. Thanks to an anonymous referee for discussion here.

[24] Or, at least, it exists in all the ways in which less present things exist, and in some in which they do not. In this context, talk of "more ways" might be misleading.

[25] I'm confident that this is a cost of Degrees Presentism so interpreted, but I'm not sure how much of a cost it is. Each of the quantifiers posited by Degrees Presentism is, in a sense, of the same ideological kind, and perhaps it is more important to count kinds here rather than members of a kind. But there are infinitely many members of this ideological kind given Degrees Presentism. See Cowling (2013b) for discussion of ideological parsimony. Thanks to Peter Finocchiaro for pushing me here.

are much older than two days old! Insofar as there is a feeling of "difference in reality," their births seem more real, more present—because they are more significant and more vividly remembered. And, similarly, as events move from the future towards the present, our anticipation of them grows greater. But to pre-theoretic intuition, all future events seem equally unreal. I suspect that these psychological facts are partially responsible for Smith's illusory belief that things are proportionately "less real" as they are distant from the present. The "levels of being" version of Degrees Presentism posits a lot of levels but without a lot of payoff.

3.5 PEP, Presentism, and Truth-Making

PEP, along with other A-theories of time, takes *the present* to be metaphysically distinguished in some way. Pre-theoretical intuition favors the A-theory. But does pre-theoretic intuition favor presentism over PEP?

A. N. Prior (1970: 245) offers this pithy formulation of presentism: "The present simply *is* the real considered in relation to two particular species of unreality, namely the past and the future." In a similar vein, albeit with less pith, Lotze (1887: 355) writes, "The history of the world, is it really reduced to the infinitely thin, forever changing, strip of light which forms the present, wavering between a darkness of the Past, which is done and no longer anything at all, and a darkness of the future, which is also nothing?" What both Prior and Lotze stress is that, according to presentism, both the past and the future are completely unreal.

But, *pace* Prior, this seems true only of future objects. That the past has some ontological status is a datum, which some philosophers have tried to respect by (mistakenly) identifying past existence with "existence in our memories or other intentional states." Consider the following remarks by Sidgwick (1894: 443):

One has to distinguish different modes of real existence. It would be absurd to say that the great study of History is not conversant with reality. So far as the historian attains truth—as doubtless he does in some degree—the past exists for him as an object of thought and investigation: but so far as it is past it has ceased to exist in the sense in which the present exists.

Note that there is an unstrained reading of this passage according to which Sidgwick endorses PEP; PEP says that past existence is a mode of *real* existence. This reading places weight on the first two sentences of the quotation. But there is also a more strained reading in which Sidgwick holds that the (only) way in which the past exists is as the object of intentional states of presently existing beings. (But in what way would this be a mode of *real* existence?) This seems to be the view defended by Augustine (1961: 266–70) in his *Confessions*, Book XI, chapters 17–21.

In order for something to be an object of an intentional state, the state must be about the object. So what makes it the case that a particular memory (or some other intentional state) is of some particular past object rather than another? And what makes that mental state a genuine memory (i.e., a true representation of the past) as opposed to a mere seeming?[26] A related concern is that memory provides us with knowledge by acquaintance rather than knowledge by description of past things.[27] But how can we be acquainted with that which in no way exists? If the past is literally nothing, it is hard to see how these questions can be answered.

I follow here Edith Stein (2009: 11), who notes that, "Past being and future being are not simply nonbeing. This implies more than that past and future have cognitive being in remembrance and expectation."

Memories are "traces" of the past, but they aren't the only kind of currently existing effect of past events. Perhaps we can appeal to these other traces in order to give the past some sort of reality. This view is suggested by Bosanquet (1897: 229), who claims that the position of the common person once it has been clarified of certain confusions is that

past and future...exist, so to speak, indirectly....The present tense alone, implying a certain duration, would predicate existence in the full sense. It would be quite agreed that past and future make a difference to the present. But they would be held to exist only in and through this difference, and would be realities only, in the case of the past, as effects, and in the case of the future, as anticipations.

A view of this sort is also defended by Łukasiewicz (1967), who holds that past truths are made true by present truths and the laws of nature, but if the laws of nature are indeterministic, then many of the propositions about the past that we take to be true are not in fact true.

I doubt both that this is the "purified view" of the common person and that this view is correct.[28] Suppose there are island universes, that is, spatially and causally isolated parts of reality, and suppose that we live in one of them. Suppose that moments from now one of these island universes will cease to be, leaving no trace at all of its ever having been, leaving no final effects on what remain. It would nonetheless be true that it existed, that it had various features, etc. The view gestured at by Bosanquet and defended by Łukasiewicz seems untenable.[29]

Intuition demands that the past must have some sort of reality. Past entities must enjoy some real mode of being. This intuition is what makes the so-called *truth-maker argument* against presentism so compelling. Let us now discuss this argument.

There are contingent truths about the past. For example, it is true that World War I was horrific. But what in the world *makes* it true? The eternalist, who believes in past, present, and future objects in all their glory and awfulness, has an easy answer: since World War I is in her ontology, she can say that World War I's being horrific is

---

[26]   See Sprigge (1992), Keller (2004), and Markosian (2004b) for discussion.
[27]   See Russell (1915) and Cockburn (1997: 54–7) for discussion.
[28]   In fairness to Bosanquet, this is not his considered view about time.
[29]   Sprigge (1992: 3) also presents an argument along these lines.

the truth-maker for the proposition that World War I was horrific. But there seems to be nothing in the presentist's ontology to serve as a truth-maker.[30]

Some presentists resist the demand for truth-makers for truths about the past.[31] I have nothing new to say to convince them to change their minds. Other presentists accept the demand, and attempt to produce *present* truth-makers for contingent truths about the past. These present truth-makers are states of affairs of the form *the world is such that it was the case that P*. The truth-maker for the claim that World War I was horrific is the state of affairs *the world is such that World War I was horrific*.[32]

A common response is to charge the presentist with *cheating*: the properties postulated by the presentist—*being such that the world was P*—are not fit to be fundamental features of reality. Yet the presentist cannot hold that they supervene on fundamental categorical properties exemplified by present objects, since two possible worlds could be exactly alike with respect to how things are (categorically) now, but differ with respect to how things were (categorically).[33] Sider (2001: 40–1) makes this point nicely:

The point of the truth-maker principle and the principle that truth supervenes on being is to rule out dubious ontologies. Let us consider some. First, brute dispositions. Many would insist that the fragility of a wine glass—its disposition to shatter if dropped—must be grounded in the non-dispositional properties of the glass, plus perhaps the laws of nature. It would be illegitimate to claim that the glass's disposition to shatter is completely brute or ungrounded. Second example: brute counter-factuals. Most would say that when a counter-factual conditional is true, for example, "this match would light if struck," its truth must be grounded in the actual, occurrent properties of the match and its surroundings.....The argument against allowing the presentist to "cheat" by invoking primitive properties like *previously containing dinosaurs*, or by invoking tenses themselves as primitive, is that this cheat seems of a kind with the dubious ontological cheats [just mentioned]. What seems common to all cheats is that irreducibly *hypothetical* properties are postulated, whereas a proper ontology should invoke only *categorical*, or ocurrent, properties and relations.

Suppose that the truth-maker objection refutes presentism.[34] Would PEP suffer the same fate? No. For PEP recognizes a fundamental quantifier that ranges over past objects. To return to our earlier example, World War I is in the domain of this quantifier, and it has the feature of being horrific. So it seems that PEP does not face the truth-making objection.

---

[30] The truth-maker argument against presentism is not a contemporary creation. For example, Brentano (1988: 96) briefly discusses it. And see Embry (2015) for a discussion of the history of the truth-maker principle in late scholastic thought.

[31] See, for example, Merricks (2007).   [32] For a defense of this view, see Bigelow (1996).

[33] This is made clear in Keller (2004). Keller discusses some other ways to defuse the objection from truth-making. I won't pursue these here.

[34] It is by no means obvious that it does; Crisp (2007), for example, presents a plausible rejoinder to this objection.

To make sure that this appearance is not deceptive, we need to think about how the ontological pluralist should formulate the truth-maker principle. The standard formulation of this principle is as follows:

(TM):   For all P, if P is true, then $\exists x$ (x *makes* P true.)

There is an intramural dispute among truth-maker theorists about what sort of relation the *makes-true* relation is. I hold that, at the very least, if x makes P true, then there is no world in which x exists and P is not true.[35] But this is all I will say about the makes-true relation here.[36]

Focus on the existential quantifier that appears in TM. Recall that the ontological pluralist believes that there is more than one fundamental quantifier. An implicit assumption in the formulation of TM is that there is exactly one fundamental quantifier. If we embrace PEP, we drop that assumption. PEP is a version of ontological pluralism that accepts two fundamental quantifiers, "$\exists_p$" and "$\exists_c$." A PEP-friendly version of TM is the following:

(PEP-TM):   For all P, if P is true, then either $\exists_p x$ (x makes P true) or $\exists_c x$ (x makes P true.)

The thought behind PEP-TM is this. If you accept that there is a close connection between existence and quantification, you will be attracted to Quine's slogan that to be is to be the value of a bound variable.[37] And if you also think that there are fundamentally different ways to exist, you will hold that there are different fundamental quantifiers. You should then hold that to be in some fundamental way is to be within the scope of a fundamental quantifier. The truth-maker principle says that whenever something is true, some existent makes it true. The generalized truth-maker principle says that whenever something is true, something existing in some way or other makes it true.[38]

PEP-TM is the proper way to formulate the truth-maker principle given PEP. PEP is consistent with PEP-TM. Since the fact that World War I is horrific is within the range of "$\exists_p$," it is the case that $\exists_p x$ (x makes it true that World War I is horrific). And

---

[35] D. H. Mellor (2003: 213–14) holds that this claim is too strong; D. M. Armstrong (2004: 10–12) suggests that truth-makers must not only necessitate their truths, they must *relevantly* necessitate them.

[36] A principle weaker than TM is sometimes appealed to, specifically, that *truth supervenes on being*. On this principle, truths are true in virtue of existing objects having properties or standing in various relations, but there needn't be an entity that *is* "an object having a property or some objects standing in a relation," and hence there need not be anything whose existence is modally sufficient for the truth of contingent propositions. (David Lewis (2001) defends a version of this view.) I believe that all of the points I want to make about presentism, PEP, and the truth-making objection could be made by way of appeal to this weaker principle.

[37] See Cocchiarella (1969: 42) for discussion.

[38] In stating the truth-maker principle, I quantified over propositions. Which quantifier was employed? The view that I prefer holds that *abstracta* do not exist in the same way as *concreta*; to use the older terminology, abstracta *subsist* rather than *exist*. So I am inclined to hold that there is at least a third fundamental quantifier in play here. But I needn't defend this here. Another plausible view is that abstract objects presently exist, and so are within the domain of "$\exists_c$."

so forth for other truths about the past. PEP does not face the truth-making objection that devastates presentism, despite the fact that PEP implies that there is a meta-physically fundamental sense in which no past objects exist.

Given PEP, reformulating the truth-maker principle as PEP-TEM is motivated. Likewise, perhaps it is not unmotivated for the presentist to reformulate the truth-maker principle as the view that truths are made true by things that *do, did,* or *will* exist.[39] *Define* the following "quantifier" as follows: $\exists_d x\ \Phi$ = df. $\exists x\ \Phi$ or $W(\exists x\ \Phi)$ or $F(\exists x\ \Phi)$. We now reformulate the truth-maker principle as:

(Pres-TM):   For all P, if P is true, then $\exists_d x$ (x makes P true).

Grant that "$\exists_d$" functions enough like a quantifier to deserve to be called one. So the friend of Pres-TM can at least mouth the slogan that "truth is determined by being." But that isn't enough. *Defined* quantifiers are cheap.[40] Suppose one believes that statements about nomic possibilities are true, but is worried that their truth requires uncomfortable additions to one's ontology on pain of violating the truth-maker principle. No need to worry! Simply *define* a new notion of *being* as follows: let "L" be the *it is nomically possible that* operator, and define "$\exists_L x\ \Phi$" as "$\exists x\ \Phi$ or $L(\exists x \Phi)$." And then reformulate the truth-maker principle as:

(TM*):   For all P, if P is true, then $\exists_L x$ (x makes P true).

But TM* violates the spirit of the truth-maker principle.[41] The lesson here is that the truth-maker principle must be formulated so as to appeal only to what exists in some fundamental sense of "exists," instead of appealing to defined or non-fundamental notions of existence. And the motivation for this restriction is straightforward. Truths about "what there is" in some non-fundamental sense must be grounded in truths about what there is in some fundamental sense. But the problem for the standard presentist is that, by her lights, there is exactly one fundamental sense of "exists" which is such that nothing that exists in that sense could serve as such ground.[42]

However, since PEP-TM appeals only to fundamental senses of "exists," PEP-TM satisfies this demand. Truth is determined by what exists in some fundamental way or other. Past existence is a genuine kind of existence, and so truths about the past are appropriately grounded.

3.6 PEP and Williamson's Present-Centrism

Another view in the philosophy of time worth considering is defended by Timothy Williamson (2002), which we will call *present centrism*. According to present

---

[39] See Gallois (2004: 649).   [40] See Turner (2010) for related discussion.
[41] Sider (2004: 679) offers a similar response.
[42] Unless the presentist appeals to "cheating properties," but doing so would eliminate the motivation for endorsing Pres-TM rather than TM.

centrism, there are past and future objects, but they have virtually none of the interesting properties that presently existing objects have:

It is said, Trajan's Column in Rome is now a trace of the Emperor Trajan, and the name "Trajan" refers to him, so various objects now stand in causal and semantic relations to Trajan. By the same token, Trajan now stands in causal and semantic relations to various objects. He still has relations, but does not still exist. Such examples are not decisive. Doubtless, *in some sense* Trajan no longer exists. Specifically, he is no longer anywhere; he lacks spatial location. Although atoms which once composed him may still be spatially located, he is not identical with those atoms. More generally, we may say that he is no longer *concrete*..... Whatever can be counted exists at least in the logical sense: there is such an item..... "Trajan does not exist" is true when "exist" is used in the nonlogical sense of concreteness, not when it is used in the logical sense. Existence in the sense of concreteness is of crucial significance for metaphysics; for logic it is just one more property, which objects may have or lack.   [Williamson 2002: 245]

On present centrism, Trajan exists, but he is neither tall nor short. In fact, he has no material parts and stands in no spatial relations. Present centrism is not a kind of Cartesian dualism: rather, Williamson's view is that Trajan is not even a person, let alone a conscious being. Given present centrism, the fundamental difference between past and present objects is *qualitative*: no past object shares any fundamental qualitative properties with presently existing objects. According to PEP, the difference between past and present things lies in how they exist, not in what sort of qualities they have. PEP's ontology is not populated with entities that are merely shells of their former selves. It might even be the case that some past objects are qualitative duplicates of present ones. (In the next section, we will discuss what the friend of PEP should say about how objects change properties over time.) This underscores the claim that, for PEP, the difference between the past and the present does not consist merely in the fact that past things lack a quality had by present ones. The difference is deeper than that.

Because present centrism strips past things of their qualities, present centrism is also subject to the truth-making objection. For what in present centrism's ontology makes it true that World War I was horrific? One apparent advantage of present centrism over presentism is that at least present centrism recognizes the existence of World War I. However, recall that on present centrism, World War I is not even a war, let alone a horrific one. It merely has the property *being such that it was a horrific war*. But this property is no less of a cheater than *being such that World War I was horrific*. Both properties are such that objects could be exactly alike with respect to categorical properties and yet differ with respect to them. Williamson (2000: 204) writes, "What distinguishes a past mountain m_1 from a distinct past mountain m_2? If one is forbidden to refer to the past, perhaps one can say only that they are distinct." I take it that the idea is that past objects are *presently* indistinguishable. According to present centrism, there are incredibly many merely past objects that are exactly alike with respect to their categorical properties, but only a few of them are such that they were horrific wars or mountains.[43]

Consider the following scenario. At *t1*, there were exactly two objects, an electron and a positron. Now, at *t2*, there is only the electron. In effect, at *t2*, the electron is the world. According to the presentist, this electron has the property *being such that it was the case that there was a positron*. Here is how the friend of present centrism describes this scenario. At *t1*, there are exactly two objects, an electron and a position. At *t2*, there are exactly two objects, an electron and something that lacks accidental intrinsic qualities. This something is an almost bare particular. According to present centrism, this object exemplifies the property *having once been a positron*. I suppose that according to present centrism, the electron also has the property *being such that it was the case that there was a positron*. And I suppose that the friend of present centrism should claim that the electron has this second property in virtue of the ex-positron having its past-tensed property. However, with respect to the categorical properties exemplified, the sole difference between presentism and present centrism seems to be the presence of an extra nearly bare particular at *t2*.

Does this difference make a difference? If the concern is cheating properties, is it better to have a bunch of entities instantiate cheating properties rather than have the presently existing universe instantiate cheating properties? With respect to this version of the truth-making objection, present centrism fares little better than standard presentism.[44]

Let "C" be a fundamental predicate such as "is negatively charged." Let's assume (to avoid unnecessary distractions) that whenever some object presently falls under "C," that object falls under "C" as long as it is present. (Consider, for example, an electron—as long as the electron presently exists, it is negatively charged). What is the salient difference between "$\exists_p x\ (Cx)$" and "$\exists x\ (W: Fx)$"? Why does appealing to the latter cheat whereas appealing to the former does not? According to PEP, "$\exists_p x\ (Cx)$" contains only fundamental vocabulary. But similarly, according to present centrism, "$\exists x\ (W: Cx)$" contains only fundamental vocabulary, since the existential quantifier and the past operator are both fundamental notions according to present centrism.

There are two salient differences. First, the friend of PEP can claim that truths involving intensional operators, such as "W" or "$\lozenge$," should ultimately be grounded in truths not involving them. But, on present centrism, it is just a brute fact that some

---

[43] See also Williamson (1998: 265–6). For criticism of Williamson, see Zimmerman (2008).

[44] One possible advantage of present centrism over standard presentism is that the putative truth-makers involve particular things (such as Abe Lincoln) rather than the entire state of the world; thanks to Peter Finocchiaro for reminding me of this. And perhaps the friend of present centrism could hold that past objects instantiate some properties relative to times. World War I is not horrific, but it is horrific in 1917, for example. Like the standard endurantist, the present centrist would need to tell to us how she understands property-indexing, and she must understand it in such a way as to not undercut the motivations for present centrism. Thanks to Joshua Spencer for suggesting this.

object was C, ungrounded in any further fact stateable without appeal to a tense-operator. According to PEP, what makes it the case that some object x *was* C is the past existence of a fact that x is C. (In other words, "$\exists x$ (**W**: Cx)" is true because "$\exists_p x$ (Cx)" is true.) Similarly, what makes it the case that an object *is* F is the present existence of a fact that x is F. In general, given PEP, all truths stateable using tense-operators are grounded in truths stateable that do not use them.[45]

Second, consider the monadic properties denoted by the open sentence "**W**: (Fx)." Are any of these properties fundamental? If not, then in virtue of what other fundamental properties do objects have them? It is hard to see what they could be.[46] If some of them are fundamental properties, then some of these properties are intrinsic properties, since fundamental monadic properties are intrinsic properties.[47] But it doesn't seem to me that, for example, *being such that x was an electron* is an intrinsic property. Nor does it seem that *being such as to have once been an electron* is an intrinsic property.[48] Note that the friend of PEP need not countenance any fundamental properties of this sort: it is consistent with PEP that all fundamental monadic properties are intrinsic properties. This is another advantage of PEP over present centrism.

Given PEP, one might worry about what grounds the truth that a past object once was present, or the putative truth that every present object will be past. The former worry is easily quieted: the past existence of past objects suffices to ground the claim that they once were present. The latter worry is less easy to quiet. First, it is not obviously true that every present entity will one day be merely past. On the version of PEP defended here, there are no merely future existences, and so next to nothing exists to ground future contingent truths.[49] In general, given PEP, future contingents have no truth-value. If, however, every (actually) presently existing object has as part of its essence that it will one day cease to be present, then each such object grounds the truth that it will one day be past. Alternatively, if the actual laws of nature presently ensure that every (actually) presently existing object will one day cease to be, then this

---

[45]   This fact suggests that one might be able to give explicit definitions of the tense operators in terms of the modes of being countenanced by PEP. This is a project that I am more than open to exploring, but I won't explore it here.

[46]   Ted Sider has suggested to me that Williamson might hold that these properties are not fundamental but deny that they supervene on other fundamental properties. I am not sure that this response is coherent, but, in any event, I deny that there are non-fundamental properties that fail to supervene on the fundamental. Another response would be to deny that these expressions succeed in denoting properties even though they are true of some entities and not others. This response is coherent, but it is a response in which one abandons the doctrine that truth supervenes on being. Since the point of this section is to assess how well present centrism can accommodate the truth-maker objection, I set this aside.

[47]   This claim is highly plausible in itself. Note that it is also a consequence of the definition of "intrinsic property" defended in Lewis (1986).

[48]   See Cameron (2011) and Crisp (2007) for discussions of this sort of worry.

[49]   Save for those future contingents whose truth-value is entailed by facts about the past or the present. Note that views that recognize a mode of being for future existences need not worry about the grounding problem for alleged truths about the future. Perhaps this is one advantage of such a view over PEP.

claim is also grounded. However, if a putative truth is determined by neither the laws of essence nor the laws of nature in conjunction with past and present facts, then reject the claim that it is true![50]

In sections 3.5 and 3.6, I assessed whether PEP does better with respect to the truth-making objection than a variety of competitor A-theories. My judgment is that it does. If the truth-making objection moves you, seriously consider PEP.

3.7 PEP and Persistence through Time

Objects persist through time, and as they persist, they enjoy different properties at different times. How should a view like PEP accommodate these facts? Are there any views about persistence over time that are either inconsistent with or in tension with PEP?

Let x be an object that exists at $t1$, $t2$, and $t3$. $t1$ and $t2$ are past times, whereas $t3$ is the present moment. Pretend that colors are intrinsic properties, and that x is red at $t1$, blue at $t2$, and green at $t3$. According to *perdurantism*, objects persist through time by having temporal parts. On this view, x has a temporal part that exists at and only at $t1$, and this temporal part is red, and distinct temporal parts at $t2$ and $t3$ that are blue and green simpliciter.[51]

The friend of PEP could endorse perdurantism, but she faces an interesting question if she does: what is the mode of being enjoyed by entities that have presently existing and pastly existing parts? Five answers are possible: a *sui generis* mode of being, both present and past existence, present existence, past existence, and finally a merely deficient mode of being. Something has a deficient mode of being just in case no perfectly natural quantifier includes it within its domain. If something has a deficient mode of being, there is no fundamental sense in which it is real. (The idea of a deficient mode of being will be further explored in chapter 5.)

We should probably reject the view that such objects have a *sui generis* mode of being, unless in general we are attracted to the view that wholes enjoy a different mode of being than their parts. The option that such objects enjoy both modes of being seems non-arbitrary, but it also seems to me that someone attracted to this option should probably prefer the view discussed in section 3.3 called minimal Meinongian presentism. Recall that, on minimal Meinongian presentism, every present object enjoys two modes of being, one of which is also enjoyed by past objects. The sole significant difference between minimal Meinongian presentism and PEP was that the fundamental quantifiers recognized by minimal Meinongian

---

[50] For each presently existing object, it is probable that it will one day be past. But I take these truths about probability to be grounded in the nature of the objects in question in conjunction with the actual laws of nature.

[51] See Sider (2001) for a defense of perdurantism.

presentism overlap while those of PEP do not. But now we are considering a view in which there is overlap. Why not go all the way if one is going to go partway?

Suppose the choice is between past and present existence. Which? No friend of PEP can deny that this question deserves a principled answer. Unfortunately, I am without principles. My inclination is to side with present existence: to have a presently existing part suffices to be present. Intuition strongly favors that we are presently existing, and if we persist by having temporal parts, we are presently existing via having a presently existing temporal part. Moreover, if we deny this, we'll need to rethink what it even means to be present or past. (Recall that at the start of this chapter, I said that something is present just in case some moment in its lifetime is present, and that something is past just in case every moment of its existence is prior to the present moment. Were these mistakes?)

The fifth option is that sums of presently existing and pastly existing entities have a merely deficient mode of being. On this view, although things persist through time, nothing *really* persists through time.

None of these options is that great. This suggests that the friend of PEP should probably reject temporal parts. There is no inconsistency in holding PEP and the doctrine of temporal parts, but the troubling questions this conjunction raises might make embracing both claims not worth it.

Note, however, that even if the friend of PEP rejects temporal parts, there are still troubling questions in the neighborhood. Suppose that whenever there are some individuals, there is a set of those individuals. Then, given PEP, there are sets whose elements are cavemen and members of congress. In which way do these sets exist? Suppose that there are facts, which are complex entities consisting of objects and properties or relations.[52] My great-grandfather is merely past whereas I am present, but there is a fact that he is my great-grandfather. In which way do facts of this sort exist?

Note that, it is not at all obvious that mixed mereological sums, mixed sets, and mixed facts should be treated uniformly. One might hold that sets and facts enjoy a different kind of being than individuals since sets and facts form fundamentally different ontological categories than those of their constituents (that are neither sets nor facts). Meinong (1904: 85), for example, held that the mode of being of objectives—entities that are much like facts—is not necessarily the same mode of being as the "constituents" of the objectives; however, he was also cautious about taking the "constituents" of objectives to be parts of objectives.

This suggests that mixed mereological sums would be the most problematic for PEP, since there is no motivation to hold that a sum of some *xs* always belongs to a different ontological category than any of the *xs*. One possibility is to simply deny that there are any mereological sums of past and present objects. This is what I am

---

[52] Gibson (1998: 26) briefly discusses the worry about facts or states of affairs.

inclined to do. Despite the protestations of some philosophers, there isn't much to be said in favor of absolutely unrestricted composition.[53] The restriction that things have a mereological sum only if they share a mode of being is neither vague nor unmotivated, for example.

Another, more radical possibility, is to hold that even an ordinary object can have a part that differs in mode of being from the whole. Consider an arbitrary way of dividing me in two. (Merely consider!) Does this arbitrary way of dividing me correspond to arbitrary proper parts of me? Some philosophers would say "yes."[54] But perhaps the right thing to say is "yes and no": this arbitrary division corresponds to *potential* but not *actual* parts, and the distinction between potential and actual objects is a distinction in way of existence.[55] An arbitrary undetached part of me is a part of me, but it does not exist in the same way as, for example, my hands or my cells. If this is the right way of thinking of things, then even ordinary wholes do not always have the same mode of being as their parts.

Let's return to the problem of persistence over time. Suppose that we reject perdurantism, perhaps because of the above considerations. As far as I can see, PEP raises no new difficulties for endurantism. We'll discuss three endurantist views about how things change in what follows: the relationalist account, adverbialism, and a hybrid of the two.

One endurantist account of change, the *relationalist account*, holds that what we took to be intrinsic properties are really relations to times. *x* bears the *red-at* relation to *t1*, the *blue-at* relation to *t2*, and the *green-at* relation to *t3*. Some take the replacement of intrinsic properties with relations to times to be unacceptable.[56] One variant of relationalism meets this complaint not via replacing intrinsic properties with relations to times but rather by *supplementing* intrinsic properties to relations to times. On this variant, for any predicate F that something can satisfy at one time and fail to satisfy at a later time, there are two ways of being F. If one is presently F, then one is F by virtue of having an intrinsic property of Fness. If one is merely pastly F, then one was F by virtue of bearing the is-F-at relation to a past time. On this view, nearly every predicate applicable to temporal beings is analogous.

Another view, *adverbialism*, claims that, it is not the property that should be "relativized" but rather the having of it. On this view, *x is-in-a-t1ly-way* red, *is-in-a-t2ly-way* blue, and *is-in-a-t3ly-way* green.[57] In some ways, adverbialism fits

---

[53] For a defense of unrestricted composition, see Lewis (1991).

[54] See van Inwagen (1981) for extensive discussion and criticism of what he calls the *Doctrine of Arbitrary Undetached Parts*. McDaniel (2007) is also relevant.

[55] Holden (2007) provides a masterful account of the history of the metaphysics of actual and potential parts. The particular way of understanding the distinction suggested here is not one of the ones discussed, however. Stein (2009: 53–4) could be interpreted as holding the sort of view I suggest here.

[56] See Lewis (1986: 202–4).

[57] See Haslanger (2003) for a discussion of this view. Haslanger distinguishes two theories, which she calls *copula-tensing* and *adverbialism*. Both views take adverbial modification of the copula metaphysically seriously, but only the former view is explicitly committed to there being an instantiation relation that

nicely with PEP. PEP recognizes a plurality of ways to be, and adverbialism recognizes a plurality of ways to have a property. There might even be a deeper reason for thinking these views fit nicely together. As I mentioned in section 3.4, it is tempting to think that present existence is a kind of absolute existence, whereas things that exist in the past enjoy only a kind of relative existence, specifically existence relative to a time. This is why past existence is a degenerate way to exist: things whose sole mode of being is past existence do not exist in themselves but only relative to a moment. The only kind of existence Julius Caesar enjoys is existence at some times or others, whereas present things just plain exist. It would be natural to supplement this view with the idea that, just as there are two ways to exist, there are ultimately two sorts of ways to have a property: to have-at-some-time the property, or to just plain have the property. Only presently existing things can just plain have properties, whereas pastly existing things merely have-at-times properties.[58] Intuitively, having-relative-to-something-or-other a property is a less respectable way to have a property than just plain having it. On this view, we needn't say that most predicates applicable to temporal beings are analogous. We do need to say that the "is" of predication is analogous, but perhaps we should say this anyways on independent grounds.

On this view, some past objects might be intrinsic duplicates of some presently existing objects, even if they differ in how they have their properties. (It is possible that there is a past object that exists at a time t and a present object such that for every intrinsic property F, that past object has-at-t F if and only if the present object just plain has F.) Past objects are not shorn of properties, although they do have-at-times these properties. And truths about the past are still appropriately grounded: for example, propositions of the form "$\mathbf{W}(Fx)$" are entailed by propositions of the form "$\exists_p t$ (t is a time and x-has-at-t F").

Let's turn to a discussion of what I will call the *Hybrid view*, which is inspired by Solomyak (2013). I'll first briefly summarize the relevant aspects of this paper before articulating the Hybrid view. Solomyak (2013) defends a version of ontological pluralism in which actual entities enjoy a mode of being not enjoyed by merely possible entities. According to Solomyak, there are two perspectives one can take on reality, an actualist perspective according to which the actual world is the only world that there is and in which properties are not had relative to worlds, and an amodal perspective according to which the actual world is merely one world among many, and in which "properties" are really relations to worlds. On Solomyak's view, there is no ultimate fact as to which perspective one should adopt: each mode of being is equally fundamental and neither is dispensable.

---

relates objects, properties, and times. With the exception of that commitment, the views seem to me to be indistinguishable, and so I will conflate them in what follows.

[58] This needn't mean that every property had by a presently existing object is just-plain-had, but some such property must be.

Regardless of whether Solomyak's view about modality is correct, the analogous view about time is very compelling. There is a presentist perspective we take, in which the present time and its contents are all that there is, and properties like shapes are really properties rather than relations to times. But there also seems to be an "atemporal" perspective in which the present is merely one moment among many, and in which its contents have "properties" like shapes only relative to times.

Corresponding to these perspectives are two distinct modes of being. The natural analogue for Solomyak's view is minimal Meinongian presentism, but what I say below could with minor modification be adjoined with PEP as well. Either way, corresponding to these two modes of being are two ways of saturating a fact. Let's illustrate this via an example. Consider the ordinary adjective "red." Setting aside concerns about vagueness, there is exactly one feature that is the semantic value of "red." But, on the Hybrid view, there is no fundamental fact about its logical form. With respect to one mode of being, the mode that includes past objects, the value of "red" is *is red at t*. A fully saturated ascription of redness is of the form: x is red at t. According to the past mode of being, redness is a relation to times. However, according to the present mode of being, the value of "red" is *is red*. Redness, on this mode, simply is a one-place property. A fully saturated ascription of redness is of the form: x is red. More generally, there are entities within the range of one fundamental quantifier—times—that are not within the range of another fundamental quantifier. There are also facts within the range of one quantifier that are not within the range of the other. Facts are supposed to be fully saturated entities.[59] Roughly, a fact F is fully saturated just in case there is no x such that it is possible to add x to F. This is where quantification enters in to the notion of saturation. And ontological pluralism recognizes different fundamental quantifiers, allowing us to define up two different corresponding notions of saturation, neither of which is objectively the *correct* notion of saturation to use. But we can still distinguish a respect in which one kind of fact-participation is attenuated: things that exist only with respect to the past mode of being are not just flat-out red. Things that enjoy present existence can be.[60]

Why is this a Hybrid view? Well, it is similar to the relationalist view in that, with respect to one mode of being, alleged properties are relations—but remember that with respect to the other mode of being they really are properties. There's no absolute fact about which of these they are. In a way, we have something like modes of instantiation, but they are dispensed with at the ground-floor metaphysical level and

---

[59] For more on saturation, see Sider (2011: 247–65).

[60] In section 1.5.3, I noted that for many applications of ontological pluralism, not much turns on whether being and its modes are first-order or second-order properties. But it seems that, if we want to make sense of views like the Hybrid view, being and its modes should correspond to quantifiers rather than ordinary predicates.

are simulated via what is at the ground-floor level, namely, the fundamental difference in mode of being.

Ontological pluralism provides a framework for new theories concerning the nature of time and the nature of persistence.

3.8 How Do We Know We Are Present?

According to PEP, past existents are not non-entities, but rather enjoy a fundamentally different mode of being than presently existing things. This might seem to generate a skeptical puzzle: how can I know that I am present rather than past? Abe Lincoln believes that he is present; I believe that I am present. Doesn't Abe Lincoln have the same evidence that he is present as I have that I am present? Wouldn't it seem to me exactly the same if I were past rather than present? In which case, on what grounds may I conclude that I am present rather than past?

PEP is not the only view that appears to generate these worries.[61] Any view that admits a kind of ontological distinction between persons seems as apt to generate them; examples of such views include a version of modal realism in which possible people are different in kind from actual people and a type of Meinongianism in which there are non-existent people. This is not to say that each of these views will be equally successful in responding to these worries, or that a solution suitable given one of these views is also suitable given one of the others.

The worries seem most vivid for versions of PEP that hold that past objects and actual objects can enjoy the same kinds of properties in the same kind of way. Consider the following line of thought. I know that I am seeing something red right now. But Abe Lincoln doesn't, because he doesn't flat-out know anything. Instead, he bears determinates of the knows-P-at relation to some times. Since I flat-out know many things, and Abe Lincoln flat-out knows nothing, my evidence base is radically different from Lincoln's. I actually have evidence (flat-out!) for various claims, and only presently existing things do. Moreover, Abe Lincoln doesn't even believe that he is present, whereas I do; instead, there are times at which Abe Lincoln bears the believes-he-is-present-at relation.[62] Perhaps these versions of PEP should be untroubled by our worries. Let's focus on versions of PEP for which the worry seems most vivid.

In what follows, I'll focus on five kinds of responses to the worry. I'll call these responses *acceptance*, *the phenomenological response*, *the easy knowledge response*, *the appeal to theoretical virtue*, and *the indexical response*. I'll discuss them in turn.

---

[61]   See Merricks (2006) for a development of these worries.

[62]   Forrest (2004) argues that past people lack consciousness; it is a consequence of the view sketched here that something like this view is correct, but merely as a consequence of a more general view about the kinds of features that past things can enjoy.

According to *acceptance*, in general, we don't know that we are present. But this is a claim we can accept, because it is not a pre-theoretic datum that we are present. It is a pre-theoretic datum that things are happening now, that events are presently occurring, and so forth. But don't confuse what this datum attributes with the metaphysician's notion of presentness. The ordinary notion of being present or nowness is an indexical notion just like the ordinary notion of being here. The metaphysician's notion goes beyond the ordinary one: it is the notion of a special metaphysical status that all and only those things that are now in the ordinary sense possess. The ordinary person on the street does not have beliefs about whether she is present in the metaphysical sense of "present," and hence it is unsurprising that the ordinary person does not know whether she is present. What about philosophers? The hypothesis that we are present is not unreasonable, and there is no evidence against this hypothesis that is not also evidence against A-theories in general. So if we are to accept an A-theory, we might as well believe that we are present, even if we do not know that we are.

I do not accept acceptance. Acceptance is inconsistent with one of the main motivations for the A-theory, namely, the widespread belief that the present moment in the ordinary sense is metaphysically special. Without this grounding in ordinary thought, it is hard to see what else should drive one to be an A-theorist. Perhaps it is simply a metaphysical insight had by a select few? Possible, but improbable.

There is an important question though, namely, why this metaphysical belief is so widespread among ordinary people. If this widespread belief is ultimately based on illusion, then a scientific exploration of the psychological mechanisms that give rise to it is an important, albeit depressing, task. If the widespread belief is true, then an exploration of how it is that one comes to have it is also important: it is hard to see how such a belief could be widespread unless we are sensitive in some way to presentness. This is exactly what the proponent of the phenomenological response suggests.

Recall that the phenomenological motivation for ontological pluralism is that some modes of being can be presented to us, and that this is revealed by a careful examination and description of our experiences in the broadest sense of "experience." Perhaps a careful examination of our experience reveals that presentness is in some way revealed to us, where presentness is not construed simply as a property that some things have and other things lack, but rather as a mode of being. On this response, my merely past counterpart does *not* have the same evidence that he is present that I have.

We need to be careful how we state the phenomenological response. It is not that some objects look present and others don't in the ordinary sense of "look"; we don't have visual impressions of presentness, for example.[63] Rather, *all* objects presented to

---

[63] As suggested by Skow (2009) and criticized by Cameron (2015: 34–6).

us by way of ordinary sense perception are presented to us as being present (and as being actual).[64] But sense perception is not the only way in which objects are represented in conscious states. Memory or recollection is another faculty by which objects are represented, but memory does not represent objects as being present. Rather, all objects presented by memory are presented as being past.[65] They might not all be presented as being *merely* past, but many certainly are, as when I recollect past facts about my childhood. It is a leitmotif of the phenomenological tradition that different kinds of intentional states represent different kinds of objects along with their characteristic modes of being. Looking for a distinction between how modes of being are presented *within* a particular kind of intentional state, such as ordinary sense perception, was never a serious project.

On the phenomenological response, I believe that I am present and that other things are present simply by having present perceptions of my surroundings and myself: things seem to me to be present (rather than past) and unless I have reasons to distrust how things seem, I form beliefs more or less automatically that things are how they seem. The widespread belief that things are present is explained simply by noting that I am in no way unique in this respect. These perceptions also provide the basis for my knowledge that I and other things are present. That sense perception presents things as being present while memory presents things as being past explains not merely why we recognize an ontological distinction between present and past but also why we have such facility with that distinction.

I find the phenomenological response tempting. But let's see what our other options are rather than keep all our eggs in one basket. As we'll see, the phenomenological response is consistent with the remaining responses. In fact, in different ways the remaining responses are arguably strengthened when coupled with the phenomenological response.

According to the easy knowledge response, there are certain propositions—call them "easy propositions" that are incredibly easy to know. Roughly, if *P* is an easy proposition for a subject *S*, all that is required for *S* to know *P* is for *P* to be true, for *S* to believe *P*, and for *S* to have no evidence for a proposition that *S* knows is inconsistent with *P*. Easy propositions are in a sense a priori propositions in that they do not demand positive sensory evidence for their truth, but this is because they do not demand any positive evidence for their truth, but merely no known evidence against their truth. On the easy knowledge response, it does not matter whether my past counterpart has the same evidence for his being present as I have for my being present, since the possession or lack of positive evidence for presentness is irrelevant.

---

[64] Compare with Paul (2010b) and Cameron (2015: 35–6), both of whom grant that perception presents things as of being present, that is, as present. (I allow that a perception can present x as *F* when *x* is not *F*; I do not use "present as" as a success verb.) Paul (2010b) attempts to provide an explanation of why perception presents objects as of present that is of use to the reductionist who denies that being present is a special metaphysical status.

[65] See, for example, Husserl (1991: 61), among many other places. For a nice piece on Husserl on memory, see Brough (1975).

The easy knowledge response is suggested by the following remarks from Bricker (2001: 30), which appear in the context of his response to skepticism about whether one is actual:

> The most serious objection to realism with absolute actualization, as Lewis has emphasized, is that it seems to allow for a coherent skepticism about one's own actuality, whereas such skepticism is absurd. Granted, such skepticism is absurd. When asked—how do I know that I am actual?—I can give only one response: I just know it. I think that response is acceptable when dealing with a fundamental ontological category; talk of "evidence" here is beside the point. Moreover, anyone who accepts more than one fundamental ontological category, be it individuals and classes, or particulars and universals, must face the same sort of question, and, I claim, give the same answer. How do I know that I am an individual and not a class? I just know it. How do I know that I am a particular and not a universal? I just do.

On the response under consideration, there are easy propositions, and for each subject S, the proposition that S is present is one of them. I am present; I believe that I am present; I have no positive evidence for a proposition that I know is inconsistent with my being present; hence I know that I am present.

There might be an interesting connection between the easy knowledge response and the phenomenological response. Suppose that among the easy propositions for S are those propositions of the form S sees x as F. I believe that I see myself and my surroundings as present; to the extent that I lack counter-evidence for this fact, I know that I and my surroundings are present. But the easy knowledge response could be adopted independently of any putative connection to the phenomenological response.

There are two concerns one might have about the easy knowledge response. First, how can anything be known without evidence? Perhaps the friend of easy knowledge can argue that there are certain things that we know but couldn't know unless they were based on easy propositions. But, second, why would claims of fundamental metaphysics be themselves good candidates for being easy propositions? Without the phenomenological response in tow, the answer to this question is not easy to see.

Let's turn now to the appeal to theoretical virtues, which has been recently defended by Cameron (2015: ch. 1). According to this response, if P is part of our best overall theory of some phenomenon, and P is in fact true, then we can come to know P by knowing that it is part of our best overall theory of the phenomena in question. According to Cameron, the claim that we are present is part of the best overall theory of the nature of time, because it is a pre-theoretic belief that is widely held and for which we have no direct countervailing evidence, and one factor that makes for a good theory is consonance with pre-theoretic beliefs of which we have no direct reason to think that they are false. A consequence of Cameron's position, which he happily accepts, is that most people do not know that they are present, because most people have not thought about which package of views in the philosophy of time provides the best overall explanation of temporal phenomena. So perhaps most ordinary people, whether past or present, lack particularly good evidence that they are present. I find this upshot more troubling than Cameron does.

But it also not clear whether those who have done the epistemic work arrive at knowledge at the end of the day. Spot that theory T is true. Definitely, I am in a better epistemic state when I come to learn that T is better than its competitors. But it is hard for to me see why this state must be knowledge, especially if the reason why T ends up on top is that it does better merely with consonance with ordinary belief. Consonance with ordinary belief is not an intrinsic theoretical virtue, but rather is virtuous only for the following reasons. First, it is difficult to challenge all of our beliefs at one time for if we give up too much, we give up the criteria which we use to judge other beliefs. So some degree of theoretical conservatism is reasonable.[66] Second, widespread ordinary belief often tracks widespread ordinary perceptions or seemings more generally. And perceptions, seemings, and intuitions are evidence, and consonance with our evidence is intrinsically important when assessing a theory. We could tie the phenomenological response to the appeal to theoretical virtue by claiming that, in this case, widespread ordinary belief that we are present is based on widespread perception that we are present. But then why embrace the more complicated appeal to theoretical virtues as opposed to the much simpler phenomenological response?

Let me close with a discussion of the indexical response, a version of which has been defended by Bricker (2006), who focuses on the status of actuality rather than presence. According to this response, we need to distinguish our concept of being present from the ontological status of being present, and moreover hold that the concept of being present is an indexical concept while the status of being present is a non-indexical absolute status. This doesn't mean that the concept of being present as used by the metaphysician just is the purely indexical concept of being now that is the temporal analogue of being here. Rather, what makes the concept of presentness indexical is that part of what it includes is the information that (i) I am present and (ii) everything "ontologically like" me is also present.

What is it for x to be ontologically like y? A remark by Bricker (2006: 61) suggests x is ontologically like y if and only if x belongs to the same fundamental ontological kind as y. But Bricker (2006: n. 51) wants to allow that objects can fall under more than one fundamental kind. This suggests that what Bricker should mean by this expression is that x is ontologically like y just in case x and y fall under exactly the same fundamental ontological kinds. (Suppose x and y's falling under just one kind sufficed for ontological likeness, and that kinds can crisscross. A past individual and a present individual are both individuals though neither are sets; so there is one fundamental kind that they both fall under; so they are ontologically like each other; so they are both present. That's no good.)

---

[66] Compare with Lewis (1986: 133–5).

The notion of a fundamental ontological kind is not indexical; nor are the fundamental kinds themselves. Bricker draws a helpful analogy with the concept and property of water: the concept of water just is the concept of the watery stuff in my environment with which I am acquainted, and hence is a partially indexical concept, whereas the property of being water just is the property of being constituted by H_2O, which is not an indexical property.

Bricker distinguishes between merely indexical concepts and those concepts that provide us with substantial *de se* knowledge; he calls the latter concepts *perspectival*. If being present is an indexical concept, it seems that it is also a perspectival concept. As discussed in section 3.2, the two modes of being recognized by PEP can be distinguished from one another via both the tense logic that governs them and the temporal relations connecting the entities that enjoy them; call these the "tense-temporal facts" about the respective modes. For example, there are two modes of being, and one of them is such that some entities that enjoy it are non-simultaneous, while the other is such that all the entities that enjoy it are simultaneous with each other. By my lights, these differences are grounded in the modes of being themselves, but it is consistent with this claim that our concept of presentness analytically contains these differences. By Bricker's lights, this allows us to understand the concept of presentness as containing the following components: an indexical component, that I am present, an ontological component that says that anything enjoying all my modes of being is present, and finally a temporal component stating the tense-temporal facts about presentness.

The indexical response nicely explains how it can be obvious that we are present: it's conceptually true. This might suggest that any appeal to the phenomenological response is unneeded, and moreover cannot make the indexical response more appealing. However, this might be too quick. It is an interesting question why we have this particular concept of presentness in addition to the far more straightforward ordinary concept of nowness. The obvious response to this question is that we need a concept of presentness because we are sensitive to an ontological divide between things and to which side of this divide we are placed. We have indexical concepts like the concept of water because we are acquainted with a qualitative divide among things in our environment; we do not willy-nilly develop indexical concepts without having some grasp of the entities to which they are intended to apply.

If Bricker is right about ontological concepts, which are among the central concepts of metaphysics, then metaphysics as a discipline cannot be characterized in terms of the *transparency* of its concepts in the sense of Fine (2012b). According to Fine (2012b), one of the distinctive things about metaphysical inquiry is that it makes use of concepts that are *transparent*. Fine (2012b: 9) says, "Roughly speaking, a concept is transparent if there is no significant gap between the concept and what it is a concept of. Thus there *is* a significant gap between the concept *water* and the substance H_2O of which it is a concept but *no* significant gap between the concept *identity* and the identity relation of which it is a concept." Fine (2012b) later clarifies this notion of transparency, and in fact distinguishes several varieties of transparency. One of them is *modal transparency*, which Fine (2012b: 23) defines as follows: a concept of x is modally transparent just in case it is necessarily a concept of x. Fine claims that the concept of water is not modally transparent. We'll focus on modal transparency here, and thus our first question will be the question of whether our concept of existence is modally transparent.

In order for there to be an interesting question about whether a given concept is modally transparent, concepts can't be individuated simply by their worldly correlates. Otherwise, every non-empty concept will be modally transparent. For example, provided that concepts are individuated this way and that the concept of water's worldly correlate is *being composed of H_2O molecules*, there is no world in which the concept of water exists and yet is not a concept of being composed of H_2O molecules.

But the concept of water is supposed to be the paradigmatic non-transparent concept, since a world in which from an internal perspective all is the same and yet our environment differs—it contains "twin water" rather than water—is a world in which our concept of water is about a different object than what it is actually about. It seems then that a necessary condition for a concept to be modally transparent is that contingent facts about the environment of the concept's possessor cannot partially determine the worldly correlate of that concept.

If the indexical view is right about the concepts of presentness, actuality, and existence, then these concepts are not modally transparent. My merely possible twin has the same concept of actuality that I have—it is an indexical concept much like the concept of water—but I successfully grasp an ontological feature via this concept whereas my twin either does not grasp a feature at all, in which case his perspective is defective, or he grasps a different ontological feature than I do. Either way, there is distance between our concepts and what they are concepts of. Accordingly, we cannot characterize what distinguishes metaphysical inquiry from other forms of inquiry by appealing to the modal transparency of its concepts. I don't know how detrimental this observation would be to Fine's (2012b) project. It is not clear to me whether he takes the modal transparency of a concept to be *necessary* (rather than sufficient) for its status as an a priori concept, and the latter seems to be at least as important to metaphysical inquiry.

3.9 Chapter Summary

In this chapter, I developed a version of ontological pluralism that respects two common intuitions about time: that the present moment is metaphysically distinguished but not in such a way that the past is unreal. The version of ontological pluralism developed—PEP—is one in which there are two modes of being, the mode of being that present objects enjoy and the mode of being that past objects enjoy. I argued that this view fares at least as well, and probably better, than other views in which the present is metaphysically distinguished.

4

Categories of Being

4.1 Introduction

A central task of *ontology* is to discover the correct list of *ontological categories.* A central task of *meta-ontology* is to determine *what it is to be an ontological category* and *what it is to fall under an ontological category.*[1] Here I explore a traditional meta-ontology in which ontological categories are *ways of being* and objects belong to the same ontological category just in case they *exist in the same way.*

Why engage in the project of defining "ontological category"? First, as Jan Westerhoff (2005: 22–4) notes, if we don't know what ontological categories are, we don't know what ontologists are supposed to be looking for. As Gilbert Ryle (1971: 170) elegantly stated, "We are in the dark about the nature of philosophical problems and methods if we are in the dark about types or categories."

Moreover, the notion of an ontological category is theoretically useful only to the extent that it can be employed in principles that make use of it. But such principles will be unclear as long as the notion of an ontological category is unclear. I'd like to use a clear notion of an ontological category to help me think through issues in the metaphysics of modality (construed broadly) and essence (construed narrowly). More on this shortly.

"Ontological category" is a philosopher's term of art, not a bit of ordinary language. There are two kinds of projects one might mean by the phrase "providing an account of ontological categories." The first kind of project is the historical or hermeneutical project of determining what some philosopher or philosophers meant by "ontological category"—or simply "category"—and then determining the roles that their particular conceptions of what it is to be an ontological category played in their theorizing. The second is the metaphysical project of determining what philosophers *ought* to mean by "ontological category" by arguing that a particular (and perhaps somewhat stipulative) account tracks something that ontologists ought to care about.

My focus will be on the second project, although as it will turn out, I think sensitivity to the first project is important for success in the second. And, in general,

---

[1] Lowe (2006: 34) says that any system of ontology must determine what ontological categories are, and says (2006: 69) that *formal ontology* is the branch of metaphysics whose job it is to do this. (I use "formal ontology" in a different way in section 4.6.) I follow van Inwagen (2001b) and Westerhoff (2005) in distinguishing between meta-ontological questions and first-order ontological questions, which Westerhoff (2005: 20–1) calls "object-level ontological questions."

pursuing the second project is not straightforward. There are several methodological considerations worth stating explicitly at the outset. A discussion of them occupies section 4.2. Here's what will transpire in the rest of this chapter. In section 4.3, I will discuss several competing accounts of ontological categories. In section 4.4, I will motivate the view that ontological categories are modes of being. Section 4.5 will contain a discussion of the nature of so-called "category mistakes," which will be briefly mentioned in 4.2 as well. Section 4.6 is devoted to an exploration of the status of the putative discipline of *formal ontology* construed as the study of those fundamental and necessary features that objects have in virtue of being objects. There I argue that formal ontology so construed requires that *object* be an ontological category. (But, as will emerge in section 4.6 and in many other places to come in this book, it isn't.) Alternative conceptions of formal ontology will be described as well. Finally, in section 4.7, I briefly discuss whether the theory of ontological categories put forth here implies that the actual ontological categories are ontological categories at every possible world.

4.2 Methodological Considerations

There are three methodological considerations I will discuss here, which for brevity's sake I will subsume under the headings of *neutrality*, *descriptiveness*, and *functionality*. I will address each in turn, although these considerations are not independent of each other.

> *Neutrality*:   To what extent should the project of determining what it is to be an ontological category be independent of the project of defending a list of ontological categories? In other words, how independent is this branch of meta-ontology from ontology proper? If a theory of the nature of ontological categories implies that something is (or is not) an ontological category, is that a cost of the theory?

My view is that neutrality is overrated, but not everyone agrees, and so for part of the chapter I'll try to be neutral with respect to neutrality. As I see things, the goal is not merely to give a definition of a technical term that is used by two or more disputants about a given list of putative ontological categories. If this were the sole goal—to clarify the terms of a given debate—it might make sense to be neutral on which debater has the correct list. For otherwise we risk misconstruing a substantive ontological debate as a non-substantive one in which one of the participants is wrong as a matter of definition. But if this isn't the goal, what is? The other two methodological considerations are relevant to answering this question.

> *Descriptiveness*:   To what extent is the project of determining what it is to be an ontological category an attempt to describe in clearer terms a pre-theoretically recognized phenomenon?

On one line of thought, we do grasp, at least dimly, categorial distinctions between certain entities. As noted in earlier chapters, some philosophers of the phenomeno-logical tradition, such as Brentano, Husserl, Meinong, and Heidegger, are sympa-thetic to this thought, which is why, on their view, phenomenological and ontological investigations are importantly connected. I'm somewhat sympathetic to this as well, which leads me to think that, to some extent, the project is also descriptive: we should account for categorial differences antecedently recognized in our theory of onto-logical categories. One way in which these pre-theoretically recognized categorial differences manifest themselves is in our unhappiness with linguistic utterances called, appropriately, category mistakes. Consider, for example, "the number two is hungry." This is a very bad sentence, and its badness does not consist simply in its metaphysical impossibility. We'll discuss the nature of category mistakes more fully in section 4.5.

If we antecedently grasp categorial differences, then there is a question of whether this inchoate phenomenon of categorial difference can be aptly described. But how could we grasp categorial differences without having also some sort of understanding about what some of the categories are? Taking seriously the descriptive aspect of the meta-ontological project seems to require downplaying neutrality over which list of ontological categories is correct.

Functionality: To what extent is the project of determining what it is to be an ontological category an attempt to explicate a theoretical role or an explanatory job that ontological categories play?

As noted earlier, the notion of an ontological category is useful only if theoretic-ally fruitful. Accordingly, we might proceed not by asking what ontological categories are but rather what we need them to be. And we assess this by asking what theoretical role we might want ontological categories to perform. On this way of thinking, if the notion of an ontological category does no theoretical work—if it is, so to speak, purely descriptive rather than partly functional—then the meta-ontological project has no philosophical payoff. Why talk about ontological categories then? I suspect that this was the perspective of David Lewis who, despite his status as one of the greatest metaphysicians of all time, seemed to have so little use for the notion of an ontological category that such a phrase rarely if ever appeared in his writings. (I think it is appropriate to say that Lewis (1986, 1991) had, or inclined towards, a two-category ontology consisting of ur-elements and classes even though he did not put weight on the label "ontological category.")

A notion is theoretically fruitful only insofar as it appears in explanatory prin-ciples. One area in which such principles could appear is in the metaphysics of modality. Let me illustrate. Some metaphysicians concerned with questions of metaphysical possibility have embraced a principle of recombination, which is, roughly speaking, that there are no necessary connections between distinct existences.[2] Sometimes this principle is glossed as the view that any pattern of fundamental properties and relations is possible.[3] However, put this boldly, the principle is far too strong. Suppose that *x is located at R* is a fundamental relation.[4] *Being a number* and *being a region of space–time* might well be fundamental properties. But necessarily no number is located at a region of space–time, and no region of space–time is located at a number!

It seems that any plausible principle of recombination must be a restricted principle. The examples just mentioned suggest that when stating a restricted principle, the notion of an ontological category will be indispensable. In general, it is appropriate to ask for explanations of why recombination fails in a given case. In the cases just mentioned, the restriction on recombination shouldn't be brute but should rather flow from the nature of the categories. I will argue that, given the theory of ontological categories defended, even a powerful principle of recombination (such as the one alluded to earlier) needn't have the consequences it might be taken to have. If I am right, the account of ontological categories defended here is capable of doing substantive metaphysical work.

The account defended here, which identifies ontological categories with ways of being, is how plenty of historically important ontologists conceived of the nature of categories of being, although the account does not match how most contemporary analytic metaphysicians inchoately conceive them. However, in this case, analytic metaphysicians *ought* to bend to the weight of tradition: insofar as it is important to one's metaphysics to employ the notion of an ontological category, one ought to conceive of them as ways in which things exist.

In what follows, I offer an account of ontological categories that is largely neutral on the correct list of ontological categories, that respects and accounts for our pre-theoretic grasp of categorial differences, and that provides a theoretical role for ontological categories to play.

4.3 Ontological Categories: Competing Accounts

There are many questions that any account of "ontological category" should be able to sensibly interpret. Does every object belong to some ontological category? Can an object belong to more than one ontological category? Can one ontological category wholly subsume another? Can two ontological categories overlap without one subsuming the other? Is there a highest ontological category to which every object

---

[2] One of the most prominent champions of (mostly) free recombination is David Lewis (1986: 87–92). See also Nolan (1996).

[3] See, for example, McDaniel (2007) and Saucedo (2011). Note, however, that Saucedo does not put much weight on this particular formulation of the principle, but rather defends a much more precise version.

[4] That some locative relation is fundamental is defended by Hudson (2005), McDaniel (2007), and Parsons (2007).

belongs? Do objects necessarily belong to their ontological categories? Are there fundamental differences between *ontological* categories and other kinds of categories, or just differences of degree? Is there more than one "right way" of dividing the world into ontological categories?

The account of ontological categories defended here can make sense of these questions, although it provides little guidance as to how they should be answered. This is not necessarily a defect of the account. It is one of the jobs of meta-ontology to tell us what we should mean by "ontological category." It is the job of first-order ontology to tell us what ontological categories there are, and how these categories relate to one another. To the extent that we are moved by considerations of neutrality, we should be happy that our account of ontological categories does not make too many decisions about ontology for us.

In this section, I will focus on some recent work by Jan Westerhoff on ontological categories, although other views will be discussed along the way. Westerhoff's fundamental approach is diametrically opposed to mine. I seek to use the notion of an ontological category to *explain* apparent failures of recombination, whereas, as we will see, Westerhoff takes failures of recombination as the starting point in his analysis of ontological categories.

Westerhoff's (2005: 6–7, 100) preferred account takes as primitive the notion of a *state of affairs*. States of affairs have constituents that appear also as members of sets. Call a set a *form set* just in case it is a set of constituents (of states of affairs) that have the same form; two constituents have the same *form* just in case they are *intersubstitutable* in all states of affairs.

The notion of intersubstitutability in a state of affairs is also primitive for Westerhoff, but perhaps the following examples illuminate it sufficiently. Consider the state of affairs of my ball's being red. My ball could have been blue, which implies that it is possible that there is a state of affairs in which my ball is blue. Being blue is substitutable with being red in the state of affairs of my ball's being red. This is true of any state of affairs in which something is red, moreover, the converse holds as well. Being blue and being red are intersubstitutable in the same states of affairs. Just as an expression is substitutable for another expression in a given sentence only if that substitution results in a meaningful sentence, a constituent is substitutable for another constituent only if that substitution would result in a possibly obtaining state of affairs.

Among the form sets are the *base sets*. Westerhoff identifies the ontological categories with the base sets. The base sets are the minimal form sets that, via some manner of *construction*, generate *all* the other form sets. According to Westerhoff (2005: 97) to say that a set B generates a set X is just to say "that there is a certain set of operations which can be applied to the members of B to obtain any member of X." Westerhoff (2005: 118–21, 125) suggests that these operations include *mereological composition* and *set-formation* and possibly other "constructive" operations. As an example, Westerhoff (2005: 102) says that the set-nominalist constructs properties out of individuals. On this view, the set of properties does not correspond to an ontological category since properties can be generated from individuals via the constructive operation of set-formation.

One cannot use Westerhoff's account of ontological categories to *explain* failures of recombination since the account presupposes these failures. Westerhoff's notion of intersubstitutability is simply that which preserves the possible obtainment of a state of affairs. And whether it is possible to substitute a constituent of a state of affairs with another entity and still have a possible state of affairs is simply a brute fact for Westerhoff. The brute limitations on how entities can be recombined are what determine which entities go together in which form sets, which in turn determines which sets correspond to the ontological categories.

In a sense, Westerhoff's view identifies ontological categories with the behavior they engender. I think this is a mistake analogous to the mistake made by the psychological behaviorist who identifies mental states with manifestations of behavior. Just as a mental state is not to be identified with its typical manifestation, but rather should be thought of as the proximate cause of its manifestation, so too we should not analyze the notion of an ontological category directly in terms of failures of recombination or intersubstitutability of states of affairs, but should rather think of ontological categories as those which are metaphysically responsible for such failures.

What then can Westerhoff's account explain? Perhaps not much, but this might not bother him. By his lights, the notion of an ontological category does little, if any, real work for metaphysics. We employ the notion of an ontological category as a tool for systematizing fundamental features of the world, but that is its sole function.[5] By Westerhoff's lights, the project of providing an account of ontological categories is largely descriptive.

Westerhoff discusses several interesting consequences of his account; I will mention those that I take to be costs, although Westerhoff does not evaluate them this way. One consequence of Westerhoff's (2005: 123–5) view is *local relativism*: at some worlds, there might be more than one set of form sets suitable to serve as base sets, and hence there is no absolute fact of the matter concerning which form sets are the ontological categories at those worlds. A second consequence is *global relativism*: something might be an ontological category in one world but not in another, since whether something is an ontological category in world w depends on what things are in world w.[6] No ontological category is essentially an ontological category.

Westerhoff takes global relativism to imply that things might belong to their ontological categories only accidentally. Since there are plausible ontological schemes in which things do not belong to their categories necessarily, perhaps this consequence shouldn't trouble us. (We will acquaint ourselves with one such scheme soon.) But regardless of whether global relativism or local relativism have unintuitive

[5] See Westerhoff (2005: 3).   [6] See Westerhoff (2005: 132–6).

consequences, they are unintuitive in themselves. I would prefer to develop a theory that does not imply them. (Understandably, Westerhoff's preferences are different.)

Let us turn to worries that Westerhoff does not address. First worry: it is hard to see how *set* or *class* could be ontological categories on Westerhoff's account. Consider, for example, the two-category ontology articulated by David Lewis (1991) that consists of individuals and classes of individuals.[7] Trivially, every set of individuals is constructed out of individuals via set-formation, and, on Lewis's view, every other set is constructed out of sets that ultimately are constructed from sets of individuals.[8] Therefore, no set of sets is a base set, since the form set of individuals suffices to construct any set of sets via the operation of set-formation. Since no set of sets is a base set, sets do not form an ontological category. Similar remarks apply to classes. So Lewis's (1991) ontology, which recognizes two ontological categories, *individual* and *class*, is a one-category ontology on Westerhoff's account. This is odd. It is not clear to me how to revise Westerhoff's account so that this oddity does not arise.[9]

More generally, it appears to be a consequence of Westerhoff's account that entities with structure never form an ontological category. Is the formation of states of affairs from properties and universals a constructive operation? If so, then states of affairs do not form an ontological category, contrary to the views of many metaphysicians.[10] Smith (2004: 252–5) discusses a "modified Aristotelian" system according to which one of the top-level ontological categories is *combinations*, which has as subcategories *set*, *whole*, and *state of affairs*. Grossman (1973: 149) defends the view that "the notion of structure...has to be ranked as one of the ontological categories." Westerhoff's account implies that such ontological schemes are incoherent.

The second worry is a converse of the first: it is not clear how Westerhoff can accommodate an ontology containing *stuff*.[11] Westerhoff's meta-ontological machinery might be suitable for ontologies with various categories of individuals—things that can be counted or be members of sets, for example—but how to include stuff in addition to (or rather than) things is less clear. (By contrast, we discussed a version of ontological pluralism with things and stuff in section 2.5.2.)

A third worry is that Westerhoff's account seems to imply *Sommer's Law*.[12] Sommer's Law is that no ontological categories *merely overlap*: category C1 merely overlaps category C2 just in case there is some *x* that is a member of both C1 and C2,

---

[7] Although, as noted earlier, Lewis does not use the term "ontological category," this description is not inapt. Compare with Nolan (2011: 278).

[8] According to Lewis (1991), every singleton is "derived" from an individual via a singleton formation operation and classes are simply mereological sums of singletons.

[9] Perhaps on a more standard version of set theory, Westerhoff could say that the null set is the sole form set for the category of sets. Thanks to Mike Rea for discussion here.

[10] Westerhoff does not presuppose that states of affairs are "made of" their constituents, but it would be problematic were this to be inconsistent with his account of ontological categories.

[11] Thanks to Mike Rea for this worry.

[12] Sommer's Law is named after Fred Sommers, and is defended in Sommers (1963) and (1965).

but neither C1 nor C2 wholly contains the other. Here is a brief argument from Westerhoff's account to Sommer's Law.[13] Ontological categories are base sets. Base sets are form sets. Some things belong to the same form set if and only if they are intersubstitutable in all states of affairs. Assume that there are two base sets B1 and B2 that merely overlap; let B- be the intersection of B1 and B2. Everything in B- is intersubstitutable with everything in B1, and everything in B- is intersubstitutable with everything in B2. So everything in B1 is intersubstitutable with everything in B2. But then neither B1 nor B2 is a form set (rather the union of B1 and B2 is a form set) and so neither B1 nor B2 is a base set. So our assumption was false; base sets cannot merely overlap.

Why is this a worry? Westerhoff thinks that, far from being an objection, satisfying Sommer's Law is actually a good feature of an account. He is not alone: Amie Thomasson (2004, section 1.5) also claims that a minimal condition of adequacy is that the categories be mutually exclusive, which implies Sommer's Law.[14]

Westerhoff (2005: 57–9) discusses three putative reasons for endorsing Sommer's Law. First, he notes that Sommer's Law imposes a tree structure on the set of ontological categories, and this tree structure is recognized by most systems of ontological categories. Second, Westerhoff (2005: 58) discusses the work of Frank Keil (1979), which on Westerhoff's view supports the claim that "categorizations with non-overlapping categories (which are hierarchies and not lattices) are particularly psychologically natural." Third, Westerhoff claims that Sommer's Law allows us to prove that every system of ontological categories has a topmost category. (The details of the proof are not provided by Westerhoff; I cannot speak of whether it is successful.)

None of these arguments is particularly compelling. That many ontological systems have a tree structure does not show that all plausible systems must. (We will see shortly that some do not.) Second, the fact that we are attracted to systems of overlapping categories shows only that we will be psychologically hesitant to accept systems of non-overlapping categories. But does it provide a reason to think that such systems could not be ontological systems or that we are unlikely to have good reasons for endorsing them as such?[15] Third, the technical result that every system of ontological categories must have a maximal category, is not an advantage, but rather is possibly a problem, since some systems of ontological categories, such as the Aristotelian system discussed earlier, lack a unique maximal element. If neutrality

---

[13]   Compare with Westerhoff (2005: 138).

[14]   Nolan (2011: 78) by contrast refrains from insisting on exclusivity and exhaustivity. Paul (2013) also does not appear to demand the conceptual necessity of exclusivity or exhaustivity, though on her preferred ontological system, there is just one ontological category. Van Inwagen's (2014) account of ontological categories also is neutral on exclusivity; it is less clear to me whether he wishes to take a stand on exhaustivity.

[15]   Rosenkrantz (2012: 86) tells us that we should prefer systems of ontological categories in which none of them merely overlap, but he offers zero justification for this.

is a constraint on our account of ontological categories, neither Sommer's Law nor the existence of a topmost category can also be constraints. I suspect that neutrality is overrated, but I also suspect that there are some categorial schemes inconsistent with Sommer's Law and that it is more probable that one of these is true than that each of them is false.

There are plausible ontological systems that do not obey Sommer's Law. Consider the following system of ontological categories: *the actual, the merely possible, universals*, and *particulars*. These ontological categories can cut across each other: there are merely possible particulars as well as actual particulars, and there are merely possible universals as well as actual ones. Smith (2004: 253–4) discusses a Cartesian ontological scheme that recognizes two pairs of crisscrossing categories: *substance* and *attribute*, and *physical* and *mental*. It is not difficult to envision arguments that could motivate these systems. Perhaps even Aristotle toyed with an ontology inconsistent with Sommer's Law; recall that Aristotle discusses the possibility that some qualities might also be "relatives" in the *Categories*.[16] And Brower (2014: 208–11) argues that Aquinas recognizes at least ten modes of being but only three non-overlapping classes of (created) things that participate in them. That Sommer's Law rules out these ontologies by fiat is a reason to be cautious about Sommer's Law and any account of ontological categories that implies it. (A view of ontological categories that implies it is not terribly ontologically neutral.)

The bulk of Westerhoff's case for his account of ontological categories consists in showing that competing accounts fail. Westerhoff (2005: ch. 2) provides a nice survey of accounts of ontological categories. He dismisses "accounts" of ontological categories that in effect take the notion as a primitive, or merely produce examples of schemes of ontological categories.[17] Westerhoff discusses (and argues against) *generality accounts* (2005: 25–40), *intersubstitutability accounts* (2005: 40–55), and *identity accounts* (2005: 59–65).

In reverse order, identity accounts appeal to the notion of an identity condition, which is closely tied to the notion of a *de re* essential property. On identity accounts, things belong to *kinds* and part of what it is to belong to a kind is to have a certain kind of modal profile: in virtue of belonging to kind K, certain changes across time or worlds are not possible. Ceasing to be an instance of K is one of the changes that is impossible; the identity conditions of most kinds are typically richer. Say that a kind K1 *includes* a kind K2 just in case any change across times or worlds permitted by K2 is permitted by K1, but some possible change permitted by K1 is forbidden by K2.

---

[16] Aristotle's *Categories* 11a37 (1984a: 17). See Frede (1987: 13) for commentary on this passage.

[17] One philosopher who refrains from defining "ontological category" is Roderick Chisholm (1996: 1), who writes, "What a category is may be shown by depicting the table of categories that is defended here." Chisholm never attempts to define "ontological category." It would be disappointing to learn that what is meant by "ontological category" can only be shown and never said.

The notion of kind inclusion induces a partial ordering on kinds; ontological categories are those kinds that appear in the higher reaches of this ordering.[18]

Intersubstitutability accounts of ontological categories appeal to the notion of intersubstitutability of one expression for another. Roughly, x and y belong to the same ontological category just in case for all (or perhaps only for some) meaningful sentences in which an expression standing for x appears, an expression standing for y can be substituted without converting the original meaningful sentence into a meaningless one.[19]

Generality accounts identify ontological categories with "the most general kinds of entities," but do not appeal to the idea that ontological categories come with associated conditions of identity. This seems to be the account of Paul (2013: 90), who writes that "The fundamental ontological categories are the most basic kinds or natures of the world."[20]

In what follows, I will focus on two versions of the generality account, since by so doing I highlight certain difficulties facing many accounts of ontological categories. I won't discuss in much detail the intersubstitutability accounts or the identity accounts discussed by Westerhoff (2005), since the arguments he presents against them are persuasive.

What is generality? In an earlier article, Westerhoff (2002: 288) suggested the following definition along with an account of ontological categories that employ it:

Say that a class S is more general than the class T iff T is contained in S and, necessarily, if S is empty, then so is T. Ontological categories are classes such that none are more general than them.

Note that here Westerhoff (2002) talks of *classes* rather than *kinds*. Moreover, Westerhoff (2005: 18–19) suggests that many ontological systems take categories to be sets or classes. Probably this is not so. Many think that sets (and classes) have their members essentially. Suppose *material object* is a category. Then, on the assumption that categories are sets, the category *material object* exists only in worlds in which exactly the same material objects exist. This is troubling. Perhaps this is why Westerhoff (2005: 27) talks about the ontological dependence of one *property* on another, a notion which he defines as follows: F depends on G = df. Necessarily, if there are no Gs, then there are no Fs. A similar definition of "kind K1 ontologically

---

[18]   This sort of account is favored by Lowe (2006). Rosenkrantz (2012: 90) holds that things essentially belong to the categories they fall under. Gracia and Novotný (2012: 30–3) attribute a similar view to Suárez, although the notion of essential predication they appeal to might be better understood as what chapter 9 will call "strict essence" than *de re* modal predication.

[19]   Although I am not sympathetic to *meta*-ontological accounts that appeal to the notion of intersubstitutability, the positive *ontology* that I describe in section 4.5 appeals to something like the notion of intersubstitutability in order to justify a particular formulation of the principle of recombination.

[20]   Similar remarks are made by Norton (1977: 18–20) and Rosenkrantz (2012: 83). Van Inwagen (2014: 194–7) also identifies ontological categories with highly general kinds of things that "objectively go together," provided that these kinds are also sufficiently "modally robust."

depends on kind G" is possible. For now, I won't settle the question of to which ontological category ontological categories belong, or whether ontological categories are even entities at all.[21]

Westerhoff points out two problems with understanding ontological categories as the most general kinds, properties, or classes of things. The first problem is that some ontological categories can contain other ontological categories (2005: 22). For example, consider the following putative system of categories: *entity*, which has as subcategories *particular* and *universal*; *particular* has as subcategories *substance* and *event*; while *universal* has as subcategories *physical* and *immaterial*. On this scheme, *entity*, *particular*, and *substance* are ontological categories, and yet only *entity* is the most general category, since it includes *particular*, which in turn includes *substance*. Were there to be no entities, there would be no particulars or universals. This account of ontological categories as maximally general kinds guarantees that there must be exactly one ontological category, namely *entity*, or, at the very least, that every ontological category contains every being.[22] This is a result that few of those who employ the expression "ontological category" will appreciate.

It is not obvious that there is a unique "highest" ontological category.[23] Recall the Aristotelian slogan that "being is not a genus," and the ontological systems that it inspired. An implication of the claim that being is not a genus is that there is no unique "highest" ontological category. Does not the author of the *Categories* deserve better treatment than to have his system of ontological categories ruled out by fiat? Do we want an account of ontological categories on which they cannot be nested and there is a single "highest" ontological category such as *entity*? It might be true as a matter of metaphysics that there is a highest ontological category. But insofar as we care about neutrality, we do not want this to be true as a matter of definition.[24] Although neutrality is not a methodological priority for me, on my preferred metaphysics, *entity* is not an ontological category. I do not think it is true as a matter of metaphysics that there is a highest ontological category. (More on this in section 4.6 and chapter 5.)

The second problem raised by Westerhoff is that *generality* is cheap. Consider the class of elephants and the class of musical instruments, classes that have very little in common with each other. The class that is the union of these two classes is more general than either. One can always generate more general classes by disjoining more specific ones. For example, the class of universals and substances is more general than

---

[21] Lowe (2006: 6–7) denies that ontological categories are themselves entities.

[22] Joshua Spencer has pointed out to me one system of categories and an attendant metaphysical system in which there are multiple categories but all are coextensive with *entity*. Suppose that *entity*, *actual entity*, and *possible entity* are each ontological categories, but every possible entity is actualized. Then the three categories completely overlap.

[23] It is surprising that Westerhoff (2005) does not note this, since he clearly indicates in the first chapter of his book that many ontological systems do not have a topmost category. Rather, he focuses on the problems generated by the fact that categories can be nested.

[24] Van Inwagen (2014: 198) is neutral on whether *entity* is an ontological category.

the class of substances, but the latter might be an ontological category whereas the former is not an ontological category.

Westerhoff (2005: 27–8) seems to think that appealing to the notion of dependence helps eliminate gerrymandered sets from counting as ontological categories. Say that one kind K1 is dependent on another K2 just in case, necessarily, if K2 has no members, then K1 has no members. How does this notion of dependence help? All universals are universals-or-substances. And nothing could be a universal without being a universal-or-substance. So the class of universals is empty if the class of universals-or-substances is empty. So *universal-or-substance* is a more general kind than *universal* despite being gerrymandered.

If we are to identify categories with classes of entities, the classes in question must be *natural* classes as opposed to gerrymandered or "merely disjunctive" classes.[25] A putative ontological category must "carve reality at the joints." Westerhoff (2005: 27) hesitates to directly appeal to the notion of naturalness because he worries that the notion is obscure. The notion of a natural kind (or property) might be somewhat obscure but it is clear that the notion is theoretically useful. The notion of naturalness has been employed in plausible accounts of core philosophical concepts, such as *intrinsic* and *extrinsic properties, causation* and *laws of nature*, and *meaning* and *reference*.[26] Why not then appeal to naturalness directly and say that ontological categories are highly general *natural* classes, kinds, or properties? This definition correctly implies that *universal-or-substance* is not an ontological category (since it is a merely disjunctive class), but allows that *universal* might be. An appeal to something like naturalness, fundamentality, or structure is in play in Paul's (2013) account of categories, for example.

However, this construal of ontological categories suffers from what Westerhoff (2002: 288; 2005: 35–8) calls *the cut-off point problem*. There is a partial ordering of natural kinds (ordered by the *more general than* relation or by the *more natural than* relation) whose topmost node or nodes are occupied by ontological categories. But since ontological categories can be nested, these terminal categories need not be the only ontological categories. How far down the ordering can one go before one ceases to have ontological categories? It might be that *electron* is a paradigm of a natural kind, but it is probably not an ontological category.

A more sophisticated version of this view is one that holds that ontological categories are those properties that provide the best overall balance of generality and naturalness. On this view, ontological categories needn't be maximally natural kinds, since those categories that best preserve generality and naturalness might fail

---

[25] For the reason discussed earlier, we should not identify ontological categories with classes or collections of any sort. However, as we will see in section 4.3, the notion of naturalness is appealed to when formulating the account of ontological categories defended here.

[26] See, for example, Merrill (1980) and Lewis (1983a), 1984, and 1986 for a discussion of these jobs and how the notion of naturalness is employed to perform them.

to be perfectly natural. But I have two concerns about this. This first might be somewhat question-begging in this context, but it sounds odd that an ontological category cuts nature less at the joints than other kinds. Second, and also troubling, we have no guarantee that there will be properties that uniquely balance generality and naturalness. So, on a view like this, there simply might not be a fact of the matter about which kinds are the ontological categories.

The cut-off problem is a *meta-ontological* problem, and therefore should not be conflated with the first-order problem of determining when some predicate corresponds to an ontological category. It might be hard to determine when some category is an ontological category. (For example, is *material object* an *ontological category* or just a very general natural kind?) By defining "ontological category" as "highly general natural kind," one *ensures* that the notion of an ontological category is vague, just as "wealthy person" is vague.

This consequence of understanding ontological categories as highly general kinds of things was clearly seen by Bolzano (2014a: 401–2), who explicitly notes the cut-off problem, draws the conclusion that the concept of a category is therefore vague, and explicitly states that there can therefore be no determinate number of categories.

I'll admit to finding this disquieting, but if the project of determining what it is to be an ontological category is purely descriptive, one might be willing to set this disquiet aside. But if the concept of an ontological category is vague, it might not be suited for real *work* in fundamental metaphysics. How could, for example, a vague notion of an ontological category be of use in formulating and justifying a restricted principle of recombination? A principle formulated with its help would be vague as well. Is it vague which states of affairs are metaphysically possible? If we care about functionality, the cut-off problem should concern us.

One might hope to avoid the cut-off problem by adding additional conditions beyond generality. For example, perhaps an ontological category is a highly general natural kind K such that, necessarily, any *x* that falls under K essentially falls under K. However, there are potential problems with this maneuver. First, not every plausible ontological system implies that objects belong to their ontological categories essentially. For example, Bricker (2001, 2006) defends the view that *the actual* and *the merely possible* are two distinct ontological categories. Many (perhaps all) things that are actual could have been merely possible, and everything that is merely possible could have been actual. This definition of "ontological category" rules out plausible ontologies such as Bricker's by fiat. Maybe that's OK—it depends on whether neutrality is a constraint on our investigations here. (And we'll have a lot more to say about whether things belong to their ontological categories essentially in chapter 9.) Second, it might be the case that electrons are essentially electrons.[27] Being an electron is a highly natural property. But *electron* still doesn't seem to

---

[27] Compare with Westerhoff (2005: 64).

be an ontological category. Is this because it is not general *enough*? So the cut-off problem remains.

The cut-off problem is serious and Westerhoff (2005) nicely demonstrates how it problematizes most of the accounts he discusses. Although a plausible account of ontological categories will most likely appeal to the notion of naturalness, it seems that it must appeal to other notions as well. (It is clear, for example, that the identity account roughly characterized earlier in this section suffers from the cut-off problem.)

4.4 Ontological Categories as Ways of Being

It's tempting to gloss ontological pluralism as the doctrine that different ontological categories correspond to different ways of being. But why have two notions? Perhaps ontological categories just are ways of being. In which case, two things belong to the same ontological category if and only if they exist in the same way. Two things exist in the same way if and only if they are in the domain of the same perfectly natural quantifier.

The account of ontological categories as ways of being is a traditional view. Aquinas (1993: 53) seems to endorse this view when he writes that,

... existing can have different levels which correspond to different ways of existing and define different categories of thing. Thus, a substance is not some sort of generic existent differentiated by adding a certain nature, but the word *substance* expresses a special way of existing.

In this passage, Aquinas explicitly equates the "categories of things," i.e., ontological categories, with the different levels of existing that correspond to the different ways of being.[28] On his view, we shouldn't think of the category of substance as simply a highly natural kind of entity: kinds are "generics" differentiated by adding a certain nature. Rather the word "substance," understood as the name of a category, purports to stand for a specific mode of existing. And in general, the categories correspond to the modes of being.[29] As Aquinas says here, they "define different categories of thing."[30]

---

[28] The theory defended here makes no use of the notions of levels, orders, or grades of being, although it is consistent with levels and orders of being corresponding to categorial differences. We'll have more to say about grades of being in chapters 5 and 7. Brower (2014: 49, 219–22) argues that Aquinas is committed to even more modes of being than those that Aquinas calls categories, but grants that, for Aquinas, the categories do correspond to modes of being. See also Galluzzo (2014: 218–19).

[29] Knuutila (2012: 71) notes that Aquinas associates categories with modes of being.

[30] On Aquinas's view, there is a being, God, who does not belong to any of the ten categories recognized by Aristotle. But also on Aquinas's view, God enjoys a mode of being that is distinct from the mode of being of any entity within the ten categories. (God in fact enjoys being identical with His mode of being.) As it were, God is the sole member of the ontological category to which He belongs (and is identical with). Pasnau and Shields (2004: 61) note that, for Aquinas, strictly God is not a substance; see also Brower (2014) and Stein (2009: 7).

Aquinas is not alone in thinking that there is a close connection between onto-logical categories and senses of "being."[31] The popularity of the idea that there is this close connection probably stems from the influence of Aristotle, who seems to endorse it as well:

But firstly, if "being" has many senses (for it means sometimes substance, sometimes quality, sometimes quantity, and at other times the other categories), what sort of one are all the things that are, if non-being is to be supposed not to be?

[*Metaphysics* XIV.2, 1089a7–14 (Aristotle 1984b: 1721)]

In this passage, Aristotle appears to assert that the various senses of (per se) "being" correspond to ontological categories.[32] In his *On the Several Senses of Being in Aristotle,* Brentano (1981a: 58) defends several theses about Aristotle's views on being, the second of which is that

The Categories are several senses of being [*on*] which is asserted of them analogically (*kat analgoian*).

Moreover, these categories are the highest univocal concepts of being, on Brentano's (1981a: 66) reading of Aristotle. And even in 1916, decades after Brentano's sym-pathy with Aristotle's metaphysics had diminished, Brentano (1981b: 30–1) main-tained that "Aristotle also says that there are as many different senses of being as there are categories."

Moreover, some philosophers explicitly endorse a strong connection between modes of being and Aristotle's categories. For example, consider the remark by Edith Stein (2002: 126) that

in the *Metaphysics* the *categories* primarily denote modes of being and genera of beings.[33]

Contemporary interpreters of Aristotle who attribute to him the view that there are modes of being to which Aristotle's categories correspond include Witt (1989: 41–4), Shields (1999), Ward (2008: 108–31), and Loux (2012: 23–4).[34]

---

[31] The connection between senses of "being" and ontological categories was not uniformly maintained. As Bolyard (2013: 87) points out, Scotus held that "being" is univocal and yet accepted that there are different ontological categories of things. Also note that the even up into the twentieth century, the connection between categories and modes of being was maintained; see, e.g., Simons (2012b: 132) for an attribution of this view to Roman Ingarden.

[32] Aristotle seems to recognize other senses of "being" besides those that correspond to the categories; these senses are sometimes called being in the sense of being true, accidental being, and potential being. Arguably, the first two of these three senses are not fundamental existential/quantificational senses of "being," although the actual/potential distinction might correspond to one. (Recall that the view defended here is that categories are ways of being, and that ways of being correspond to *fundamental* quantificational senses of "being"). See Marx (1977: 18), Galluzzo (2013: 35–8), and Hintikka (1986) for a comprehensive discussion of interpretations of Aristotle's views on being, senses of "being," and the categories.

[33] See also Stein (2009: 89, 92).

[34] Note that Shields (1999: ch. 9) argues that Aristotle's arguments for a plurality of modes of being are unsound, and that there were reasons available to Aristotle for rejecting the claim that there are modes of being. Ward (2008: section 4.4) is more sympathetic to Aristotle's position. We'll examine their views more

Incidentally, that there is a close connection between categories and modes of being has been defended by philosophers outside of the Western tradition. Gajendragadkar (1988) is an interesting study of the ancient Indian philosopher Kanāda, and in this book he defends the view that for Kanāda the *Padārthas*, which Gajendragradkar translates as "categories," are modes of being. Gajendragadkar (1988: liii) tells us that each category is a distinct mode of existence with distinct logical behavior, that Kanāda's doctrine of categories runs parallel to Aristotle's (Gajendragadkar 1988: 1), that, like Aristotle, Kanāda distinguishes different senses of being (Gajendragadkar 1988: 5), and that modes of being cannot be thought of as classes and category-words do not denote classes of things (Gajendragadkar 1988: 11). However, unlike Aristotle, Kanāda denies that any one of the categories is metaphysically prior to the others (Gajendragadkar 1988: 156–7).

On the theory defended here, there is a connection between ontological categories and potential senses of "being": although in ordinary English, "being" might be univocal, there are as many possible *perfectly natural* meanings for "being" as there are ontological categories. These senses of "being" are *potential* senses twice over: they are available to be meant, and, on some views of meaning, they *strive to be meant*.[35] These potential senses of "being" correspond to the modes of being.

However, no other contemporary view of ontological categories implies that there is even an interesting connection between the plurality of ontological categories and the (potential, natural) senses of "being."[36] For example, if ontological categories simply are highly natural classes, properties, or kinds of things, the connection between them and potential senses of "being" is tenuous at best.[37] Perhaps contemporary metaphysicians will take this fact to reflect favorably on their view. It does indicate that their use of "ontological category" has abandoned the tradition that gave birth to the expression.

The view defended here respects the intuition that the fact that an object belongs to a particular ontological category is a deeper fact than any fact concerning the properties had by that object. The category that an object belongs to is not just another property among many had by the object, but rather is ontologically prior to

---

in section 7.5. Hintikka (1986: 100–1) indicates sympathy with linking categories to different existential senses of "being." Hoffman (2012: 142) also links categories with senses of "existence" in Aristotle. Kahn (1986: 14) sounds a cautionary note. See Pini (2005: 70–3) for a discussion of medieval doctrines on categories and modes of being.

[35] This admittedly Leibnizian remark is not hyperbole given the view that the naturalness of a meaning-candidate is a factor that determines whether that candidate succeeds in being meant. See Sider (2009) for discussion, as well as Lewis (1984) and Merrill (1980) for inspiration for the view.

[36] Von Solodkoff and Woodward (2013: 560, fn. 3) also suggest a link between having a way of being and belonging to an ontological category. Russell (1971: 268) does not talk in terms of categories, but does say that there are two senses of "there is," one that applies to non-sets such as chairs and another that applies to sets.

[37] We could reconcile their views and my own by holding that a kind is general in the relevant sense just in case it corresponds with a way of being. Thanks to Joshua Spencer for discussion here.

any property had by the object. Properties partition the beings in the world. Ontological categories partition *being itself*.

Let me state other noteworthy features of the view. First, in formulating the view, the notion of naturalness was appealed to. In section 4.3, we noted that any plausible view of ontological categories would probably need to appeal to the notion of naturalness, but would also need to appeal to other concepts. Since the view defended here does not identify ontological categories with highly natural classes, first-order properties, or kinds of things, it does not suffer from the meta-ontological cut-off problem that plagued the views previously discussed. Electrons, despite forming a highly natural class, need not form an ontological category, because (I presume) there is not a special way of existing unique to electrons. Either there is a unique way of existing had by (and only by) some *x*s or there is not. When there is, they form an ontological category, and when there isn't, they don't. And so the notion of an ontological category is not vague on the view defended here.

More carefully, the notion of an ontological category is not *semantically* vague on this view; no underdefined notions such as "highly general" appear in the statement of what it is to be an ontological category. Nothing in the framework developed here rules out the view it is *ontologically vague* whether some entity is a member of some ontological category. I would reject such a view; just as it is never indeterminate whether something exists, it is never indeterminate how it exists. But for better or worse the framework developed here is consistent with genuine ontological vagueness.

There is still the question of why electrons don't form an ontological category. But this is not a *meta*-ontological question. Rather, the task of answering this question belongs to ontology proper. The view defended here can sensibly interpret the question, and this is all that it is required to do. It is important to keep in mind the wide diversity of ontological schemes that philosophers have proposed. At one end of the spectrum there is the radical nominalist who recognizes only the category of *individual thing* and Paul's (2013, 2017) one category of qualitative characters. Nearing the other end of the spectrum is the ontological scheme defended by Heidegger (1962, 1988), according to which *person (Dasein)*, *equipment*, *parcel of matter*, *living thing*, and *abstracta* each enjoy different modes of being.[38] The most radical view of all is that every individual belongs to its own ontological category.[39] None of them is ruled out by the meta-ontological scheme defended here.

The account of ontological categories defended here is silent on a large number of first-order ontological disputes. It does not tell you, for example, whether substances, or abstract entities, or modes, or events, belong to distinctive ontological categories. Note that the account does not in itself require that one believe in any entities that are the ontological categories.[40] (Unlike, for example, Westerhoff's account, which is

---

[38] See Heidegger (1962: 67, 97–8, 121, 258–9, 285; and 1988: 28, 282, 304).

[39] We'll explore the view that each person enjoys her own mode of being in section 6.7.

[40] Lowe (2006: 6–7, 41–3) says that ontological categories are not entities of any sort.

committed to the existence of states of affairs and sets of them and their constituents.) This neutrality also extends to the claim that sets, wholes, structures, or other
compounds belong to different ontological categories than their constituents.[41]
Recall that Westerhoff's account of ontological categories implies that, for example,
sets and other constructed entities never form ontological categories.

A second noteworthy feature of the view is that it does not imply Sommer's Law,
but it is consistent with it. Recall that Sommer's Law is that no two ontological
categories merely overlap. The interpretation of Sommer's Law in the framework
defended here is that the domains of perfectly natural quantifiers never merely
overlap. There is nothing in the framework that implies this, but one is free to
adopt it if one wishes. (Earlier, we saw that some plausible ontological schemes
have ontological categories that merely overlap.) Relatedly, the view takes no stand
on whether there is a unique topmost ontological category: there is if the unrestricted
quantifier is perfectly natural. But on the specific first-order ontology I am attracted
to, the unrestricted quantifier is not perfectly natural. (More on this shortly.) Another
way for there to be one topmost ontological category is for there to be a fundamental
mode of being that includes in its domain everything that enjoys some fundamental
mode of being or other.

Third, the account is consistent with the claim that some objects belong to no
ontological category. An object belongs to no ontological category just in case there is
no natural quantifier that ranges over it. Holes, cracks, and shadows are such objects.
Although they exist (they are within the range of the ordinary English unrestricted
quantifier), they do not "fully" exist (since the unrestricted quantifier is not a natural
quantifier, and no natural quantifier ranges over them). We'll have more to say about
this in chapter 5.

Fourth, the account does not imply that, if something belongs to an ontological
category, it necessarily belongs to that ontological category, although one could
endorse this additional thesis. Although most plausible ontological schemes are
such that every entity belongs to its ontological category essentially—could a substance have been a property or a proposition?—not every ontological scheme has this
feature. Recall the scheme defended by Bricker (2001) according to which the
possible and the actual form different ontological categories. But nothing merely
possible is essentially merely possible, and much if not all of what is actual could have
failed to have been actual. Similar remarks apply to Meinongian ontological schemes
according to which *existent* is an ontological category: some of what exists could have
been objects while failing to exist, and some of what merely is an object could
have existed.

Note that other accounts of ontological categories struggle to make sense of
Bricker's (2001) ontological scheme. For example, identity accounts, which imply

---

[41] As noted in section 3.7, I doubt that sets and states of affairs/facts belong to the same ontological
category as their elements or constituents, but perhaps mereological sums do.

that objects belong to their ontologically categories essentially, cannot. And, if one is suspicious of "absolute" *de re* modal properties, one might be suspicious of identity accounts as well. For example, suppose one is attracted to a kind of *counterpart theory* according to which objects in the actual world have *de re* modal features in virtue of being similar to objects in other possible worlds. One prominent champion of counterpart theory, David Lewis (1986: 251), seems to believe that in some contexts it is true to say you couldn't have been an angel while in other contexts it is true to say that you could have been an angel. An angel is a very different kind of thing from a human being. Why then not allow for a context in which it is true to say that you could have been, for example, a property or a set? (How much freedom does counterpart theory allow?) However, someone who holds a counterpart theory of this sort might still hesitate to say that what ontological category I actually belong to differs from context to context. And so a counterpart theorist might reject an identity account of ontological categories.

Fifth, the account defended here is consistent with the claim that individuals of different ontological categories can be alike with respect to every perfectly natural property. On Bricker's (2001, 2006) ontological scheme, some merely possible objects are *duplicates* of actual objects even though they belong to different ontological categories. (Bricker and I adhere to Lewis's (1986: 61–2) view that things are duplicates just in case there is a one–one correspondence between their parts that preserves natural properties and relations.) This additional thesis is not ruled out by the ontological scheme defended here. Were ontological categories to be identified with natural properties, this additional thesis would be inconsistent. The best that someone attracted to Bricker's scheme could say is that it is possible for objects from different ontological categories to be alike with respect to all natural *qualitative* properties.[42] But this puts quite a lot of weight on the difference between the qualitative and the non-qualitative—perhaps more weight than this distinction can bear.

Finally, because the account of ontological categories defended here does not simply define *ontological category* in terms of failures of intersubstitutability in states of affairs, one can appeal (without threat of circularity) to the notion of an onto-logical category to explain why and how the principle of recombination must be restricted. In the next section, we will look at how one might use the framework defended to formulate and justify a restricted principle of recombination. Similarly, because the account of an ontological category does not appeal to the notion of an essence, it might be of use in explaining why things have the essences they have. The connection between essences and modes of being will be explored extensively in chapter 9.

---

[42] In fact, this is what Bricker (2006) ends up saying.

4.5 Restricting Recombination

I'll now explore how someone could use the meta-ontology defended here to articulate and justify restrictions on the principle of recombination. A friend of the meta-ontology needn't follow me here, and there might be other ways of appealing to modes of being when formulating and justifying various principles of recombination. But it is useful to see whether a way is possible.

Consider this powerful principle of recombination: every logically consistent sentence wholly composed of perfectly natural expressions is possibly true. (It is much like the principle of recombination roughly stated in section 4.2.) This powerful principle seems to quickly lead to trouble. On the assumption that "is a member of," "is a material object," and "something" are perfectly natural expressions, this principle delivers the verdict that it is possible that some material object has a member. This seems absurd: it is a "category mistake." The principle must be restricted in some way to rule this out. The hard task is to justify some particular way of ruling this out.[43]

What should we think of "category mistakes"? Gilbert Ryle (1949, 1971) introduced the technical term "category mistake." What did he mean by it? Some of Ryle's examples suggest the following explication: one commits a category mistake when one believes that a term functions as a referring expression (when in fact it does not) and uses that term accordingly. Suppose you and your friend, Dr. McX, attend a football game. You comment on how impressed you are with the team's spirit. Dr. McX sees the team, sees the team's coach, but is unable to see the team's spirit. He then concludes that the team's spirit must be an entity that he can't see (perhaps the team's spirit is an immaterial substance) but nonetheless causally interacts with the team. After all, when the team's spirit is strong, the team plays well, and when the team does poorly, the team's spirit suffers. Dr. McX has committed a paradigmatic Rylean category mistake.[44] And it also seems that Dr. McX's mistake stems from (if it is not identical with) his using a non-referring expression as if it were a referring expression. (We use expressions like "the team's spirit" to say something about the behavior of the team, but we do not use the expression as a referring expression. There is no intention to refer to any entity at all with that term.)

However, although this explication of "category mistake" is serviceable for certain purposes, this doesn't seem to be what Ryle meant.[45] Recall that Ryle held that

---

[43] The principle of recombination formulated above is very powerful, and might generate both *de dicto* and *de re* modal possibilities, depending on what is in the metaphysically perfect language. We might wish to focus on a principle of recombination that yields only *de dicto* possibilities. A weaker principle of recombination, one that yields only *de dicto* possibilities, is this: every logically consistent sentence in which no proper name or other rigid designator appears that is wholly composed of perfectly natural expressions is possibly true.

[44] Compare with Ryle (1949: 17).

[45] As Magidor (2013: 9–10) notes, it is difficult to understand what Ryle means by "category mistake" and also what exactly the category mistake committed by Cartesian Dualism consists in.

there are several senses of "there is," "exists," "being," etc. in ordinary English.[46] It is perfectly proper, on Ryle's view, to say that teams exist, and it is perfectly proper to say, in what Ryle (1949: 23) would call a "different logical tone of voice," that team spirits exist. However, on Ryle's view, it is not proper to say that both teams and team spirits exist: the sense of "exists" in which one can truthfully say "teams exist" is not the same sense of "exist" in which one can truthfully say that "team spirits exist," and there is no sense of "exists" in which one can meaningfully utter "both teams and team spirits exist."

If there are many senses of "exists," then presumably there are also many senses of "refer." If there are (in some sense of "there are") team spirits, then "the team's spirit" refers (in some sense of "refers") to the team's spirit. So whatever mistake Dr. McX is making, it is not as obvious that he is making the mistake of thinking of some term that it is a referring expression (in some sense of "referring expression") when in fact it is not.

It is not easy to make sense of Ryle's (1949) view of category mistakes. Here is one way that captures the gist of the view. First, there are several senses of "exist," but there is no "generic" sense of "exist." Recall that there is a generic sense of "exist"— "exist*" if you like—just in case, for any sense of "exist," if one can truly say "a exists" in that sense of "exist," then one can truly say "a exists*." There can't be a generic sense of "exists" for Ryle, for then it would be perfectly proper to say "Minds and bodies exist."[47]

Second, certain kinds of univocal expressions in the English language are associated with exactly one sense of "exist." (If an expression of one of these kinds is ambiguous, its potential disambiguations are each associated with exactly one sense of "exists.") These expressions include one-place predicates, names, definite descriptions, and perhaps complex demonstratives (such as "this dog"). Expressions not associated with exactly one sense of "exist" are the truth-functional logical constants, such as "and," and probably other sentential connectives that are not straightforwardly defined in terms of ordinary predicates. Let e be a sense of "exists" and let "exists(e)" be a univocal expression with e as its sense. A name (or complex demonstrative) n is associated with e just in case there is a meaningful sentence whose constituents are n and "exists(e)" in that order; a one-place predicate F is associated with e just in case there is a meaningful sentence whose constituents are "an," F, and "exists(e)" in that order.

Say that some expressions are *co-categorial* just in case they are associated with the same sense of "exist." We also want to have a notion of "association" for polyadic predicates. An expression e is co-categorial with a polyadic predicate with respect to a slot s just in case (i) there is a meaningful sentence containing that predicate in which

---

[46] See Ryle (1971: 206–7; 1949: 23).
[47] As noted in section 1.2, Ryle's failure to recognize a generic sense of "exists" makes him vulnerable to the argument of van Inwagen (2001b).

e occupies *s* and (ii) there is no meaningful sentence that contains that predicate in which an expression not co-categorial with *e* occupies *s*.

In Ryle's "Categories," which is reprinted in Ryle (1971), Ryle claims that category mistakes are absurd sentences—sentences that lack both meanings and truth-values—that result from conjoining expressions from different "logical" types. My hypothesis is that for Ryle around the time of *The Concept of Mind*, the various logical types are correlated with the senses of "there is," "exists," and "being" that Ryle believes in. We can think of a *Rylean category* as a *maximal* set of co-categorial terms. "Red is sleeping" commits a category mistake because "red" and "is sleeping" belong to incompatible logical types; moreover, the sense of "exists" associated with "red" is a different sense of "exists" than that associated with "is sleeping." This suggests that a putative atomic sentence is actually a category mistake when it consists of noun-phrases and predicates that are not co-categorial (or not co-categorial with respect to a slot). A putative molecular sentence is actually a category mistake when it contains an atomic category mistake.

As just noted, on Ryle's (1971: 179) view, category mistakes are literally meaning-less sentences.[48] Category mistakes do seem worse than merely false. Consider the difference between the following claims: "The number two is blue" and "That cat is canine." Both are admittedly odd, perhaps even absurd, but many have the intuition that the first is far worse than the second. If Ryle is right, the difference is that category mistakes are worse than being false by virtue of being nonsensical.

I don't think that category mistakes are meaningless sentences.[49] As I have stressed in section 2.2, the view that there are modes of being, i.e., many *possible* perfectly natural senses of "exists," is consistent with the claim that, in English, the word "exists" is univocal. In fact, I suspect that "exists" is univocal in English, and so (in English) every term is "co-categorial."[50] Sentences like "The number two is blue" and "That man is an abstract object" are meaningful, although obviously false and bizarre. So my explanation of why such sentences are worse than false must be different than Ryle's.

Magidor (2013: 14) notes that typically those who think that category mistakes are meaningless think that the notion of a category mistake is of crucial importance to philosophy of mind or metaphysics more broadly, whereas those who think they are meaningful but false typically dismiss the importance of category mistakes. We'll consider a middle path: category mistakes in English are meaningful (yet false) but our reaction to them indicates something important about the underlying metaphysical situation. Ryle is wrong about English, but a Rylean view about the

---

[48] Magidor (2013: 10, fn. 24) notes that sometimes Ryle appears to think of category mistakes as being false. But this strikes me as mere appearance.

[49] Magidor (2013) makes a persuasive defense of the meaningfulness of category mistakes.

[50] Quine (1976: 229) defends this. This is also the view of Magidor (2013). Van Inwagen (2014: 65–6) also presents strong evidence that "exists" is a univocal English word.

metaphysically perfect language might well be right. I appealed to the notion of a natural expression when formulating the doctrine that there are modes of being. In a metaphysically perfect language, every expression is a perfectly natural expression. On my view, a metaphysically perfect language will contain multiple quantifiers. Given a commitment to multiple fundamental quantifiers, it is natural to hold that there are distinct sets of variables associated with these quantifiers. That is, the metaphysically perfect language is multi-sorted.[51] For each set of variables, there will be a maximal set of terms that are their possible substitution-instances. These sets need not overlap.

Secondly, the metaphysically perfect language will contain two kinds of predicates, *intra-categorial* predicates and *inter-categorial* predicates. An intra-categorial predicate is such that it can meaningfully prefix only terms from exactly one maximal set of terms. An inter-categorial predicate can meaningfully prefix terms from more than one maximal set, but for each such predicate there will be syntactic rules governing how that predicate can combine with these terms. Whether a predicate is an intra-categorial predicate or an inter-categorial predicate is as much a function of its logical form as whether that predicate is, for example, a one-place or two-place predicate.

The logical form of a predicate is shown by the range of open sentences one can construct with the predicate. "x_1 is to the left of x_2" is an open sentence in which the predicate "is to the left of" appears. "x_1 is to the left of" fails to be an open sentence. On the view under consideration, the *sort* of variables matters as much as the number of variables. One can begin with an open sentence, replace a variable of one sort with a variable of another sort, and end with something that fails to be an open sentence. So, for example, "x_1 is to the left of n_1" fails to be an open sentence, since "n_1" is not a variable of the right sort.

One makes a *metaphysical category mistake* when one constructs a pseudo-sentence by either prefixing an intra-categorial predicate to some terms from the wrong maximal set of terms (or to variables from the wrong class) or by prefixing an inter-categorial predicate to some terms in violation of the syntactic rules of the metaphysically perfect language.

This is a bit abstract. An example should help. Suppose that the correct ontology has two ontological categories: *individual* and *set*. There is a fundamental quantifier, "$\exists_{ind}$," that ranges over all and only individuals, and a fundamental quantifier, "$\exists_{set}$," that ranges over all and only sets. Associated with the first quantifier are the variables "$x_1 \ldots x_n$" and associated with the second are "$s_1 \ldots s_n$."

---

[51] Turner (2010) explicitly discusses multi-sorting, but, as I did in McDaniel (2009b), opts to focus on a version of ontological pluralism that makes use of single-sorted variables. He also briefly indicates that one nice feature of multi-sorting is the possibility of explaining category mistakes. Norton (1977: 62–5) extensively discusses Carnap's use of a multi-sorted language to make what are intuitively categorial distinctions; see also Norton (1977: 101–2, 154–6).

Let us pretend that the only fundamental predicates of individuals are shape predicates, e.g., "is a triangle," "is a square," and the only fundamental predicate of sets is the subset predicate. The set of shape predicates is an intra-categorial set of predicates, and the singleton set of the subset predicate is an intra-categorial set as well. The shape predicates are all monadic, and their logical form permits construction of open sentences of the same kind as "Fx_1." There is one inter-categorial predicate, namely, the two-place predicate "is a member of." It is a dyadic predicate, and its logical form permits the construction of the following kinds of open sentences: "x_1 is an element of s_1" and "s_1 is an element of s_2."

The syntactic rules of this language prohibit each of the following:

(i) $\exists_{ind} x_1, \exists_{ind} x_2: x_1$ is a member of x_2.
(ii) $\exists_{set} s_1: s_1$ is a square.
(iii) $\exists_{ind} x_1, \exists_{set} s_1: s_1$ is a member of x_1.

Each of (i)–(iii) is a category mistake. In a metaphysically perfect language, they are utterly without meaning, since the syntactical rules of the language disallow any of (i)–(iii) from being well-formed sentences. These pseudo-sentences fail to respect the logical forms of the predicates that appear within them.

Taking on board the full generality of the notion of a natural expression allows us to provide a justifying rationale for the feeling that something is terribly wrong with sentences like "my table has three subsets." There are many ways for a language to fall short of metaphysical perfection. One way is by having the wrong primitive predicates. A language that has, for example, "is grue" and "is bleen" as primitive predicates is less than ideal. Another way in which a language can fall short is by having the wrong primitive quantifiers. A third and related way a language can fall short is by having, in a sense, the right predicates, but having predicates whose surface logical form does not match the logical form of the underlying properties they stand for.

We have a predicate in English, "is simultaneous with," and the apparent logical form of this predicate is shown by open sentences such as "x is simultaneous with y." Let us suppose that *simultaneity relative to a reference frame* is a perfectly natural three-place relation. There is still a strong temptation to think that our predicate "is simultaneous with" refers to this relation. We learned that simultaneity does not have the logical form we thought it had. We did not learn that "simultaneity" is like "filled with phlogiston" in that neither corresponds with something in the world. Accordingly, we can't complain that "is simultaneous with" is defective in virtue of failing to stand for something natural. But *how* it stands for something natural is defective: it would be metaphysically better to have a predicate that matches the logical form of the relation that is its content.

Similarly, perhaps, "is a member of" stands for a perfectly natural relation, *is a member of*. It would be better to have a predicate that stands for this relation whilst simultaneously not allowing sentences in which, as it were, material objects have members to be formed. The logical form of the membership predicate in English does not match the logical form of the membership relation. In the metaphysically perfect language, these two would not come apart.

A Rylean view of the metaphysically perfect language is attractive. What makes a "category mistake" such as "my table has three subsets" worse than other falsehoods is that no paraphrase of such a sentence into the metaphysically perfectly language is even in principle possible. (Sometimes what can be said should not be said.) Any purported paraphrase of that sentence would require conjoining incompatible intra-categorial expressions. Our language would be better off (metaphysically speaking) were Ryle to be right about it.

Recall the general principle of recombination we first considered: any logically consistent sentence in the metaphysically perfect language is possibly true. Assume that "is a member of" is a perfectly natural expression, as are the proper names of fundamental particles. It might initially seem then that this principle of recombination licenses the claim that "this electron is a member of this proton" is a possibly true sentence. However, on the picture described moments ago, this sequence of expressions is not even a sentence in the metaphysically perfect language, let alone an atomic sentence. And so the powerful principle of recombination does not license the claim that some electron is a member of some proton.[52]

On a view like this, there is an intimate connection between logical possibility and metaphysical possibility: all logically consistent sentences in the metaphysically perfect language express metaphysically possible propositions. In short, in the metaphysically perfect language, logical possibility suffices for metaphysical possibility.

However, one cannot straightforwardly claim that a proposition is metaphysically possible if and only if it is expressible by a logically consistent sentence in the metaphysically perfect language. The English sentence "No electron has a member" expresses a metaphysically necessary, and hence metaphysically possible, truth. Yet this truth is *not* expressible in the metaphysically perfect language. So we need further principles to bridge logical possibility and metaphysical possibility if we hope to offer a reductive analysis of metaphysical possibility in terms of logical possibility. My hope is that pursuing such principles might be a fertile research project.

Note that for similar reasons we can't say that a *necessary* condition for being metaphysically possible is having a logically consistent translation in the metaphysically perfect language, since, as just noted, "no electron has a member" is necessarily true (and hence possibly true) and yet lacks a translation.[53] In the remainder of this section, I will focus on strategies for formulating an appropriate necessary condition for metaphysical possibility. Finding such a condition would be a good first step

---

[52] Recall that we might wish to restrict this principle further, so that it generates only *de dicto* modal truths. As suggested earlier, one plausible way of restricting it is to have it apply to sentences without proper names or other rigid designators.

[53] Such sentences lack what Sider (2011) calls a metaphysical semantics.

towards the greater goal of providing necessary and sufficient conditions for meta-physical possibility.

One tempting move is to distinguish between positive category mistakes and negative category mistakes. A positive category mistake is a sentence that (i) ascribes a property to an object (or a relation to some objects) and (ii) has no translation into the metaphysically perfect language. A negative category mistake is the negation of a positive category mistake. Now state that all positive category mistakes are necessarily false and all negative category mistakes are necessarily true, or at least are true in any world in which the object in question exists.

This tempting move is too crude. There's the question about what to say about sentences with predicates such as "non-charged." Consider, "this set is non-charged." It's true, and yet it seems that it will lack a translation into the metaphysically perfect language as well. The idea is that the translation of "charged" into metaphysically perfect language is a predicate that is explicitly typed, i.e., an intra-categorial predicate in the sense defined above. So the translation of "non-charged" into the metaphysically perfect language should be the result of prefixing this typed predicate with predicate-negation, and therefore the result should be another typed predicate.[54] This is assuming that the metaphysically perfect language has a negation operator that can attach to predicates; it might not, for if it does, it will contain complex predicates that express less than perfectly natural properties! (We could refine the idea of a metaphysically perfect language by saying that it is one in which all simple expressions correspond to perfectly natural entities if they correspond to anything at all.) It looks like then we should classify "this set is non-charged" as a positive category mistake, and accordingly hold that it is necessarily false, even though it is true!

Alternatively, it might be that one function of the predicate-negation operator in the metaphysically perfect language is to remove type-restrictions: if this is so, then prefixing this operator to an intra-categorial predicate would result in producing an inter-categorial predicate. Things would be a bit easier if this were the case.

The metaphysically perfect language can't say some of the things our imperfect language can, and this is the source of the difficulty we are facing here. I do not take the lack of "expressive power" to be a defect of this language, since the things it can't say are not worth saying, at least not in what van Inwagen (2014) calls "the ontology room." And the metaphysically perfect language is not the appropriate language to use outside this room. But perhaps we should consider a Wittgensteinian move, and distinguish between what the metaphysically perfect language can *say*—that is, what propositions can be expressed via it—and what that language can *show*.[55]

---

[54] See Magidor (2013: 95–9) for a relevant discussion of a similar problem for some treatments of category mistakes in natural language.

[55] The distinction between what a language can say and what it can only show comes from Wittgenstein (1966). But interestingly, McManus (2013: 668–9) suggests that to understand some of the later Heidegger's thought about being and its modes, it might be useful to make a similar distinction.

The tempting thought is that a necessary condition for an English sentence to be metaphysically possible is either for it to have a translation into the metaphysically perfect language or for the metaphysically perfect language to *show* that it is true. Once we understand the rules and limitations of the metaphysically perfect language, we can see that it shows that no electrons have members and that all sets are non-charged. I'm hesitant to rest things on this distinction, but it would be interesting if this were the best move to make.

Before moving on, let us raise the interesting, albeit largely terminological, question of whether we should reserve "ontological category" for those modes of being that impose type-restrictions of the sort used here or rather use the phrase interchangeably with "mode of being." (We could, if we liked, call the former "strict ontological categories.") Adopting this terminology might bring the view explored here closer to the Aristotelian tradition that inspires it. I think Aristotle's notions of *potentiality* and *actuality* correspond to modes of being, but he does not call them "categories"; those are reserved for the modes of being of substances and the various kinds of accidents.[56]

Finally, as noted in section 1.5.3, for many applications of ontological pluralism, it doesn't matter much whether modes of being are understood in terms of first-order properties or in terms of kinds of quantification. But if we want to defend a view like the one defended in this section, it seems that we are better served by taking modes of being to correspond to kinds of quantification.

4.6 Formal Ontology

Let's now discuss the ramifications of the neo-Aristotelian view of ontological categories for the putative discipline of *formal ontology*. The key question is whether formal ontology ineliminably presupposes that *object/entity/thing*, understood as the most general covering kind for anything that there is, is an ontological category. On the neo-Aristotelian view, it is not, and hence the possibility for tension.

What then is formal ontology? There are many reasonable things one could mean by this expression. Formal ontology as I will understand it is *not* merely the discipline of philosophy that applies formal methods to ontological questions. I have no qualms about the applications of formal methods to ontological questions, and the neo-Aristotelian view does not in itself imply that such an application would be methodologically improper.[57] Rather, I construe formal ontology as the putative discipline that describes the perfectly natural topic-neutral features that are

[56] Similarly, Witt (2003: 3) distinguishes between what she calls "kinds" of being that correspond to categories and "ways" of being that include potentiality and actuality.

[57] Nor do I have qualms about the discipline called "formal ontology" by Cocchiarella (1969, 1972), which studies the foundational principles governing the various modes of being. I welcome such a discipline!

applicable to objects of any ontological category that entities enjoy *simply in virtue* of being entities. Formal logic studies those features that the objects of logic have in virtue of their form alone—validity being a paradigmatic logical feature an argument has not in virtue of content but rather in virtue of form.[58] Similarly, formal ontology studies those features that objects have simply in virtue of their form, that is, in virtue of their being an object rather than their being an object of a specific type.[59] Sub-branches of this putative field allegedly are the theory of identity, the theory of plurals, mereology, and the study of ontological dependence and ground.

This way of thinking of formal ontology appears to be Husserl's around the time of the *Logical Investigations*.[60] Formal ontology is the theory of objects *as such*.[61] In order for formal ontology to be a science, it must not be a hodgepodge collection of truths but rather its subject matter must be governed by *laws* that are in turn grounded in the essences of the things that science studies.[62] If formal ontology is to be a science, then objects *as such* must be law-governed in virtue of the strict essence of objects *qua* objects.[63] Husserl conceives of formal ontology as a proper part of the science of pure logic he articulates; the complementary part is formal logic construed as the science of the relationships that pure meanings bear to one another, where meanings themselves are ideal, abstract objects not located in space or time, and include propositions and their constituents.[64] The following are some of the reasons that formal ontology and formal logic are appropriately subsumed under pure logic. First, in some sense, meaning and object are connected notions, since meanings are directed towards objects.[65] Second, both disciplines are bodies of necessary truths. Third, these truths have the same evidential basis, which for Husserl is the intuition of essences, and accordingly are both appropriately classified as a priori sciences.[66] Fourth, both sciences concern notions that are applicable with

---

[58] In the tradition I am discussing, the objects of formal logic are not components of a natural language, but rather meanings and propositions construed as mind-independent abstract objects.

[59] See Poli (1993: 10).

[60] In his introduction to Husserl (2005a: xii), Moran says that formal ontology is the theory of the *nature* (my emphasis) of objects in general. See also Poli (1993) and Varzi (2010).

[61] Husserl (2005b: 3). See also Husserl (1973: 11), where formal ontology is characterized as "the theory of something in general and its derived forms."

[62] See Husserl (2005a: 17–21). See also Smith (1989) and Smith and Smith (1995: 29) for discussion of formal ontology as a science.

[63] By "strict essence" I mean a notion of essence not straightforwardly equivalent to the standard notion of a *de re* essential feature, but rather the kind of notion articulated by Fine (1994a and 1995b), among others. This notion will be the focus of chapter 9.

[64] Bell (1999: 94) agrees that formal ontology is a part of logic.   [65] Husserl (1969: 78–9).

[66] Smith (1995: 330) says that formal ontology concerns itself with formal essences. I concur with this claim as well; according to Husserl, it is of the essence of an object that it stand in part–whole relations and relations of dependence, that it be a constituent of states of affairs and propositions, that it have properties and stand in relations, and so forth. Each of these features appealed to in the statement of an object's essence is appropriately titled a "formal essence." Note that Husserl is arguably *not* the first philosopher to approach formal ontology via phenomenological investigation. Crusius, an important precursor of Kant, understands ontology to be the universal science of objects as such, whose principles are discovered via "investigation" but because these principles are universal, any particular *exemplar* of them is an apt starting

respect to every subject matter; this is one sense in which the features to which they pertain are topic-neutral. Because these disciplines are topic-neutral, they are both aptly labeled *analytic* sciences.[67] Finally, these sciences both have a *fundamental* subject matter and are thereby genuinely unified sciences rather than mere hodge-podges of necessary truths concerning gerrymandered features.[68]

Formal ontology studies those features of objects (or entities) that objects have *qua* objects, that is, in virtue of being objects. But *to be an object* just is *to be*: formal ontology purportedly studies entities as such rather than a specific subclass of entities. But by my lights *being an object* does not rank very highly on the naturalness scale, since it is defined in terms of *being*, which does not rank particularly highly on the naturalness scale. *Being an object* is at best an analogous property, but as will emerge in chapter 5, it might not even be that.

There are accordingly two concerns about formal ontology so construed. First, if non-fundamental features lack essences in the strict sense, there is no essence of *being an object* to be the object of an intuition that is purportedly the evidential basis of formal ontology. Whether non-fundamental things have essences in the strict sense will be discussed in section 9.2. Second, formal ontology so construed purports to study the fundamental features that objects have in virtue of being objects. But I do not see how a fundamental feature of an object could be had *in virtue of* a non-fundamental feature of that object. Since *being an object* is not fundamental, no fundamental feature can be had in virtue of it.

Given the meta-ontology I accept, the pursuit of formal ontology so construed is a doomed project. This does not mean that there is no viable project that deserves to be called "formal ontology." For example, we could entertain the possibility of *formal ontology**, which is the putative discipline that describes the perfectly natural topic-neutral features that are applicable to objects of any ontological category. I have no in-principle objection to such a science, at least on the assumption that ontological categories are fundamental modes of being. But two reservations are worth mentioning. First, formal ontology* will not be a universal science, since there are entities, such as holes and shadows, that do not enjoy fundamental modes of being and hence are not within the scope of this discipline.[69] Second, we cannot look to *being an object* in order to assess from the top down, as it were, whether there are such fundamental, topic-neutral features. Perhaps there are, but each putative example of a fundamental topic-neutral feature must be assessed on its own merits.

---

point for their investigation: from "any actually present object that comes before our senses" all the truths of ontology may be discerned; see Watkins (2009: 139).

[67] See Husserl's Third Logical Investigation (in Husserl 2005b) for his reconstruction of the analytic/synthetic distinction.

[68] For further discussion of Husserl's notion of formal ontology, see Bell (1999: 93–101) and Smith (1998).

[69] Such entities will be the focus of chapter 5.

4.7 The Necessity of Ontological Categories

Let's close this chapter with a brief discussion of whether what ontological categories there are is necessary or contingent. Westerhoff (2005) is committed to contingency; the account I've offered is consistent with both.

In order to make the discussion more tractable, let's first take modes of being to be higher-order properties and let's assume that properties have their grade of naturalness essentially. Given these assumptions, ontological categories are essentially ontological categories.[70] But it is still an open question whether ontological categories necessarily exist.

If properties in general necessarily exist, then ontological categories necessarily exist even if nothing is a member of them. But, if properties exist only if they have instances, then an ontological category exists only if some first-order property exemplifies it. And this in turn is the case only if some member of that ontological category exemplifies that first-order property. Perhaps there are some ontological categories that are necessarily non-empty; the putative category of mathematical entities is plausibly such a category. But it is also plausible that some actual category could have been empty; both the category of physical object and the putative category of tropes are plausibly possibly empty.

As discussed in chapter 2, our concept of existence—assuming that we have a unique concept of existence—is at best an analogous concept. (We will further complicate our picture of existence in chapter 5.) The feature that it represents is less natural than the various modes of being that are its analogue instances. Analogous properties are akin to disjunctive properties but more natural than merely disjunctive properties. But perhaps thinking first about disjunctive properties will be illuminating. Does a disjunctive property exist only if its disjuncts exist? If a disjunctive property is literally composed of its parts, then, if mereological essentialism holds for properties, the answer is "yes"; otherwise perhaps not. Another possibility is that a disjunctive property exists in any world in which at least one of its disjuncts exist. Fine (1994b) recognizes a mode of composition that functions in this way. And given Lewis's (1986) view that a property is a set of actual and possible instances, a disjunctive property is simply a set that is the union of its disjuncts. On Lewis's view, a disjunctive property can have an instance at a possible world even if one of its disjuncts does not. (In general, on Lewis's view, a set can have an instance at a world even if not all of its instances are to be found at that world.)

So it is hard to settle the question of the modal status of existence without taking a stand on the nature of properties in general. What we can see though is that, on one theory of properties, existence exists only if each of its analogue instances exist; and hence there are worlds in which some things enjoy a mode of being without enjoying existence. This is a strange but coherent view. But I think the right view is that a

---

[70] We will reconsider whether properties have their degree of naturalness essentially in section 9.7.

sufficient condition for a disjunctive property to exist is that at least one of its disjuncts exists, and this might not even be a necessary condition. Similarly, it is sufficient for an analogous property to exist that one of its analogue instances exist, and it is sufficient for a determinable property to exist that one of its determinates exist. Provided that, in every world, some fundamental mode of being is instantiated, existence is sure to be found.

4.8 Chapter Summary

In this chapter, I focused on the nature of ontological categories. I argued that, insofar as the notion of an ontological category is theoretically fruitful, we should take ontological categories to be modes of being. I discussed one way in which ontological categories as modes of being could be used to formulate interesting and powerful principles about what is metaphysically possible. I also discussed whether it is necessary which ontological categories there are, and the prospects for a putative discipline of formal ontology construed as that which studies the essence of an object qua object.

5

Being and Almost Nothingness

5.1 Introduction

We appear to be ontologically committed to what I will call *almost nothings*. Examples of almost nothings include *holes*, *cracks*, and *shadows*; almost nothings thrive in the absence of "positive" entities such as donuts, walls, and sunlight. Let's focus on holes, since the literature on them is voluminous.[1] We quantify over holes, and even count them: we say, for example, that there are some holes in the cheese, seven to be precise. We ascribe features to them and talk as though they stand in relations: that hole is 3 feet wide, much wider than that tire over there. Holes apparently persist through time, as evidenced by the fact that my sweater has the same hole in it as the last time you saw me wear it. We even talk as though holes are causally efficacious: I badly sprained my ankle because I did not "mind the gap," and fell into the gap between the train and the walkway. We see holes in the roads and swerve to avoid them.[2] We believe in holes. If our beliefs are true, holes must enjoy some kind of reality.

For the ontological pluralist, there is more to learn about an object's existential status than merely whether it is or is not: there is still the question of *how* that entity exists. The ontological pluralist can happily say that there are holes and then diligently pursue the question of in what way there are holes. By contrast, according to the ontological monist, either something is or it isn't, and that's all there is say about a thing's existential status. This puts the ontological monist in an uncomfortable position. According to her, everything that there is enjoys *the same kind of reality*, which is the kind of reality enjoyed by full-fledged concrete entities such as ourselves. She is committed to the unpleasant claim that *holes are just as real as their hosts*, a claim that is apt to be met with incredulous stares by those not acquainted with contemporary metaphysics. Roy Sorensen (2008: 19) notes the tension almost

---

[1] Lewis and Lewis (1970) began the contemporary discussion. See Casati and Varzi (1994) for a book-length treatment. Lewis and Lewis (1996), Casati and Varzi (2004), and Sorensen (2008) continue the discussion. But, as we will see, concerns about the ontological status of holes, privations, and the like predate the 1970s by a considerable margin!

[2] Potter (1977: 144–5) discusses the positions of various schools of Indian metaphysics on whether absences are perceivable. Sorensen (2008: 127–9) argues that holes can be perceived, and that this fact need not violate a causal theory of perception.

nothings generate for ontological monists: "It feels paradoxical to say that absences exist—but no better to say that absences do not exist." And later (2008: 189) he writes, "Holes do not sit any more comfortably on the side of being than of nonbeing."

Holes and other almost nothings, although real, are not real in the same way as concrete objects. Moreover, it seems that the kind of reality enjoyed by holes is in some sense *degenerate* or *less robust* than the kind of reality enjoyed by "positive" entities. In fact, it is hard to see what could be meant by claiming that holes and other "absences" are in any sense "absences" if the kind of existence they enjoy is the same as the kind of existence of "presences." The fact that every "absence" necessarily exists only if some "presence" exists does not suffice to ensure that these labels are appropriate: perhaps every concrete object necessarily depends on the existence of a God, but this would not make it the case that we are absences while God is a presence. Nor does the fact that every "absence" necessarily excludes some "presence" suffice to ensure that these labels are appropriate, for "presences" might also necessarily exclude each other.[3]

The ontological pluralist has it easier: since she believes that there are different modes of being, she is under no pressure to hold that almost nothings exist in the same way as presences. However, questions remain. First, what mode of being do almost nothings have? Second, in what way is this mode of being degenerate or less robust? Recall that in the introduction I noted that there are at least three different kinds of ontological degeneracy: almost nothings might be (1) degenerate because they enjoy a lower level on the hierarchy of being, (2) degenerate because they enjoy a relational mode of being (such as being-in), or (3) degenerate because they enjoy a low degree of being; this third kind of degeneracy will be articulated in section 5.4. Identifying the kind that almost nothings suffer from is the primary task of this chapter.

In section 5.2, I discuss whether we should understand the way in which holes are ontologically degenerate in terms of levels of being, and argue that we shouldn't.

In section 5.3, I articulate and motivate the thesis that the mode of being of almost nothings is *being-in*, a mode of being also exemplified by attributes. Although it is somewhat plausible that the mode of being of almost nothings is being-in, there are reasons to be not fully satisfied with this thesis. I will consider a view on which almost nothings have a lower order of being than attributes, which in turn have a lower order of being than substances. But, as we will see, this is also not the right model of how almost nothings are ontologically degenerate.

This leaves us with the third kind of ontological degeneracy: grades or degrees of being. In section 5.4, I articulate and motivate the thesis that the mode of being of

---

[3] According to the position defended in Casati and Varzi (1994), holes are immaterial particulars, equal in reality but differing in constitution to material particulars. But being immaterial does not suffice for being a privation: Cartesian souls are immaterial *substances*, not absences.

almost nothings is something I will call *being-by-courtesy*, which we shall see is a truly degenerate way to be.

In section 5.5, I explore whether other putatively possible entities are plausibly thought of as enjoying being-by-courtesy. In section 5.6, I turn to the question of whether recognizing being-by-courtesy makes certain ontological questions "easy." Finally, in section 5.7, I discuss how the notions of ontological reduction and being-by-courtesy might be connected, and whether things that enjoy being-by-courtesy are capable of exemplifying fundamental features.

In what follows, I do not defend the intuition that holes and other almost nothings exist but are less than fully real. The goal of this chapter is to explore and develop plausible accounts that can be used to explicate the intuition that almost nothings are less than fully real. If you do not share the intuition that motivates this project, there is almost nothing I can do to make you have it. I would ask you to look within once more to be sure—you are decidedly in the minority if you lack it! But regardless, it will still be worthwhile for you to see the extent to which the accounts offered here are plausible, since the questions discussed pertain to fundamental issues in metaphysics.[4]

5.2 Almost Nothings and Levels of Being

The first model of ontological degeneracy that we will consider employs levels of being, the application of which to Meinongian presentism and degrees presentism was discussed in sections 3.3 and 3.4. Here's what the model proposes. There are two fundamental quantifiers that range over concrete objects, one of which includes "positive" material objects, such as persons, living organisms, quarks, and so on, but does not include almost nothings. The other quantifier is more inclusive, containing everything included in the "inner" quantifier as well as almost nothings. On this model, the ontological degeneracy of almost nothings is putatively captured by the fact that positive entities have more being than they do: there is a kind of being enjoyed by positive entities that almost nothings lack, but the converse is not the case.

This sounds initially promising. But for the following reasons levels of being do not provide the right model. First, it seems misguided to multiply the number of modes of being a positive entity enjoys simply in order to capture the way in which the being of almost nothings is impoverished: instead of capturing how the mode of being of a hole is deficient, this model suggests that the ontological status of its host is even better than we thought. We are in effect rethinking the ontological status of positive entities rather than almost nothings, and that's why I say this model is misguided: it "adjusts" the wrong target.

---

[4] Metaphysics and ontology have never been concerned *only* with the nature of what is fundamental or rock bottom, as even a superficial examination of texts such as Suárez (2005) would confirm.

Second, the existence and qualitative nature of almost nothings is completely determined by the existence and qualitative nature of positive entities.[5] But, on this model, this fact is surprising. For, on this model, almost nothings enjoy a fundamental mode of being that they share with positive entities. There is a fundamental way in which almost nothings exist. Consider two other views that are structurally similar to the model discussed here: minimal Meinongian presentism and full-on Meinongianism. These views distinguish a fundamental inner quantifier and a fundamental outer quantifier.

The outer domain of minimal Meinongian presentism contains merely past objects as well as presently existing ones, whereas its inner domain contains only present objects. But since past objects do enjoy a fundamental mode of existence, it is unsurprising that their existence and nature needn't be exhausted by the existence and nature of presently existing objects: they have an existence in their own right. And this is why fundamental facts about the past needn't supervene merely on fundamental facts about the present. If past objects did not enjoy a fundamental mode of being, their existence and nature would be determined by that which does enjoy a fundamental mode.

Similarly for less minimal Meinongianism. Meinongians recognize an outer domain of objects whose nature—or *Sosein*, to use the popular technical expression—is not across the board constrained by the existence and nature of those items in the inner domain. They think that the truths about objects in general can float free of the truths about existing objects.[6] Now Meinongians might try to avoid saying that the outer-quantifier corresponds to a manner of being, but, as discussed in section 1.5.2, I think that they are mistaken to do so. Objects *are* in some fundamental way, and that is why it is unsurprising that their natures are not completely exhausted by the natures of the existent. If this weren't the case, one would expect that, even if there are (in some sense) non-existent objects, nonetheless all the facts about them are determined by facts about the existing ones.

This is why I think this model makes surprising the fact that the existence and nature of almost nothings is fixed by the existence and nature of positive entities. This is not a decisive reason to reject the model, but it is a cost of it, and it should motivate us to look carefully at the alternatives to it.

5.3 Almost Nothings and Being-In

In section 2.4.2, we discussed a mode of being called *being-in*. This is the mode of being enjoyed by attributes. Perhaps it is also the mode of being of other entities that

---

[5] That facts about holes are fixed by facts about material objects is granted by Casati and Varzi (2004) and Lewis and Lewis (1996). According to Weidemann (2002: 85–7), Aquinas would accept this principle, as it follows from a more general principle that beings in the sense of being true supervene on genuine beings; we will discuss what "beings in the sense of being true" means in section 5.4.
[6] Von Solodkoff and Woodward (2013) argue for this interpretation of Meinongianism.

depend in some way on substances. In this section, I assess whether almost nothings enjoy being-in as their mode of existence.

We begin with the positive case for the proposal. First, let us note that holes are ontologically dependent on some host or other, but it is not the case that each particular hole is ontologically dependent on some particular host or other. Consider a sweater with a single small hole in its left-hand side. If you destroy most of the fabric except for a small amount that surrounds the hole, then you will have destroyed the original host of the hole (the sweater) and yet the hole will persist.[7] Similarly, attributes require the existence of some substance or other, but needn't require the existence of any particular substance.[8]

Second, just as we talk of attributes as being in substances, we talk of holes as existing in or residing in their hosts. And just as we have the option of taking this talk strictly and literally by holding that the logical form of the kind of existence enjoyed by attributes is two-placed, we can take this talk literally with respect to holes.

Third, we can provide content to the inchoate intuition that holes enjoy "less reality" than their hosts. I hesitate to give a *definition* of the expression "*x* is more real than *y*," since I think that there are multiple good notions of ontological deficiency to be explored, each of which is a genuinely *ontological* rather than, for example, a modal, causal, or essential kind of deficiency. But, as noted earlier, the following seems reasonable: *x* is more real than *y* if (i) the mode of being of *x* has an *n*-placed logical form whereas the mode of being of *y* has an *n* + *m*-placed logical form (*n* and *m* are positive integers), and (ii) all entities that have *y*'s mode of being have being relative to some entity that has *x*'s mode of being. The intuition behind this condition is that modes of absolute being are more real than modes of relative being, and so if your mode of being is relative to something else, then you are less real than that something else.

On this account, holes have less reality than their hosts. The mode of being of a hole is 2-place, whereas the mode of being of its host is 1-place, so the first clause is satisfied. And since every hole exists in some host or other, the second clause is also satisfied. It is nice that we can give an account of the intuitions that (i) although holes exist, they do not exist in the same way as positive entities such as their hosts and (ii) holes enjoy a kind of reality less robust than that of their hosts. Moreover, unlike the account explored in section 5.2, we don't need to rethink the mode of being of positive entities in order to come to grips with the mode of being of almost nothings.

But there are also reasons to be concerned with the view that the being of holes is being-in. First, perhaps the defining feature of an ontological category is that two

---

[7] See Casati and Varzi (1994: 19) for discussion. Perhaps it would be more careful to say that the hole had more than one host to begin with, specifically the whole piece of cloth and any proper parts of that cloth that "contain" the hole. Note that the conclusion that holes are not ontologically dependent on any particular bearer still follows. Thanks to Ross Cameron for discussion here.

[8] For a recent defense of Aristotelian realism, see Armstrong (1978).

entities belong to the same ontological category if and only if they exist in the same way, i.e., share the same mode of being. This was the view explored in section 4.4. If this is right, then the proposal articulated here implies that attributes and almost nothings belong to the same ontological category. This seems mistaken. As Casati and Varzi (1994) argue, holes and other almost nothings are dependent particulars, not universal attributes. (I don't think that holes are particular attributes either.)

One response to this objection is to deny that attributes and almost nothings exist in the same way, but grant that both modes of existence have the same logical form and structure: both are kinds of relative existence, one of whose relata is always some substance. If we go this route, in order to avoid confusion, we should stick to using "being-in" to designate the mode of being of attributes, and use some other locution to designate the mode of being of almost nothings.

A deeper worry stems from the intuition that, even if holes and attributes enjoy different modes of being, attributes enjoy more reality than holes and other almost nothings. Attributes might be mere modifications of substances, and because of this less real than substances, but their reality is at least a positive kind of reality, whereas almost nothings seem less real than even attributes. Light is more real than shadow, noise is more real than silence. However, it is hard to see what grounds this judgment if we understand comparative reality in the manner articulated above. The sufficient condition articulated above implies that substances are more real than attributes and substances are more real than holes. However, on the natural way of extending the sufficient condition above so as to compare the reality of attributes and holes, attributes and holes come out as equally real. Let x and y be entities and $B(x)$ and $B(y)$ be their respective modes of being. Suppose that (i) $B(x)$ and $B(y)$ have the same adicity and (ii) if $B(x)$ and $B(y)$ are kinds of relative being, then every kind of entity to which $B(x)$ is relative is also a kind of entity to which $B(y)$ is relative. If these conditions are met, then x and y are equally real. The idea is this: modes of being that are "absolute," i.e., 1-placed, are the highest degrees of reality. Modes of being that are $1 + n$-placed are less real modes than absolute modes. The absolute modes of being are the "central" points, whereas relative modes of being are to some extent distant from these "central" points.

Admittedly, intuitions here are somewhat woozy, and the sufficient condition for equal reality articulated above is not one we are forced to endorse. But it is attractive, and if it is true, then on the current proposal attributes and almost nothings enjoy the same amount of reality. Both attributes and almost nothings are the same "onto-logical distance" from that which is maximally real, namely substances, since both attributes and almost nothings enjoy a mode of being that is relative in the same way to substances. But, as noted, this is intuitively incorrect: attributes are a kind of positive reality, whereas almost nothings are mere privations, and so should have less reality than attributes.

Fortunately, there is another proposal worth considering that is in the neighbor-hood. Perhaps the mode of being of an absence is relative not only to substances (their hosts) but also to their modifications, such as their surfaces or other attributes of the host. The mode of being had by an almost nothing, on this proposal, is doubly indexed: *x exists in substance S relative to attribute A*. On this view, an absence exists in a modified substance. This proposal is more attractive than its predecessor, for not only can no absence exist without a presence, no absence can exist without that presence being positively modified in some way or other. The donut has a hole, after all, because it has a positive modification, specifically its shape.[9]

Note that, on this view, the sufficient condition for equal reality articulated earlier is not satisfied. Note also that the sufficient condition for greater reality is satisfied: on the proposal just articulated, substances enjoy the fullest kind of reality, attributes are less real than substances, and almost nothings are less real than attributes. This is a pleasing consequence of the proposal.[10]

Still, I don't think that this is the right model for understanding the deficient ontological status of almost nothings. My primary concern is that even if the mode of being of almost nothings is polyadic, and hence in this respect attenuated, it is nonetheless a fundamental mode of being, and so it is still surprising that the existence and nature of almost nothings is exhausted by the existence and nature of positive entities. The nature of an attribute is not simply exhausted by the nature of what it modifies: attributes have a quiddity all of their own, and this is why it is right to think of them as forming a distinct ontological category. But almost nothings lack even this. The qualitative nature of an almost nothing is fully determined by the qualitative natures of positive entities. Moreover, the non-qualitative aspect of an almost nothing is also fully determined by that of positive entities: fix which positive entities exist and how they are qualitatively, and you thereby fix *which* almost nothings exist.

We should examine the third model of ontological degeneracy. This third model, as we will see, is not only metaphysically appropriate. It also has a strong historical pedigree.

5.4 Being-by-Courtesy

Recall (from section 1.5) my minimal formulation of ontological pluralism as the view that there are possible languages with semantically primitive restricted quantifiers that are at least as natural as the unrestricted quantifier. A "neo-Aristotelian" version of this view was also discussed, which holds that these semantically primitive

---

[9] Why not say instead (or also), "The donut has a certain shape because it has a hole"? The answer is that it is intuitive that the shape of the object is primary: the object has a hole *in virtue of* the fact that the object has that shape. The *in virtue of* relation is asymmetric: since the object has a hole in virtue of the object having that shape, it does not have the shape in virtue of the object having a hole. I thank an anonymous referee for raising this question.

[10] As Galluzzo (2014: 222) notes, Aquinas thinks of the mode of being of privations as far "weaker" than the mode of being of attributes.

restricted quantifiers are *more* natural than the unrestricted quantifier. The view that will be articulated in this section will presuppose the neo-Aristotelian version of ontological pluralism.

In order to make the exposition of the view as straightforward as possible, I will assume that the unrestricted quantifier is semantically primitive.[11] There is a simple sense of "being" present in ordinary English that is fully captured by the "$\exists$" of first-order logic. If there are other senses of "being" present in ordinary English, the sense of "$\exists$" is not decomposable into those senses. I want to remain neutral on whether there are other senses of "being" in ordinary English. As we saw in chapters 1 and 4, many historically important friends of modes of being held that there are senses of "being" corresponding to them present in ordinary language.

However, it will expedite matters to explicitly introduce quantifiers that stand for the modes of being. Let's provisionally assume a meta-ontology according to which concrete objects, such as tables, chairs, and human persons, enjoy one mode of being, represented by "$\exists_m$," while attributes and other abstracta enjoy a different mode of being, represented by "$\exists_a$."[12] Let's assume that these are the only two modes of being. On the neo-Aristotelian account, "$\exists_m$" and "$\exists_a$" are more natural expressions than "$\exists$." It is tempting to think that, given this meta-ontology, "$\exists$" is something like the quantificational equivalent of a disjunction of "$\exists_m$" and "$\exists_a$." This temptation is increased if we hold that the domain of "$\exists$" contains all that is in the domains of both of "$\exists_m$" and "$\exists_a$" and nothing more, i.e., that the domain of "$\exists$" is simply the union of the domains of "$\exists_m$" and "$\exists_a$."[13]

The domain of "$\exists$" must *include* everything that is within the domain of "$\exists_m$" and "$\exists_a$." "$\exists$" is the *unrestricted* quantifier after all, and its job is to range over everything there is regardless of what kind of thing it is. But it is not obvious that the domain of "$\exists$" must contain *only* that which is in the domain of either "$\exists_m$" or "$\exists_a$." Suppose that the domain of "$\exists$" contains *more*. If this is the case, then there are some things such that there is no fundamental way in which these things exist: there are things that enjoy no fundamental mode of being. Let us call any such entities *beings by courtesy* and the derivative mode of being they enjoy, a kind of mode of being that may be defined purely negatively, *being-by-courtesy*. Being-by-courtesy, represented by "$\exists_b$," can be defined as follows: $\exists_b x\ \Phi$ = df. $\exists x\ \Phi\ \&\ {\sim}(\exists_m x\ \Phi$ or $\exists_a x\ \Phi)$.

Being-by-courtesy is a truly degenerate way to be. On the one hand, things that are beings by courtesy can be truly said to exist, i.e., they fall within the range of the unrestricted quantifier of ordinary English. On the other hand, in no language with

---

[11] Recall that the assumption that "$\exists$" is semantically primitive does not imply that "$\exists$" is a natural expression.

[12] I provisionally assume here that the being of attributes is not a kind of relative being. But this is in order to keep the discussion relatively streamlined.

[13] Probably "$\exists$" is not a merely disjunctive expression. Probably "$\exists$" is an *analogous* expression, where analogous expressions (recall section 2.2) are more natural than merely disjunctive ones but less than perfectly natural.

only perfectly natural quantifier expressions are beings by courtesy quantified over. This gives us a different way of articulating the claim that some entities are more real than others: x is more real than y if x enjoys a fundamental mode of being while y is merely a being by courtesy.

The hypothesis to be explored is that almost nothings are beings by courtesy. We have seen that this hypothesis accommodates the idea that almost nothings exist in a different way than concrete material things (but they do not exist in a *fundamental* way at all.). It also gives us a way of articulating the intuition that almost nothings are *privations*: even their mode of being is to be understood negatively, as a remainder of what is left in the domain of "∃" once one subtracts from it what is "fully" real.

Is being-by-courtesy really possible? How could it come to be that the unrestricted quantifier ranges over things that exist in no fundamental sense?

Let's start with the banal observation that we could have meant something else than we actually do by "∃." Some of these possible meanings are such that, had we meant one of them by "∃," it would still be appropriate to think of "∃" as something like an existential quantifier. The possible semantically primitive restricted quantifiers appealed to earlier are expressions whose meanings are among those possible for "∃." There are also possible meanings for "∃" that we can think of as "super" meanings in the following sense. Let s be a possible meaning for "∃" and let "$∃_s$" be a quantifier-expression with that meaning. Say that s is a "super meaning" for "∃" just in case it is true that, for all Ψ, "$∃x\ \Psi$" is true only if "$∃_s x\ \Psi$" is true, yet for some Φ, "$∃_s x\ (\Phi\ \&\ \sim ∃x\ \Phi)$" is true. (The "∃" appearing in this formula has the meaning that it customarily has: it is *our* unrestricted quantifier.) "$∃_s$" is a semantically primitive quantifier expression, as is "∃." What is interesting about "$∃_s$" and other "super" meanings is that any speaker of a language in which such a quantifier-expression is the primary expression ought to think of our language as containing only *restricted* quantifiers.[14]

What makes it the case that "∃" has the meaning it has rather than any of these possible alternatives? Recall that Merrill (1980), Lewis (1983a, 1984), and Sider (2001, 2011) have suggested that two factors are relevant to determining the meaning of an expression: how we use that expression and how natural the candidate meanings are.[15] Our use of an expression consists in our dispositions to utter sentences in which that expression appears: roughly, a possible meaning for an expression fits with our use of that expression to the extent that it makes those sentences that we are apt to sincerely assert come out as true. Fit with use is a matter of degree.

---

[14] Note that, in order to state the thesis that "super" meanings are possible, one must assume that the meaning of a quantifier expression is not simply its domain. The unrestricted quantifier, by definition, ranges over the most expansive domain there is. For more on this point, see Sider (2001).

[15] Also recall that I don't think these factors are the only two factors. Causation also plays a role. But it is hard to see exactly what role it plays in determining the meaning of "∃." I will accordingly ignore causation in what follows, but I am aware that it might be a mistake to do this.

The naturalness of a meaning is also a matter of degree. Fit with use and naturalness are independent and often competing factors: the meaning that most fits with use needn't be the most natural, and vice-versa. In addition, neither factor invariably trumps the other: perfect naturalness can trump even high fit with use.

On the neo-Aristotelian version of ontological pluralism we have been considering, there are two perfectly natural quantifier expressions, "$\exists_m$" and "$\exists_a$." But the meaning of neither expression fits with use at all well. Presumably this is why "$\exists$" is not synonymous with either "$\exists_m$" or "$\exists_a$." (Perhaps we don't even have a use for "$\exists_m$" and "$\exists_a$," although those friends of the distinction between *existence* and *subsistence* might disagree. Perhaps both senses are represented in ordinary English, and this is why some people are inclined to say, "Tables and numbers do not exist in the same sense of 'exist'.") However, on the neo-Aristotelian view considered here, there are no other perfectly natural meanings for "$\exists$" to take. Any remaining candidate meaning for "$\exists$" must be less than perfectly natural.

There might well be a *most natural* (but less than perfectly natural) meaning for "$\exists$." Perhaps it is the meaning such that, were "$\exists$" to mean it, each substitution instance of Φ in "$\exists x\ \Phi$ if and only if ($\exists_m x\ \Phi$ or $\exists_a x\ \Phi$)" would yield a true sentence. If this meaning is the meaning of "$\exists$," then it is true that the unrestricted quantifier ranges over all and *only* those things that enjoy some fundamental mode of being. Let "$\exists_d$" be a possible quantifier with this meaning, and let "$m('\exists_d')$" stand for its meaning. $m("\exists_d")$ is probably more natural than any other candidate meanings for "$\exists$." But this fact does not actually tell us *how* natural it is. (Is it a mere disjunction or is it analogous?)

Note that $m("\exists_d")$ also does not fit terribly well with our use of "$\exists$." As noted earlier, we happily and frequently quantify over almost nothings, which are neither abstract objects nor concrete realities. Instead, they are privations of concrete realities. If the meaning of "$\exists$" is $m("\exists_d")$, then "$\exists x\ x$ is a hole" is false.

Presumably, there are other candidate meanings for "$\exists$" that have a better fit with our use of "$\exists$" than $m("\exists_d")$. Such meanings would make "$\exists x\ x$ is a hole" express something true. These candidates are not as natural as $m("\exists_d")$, but sometimes fit with use trumps naturalness, especially when the degree to which a meaning fits with use is high and the degree of naturalness of alternative meanings is relatively low. The hypothesis entertained here is that fit with use has trumped naturalness in this case: the meaning of "$\exists$" is *not* $m("\exists_d")$, but is rather something relative to which "$\exists_d$" is a restricted quantifier. If this is the case, then there are things such that they exist in no fundamental way. In other words, on this hypothesis, there are things that are mere beings by courtesy.

This hypothesis gives content to the intuition that beings by courtesy are less real than, e.g., concrete material beings. We can "define" the notion of degree of reality as follows: x is less real than y to degree n just in case (i) "$\exists_1$" is the most natural quantifier that ranges over x, (ii) "$\exists_2$" is the most natural quantifier that ranges over y, and (iii) "$\exists_2$" is a more natural quantifier than "$\exists_1$" to degree n. Given this "definition," it follows that beings by courtesy are less real than concrete material beings.[16] They are also less real than attributes, assuming that attributes enjoy a fundamental mode of being. The third model gives a scale on which holes are less real than attributes even given the assumption that the mode of being an attribute is polyadic.[17]

There are precedents to the position defended here. Recall that Fine (2001: 2–3) argued that we should distinguish between *what is* and *what really is*. There is a special propositional operator, *it is really the case that* ("**R**"). Perhaps there are some true existentially quantified propositions that are not *really* true. Fine's proposal enables us to distinguish beings by courtesy from genuine beings: both exist, but only the latter *really* exist. Fine does not explicitly discuss almost nothings, but the position that almost nothings are real without being really real is a natural view for him to endorse. (Recall that in section 1.5.4, we discussed a way to formulate the doctrine that there are modes of being using Fine's "reality operator.")

Ross Cameron (2008) also distinguishes between what exists and what "really" exists. According to Cameron, things that really exist are minimal truth-makers for existential sentences. But a true existential sentence such as "*a* exists" can be made true by something other than *a*: if *a* is not a minimal truth-maker for "*a* exists," then *a* exists but does not really exist. Cameron does not explicitly discuss almost nothings, but rather applies his framework to questions concerning composition and mathematical objects. But the extension of his framework to almost nothings is, if anything, even more apt.

These are modern precedents to the model staked out here. But the model has a much longer lineage. This distinction between *a*'s existing in the sense of there being a true sentence of the form "*a* exists" and *a*'s *really* existing is foreshadowed by these remarks by Aquinas:

We should notice, therefore, that the word "being," taken without qualifiers, has two uses, as the Philosopher says in the fifth book of the *Metaphysics*. In one way, it is used apropos of what is divided into the ten genera; in another way, it is used to signify the truth of propositions. The difference between the two is that in the second way everything about which we can form an affirmative proposition can be called a being, even though it posits nothing in reality. It is in this way that privations and negations are called beings; for we say that affirmation is opposed to negation, and that blindness is in the eye. In the first way, however, only what posits

---

[16] I tend to think of entities as something like determinations of their modes of being. The analysis offered here provides an interesting analogy between entities and their most natural mode of being and determinates and determinables. Just as determinates and their corresponding determinables are equally natural/equally real (see section 2.2 and chapter 7), entities are as natural (real) as the most natural mode of being that they determine.

[17] Korman (2015: 306) suggests that we should distinguish the question of which objects are fundamental from the question of which modes of being are fundamental. I agree that the questions are distinct, but I see no reason to think that there are independent scales of fundamentality. On the contrary, our total theory is much simpler if the scales are linked. And the particular way of linking them defended here has an impressive historical lineage, as we will shortly see.

something in reality can be called a being. In the first way, therefore, blindness and the like are not beings.[18]

The ten genera referred to by Aquinas are Aristotle's ten categories, which for the sake of convenience have been here compressed into two.[19] According to Aquinas, there is a sense of "being" whose job is to range over the entities that fall under the ten categories. This sense is like our $m(\text{"}\exists_d\text{"})$.[20] There is also a sense of "being" that ranges over *more*, according to which privations such as blindness and the like (which presumably include holes and other almost nothings) are beings. This sense of "being" is "being-true."[21] I am inclined to think that Aquinas's beings in the sense of being-true are beings by courtesy.

The sort of distinction Aquinas draws does not seem to be unique to "Western" philosophy. Potter (1977: 140–6) discusses various schools of Indian metaphysics that made a distinction between the real categories of things and absences, and argued over whether absences are "really" there. Similarly, McDermott (1969: 62–3) claims that the metaphysicians of the Nyāya-Vaiśeṣika traditions recognized a similar distinction between entities like substances, tropes, and motions, which enjoy existence in the strict sense, and absences, which do not exist in the strict sense (but which are nonetheless quantified over and theorized about).[22]

There are apparent and important differences between Aquinas's view and the one defended here. First, the view defended here is consistent with the claim that, as a matter of fact, "being" has exactly one sense, i.e., "being" is not polysemous. Call the putatively sole meaning of "∃," "$m(\text{"}\exists\text{"})$." "∃" is semantically simple, i.e., $m(\text{"}\exists\text{"})$ does not have other meanings as parts. Likewise, $m(\text{"}\exists_d\text{"})$, a merely possible meaning for "∃," is semantically simple. Part of what is meant by saying that m ("∃") is simple is that sentences of the form "$\exists x\ \Phi$" will not be identical in meaning to sentences containing "$\exists_d x\ \Phi$" plus additional operators or other linguistic machinery. There is a sense in which $m(\text{"}\exists\text{"})$ is an *extended* sense of "∃" relative to $m(\text{"}\exists_d\text{"})$, in that "∃" contains more in its domain of quantification than "$\exists_d$."

---

[18] See Aquinas's *Being and Essence*, section 4 (Aquinas 1965: 21). Similar passages are translated and discussed in Klima (1993). See also Kenny (2005a: 3–4).

[19] I have ignored other ontological categories besides *substance* and *attribute* here. And perhaps an accurate picture of Aquinas will postulate further modes of being beyond those of the ten categories; this is persuasively argued in Brower (2014).

[20] As noted in section 4.4, Aquinas also sometimes speaks as though, for each category of being, there is a sense of "being" associated with it. For example, Aquinas (1993: 92) says that "being" is used in one sense to stand for substances and in another sense to stand for properties. See also McInerny (1961: 39) and Miller (2002: 16). Brentano (1981b: 90) attributes this claim to Aristotle: "This much is certain: he thought that there was a sense of the term being for each category; and in making the classification, he wanted to distinguish as many different senses of being."

[21] The inspiration for this doctrine in Aquinas is Aristotle's *Metaphysics*, specifically IV.2, 1003b5 (Aristotle 1984b: 1584). Similarly, Kukkonen (2012: 56) notes that Averroes recognizes a distinction between the metaphysically important sense of being applying to entities belonging to categories and an impoverished sense applying to privations. See Kenny (2005a: 3–5) for discussion of Aquinas.

[22] See also Matilal (1982: 100).

But "∃" is not to be understood in terms of "∃ₐ," despite the fact that the latter expression is more natural.

The view defended here, namely that almost nothings are beings by courtesy, is also consistent with the claim that "being" is polysemous in the ways Aquinas suggests. Perhaps the following facts jointly suffice for "being" to be polysemous: (i) $m($"∃ₐ"$)$ is relatively natural but is not a terrific fit with use, (ii) $m($"∃"$)$ fits with use very well but is comparatively less natural, and (iii) no other candidate meanings for "∃" balance these two factors as well as either $m($"∃ₐ"$)$ or $m($"∃"$)$.

Casati and Varzi (1994: 178–84) argue persuasively that claims about the existence of holes cannot be paraphrased away.[23] We are committed to the literal truth of "∃x x is a hole." That there is no paraphrase of sentences in which quantification over holes occurs into sentences in which such quantification does not occur is what we should expect given that that sentences of the form "∃x Φ" are not identical in meaning to sentences containing "∃ₐx Φ" plus additional operators or other linguistic machinery. When one truly says that holes are beings, or that they exist, one is not using "being" or "exist" in an attenuated or metaphorical sense.[24] It does not follow, however, that holes are genuine beings rather than beings by courtesy. On the view articulated here, strictly and literally, holes exist, but they are less real than their hosts.

Let us return to contrasting the view here with the view that was plausibly attributed to Aquinas. A second difference is that, according to a popular interpretation of Aquinas's *Being and Essence*, those things whose sole mode of being is being-true exist "only in the mind."[25] One way of understanding this claim is as the view that those entities whose sole mode of being is being-true are such that, were there no minds, they would not exist.[26] Those objects whose mode of being is being-true are "beings of reason," creatures whose existence is the product of our cognitive structure or intellectual activities.

Suárez also makes similar distinctions and claims about almost nothings. Suárez (like Aquinas) does distinguish (at least) two uses of the word "being." In Suárez's (2005: 70) commentary on Aristotle's *Metaphysics*, he writes:

[23] This claim is consistent with the plausible claim that facts about beings by courtesy supervene on facts about real beings.

[24] This view differs greatly from the position of Brentano (1981b), who argues that there is a difference between the strict sense of "being" and many "extended" senses of "being," but claims that truths stated using an extended sense can be paraphrased in terms of the "strict" sense. "Being" in the sense of "being-true" is one such extended sense that he recognizes. It is also in contrast to the view of van Inwagen (2014: 5–12), who distinguishes between the proposition expressed by "shadows exist" in what he calls "the ontology room" from the proposition that sentences expresses outside the ontology room. He does not, however, explicitly tell us whether "shadow" is ambiguous and denies that "exists" is ambiguous.

[25] See, for example, Bobik (1965: 36, 57) and McInerny (1961: 39–40). This interpretation of Aquinas is also suggested by Klima (1993).

[26] Klima (2014: 109) says that thinkers before Ockham thought of beings of reason as mind-dependent things.

We...speak about being in two ways: in one way, as it comprehends only true real beings—and it transcends and contains under itself all of those. In another way, it is extended to many things which are not truly and intrinsically and which are called beings only by a certain extrinsic attribution, for example, privations, or beings which are entirely by accident, or beings of reason.

And like Aquinas, Suárez thinks that almost nothings are in some way mind-dependent.[27] In Suárez (2005: 75), he tells us that "It must be said, therefore, that a being of reason properly comes to be through that act of the intellect by which something that in reality has no entity is conceived in the manner of a being."[28]

Regardless of whether one should attribute this view to Aquinas, Suárez, or other scholastics, I would like to distance myself from it. Beings by courtesy needn't be mind-dependent. If there is a hole in the center of the earth, it would exist regardless of whether there were any minds to think about it. Holes (and other absences) are no more dependent on human cognition than the material bodies in which they reside.[29]

One response to this objection is to argue that, although holes are mind-dependent, material objects could be perforated independently of the existence of any minds. One problem with this response is that it makes some apparently analytic or conceptual truths turn out false. For example, "If there are holes, then necessarily a material object is perforated if and only if it has a hole" is conceptually true: anyone who understands what "holes" means ought to agree with it. However, on the view suggested by Aquinas and Suárez, this sentence is not conceptually true. There are holes, but it is possible for something to be perforated without having a hole. A world in which there are no finite intellects is, on this view, a world that is holeless, but it might for all that be a world that has perforated objects. One can consistently (albeit incorrectly) deny that there are holes. One can't coherently say that there are holes but material objects could have been holed without them.

Although holes and other absences are not dependent on our minds or our conceptual schemes, we can try to soothe the intuition that some seem to have that they are mental constructions or products of reason. The worry seems to be that beings by courtesy are not truly *objective* beings. The concept of *objectivity* is intimately tied with the concept of *parochialism*. There are at least two ways in which a classificatory scheme can be parochial. First, it might demarcate entities on the basis of features that are dependent on human minds. Second, a classificatory scheme can be parochial when that scheme is not *required* by the world. If our conceptual scheme is like this, then it is very reasonable to fear that the explanation

---

[27] This is affirmed by Coffey (1938: 44).

[28] For further discussion of being in the sense of being-true, see Kenny (2005a: 3–6). Normore (2012: 78) says that, for Ockham, beings of reason are mind-dependent. Midtgarden (2012: 208–9) claims that beings of reason were acknowledged by Peirce.

[29] In a similar vein, Sorensen (2008: 18, 248–9) criticizes Sartre for making absences dependent on the human mind. John Doyle (2005: 29–30), in his introduction to Suárez (2005), discusses this objection as well.

for our *having this scheme* as opposed to some other turns more on facts about us than facts about the content of the scheme.[30] And on the hypothesis that we are considering, to some degree this is the case: "∃" has the meaning it has largely because of how we use the term. There were other, *metaphysically better*, meanings available for "∃," and if we had meant one of them, we could not have expressed a truth with "holes exist." Holes are "conceptual projections" or "beings of reason" or "social constructions" not in the sense that they depend for their existence on concepts or rational activities or societies, but rather in the sense that a conceptual scheme that recognizes them is not mandated by the world.[31] A conceptual scheme is parochial to the extent that it recognizes beings by courtesy.

Suárez and other scholastics were wrong to think that almost nothings are creatures of reason in the sense that they are created by acts of reason. We can create holes in bodies by pushing a finger through clay or a sword through a person, but we can't create a hole in a body through thought alone, even if we try really hard. What we can do is speak in such a way that a metaphysically dodgy meaning for "exist" is selected on which it is true that holes exist.

That almost nothings are beings merely by courtesy has proved to be a coherent and fruitful hypothesis. Perhaps other putative entities are best thought of as beings by courtesy. In the next section, we will briefly explore some of the possibilities.

5.5 Diminished Beings

How big is the class of beings by courtesy? As we saw earlier, the temptation to identify almost nothings with mind-dependent entities, so-called "beings of reason," should be resisted. I suggest that we consider the opposite approach. Some of the entities that have been called "beings of reason" might be better thought of as beings by courtesy.[32]

For example, some medieval philosophers who wrestled with questions about the ontological status of relations concluded that they are mere beings of reason.[33] However, this view is very implausible. For example, x could be 5 feet from y even in possible worlds that contain no minds. But, necessarily, x is 5 feet from y if and

---

[30] Suárez (2005: 82–4) wonders whether the cognitive activity of God or angels produces beings of reason. Suárez argues that only imperfect intellects are productive of beings of reason, and hence God does not produce them (and probably angels do not either).

[31] Recall Hirsch's (2005) *quantifier variance*, according to which questions about which composite objects exist or whether objects have temporal parts are bankrupt. The world does not mandate any answer to these metaphysical questions. The reason Sider (2011) appeals to the naturalness of quantifiers is that he believes these metaphysical questions are genuine (and difficult).

[32] Suárez (2005), for example, takes privations to be a species of beings of reason. I have argued that it is better to think of privations as beings by courtesy.

[33] See Brower (2005) for an impressive overview of the terrain. One of the strategies adopted by these philosophers was to dispense with the full-blooded existence of relations while appealing instead to properties of the relata to ground the truth of statements that apparently attribute relations to things.

only if x bears the *being 5 feet from* relation to y. So the relation *being 5 feet from* is not mind-dependent.[34] Still, it might be a mere being by courtesy. One who is tempted by Aristotle's claim that "the relative is least of all things" should consider whether relations are beings by courtesy.[35]

I doubt that relations are beings by courtesy because some facts about relations seem metaphysically fundamental. (It's hard to see how all relations could be beings by courtesy if some relational facts do not supervene on non-relational facts.) Rather, (some) relations enjoy the kind of reality enjoyed by other attributes. But here I merely wish to explore possibilities.

If relations are beings by courtesy, then perhaps objects that exist only when certain relations are exemplified are also beings by courtesy. Indeed, perhaps many of those things that we now take to be genuine realities are mere beings by courtesy. For example, it is plausible that some things compose a whole only if they are really related to one another in some way. If we subtract genuine relations, we subtract the composites that require them. Mereological nihilism is the view that no complex object exists. This is a hard view to defend.[36] These reflections suggest that a more moderate view according to which no complex object is fully real might be more defensible. Perhaps the only material objects that are fully real are microscopic simples; one might be attracted to this view if one thought that, necessarily, all facts about composite objects obtain in virtue of facts about microscopic simples.[37]

A related view is a kind of *existence monism*. Schaffer (2007a, 2007b, 2010) has defended a kind of monism according to which, although the many are as real as the One, the One is *prior* to the many. Schaffer calls his view "priority monism," and contrasts it with the view he calls "existence monism," which holds that the One is the only thing that exists. Existence monism seems at least as hard to defend as mereological nihilism. However, perhaps a kind of existence monism construed as the view that exactly one entity, namely Reality-as-a-Whole, is a genuine being might turn out to be defensible. This version of monism is neither Schaffer's priority monism nor his existence monism but rather lies somewhere between them in logical space.[38]

Other contentious entities are *possibilia*, i.e., merely possible individuals or worlds. In his interesting article on the status of the merely possible in late scholastic thought, Jeffrey Coombs (1993) articulates the views of John Punch. According to Coombs (1993: 450), "Punch's difficulty is to explain how possible entities can be entities

---

[34] Brower (2005: 11) discusses something like this argument.

[35] See Aristotle's *Metaphysics* XIV.1, 1088a23 (Aristotle 1984b: 1719). We will discuss this passage further in section 7.5.

[36] But it has been defended. See Rosen and Dorr (2003).

[37] For what it's worth, I don't think that, necessarily, all facts about complex objects obtain in virtue of facts about simples. I accept the possibility of genuinely emergent properties had by complex objects; facts about such properties do not obtain in virtue of facts about the properties and relations enjoyed by simples.

[38] Gibson (1998: 21) attributes a view in this neighborhood to F. H. Bradley. Della Rocca (2012: 157–64) argues that Spinoza held this sort of view as well.

without claiming that they are eternally actual." Coombs (1993: 450) quotes Punch as holding that the solution lies in positing "a certain diminished being, so to speak, an intermediate being between beings of reason and actual being without qualification." It is not plausible to identify possibilia with beings of reason. However, we can develop a view inspired by Punch's remarks. Let us distinguish between two versions of the most extreme kind of modal realism. Both versions agree that concrete possible worlds other than the actual one exist, but one version demotes the mode of being of non-actual concrete possible worlds to being-by-courtesy, whereas the other grants them full reality. The former view holds that possible beings enjoy a "diminished" kind of being. Note that the question of whether concrete possibilia are mere beings by courtesy is not settled by any of the arguments Lewis (1986) gives for the existence of concrete possible worlds. (In section 2.5.4 I discussed a kind of modal realism in which the possible and the actual have different modes of being, but did not take the further step of arguing that the possible have an inferior mode of being.)

Fictional entities are beings by courtesy. In fact, they are excellent examples of beings of reason in the medieval sense. As I see things, all beings of reason are beings by courtesy, but the converse doesn't hold. Many scholastics mistakenly held that almost nothings are beings of reason, but they were not mistaken in thinking that there were beings of reason. Chimeras and other imaginary objects, creatures of myth and fiction, and characters of dreams all are excellent candidates for being less than fully real as well as being mind-dependent in exactly the way the scholastics thought.[39]

We can entertain a further expansion of being-by-courtesy to include merely intentional objects of all varieties, even those for which it is metaphysically impossible that they be actual. A kind of qualified Meinongianism in which the merely intentional enjoy being-by-courtesy might prove to be a defensible position.[40] As noted in section 1.5.2, I don't think that this is a view that the historical Meinong could accept, since by my lights he held that the outermost quantifier—the one that ranges over absolutely everything there is—is a perfectly natural expression, whereas on the view discussed here, it is not. On my preferred interpretation, Meinong also makes use of two other perfectly natural semantically primitive quantifiers, a subsistence quantifier that ranges over obtaining abstracta and an existence quantifier

---

[39] Sol Kim has suggested to me that the mode of being of holes and the mode of being of fictional entities should not be conflated, since holes are spatiotemporally located, causally potent, and mind-independent, whereas fictional entities are none of these. Moreover, these differences could be explained by the difference in mode of being. Intuitively this is right. Fictional entities *exist in* stories, dreams, etc. This suggests a fourth model for fictional characters, one that combines grades of being with orders of being. On this fourth model, the mode of being of fictional characters is both relative and non-fundamental. Like attributes, fictional characters *exist in* something else, but unlike attributes, their relative mode of being is not particularly natural. If we want to distinguish the mode of being of holes, shadows, etc. from that of fictional characters, this is one way to do this—holes have a not particularly natural yet absolute mode of being, while fictional entities have a not particularly natural and relative mode of being.

[40] Berto (2013: 74–6) alludes to but rejects something like the position developed here.

that ranges over obtaining concreta. But Meinongians needn't follow the historical Meinong here. If they don't, they should also say that Soseins of the intentionalia are determined by the features of those things within the inner quantifier. But this seems actually to be the intuitively correct view. There is not, for example, any more to Sherlock Holmes than what is determined by the goings-on of concrete reality.[41] We'll have a bit more to say about creatures of fiction in section 5.6.

This sort of view would not be without precedent. According to Friedman (2015: 143–5), Peter Auriol held that there is a mode of being that all intentional objects enjoy, but that it is a kind of *diminished* mode of being.[42] Friedman's remarks suggest that this mode of being is diminished in two respects: it is not fundamental and it is not absolute but rather a relational kind of existence, existence-in-a-mind. One interesting feature of Auriol's position is that some objects enjoy more than one mode of being. Socrates, for example, enjoys the existence characteristic of substances but also this diminished mode of being given that he is an intentional object. So there are not two entities, Socrates and a representation of Socrates, but only Socrates existing in two manners.

Does the fact that Socrates enjoys a non-fundamental, non-absolute mode of being compromise his status as a substance? No. We can suppose that a necessary and sufficient condition for being a substance is enjoying at least one mode of being that is both fundamental and absolute, and the position of Peter Auriol is not inconsistent with this. Some attributes might enjoy a fundamental mode of being, if *being-in* is perfectly natural, but they do not qualify as substances by virtue of that enjoyment, since the mode of being is not absolute. And these attributes might also enjoy a non-fundamental and yet absolute mode of being; perhaps the generic mode of being that everything enjoys is such a mode. And yet this also does not elevate the attribute to a substance. Conversely, the ontological status of a substance is not compromised by its enjoying a non-fundamental mode of being; everything does. Nor is it compromised if some of those non-fundamental modes are also relational modes. Only if a substance enjoys a fundamental and relational mode of being should we pause for concern.

Let us return to the discussion of potential candidates for being beings by courtesy. Schiffer (2003) has argued that propositions and properties are "pleonastic" entities. Pleonastic entities exist but they have a kind of "diminished" ontological status: they are "thin" entities in some sense. They are "shadows" of sentences and predicates.[43] We know that they exist because there are true sentences that imply the existence of such entities. Moreover, Schiffer (2003: 66) is explicit that they are not mind-dependent or language-dependent entities, since propositions exist in possible worlds

---

[41] See Schiffer (2003: 51–2), who argues that this is a conceptual truth about fictional entities.
[42] See also Friedman (2014).
[43] See Schiffer (2003: 59–64). Armstrong (1989: 77–8) also employs this expression, though he does not accept that all universals are mere shadows of predicates or concepts.

in which no minds or languages depend. Schiffer's pleonastic propositions sound like a species of beings by courtesy.

Part of Schiffer's motivation for thinking that such entities have a diminished status is that their existence is known via trivial inferences.[44] Given the truth of "Fido is a dog," Schiffer claims it trivially follows that "Fido has the property of being a dog" is true.

Recently, Thomasson (2016) has criticized this part of Schiffer's motivation, since she thinks that the existence of ordinary physical objects can also be known via trivial inferences, and yet we do not ascribe a diminished status to them automatically. For example, according to Thomasson, given the truth of "the particles are arranged tablewise," it trivially follows that "the particles compose a table" is true. Regardless of whether Thomasson is correct about the triviality of this inference, I think Thomasson's criticism of Schiffer is apt: from the fact that an object is known via a trivial inference of this sort, we shouldn't automatically conclude that it has a diminished ontological status. (I will provide my own reason for not concluding this via a discussion of properties in a moment.)

On the other hand, I am willing to grant that propositions might be mere beings by courtesy, and that we can know this to be the case via metaphysical inquiry. This is how it is with holes: the arguments that there are holes are in some sense trivial, e.g., (i) some objects are perforated; (ii) perforated objects have holes in them; (iii) so there are some holes in some objects; (iv) so there are holes. But my knowledge that holes have a diminished ontological status is not via my knowing that holes are known via inferences of this sort. Rather, my knowledge is based on a direct awareness of the deficient ontological status of holes. The point of trivial arguments of this sort is not to provide a route to knowing the ontological status of the entities in question, but rather to talk us out of an unwarranted eliminativism about these entities that might tempt us *because we antecedently implicitly recognize their deficient ontological status.*

What about properties? Here again caution is warranted. It might be that the existence of properties in general is known via trivial arguments, and it might be that trivial arguments of this sort support a view on which there is an "abundance" of properties, i.e., more or less a property for every meaningful predicate. It does not follow that each property has the same diminished ontological status. On the contrary, we might wish to hold that although all properties exist, some properties exist more than others. In fact, I do hold exactly this thesis, and it will be the focus of chapter 7.

So Thomasson's criticism of Schiffer is correct. But, as should be obvious, I disagree with Thomasson's suggestion that all things have the same ontological status. Trivial arguments for Fs do not *establish* a deflated ontological status for the

---

[44] Mulligan (2006a: 42) also discusses Schiffer's "nothing to something" inferences but argues that they are to be justified by a theory of intentionality.

Fs, to be sure. But the fact (if it is one) that the existence of ordinary objects can be established via similar arguments also does not *establish* that the Fs and ordinary objects have the same ontological status. Even if the existence of material objects and the existence of holes are both guaranteed by trivial arguments, all holes have a poorer form of existence than (some) material objects. It is a defect of Thomasson's meta-ontological system if it cannot recognize this.

Is it possible that everything is a being by courtesy? I have to confess to a strong inclination to deny this possibility: it is a fundamental metaphysical truth—an axiom if you like—that something is genuinely real. I doubt this truth is capable of proof. But my inclination does not lead me to think that the alternative is either incoherent or should be decisively rejected, or that we should ignore arguments to the contrary. Turner (2011) provides an interesting defense of something like this view, on which the fundamental structure of reality is one without entities.[45] On such a view, nothing *really* exists.

I suspect that there are precedents for such a view in the philosophy of Nāgārjuna. One of the key technical terms in his metaphysical system is "emptiness" and one of the most profound of his doctrines is that *everything* is empty.[46] Unsurprisingly, in the extant secondary literature, there is much debate about what is meant by "emptiness." Here are five of the candidates: to be empty is to fail to be a substance[47]; to be empty is to lack an essence in the strict sense[48]; to be empty is to lack an intrinsic nature[49]; to be empty is to not exist at all, i.e., for it to be illusory that one exists[50]; to be empty is to exist merely conventionally.[51] I would add a sixth candidate for consideration: to be empty is to be a mere being by courtesy, i.e., to exist but not to *really* exist.[52] (And another possibility is that the right conception of emptiness is some combination of the previously mentioned options.)

---

[45] See also Bliss (2013, 2014) for critical examination of the arguments for the claim that there must be fundamental entities.

[46] This is the principal metaphysical thesis of Nāgārjuna (2010 and 2013).

[47] Westerhoff (2009: 24–44) discusses an interpretation of the technical term "svabhāva," which seems to stand for that which exists in the primary way vs. a second-class way of existing. If there were substances, they would exist in a primary way. In Nāgārjuna (2010), Westerhoff opts to translate this term as "substance." Garfield (2002: 10) says that empty things are "devoid of substance"; see also Garfield (2002: 38).

[48] See Garfield (2002: 24, 50–1). I admit I am not sure what "essence" means in this context. By "essence in the strict sense," I mean the non-modal notion of essence defended by Fine (1994a, 1995b) and others; this notion will be the focus of chapter 9. Perhaps it is better to attribute to Garfield the view that empty objects lack intrinsic natures instead (or in addition). See also Westerhoff (2009: 20–3).

[49] See Napper (1989: 3), who writes that all things are empty of "being autonomous entities, of having some 'own thing,' some intrinsic nature that comes from their own side without depending on external causes and conditions or on a subjective factor of those who observe them." See also Garfield (2002: 60–8).

[50] Burton (1999: xi, 4, 39) notes that Nāgārjuna rejects nihilism, but argues that nonetheless Nāgārjuna is committed to it. Westerhoff (2009: 186) notes that many of his competitors attribute nihilism to Nāgārjuna, but that he does not hold it. See also Napper (1989: 4–5).

[51] See Burton (1999: xi, 37) and Siderits (2007: 143–4).

[52] Westerhoff (2009: 24) does identify those things with svabhāva as primary existents rather than secondary ones.

By my lights, there are interesting connections between these various candidate interpretations of "emptiness." I claim that not *really* existing implies not being a substance and not having an essence in the strict sense. (The latter will be discussed in section 9.2.) However, if something is a being by courtesy, it is not an illusion that it exists. And it *might* have an intrinsic nature in some sense, though it certainly does not have a fundamental intrinsic nature. (It might be part of one's intrinsic nature that one lacks a fundamental intrinsic nature.) However, it might be that if *everything* is a being by courtesy, then nothing has a fundamental intrinsic nature; see Turner (2011) for an argument that ontological nihilism understood as the view that nothing really exists implies a kind of holism. Finally, I take it that if something exists merely conventionally—that is, it exists in virtue of our conventions—then it is a being by courtesy, although the converse needn't hold. Nāgārjuna interpretation is *very* hard and I am not prepared to defend here an interpretation on which he holds that nothing *really* exists—but from my amateurish readings, such an interpretation looks tempting, and given the interesting connections between being-by-courtesy (emptiness?) and non-substantiality, lack of essence, and so forth, this interpretation stands posed to make sense of a lot of the positive data for its apparent competitors.[53] A big part of assessing this involves determining how much of Nāgārjuna's interpretation of Buddhist normative theory and its accompanying practice is either really justified by or requires understanding emptiness as conventional existence rather than being-by-courtesy.[54]

If there must be some fully real things, which things are they? Perhaps the entities of our most fundamental scientific theories are good candidates. But what about *us*? It is a Moorean fact that I have hands, that is, that my hands exist. But are there Moorean facts about the *mode of existence* had by hands? Perhaps it is a Moorean fact that my hands do not *subsist*—this is the mode of being had by *abstracta*—but it is not a Moorean fact that my hands are not mere beings by courtesy. Similarly, we can grant that "I think, therefore I am" is a certainty, while denying that "I think, therefore I am a genuine being rather than a being by courtesy" is certain. That I might be a mere being by courtesy is especially disturbing. Our own ontological status is the focus of chapter 6. Unfortunately, we will find in that chapter nothing to conclusively calm our disquiet.

We have seen that there are interesting metaphysical questions about being-by-courtesy. Mapping the realm of being-by-courtesy is apt to be a fruitful project. In this respect, I once again side with Suárez (2005), who thought that one of the tasks of metaphysics is to classify various kinds of beings of reason under different headings.[55]

---

[53] It might be that "emptiness" has no precise translation, and at best what I have a suggested is a good philosophical model in the sense of McDaniel (forthcoming-a).

[54] Interestingly, if being empty just is being a being by courtesy, then we can see why *being empty* is itself empty. As will be discussed in section 5.7, plausibly beings by courtesy enjoy no perfectly natural properties. If being empty were non-empty (if it were a real property), then empty things would enjoy it.

[55] Perhaps to fully complete this task, we must further distinguish between ways of being a being-by-courtesy. For example, Stein (2002: 121–5) discusses the mode of being of privations, but holds that it

Before we move on, one last disturbing possibility should be at least mentioned. This is the possibility that, in a sense, there might be *more* to reality than what is ranged over by the absolutely unrestricted quantifier. Just as we can make sense of the claims of the form *there are Fs but there really aren't Fs*, we can make sense of the claim *there are no Fs but there really are Fs*. The key is to explain what "really" is doing in these sentences. In section 5.4, we briefly discussed the possibility of "super" meanings for "∃." Let $m("∃_s")$ be a "super" meaning for "∃," and let "$∃_s$" be a primitive quantifier with that meaning. $m("∃_s")$ is a "super" meaning in the sense that, for some $Φ$, "$∃_s x\ Φ$ & $\sim∃x\ Φ$" expresses a truth. Suppose that "∃" is not a perfectly natural expression, but not because some semantically primitive restricted quantifier is more fundamental, but rather because the most natural meaning for "∃" is $m("∃_s")$. Relative to "$∃_s$," "∃" is a *restricted* quantifier. Since $m("∃_s")$ is more natural than $m("∃")$, somehow $m("∃_s")$ must fit with use much less than $m("∃")$. I do not believe this possibility obtains, but I have no proof that there is no such meaning as $m ("∃_s")$.[56] If there is, then there is a sense in which there are *more* entities than those ranged over by our most unrestricted quantifier.[57]

5.6 Easy Ontology?

Does recognizing being-by-courtesy have implications for whether certain ontological disputes over the existence of Fs are "easy" in the sense of being easy to settle in favor of the Fs?

Certainly not for all ontological disputes. To take an extreme example, consider the dispute about whether there is a God. It is built into the very concept of God that nothing could be both a God and a mere being by courtesy. There is a God only if there *really* is a God in the peculiarly metaphysical sense of "really."

However, this is not the case for other putative kinds of entity. It is, I think, built into the concept of *substance* that substances are not beings by courtesy. But it is not built into the concept of *table*, *chair*, or even *person*, that these entities are substances. It is not part of the concept of number that numbers have a certain ontological status; nor is it a part of the concept of proposition, or set, or property. Each of these entities might turn out to be mere beings by courtesy. The most compelling arguments for these entities are based on the idea that we cannot avoid quantifying over them, but these arguments do not by themselves also license the claim that the kind of

---

differs from that of negations and that of states of affairs, even though all of these entities are beings of reason, and all of them have their foundations in real things.

[56] Peter Finocchiaro has suggested to me that a certain kind of compositional universalist who also holds that "the folk" speak truly but not restrictedly when they deny there are fusions of trout and turkeys should find this view attractive.

[57] I cannot tell whether these observations should be comforting to those who reject the possibility of unrestricted quantification because of the set-theoretical paradoxes. On the puzzles and perplexities concerning unrestricted quantification, see the papers in Rayo and Uzquiano (2007).

quantification is fundamental.[58] Once we recognize that these entities might be beings by courtesy, should we shift focus away from the questions of whether these entities exist and focus instead on the question of how they exist? Yes.

Let me illustrate this by way of a fable.[59] Our ancestors lived in a linguistic Eden in which, for want of a better phrase, only actual concrete objects were named and quantified over. Perhaps they quantified over types of concrete objects as well, if these entities are not concrete themselves. But this won't play a role in what follows.

But eventually they started telling stories to one another, perhaps in order to make their nights in firelit caves more bearable. At first, these stories were all true stories about actual objects, but soon they began to tell fictional stories. And as these stories became more popular, people began to say things like, "the characters in story A are more interesting than the characters in story B" and "there was some character in that story you told me last night that really stuck with me, but I can't remember the character's name, what was it again?" And thus came the Fall.

Things got worse after that. Soon our ancestors were happily counting holes in blocks of cheese, measuring the lengths of their shadows, describing hallucinatory objects, and quantifying over all manner of unsavory creatures of darkness. We never returned to paradise. Even today, we say things like, "there are seven holes in the cheese," and what's even worse is that these sentences we utter are strictly and literally true. Those among us who have studied our language have found little reason to think that our phrase "some" has a different meaning when used in "some pieces of cheese are stinky" than when used in "some holes are larger than others." And no plausible definition or analysis of this phrase (or others of its ilk) is available to us. It is a semantically primitive quantifier in my sense.

In my parable, phrases can acquire different meanings in response to changes in how they are used.[60] And this has happened with "some," "there is," "exists," and other "ontological expressions." What we mean by "there is" is not what is meant by "there is" in the mouths of our Edenic ancestors. We have forgotten the primordial meaning of "being."

And we cannot go home again. The expressive power of our current language is far too addictive. Think about how one of our ancestors, if she could somehow communicate with us now, would try to express, in her language, "There are as many holes in the cheese as there are colors in the coat of the unicorn I dreamed about last night, but some of these holes are larger than any mouse I've ever seen." We cannot

---

[58]   Thanks to Peter Finocchiaro for discussion here.

[59]   This fable has some important similarities to the fable told in Yablo (2005), but the lesson I draw from it is very different.

[60]   Note that in order for speakers to use "exists" differently, they needn't in advance have a theory about what exists. Our Edenic ancestors did not need to believe that fictional characters exist prior to changing the terms in their language so that they could express that fictional characters exist. Accordingly, I reject van Inwagen's (2014: 69) argument against the possibility of different meanings for ontological expressions, which requires the truth of what I have just denied.

recover our innocence, and each generation born and raised with this augmented language inherits our original metaphysical sin. So endeth the lesson.

Now for the maxims. Language did not evolve so that we could do metaphysics.[61] Communicating efficiently about the wonders of our internal worlds and the dangers of our shared common world are of much more practical interest to us than having a language that corresponds with the ultimate structure of reality, and so it is unsurprising that meanings for our expressions—even those cherished by ontologists— were determined at least as much by the former as by the latter. There are meanings available that serve these practical purposes and enable us to truthfully communicate about dream characters, fictional entities, holes and shadows, and so on. If there are purely linguistic considerations that mandate not taking sentences like "there are holes" or "there are numbers" at face value, so be it—but I doubt that there are. Do not let concerns of ontology determine your theory of the semantic values of natural language expressions. If there is widespread apparent acceptance of various "problematical ontological commitments," seek not paraphrases of them but rather accept them as they are unless other linguistic data decisively tell against the appearances. Rather, fight the ontological fight on the ontological playing field: I do not doubt that there are holes—there are—but I also do not doubt that there are not *really* holes.

Similarly, do not doubt whether there are numbers, properties, or propositions. There are prime numbers between 2 and 9; so there are prime numbers. Wolves and whales have many anatomical properties in common; so there are properties. Ross believed what Elizabeth said; there is something that can be both believed and said, i.e., a proposition. In each case, the premise is true and the inference valid. Believe the conclusion. Then turn to the pressing question of what manners of being these entities enjoy.[62]

It might even turn out that a quantifier that includes numbers, properties, propositions, as well as concrete entities, is more fundamental than the one employed by our Edenic ancestors. From their perspective, then, there *really* are things that there are not—a possibility discussed in section 5.5. Ontological discovery and semantic change of ontological vocabulary can go hand in hand. If an extended meaning relative to the meaning for the quantifier we have actually selected is more natural, and sufficiently many members of our linguistic community discover this fact even if inchoately, we should expect a meaning shift.

(Note that though there is a formal possibility of it being true that there are really things for which there are not, I think it is unlikely that this possibility obtains. Suppose for the sake of argument that there are two meanings for an existential quantifier, the one that we have actually selected and the extended one that by assumption is more natural. Suppose that the range of our actual quantifier is exhausted by entities of kinds K1–K10. Unless there are widespread, frequent, sincere

---

[61]   As van Inwagen (1990: 130) points out, that's not what natural languages are for.
[62]   Compare with Schaffer (2009).

utterances of claims such as "everything belongs to one of K1–K10," the acceptance that everything is one of these kinds is not among the facts about usage relevant to selecting the meaning of the quantifier expressions of our language. But in which case the extended meaning for the quantifier fits with use as well as the putatively actual one—and since by hypothesis it is more natural, on the whole *it* is the better candidate for being the meaning of our quantifier expressions rather than the putatively actual candidate.)

Since the position that certain ontological questions are "easy" is now not uncommon, it might be worth briefly indicating similarities between the view I am attracted to and others extant in the literature.

The most obvious similarity is with Schaffer (2009), who thinks that the interesting questions in ontology concern grounding rather than existence.[63] He thinks that there is an irreducible relation of grounding that can relate entities of all sorts of ontological categories and that structures what there is. My main disagreement with Schaffer, which will become clear in section 8.2, is that I do not think that his notion of grounding is metaphysically fundamental. Rather, it does no work over and above what is done by degrees of being and the other structuring relations (not reducible to grounding!) that multi-category ontologies must recognize. Since all this will be discussed in section 8.2, I will move to other views now. Suffice it to say then that I more or less agree with Schaffer about the status of many ontological questions, while I disagree with the underlying meta-metaphysics he uses to describe their status.

I have already mentioned some of the work of Amie Thomasson (2007, 2015, 2016) earlier in this chapter; she is one of the most prominent and prolific proponents of the easiness of ontological questions. Our positions diverge in several respects. Most importantly, Thomasson does not recognize differences in ontological status between entities, whereas I think it is crucial that we do! If we don't recognize both that holes and their hosts exist in different ways and that holes exist in a less robust way than their hosts, we are not recognizing all the ontological facts. This is the fundamental *ontological* disagreement. But there are also smaller differences about the philosophy of language. For example, I needn't accept that the inference from "there are particles arranged tablewise" to "there are tables" is conceptually or analytically valid. I needn't deny it either; it's just not part of the view I advocate, whereas it is arguably a central part of Thomasson's view.

---

[63] Interestingly, Norton (1977: 88–99) also argues that traditional ontological debates are not about what things exist but rather are about which things can be reduced to other things, and which things cannot be so reduced. This argument forms the basis for Norton's complaint against Quine's conception of ontology. Norton (1977: 98) even employs a notion of ontological priority, although this notion does not appear to be the same as Schaffer's notion of entity grounding. That ontological questions are not simply very general questions about what there is forms the basis for Norton's complaint against Quine's conception of ontology.

Thomas Hofweber (2009: 275–9) argues that natural language quantificational expressions are polysemous. He distinguishes between two readings of quantificational expressions: an inferential reading, in which they are characterized by inferential role, and a second reading in which they are characterized in terms of domains of entities. Consider the question, "are there numbers?" According to Hofweber, if the quantifier in question has the meaning characterized by inferential role, the question is trivially answered with a yes. (Interestingly, Hofweber also has an argument that the answer is "no" if the quantifier expression is intended in the second sense.)

There are many apparent points of conflict between Hofweber's views and my own. First, for me, quantifier expressions are all primarily characterized by their syntactic and inferential roles—a quantifier is something that behaves syntactically and inferentially like the unrestricted existential quantifier of ordinary language. (I am happy to talk in terms of domains as well; but since there are ways of *being,* there are also ways of *being a domain,* and hence the syntactic and inferential characterizations seem more fruitful.) This characterization presupposed that there is one thing that can be identified as *the* unrestricted existential quantifier of ordinary language.[64]

This leads to the second point of difference: as discussed in section 2.2, it is ultimately a matter of indifference to me whether ontological locutions in ordinary language are polysemous or univocal. I am happy to accept that, in ordinary language, "being," "some," "there is," "exist," are basically interchangeable and that all are to be understood in terms of an unrestricted existential quantifier. Whether or not this is the case is to be settled more by linguistics than metaphysics, but it is ultimately an orthogonal issue to what most concerns me: whether there are modes of being and whether some modes are "superior" in some way to others. Linguistic inquiry is relevant to this metaphysical project only in the following ways. First, our patterns of language use *might* track intuitions about modes of being, and insofar as this is a possibility, it would be good to have insight into what those patterns are. Second, philosophical linguistics can provide us with descriptions of possible structures for languages to consider, and some of these structures might be exemplified by metaphysically better languages than English even if they are not exemplified in English itself.

But for Hofweber, it is important that, "there are more numbers than there are planets in the galaxy" is semantically ambiguous, and that on one of its disambiguations, it is false. Maybe that's the case, but the sentence doesn't seem ambiguous. (This is *not* to say that numbers and planets exist in the same way!) Again, this is a matter for linguistics to settle, provided that the linguistics is not constrained by antecedent ontological qualms. I'd be fine if ontological expressions are polysemous

---

[64] This is a presupposition I am happy to accept, but as we will see shortly, I am also in principle willing to reject.

in ordinary language, but my explanation of why certain ontological questions might be "easy" in no way commits me to claims of this sort about ordinary language.

As noted above, there are important differences between the view I like and the views of Schaffer, Thomasson, and Hofweber. But the important similarities should also be stressed. We each believe in readings of "there are numbers" or "some holes are in the cheese" that are straight-up literally true, rather than merely metaphorically true, merely true only given some pretense, or merely true-in-a-fiction.[65] Proponents of such views are motivated by ontological qualms, and perhaps they are right to have such qualms. In the case of almost nothings, qualms are appropriate to be sure! However, such views are *not* justified by these qualms since there are alternatives that better accommodate the qualms without sacrificing the literal truth of what is said in ordinary contexts.

5.7 Metaphysical Reflections on Being-by-Courtesy

In this section, I will briefly discuss some intriguing questions raised by the possibility of beings by courtesy.

First, the main goal of this chapter was to provide a theory that accounts for the intuition that holes and other absences are in some sense real but less real than their hosts. In order to do so, I articulated a distinction between what I call "genuine beings" and "beings by courtesy," and argued that the theory that almost nothings are beings by courtesy satisfies this intuition. But I didn't articulate general principles about when some entity is a mere being by courtesy. We will now consider principles of this sort.

Facts about holes and other almost nothings supervene on facts about "positive" entities.[66] Holes and other almost nothings are mereologically distinct from their hosts. What is suggested by these observations is that in general facts about beings by courtesy supervene on facts about genuine beings. Suppose we learn that the xs are mereologically distinct from the ys but asymmetrically supervene on the ys. Should we conclude that the xs are mere beings by courtesy?

One is reminded of Armstrong's (1982) dictum that that which supervenes is no addition to being.[67] But we must be careful. Suppose there is an omnipotent God such that all else supervenes on the divine will. Is God then the only genuine being? Worse, facts about mathematical and logical entities supervene on facts about concreta, since mathematics and logic are realms of necessary truth. Do mathematica

---

[65] Pace Yablo (2005).

[66] There is one possible exception to this claim. If "global absences" are possible—that is, absences that are the absence of anything positive—then in worlds in which they exist there are no positive entities on which they supervene. But they might still be said to supervene in an indirect way on positive entities, since if they were to exist, the global absences would not. See McDaniel (2013b) for a discussion of global absences and ontological pluralism.

[67] This dictum will receive critical scrutiny in section 7.3.

form a merely superficial superstructure of beings by courtesy?[68] Perhaps a stronger relation than asymmetric supervenience, such as the grounding relations appealed to by Fine (2001) and Schaffer (2009) or the *in virtue of* relation, would be more appropriate to consider.[69]

Suppose that we cannot paraphrase statements about holes and other almost nothings in terms of statements about "positive" entities alone. Perhaps this is because of the limits of our language: there are no infinitely long sentences in English, and the only way to paraphrase talk about holes would be via infinitely long constructions. However, suppose we can conceive of how such a paraphrase might go in an augmented version of English. I think this is the case with holes: with sufficient expressive resources—ones that go far beyond any language we could speak or think—"explicit paraphrases" of talk of holes could be systematically given. If we think this augmented version of English would be a metaphysically better language to speak than ours, even though no quantifier in that language ranged over holes, then we have a reason to think that holes are mere beings by courtesy. Ontological *reduction*, on this picture, amounts to identifying some entity as a mere being by courtesy. Ontological *elimination*, by contrast, consists in denying any sort of reality to the entity in question.[70] Except in very rare cases, such as those in which the positing of any kind of reality to a putative entity would suffice for paradox, it is more warranted to seek an ontological reduction of an entity rather than an ontological elimination.

Once we take seriously that *being* might not be perfectly natural, we need to re-examine other metaphysical notions. Can beings by courtesy exemplify perfectly natural properties or stand in perfectly natural relations? A negative answer to this question is the contemporary analogue of Suárez's (2005: 65–6) claim that "common concepts" cannot apply to both beings of reason and real beings. It is also similar to a view endorsed by Ratnakīrti, according to which (1) there is a distinction between real and less than fully real attributes, (2) there is a distinction between real and non-real entities, and (3) non-real entities cannot exemplify real attributes.[71]

Holes (and other almost nothings) have proper parts and can stand in spatial, temporal, and causal relations with other beings by courtesy and even genuine beings. (When driving, it is very important that one not get too close to a hole in the road.) Parthood, spatiotemporal distance, and causation initially seem to be good candidates for being perfectly natural relations that do not supervene on other perfectly natural properties and relations. Note that all facts about beings by courtesy supervene on and are grounded in facts about genuine beings. So none of those

---

[68] See Eddon (2013) and Wilson (2012) for further reasons to doubt that supervenience and non-fundamentality go hand in hand.

[69] However, as we will see in sections 8.2 and 8.3, there are reasons not to (merely) use a notion of ground to illuminate whether something is a being-by-courtesy.

[70] Compare these remarks with those of Fine (2001).

[71] See McDermott (1969: 40, 70) for a presentation and discussion of this view and the arguments for it.

perfectly natural properties that do not supervene on other perfectly natural properties is enjoyed by beings by courtesy.

I tentatively conclude that parthood, spatiotemporal distance, and causation are not perfectly natural relations. Instead, the perfectly natural relations are parthood*, spatiotemporal distance*, and causation*. These latter relations are each *restricted* relations in that they are exemplified only by genuine beings. The lesson I am inclined to draw is this: if we accept a kind of ontological pluralism that recognizes being-by-courtesy, then we should also accept a kind of pluralism about these relations as well. Just as there are modes of being, some of which are degenerate, there are different kinds of parthood, modes of spatiotemporal relatedness, and so forth.

What about those perfectly natural properties and relations that do supervene on other perfectly natural properties and relations? Could almost nothings enjoy these perfectly natural properties and relations? The most plausible candidates for such properties are higher-order properties: properties enjoyed by abstract objects. Eddon (2013), for example, argues that some fundamental properties (among them quantitative determinates) themselves enjoy fundamental properties. But the paradigmatic beings by courtesy are not abstract objects, but rather are concrete: holes, shadows, heaps of things, arbitrary undetached parts, and so on.[72] As far as I can see, the only potential candidate for being a supervening but fully real property or relation enjoyed by almost nothings is the identity relation. And even then it is not clear to me that the identity relation is a *supervening* relation: if all other perfectly natural properties and relations are not haecceities, then it fails to supervene as well. (We'll discuss haecceities more in section 6.5.)

But I also don't see a particularly compelling reason to think that identity per se is perfectly natural (rather than identity*), and it might be a cleaner theory to follow Suárez all the way and deny that beings by courtesy and genuine beings enjoy "common concepts."[73]

5.8 Chapter Summary

Holes, shadows, and other almost nothings fittingly show the cracks of many ontological theories. Their reality must be recognized, but their way of being must also be recognized as in some way deficient. In this chapter, I discussed several ways

---

[72] Whether there are abstract objects that are also beings by courtesy will be discussed further in chapter 7.

[73] Note that I do not endorse the claim that fundamental objects can't instantiate non-fundamental properties. There is an interesting middle position worth considering, namely that fundamental quantifiers cannot be attached to non-fundamental predicates. That is, if "E" is a fundamental quantifier and "F" is a non-fundamental predicate, then neither "Ex Fx" nor "~Ex Fx" expresses a proposition. A position like this is inspired by some remarks in Siderits (2007: 61–3), who writes at page 62, "at the level of ultimate truth, no statement about persons could be true; all such statements are simply meaningless." The view suggested by these remarks is also similar to what Sider (2011) calls *purity*.

of accounting for the deficiency of the mode of being of almost nothings before settling on the claim that almost nothings have a lower grade or degree of being than other objects. I developed a view on which the degree of being of an object is proportionate to the naturalness of the most natural quantifier that ranges over that object. Beings by courtesy are those beings for which no fundamental quantifier ranges over them. Almost nothings are species of beings by courtesy, but I also discussed whether other kinds of objects might be as well.

6

Persons and Value

6.1 Introduction

I exist and so do you. But in what way (or ways) do we exist? And do we exist to the fullest degree? These questions are not pressing for those philosophers who think that there is only one way to exist, and that there is no distinction between existence, being, and being one of what there is, and who deny that any entity enjoys any more existence or being than any other. For these philosophers, who perhaps are the majority of those who think about these questions, there are still interesting questions about what kind of properties creatures such as ourselves have, but there are no interesting questions about our existential status per se. But, for the reasons articulated in the previous chapters, I am not one of these philosophers, and so the questions are pressing for me. These are the questions I pursue here.

I will focus here on whether we exist to the fullest extent. To recall the results from the previous chapter, an entity exists to the fullest extent just in case it enjoys a fundamental mode of being. A fundamental mode of being is a perfectly natural mode of being. One enjoys a mode of being just in case one falls within the range of the possible quantifier that corresponds to this mode. In general, the degree of being enjoyed by some entity is proportionate to the naturalness of the most natural mode of being enjoyed by that entity.

In what follows, I will distinguish three different views on which persons enjoy a fundamental mode of being. On the first view, persons enjoy a fundamental mode of being that is also enjoyed by other entities that are not persons. On the second view, there is a distinctive fundamental mode of being that is enjoyed by all and only persons. The third view is the most radical: on it, each person enjoys a fundamental mode of being that is enjoyed by *only* that person.

Note that I am primarily interested in the question of whether those things who are persons are fully real, and am only derivatively interested in the questions of whether persons are essentially persons or whether being a person is itself a fundamental property.

It turns out to be very difficult to defend the view that we are fully real, but perhaps not impossible. The primary goal of this chapter is to show just how complex the issues involved are.

But before we dive into the question of our ontological status, let us consider why we should care to dip into these waters at all. The short answer is that there are interesting connections between normative and evaluative status and ontological status. These connections will be sketched in the next section. In the remaining sections of this chapter, we'll focus on whether we are fully real and on various routes towards establishing our full reality.

6.2 Being and Value

A certain evaluative conception of ourselves and our place in reality presupposes that we are fully real, and to the extent that our ontological status is dubitable so too is this evaluative conception. I doubt that this evaluative conception can be lightly surrendered. But let's begin by first describing it and then assessing how this self-conception is connected to other normative and evaluative judgments.

We take ourselves to be beings that matter. We are persons, and persons *count*. Among other things, this implies that persons *are to be counted*. If we are beings by courtesy, a more objective ontological scheme would not countenance us. Fundamentally, we would not be counted. We would not count.

I do not think that this line of reasoning simply equivocates on what "are to be counted" means but rather captures that a necessary condition for persons mattering in the way that we take them to matter is that they are really to be counted, that is, they are fully real.

To see this, let's put a theological spin on the issue. Whether God cognizes beings of reason is a thorny theological question unsurprisingly addressed by Suárez in his comprehensive *Metaphysical Disputations*.[1] On the one hand, we have knowledge of beings of reason, and God is omniscient, so God must have knowledge of what we have knowledge of.[2] Knowledge of a thing requires cognition of a thing, and so God must cognize beings of reason. On the other hand, cognition of beings of reason is no perfection, but rather manifests imperfection and weakness. As I noted in the previous chapter, the explanation of why we think in terms of beings of reason (or, as I would prefer to put it, why we think in terms of beings by courtesy) ultimately rests on our essential finitude. God is essentially infinite and perfect, and hence God does not cognize beings of reason. Suárez sides with the latter opinion: God cognizes us as we are—finite, weak, imperfect—and this suffices for God to be attributed knowledge of beings of reason even though God does not cognize beings of reason. But God does not think in terms of beings of reason. They are beneath God's

---

[1] Specifically, Disputation 54, section 2, subsections 19–24 (Suárez 2005: 79–84).
[2] Recall that beings of reason were extensively discussed in sections 5.4 and 5.5. Since I take beings of reason to be a subspecies of beings by courtesy, I should at least note that I see the theological considerations pondered by Suárez as being sufficiently general to cover all beings by courtesy rather than a mere subset of them.

contemplation. Suárez's resolution of this dilemma presupposes that we are not beings of reason—God after all does cognize us. On Suárez's view, we are beings in the eyes of God. But, if we are mere beings by courtesy, we are not fit objects for divine cognition. We are not beings in the eyes of God. From the point of view of God, we would be nothing. Far from being created in the image of God, we would be mere shadows of God's true creations.

Suárez had the idea that beings of reason are not fit objects of God's cognition. A more general view is that cognition should be directed away from beings by courtesy and towards the fully real to the extent that this is possible. This seems to be the attitude of Kant. Recall that, for Kant, given the natures that we in fact have, ignorance of things in themselves is inescapable. This is a fact to be regretted rather than merely acknowledged. In some way, it would be better (or perhaps we would be better off) if we were to know things as they are in themselves.[3]

Kant famously distinguishes between *things in themselves* and *appearances*.[4] Let us say that *mere phenomena* are those appearances that are not numerically identical with something that can be properly considered as it is in itself. Those interpreters of Kant who hold that the distinction between appearances and things in themselves is merely a distinction between two ways of considering one and the same set of objects will deny that there are mere phenomena in my sense, as will those interpreters who think that the distinction is one between two sets of properties of one and the same set of entities.[5] There might be some appearances that are not mere phenomena, but my current view is that some appearances are mere phenomena. Among the mere phenomena are the objects of outer sense. My current inclination is to think that *mere phenomena* are beings of reason. They are derivative entities, that is, entities that enjoy a deficient mode of reality, which Kant calls *empirical reality*, whereas those things that are not mere phenomena enjoy a better mode of being. Things in themselves enjoy *transcendental reality*.[6] It sucks for us that our knowledge is limited to mere phenomena or to aspects of things that do not inform us of the fundamental features of that which they are aspects of. In the Kantian philosophy, there is a connection between a kind of ontological status and a kind of evaluative status: things in themselves would be better to know, and we unfortunately must settle for (genuine) knowledge of appearances.[7] If we ourselves are mere phenomena, then we are not the best objects of our own knowledge. This would be a disquieting result.

---

[3] Langton (1998: 13–14, 30, 42–3) stresses Kant's expressions of loss and dismay at our ignorance of things in themselves.

[4] The distinction appears early in the B-edition of the *Critique of Pure Reason* (Kant 1999a: 112, Bxx) and is frequently appealed to thereafter in both versions.

[5] See Alison (2004) for a classic defense of a "one-world view." Langton (1998) is another. For a recent and sophisticated defense of the two-worlds view, see Stang (2014).

[6] Gibson (1998: 23) also suggests that Kant believes in two kinds of existence.

[7] Witt (2003: 5, 94–6) suggests that Aristotle also accepts a normative hierarchy that goes hand in hand with an ontological hierarchy. The actual is ontologically prior to the potential and is prior in value as well.

The idea that the direction of our cognition should be towards the fundamental still informs contemporary metaphysics. Sider (2009: 401), for example, writes:

Structure has an evaluative component. The goal of inquiry is not merely to believe many true propositions and few false ones. It is to discern the structure of the world. An ideal inquirer must think of the world in terms of its distinguished structure; she must carve the world at its joints in her thinking and language. Employers of worse languages are worse inquirers.

Note how many normative or evaluative concepts are expressed in this single paragraph: *goal of inquiry*, *ideal inquirer*, *must*, and *worse*. Far from pinning down a single evaluative component of the notion of structure, Sider invokes several, and it is not clear which among them, if any, he takes to be most central.

My preference would be to focus on a notion that Sider does not explicitly invoke, that of *correctness*. This normative notion plays a central role in the meta-ethical system of Franz Brentano, who uses it to provide a reductive account of intrinsic value. According to Brentano (1969: 18, 25–6), something is intrinsically good if and only if an act of love that takes that thing as its object is correct; something is intrinsically bad if and only if an act of hate that takes that thing as its object is correct; and one thing is intrinsically better than another just in case a preference for the first over the second is correct. Do not let the terminology of love and hate distract you: for Brentano, any pro-attitude directed towards an object is an act of love and any con-attitude directed towards an object is an act of hate.[8]

Here are some intuitive examples. The pleasure that I take in my older daughter's delight in learning how condensation works is a correct act of love. The pain that I take in the physical pain experienced by the same daughter when she falls face first into the sidewalk is a correct act of hate. Finally, my preference for knowledge over ignorance is a correct preference.[9] For Brentano, a notion of correctness also provides an account of truth: a belief is true if and only if it is correct.[10]

The notion of correctness is sufficiently clear for Brentano's accounts to be intelligible and worth considering. Moreover, we can (and should) accept the biconditionals linking correctness to intrinsic value and truth even if we deny them the status of reductions. But we can go beyond Brentano as well. Brentano

---

As Witt (2003: 95) puts it, "what is prior in being turns out also to be what is better and more valuable," and to be clear this is no accident; for Witt (2003), Aristotle's hierarchy of being is intrinsically normative.

[8] For example, in Brentano (1973) examples of acts of love include instances of pleasure, of desire, and even of preference. Moreover, Brentano (1973: 200) tells us that *every* emotion is "principally distinguished by being one of love or of hatred."

[9] Note that Brentano (1969: 20–2) also holds that in each of these examples I not only have correct emotions but also I experience them as being correct. It is *self-evident* that it is correct to prefer knowledge to ignorance.

[10] See Brentano (1969: 18). Note that one can accept that a belief is true if and only if it is correct as well as further biconditionals, e.g., that a belief is true if and only if the object of the belief exists. Brentano (1969: 74–5) defends this as well.

employs the notions of correctness to whole propositional attitudes such as desires, preferences, and beliefs. I suggest that we can also assess the correctness of sub-propositional objects. I offer for consideration the following: a *concept*, which, as Kant told us in the first *Critique*, is a predicate of a possible judgment, is correct to the extent that it is a concept of something fully real.[11] In general, one might hold that any sub-act of a propositional attitude that has content is correct to the extent that the object of that act is fully real. The most fit objects of our thoughts are those that are fully real.

This is not to say that every object-oriented attitude is correct *only* to the extent that its object is fully real. Some emotions are directed towards objects rather than propositions or states of affairs; one kind of love is directed towards objects. One might love Hitler; perhaps Hitler, like all persons, is fully real; and yet one's love of Hitler is not clearly thereby correct. But there is one object-directed attitude that is maximally correct if and only if its object is fully real: the attitude of attending to. On this way of thinking, some objects are fit for attention and others are not. Beings by courtesy are not cognized by God because a perfect being attends only to those objects that are most fit for attention.

If we are mere beings by courtesy, then we are not ourselves fit objects for our thoughts. There is a sense then in which our self-conceptions are irredeemably flawed. Moreover, if we accept that there is a connection between correctness and value across the board—which I am also inclined to do, even without accepting that this connection amounts to a reduction—then there is also a sense in which being is a kind of value: it is metaphysical goodness. Fully real beings enjoy a certain kind of metaphysical goodness that beings by courtesy lack. If we are beings by courtesy, we are less good qua beings than we might have hoped to be.

I have stressed the importance of our full reality to our evaluative self-conception. However, perhaps our self-conception is something we should give up. In section 5.5, we discussed the philosophy of Nāgārjuna, who held that everything—which includes us!—is *empty*. I tentatively suggested that we might take *emptiness* either to be or to imply lack of full reality. According to this tentative interpretation of Nāgārjuna's philosophy, our ignorance of our own ontological status is one of the barriers to achieving liberation from suffering.[12] And more generally, the doctrine of "no-self" has been taken to be central to various strands of Buddhist philosophy.[13] One way of interpreting the doctrine of no-self is that there are two kinds of existence: conventional existence, the kind had by ordinary things including ourselves, and fundamental existence. Various strands of Buddhism

---

[11] See Kant (1999a: 205, A69/B94).

[12] Fenner (1990: 37) says that, for Nāgārjuna, a necessary condition of liberation is recognizing the emptiness of everything; according to Fenner (1990: 42), "intrinsic existence" is what empty things lack. Westerhoff (2009: 157) says that no longer thinking of oneself as substantial is essential to liberation.

[13] See Siderits (2007: 26–7, ch. 3).

might disagree on whether anything has the latter kind.[14] But the dominant view is that we do not.[15]

There are also strands of the no-self doctrine in Western philosophy. Hume (1958: 251–3) notoriously raised skeptical doubts about a real self. In the tradition of British Idealism, the question of whether persons or selves are in some way less than fully real marked a real divide. Personalists accepted the fundamentality of persons. Prominent examples include Calkins (1927) and McTaggart (1927a, 1927b).[16] On the other side of the divide were Bosanquet et al. (1917–18) and Bradley (1930); Bosanquet (1917–18) treated persons (and other finite entities) as something like attributes of the universe as a whole, while Bradley (1914: 448) endorsed an ontology with degrees of being.[17]

These are important counter-perspectives to the one defended here.

6.3 Being as a Fundamental Mode

As noted in section 5.5, I grant the soundness of the *Cogito* argument: one can infer from the claim that one thinks to the claim that one is, i.e., has being. But it would be a mistake to then immediately infer that one is fully real. One can infer that one exists but not how one exists from the mere claim that one is thinking. This point is intimately related to Kant's criticism of rational psychology: one is not entitled to infer that one exists as an *unconditioned* substance from the mere claim that one is thinking. In general, the conclusions deliverable by the *Cogito* are limited. The *Cogito* cannot by itself teach us that we are substances, or that we are simple, or even that we persist over time. To think otherwise would be to succumb to what Kant calls *paralogisms of pure reason*.[18]

There are many genuine modes of being. But we needn't determine which among them persons enjoy to determine whether persons are fully real if being itself is a fundamental mode of being. For then the *Cogito* in conjunction with this claim would quickly deliver one's own fundamentality. And each person could run the same argument for herself. My question would be answered, and this chapter would be finished.

---

[14] Siderits (2007: 53–5) notes that in early Buddhist philosophies there is a kind of ontological bias against composite objects: "wholes are not really real, only their parts are." (Note the peculiar phrase "really real," which was the subject of much discussion in sections 5.4 and 5.5.) Siderits (2007: 69) also distinguishes between things that do and do not exist in a strict sense. See also Siderits (2007: 111–13).

[15] One school of Buddhism, the Puggalavadins, did affirm the full reality of human persons. See Laumakis (2008: 137–8) for a brief discussion.

[16] See McDaniel (forthcoming-c and 2009d) for overviews of their respective philosophies.

[17] See Mander (2011: 384) for further discussion of Bosanquet.

[18] See Kant's *Critique of Pure Reason*, specifically the subsection of the transcendental dialectic titled "The Paralogisms of Pure Reason." This begins at A341/B399 (Kant 1999a: 411).

Unfortunately, in the previous chapter, I argued from the premise that shadows, holes, cracks, and other entities that I called "almost nothings" exist to the conclusion that being itself is not fundamental.

However, we belong to many different kinds: we are persons, we are animals, we are living beings, we are physical objects, and we are concrete beings. If any of those kinds corresponds to a fundamental mode of being, then we are fully real. One plausible candidate for being a kind corresponding to a fundamental mode of being is the kind *concrete object*, since on some traditions, the distinction between the concrete and the abstract marks a genuine ontological divide: the mode of being of concreta is *existence*, whereas abstract objects, strictly speaking, do not *exist* but rather enjoy a different mode of being, such as *validity* (in Lotze 1889) or *ideal being* (in Husserl 2005a and 2005b), or *subsistence* (in Russell 1997 and Meinong 1904).

Unfortunately, the domain of concreta appears to contain mere beings by courtesy as well. The obvious examples of beings by courtesy are mere aggregates of substances such as piles of trash or heaps of sand, arbitrary undetached parts, and arbitrary fusions of entities. Similar worries arise about the kind *material object*: each of the above objects is a material object. The judgment that these entities exist at all is somewhat contentious, at least among philosophers, although no parent of small children can deny that they create numerous heaps and piles of other entities on a daily basis. (At the end of each day, I disassemble many such piles of clothing, drawings, toys, pets, and miscellaneous recyclables.)

It's not nuts to think that all simples and composites of simples are ontologically on a par, all enjoying equal reality, and hence heaps and piles are fully real, as well as arbitrary undetached parts of things. But if you are like me, you smell more than a whiff of unreality about some of these entities, and you think that neither *concrete object* nor *material object* corresponds to a fundamental mode of being.

Mere aggregates and arbitrary undetached parts are not living beings, animals, or persons. So the possibility that *living being, animal*, or *person* correspond to fundamental modes of being is not yet eliminated. I won't examine whether being alive or being an animal correspond to a fundamental mode of being here, but in the next section I will briefly discuss whether being a person corresponds to a fundamental mode.[19]

6.4 Interlude: Personhood as a Fundamental Mode of Being or as a Fundamental Property

There are two strategies for arguing that being a person is a fundamental mode of being that I will not defend, but which, due to their historical importance, deserve at least a brief discussion.

---

[19] In section 1.2, we briefly mentioned Heidegger's (1962: 285) view that living beings that are not Dasein have as their mode of being *Life*.

The first strategy is via arguing for a kind of idealistic metaphysic on which everything is a person, or is at least intimately related to a person in some way. McTaggart's (1927a, 1927b) staggeringly immense work, *The Nature of Existence*, defends the view that, as a matter of necessity, reality consists of persons, parts of persons, states of persons (such as perception and love), and nothing else. Now McTaggart does not believe in degrees of being, and he is not inclined to give much weight to commonsensical judgments about what there is.[20] On McTaggart's view, it is just flat out false that there are holes, mere aggregates, and so forth, so it is just flat out false that there are the sort of counter-examples that I worried about earlier to the claim that being is fundamental. We have a radically false view of what beings there are. Strictly, on McTaggart's view, being a person does not correspond to a fundamental mode of being, but being either a person, part of a person, or state of a person does, since it corresponds to being, the only mode that there is.

A second McTaggartian route towards the conclusion that persons are fully real is via the claim that *personality* is a fundamental property. This route is an instance of a more general strategy that will be pursued in detail in section 6.5. The strategy relies on the claim, made in section 5.7, that instantiating a fundamental property suffices for being fully real. For now, we will focus specifically on the claim that personality is fundamental. Personality is the property of being a self. According to McTaggart (1927b: 62; 1996: 88), the quality of personality is both simple and indefinable, and is known to us via self-perception of something that has this quality. I submit that if a property is both simple and indefinable, then it is a fundamental property in the sense at issue. Unfortunately, McTaggart does not have an argument that personality is simple and indefinable, but merely rests on the claim that it appears to be so. The general idealism of McTaggart and McTaggart's claim that personality is simple and indefinable do not strike me as promising. Let's move on.

The second strategy relies not on argument but rather on phenomenological description. In Heidegger's *Being and Time*, we are confronted with, among other things, the task of accounting for the various fundamental modes of being and determining how those modes relate to one another and to being itself. The task of phenomenology is to describe what is given in experience as it is given, and Heidegger thinks that among what is given are the modes of being of various entities encountered in experience. Recall that among the modes encountered are *readiness-to-hand*, the mode of being of tools; *presentness-at-hand*, roughly, the mode of being of lumps of matter; *life*, the mode of being of living things that are not persons; and *Existenz*, which is the mode of being of Daseins, which is the kind of thing we are.[21]

Although Heidegger would be unhappy with the claim that "Dasein" just means "person," I believe we can set aside this worry. Here's why: something is a Dasein *only*

---

[20] See McTaggart (1927a: 4) on degrees of being, and McDaniel (2009d) for brief discussion, as well as an overview of McTaggart's methodology for metaphysics.

[21] On these modes of being in Heidegger (1962), see pp. 67, 97–8, 121, and 285 respectively.

if it is a being who enjoys intentional states, who is capable of language use, who has social interactions with other Daseins, and who is governed by norms of various kinds. These *necessary* conditions on being a Dasein are, I believe, *sufficient* conditions for being a person. So, if Daseins enjoy a fundamental mode of being, *Existenz*, then at least some persons do as well. If one could show that all persons are Daseins, one will thereby have established that being a person corresponds to a fundamental mode of being. Moreover, even if I am wrong that being a Dasein suffices for being a person, at rock bottom what matters most is that we are fully real rather than that we are fully real persons. It is sufficient to satisfy our existential concern that we are Daseins who each enjoy a fundamental mode of being.[22]

At this point, it is worth mentioning an interesting position in Heidegger interpretation according to which we are not Daseins but rather what we are is *cases* of or *instances* of Dasein.[23] Don't think of Dasein, on this interpretation, as a type of thing of which we are tokens, but rather think of the relation between Dasein and us as akin to the relation between cancer and cases of cancer. For our purposes here, it suffices to note that, on this interpretation, the full reality of Dasein might not suffice for our full reality. It depends on whether a case (in the sense at issue) of something is guaranteed to be as real as that of which it is a case.

It is not clear what role phenomenology should play in ontological investigation. As noted in the introduction, one historically prominent motivation for ontological pluralism is that ontological pluralism is (allegedly) a consequence of the correct phenomenological description. I find this motivation incredibly intriguing, but at the end of the day I am not sure what to make of it. For this reason, I will set it aside here and return to a consideration of speculative arguments.

6.5 Real Beings and Real Properties

One way to make headway on the question of whether one is fundamental is to consider additional metaphysical theses concerning the fundamental in general. Let's consider the principle, articulated in section 5.7, that only fully real entities can enjoy perfectly natural properties and relations. (Note that this principle states a necessary condition for enjoying perfectly natural properties, not a necessary and sufficient condition, although in the course of things we would eventually consider the logically stronger principle as well.) If this principle is correct and persons do enjoy perfectly

---

[22] In a similar vein, consider the remark by Merleau-Ponty (2000: xiii) that "I certainly do not exist in the way in which things exist." Persons are not things; they exist in fundamentally different ways. And since we are free in a way that things are not, we are not "to be counted among things" (2000: 435). Rashdall (1902: 382–4) also distinguishes between the being of persons and those of things; see Mander (2011: 367, 405) for further commentary. (Rashdall and Mander both mention the being of persons vs. that of things and the essence of persons vs. those of things. The connection between being and essence will be further explored in chapter 9.)

[23] This interpretation is defended by Haugeland (2013). We'll revisit his interpretation in section 9.5.

natural properties, then persons are fully real. In what follows, I'll presuppose the principle and focus on whether persons enjoy any such properties. (If the principle is false, we lose one further route to showing the full reality of persons, so our case is *not* strengthened if it fails.)

Some candidate properties spring to mind. First, consider shape properties, such as being three-dimensional or being triangular. Shape properties might seem like good candidates for being perfectly natural properties, and persons have shapes. So here are the makings for a quick argument for the full reality of persons.

Unfortunately, this quick argument fails for multiple reasons. First, I don't think that the shape properties of persons are perfectly natural properties because, in general, the shape properties of any material objects are not perfectly natural. Rather, a material object has the shape that it has in virtue of occupying a region (or regions) of space–time.[24] The shape properties of regions of space–time might (or might not) be perfectly natural, but if the shape properties of material objects are instantiated in virtue of occupying regions with certain shapes, then the shape properties of material objects are extrinsic properties. And I do not think that extrinsic properties can be perfectly natural properties.[25]

Second, and perhaps as troubling, holes and shadows also have shapes. But holes and shadows are not fully real. And so, at the very least, the shape properties that they enjoy cannot be perfectly natural properties. (Recall the discussion of section 5.7.) It would be good to have an independent reason for thinking that the shape properties had by persons are perfectly natural. Otherwise the argument for the full reality of persons will be pretty weak.

Note that a similar worry can be raised about an appeal to spatial (or spatiotemporal) relations, upon which one might reasonably assume shapes to supervene.[26] Persons stand in distance relations to other things. If distance relations are perfectly natural—if they are real relations—then persons must be fully real. But holes also stand in distance relations to other things—and so the distance relations that they enjoy must not be perfectly natural. Similar remarks apply to the idea that *occupation* is a perfectly natural relation that relates occupants of space–time to space–time itself.[27]

What about the properties that are postulated by physics? Persons have mass, for example, although they have the mass property that they have in virtue of having parts that have certain mass properties. (Let's distinguish this claim from the stronger, and perhaps empirically false, claim that the mass of a composite object

---

[24] See McDaniel (2007) for a defense of this claim.

[25] This is a consequence of Lewis's (1986) account of the extrinsic–intrinsic distinction. But I regard it as plausible independently of whether Lewis's view is true.

[26] I do not think this is quite right: the shapes of regions of space–time might supervene on the distance relations between their parts, but, in general, the shapes of the occupants of space–time regions supervene on the shapes of the regions they occupy.

[27] I advocated that occupation is perfectly natural in McDaniel (2007).

is always the sum of the masses of its parts.) That said, as noted in section 2.2, I think that all determinates of a given determinable are equally natural and as natural as the determinable itself. So if the mass property enjoyed by a person is a determinate of the same determinable as the mass property enjoyed by, for example, a fundamental particle, then that person is fully real if that mass property enjoyed by that fundamental particle is fully real. So, for me, the issue is whether the mass property enjoyed by a composite object really is a determinate of the same determinable as that enjoyed by a fundamental particle. I don't know how one goes about settling this. (Does the fact that it makes good sense to assign numbers to quantities of mass and perform algebraic operations on those numbers settle the issue?) Similar remarks apply to other putatively fundamental properties postulated by physics. Persons have a net-charge in virtue of having parts that enjoy various charges. Is the net-charge of a person a determinate of the same determinable as the charge of one of the electrons that are among her parts?

Net-charge and net-mass are good candidates for being perfectly natural properties, and, moreover, holes cannot enjoy such properties, unlike shape. This is good, since it is a constraint on my project that any argument for the full reality of persons not generalize to an argument for the full reality of holes. However, arbitrary undetached parts and mere aggregates of material objects also enjoy net-charge and net-mass. I am more willing to accept the full reality of these things than I am of holes. But that this argument would generalize to cover arbitrary objects does give me pause.

What about causation, or power, or some other notion of efficacy? Trenton Merricks (2003) endorses a metaphysics on which all composite objects have non-redundant causal powers. He argues that alleged composites such as baseballs do not enjoy novel causal powers over and above those enjoyed by their parts and hence do not exist. But on Merricks's view, persons do enjoy novel causal powers. Now although the *fundamental* ontology I find attractive is similar to Merricks's metaphysic in that the only material things that are *fully* real are persons and the objects of successful scientific discourse (which would include the objects of biology), I do not follow Merricks in *eliminating* things such as baseball bats or cars. Although perhaps they are not fully real, they do enjoy some degree of reality. Still, maybe we can use Merricks's appeal to novel causal powers as a way to argue for the full reality of people.

My inclination is that causal powers are not perfectly natural, and that things do not have causal powers independently of the properties that they enjoy. So if a person has causal powers that are not had in virtue of the powers of her parts, it must be because the person has properties that are genuinely novel, i.e., are intrinsic properties that do not supervene on the perfectly natural properties or relations of her parts. And it is these novel properties that underwrite any novel causal powers that the persons might enjoy.[28] For this reason, in

---

[28] Compare with Merricks (2003: 93–117).

what follows, I will focus not on emergent causal powers but rather on emergent properties.[29]

What could those novel properties be? One candidate class of properties is the class of *qualia*, which we will turn to next. Qualia are properties like *the feel one has when one tastes an orange* and *the way cinnamon smells*.

Let's start with the putative case for the fundamentality of qualia. The case will unsurprisingly be very contentious. For now, let's use the label *physical properties* for the natural properties discoverable via fundamental physics. First premise: there is a possible world that is just like the actual world with respect to the distribution of the perfectly natural physical properties and relations but that differs with respect to the distribution of qualia. One such world is a world in which all qualia are absent, even though there are biological creatures much like us.[30] Let us grant for now that there is such a world.

Second, the case for the fundamentality of qualia employs a putative sufficient condition for being a perfectly natural property: P is a perfectly natural property if P is a qualitative property and the distribution of P fails to supervene on the distribution of all other perfectly natural properties and relations. (What is a qualitative property? Hard question—we'll discuss it briefly in section 6.7. For now, it suffices to note that on any acceptable account of the qualitative/non-qualitative distinction, qualia are qualitative properties.) Note that, if the first premise is true, then some qualia fail to supervene on the distribution of all of the perfectly natural *physical* properties and relations.

Third, the case depends on the plausible hunch that there are no other perfectly natural properties and relations than the perfectly natural physical properties and relations that are good candidates for being among the supervenience base of qualia.[31] So some qualia fail to supervene on the distribution of all other perfectly natural properties and relations, hence, given our sufficient condition, are themselves perfectly natural properties and relations.

So far, (perhaps) so good. But even if we grant each step in the argument, we aren't yet in a position to conclude that persons are fully real. True, no less-than-fully-real object can enjoy a perfectly natural property or stand in a perfectly natural relation: but even if we have established that qualia are fundamental, we haven't yet established that it is *persons* who instantiate the qualia. And this is the next thing that would need to be established in order to successfully argue that persons are fully real.

---

[29] Note that it does not strictly follow from the fact that causal powers supervene on properties that certain causal powers are not themselves perfectly natural properties. However, I will assume that they are not.

[30] These are philosophical zombies in Chalmers's (1997: 95) sense. The argument presented here is heavily indebted to Chalmers's work.

[31] In short, I reject the hypothesis floated by Chalmers (1997: 126–7) that there are "proto-phenomenal" properties.

Here is one place where considerations of how things persist, and specifically how *persons* persist, come into play. Let me say at the outset that it is compatible with the doctrine of temporal parts that persons are fully real. But the doctrine of temporal parts does undercut one way of establishing that persons are fully real. On the strongest version of the doctrine of temporal parts, a persisting thing has a temporal part corresponding to every sub-interval of the interval of time across which that entity persists. On the weakest version of the doctrine of temporal parts, the possession of temporal parts coincides with the possession of changing intrinsic properties: in effect, an entity has distinct temporal parts only to the extent that its possession of them suffices to avoid the problem of temporary intrinsics. Consider a world that consists of a persisting spherical ball that changes from blue to red. Suppose the ball is blue for one hour before the change begins, and suppose that the change is instantaneous and that the ball is red for one hour afterwards. On this weaker version of the doctrine of temporal parts, the persisting ball is composed of two temporally smaller entities: a persisting temporal part that is blue and a persisting temporal part that is red. The persisting ball has no temporally smaller temporal parts than these two. And there are many intermediate versions of the doctrine of temporal parts that are worth considering.

But, on any version, the doctrine of temporal parts raises trouble for the argument from the naturalness of qualia to the fundamentality of persons. Qualia are supposed to be intrinsic properties, and moreover, they are temporary properties: that qualitative chocolatey taste disappears so quickly, which is why I must eat chocolate chip cookie after chocolate chip cookie. On even the weakest version of the doctrine of temporal parts, I have distinct temporal parts corresponding to each distinct episode of chocolatey enjoyment. Moreover, it is these temporal parts that are the bearers of the qualia: a persisting thing can be said to have the qualia *at a time* just in case it has a temporal part that is located at that time and has that qualia period. Now it is true that temporal parts theorists do not accept in full generality the claim that an object is F at time *t* just in case it has a temporal part that is located at *t* which is F. But the exceptions to this principle are, in general, extrinsic properties. With respect to temporary intrinsic properties like shapes or qualia, the principle holds.

So, if four-dimensionalism is true, at best considerations from qualia support that persons have some fundamental person-like temporal parts, but not that persons are fully real. I suppose that, if one such person-like temporal part were to exist without being part of a larger person, then *it* would count as a person. However, such an occurrence is at most merely possible. But perhaps the qualia argument can promise the possibility of fully real people, albeit very short-lived ones.

Perhaps there are qualia that last long enough that they can be attributed to whole persisting persons directly rather to any of that person's temporal stages. Recall that Hume's (1958: 251–3) skepticism about our possessing an idea of a self was driven by his inability to locate any permanent impressions that could correspond to such an idea. One early responder to Hume was Henry Home (2000: 123–4), who argued that each of us has an original feeling of selfhood from which our idea of selfhood derives. Unfortunately, Home thought that this original feeling is not one that is constantly possessed. Similarly, perhaps the feeling of being embodied is a persisting qualitative experience that a person has throughout her existence.[32] But this also does not seem to be the case, since we seem to continue to exist while in a dreamless slumber, and I doubt that we feel embodied in these scenarios.[33]

But set these worries aside. Even if we grant that there is a permanent sense of the self or a permanent feeling of embodiment, and hence that some qualia can be assigned directly to the whole persisting person rather than via their temporal parts, there is still a further issue. Even if some qualia are perfectly natural, it is not obvious that all of them are. Perhaps there are some qualia that supervene on other qualia, and if so, we at least need a reason to think that the supervening qualia are themselves perfectly natural, since they do not satisfy the principle for being perfectly natural that I articulated earlier. I don't know about a sense of the self, but the sense of embodiment is a plausible candidate for being a quale that supervenes on other, shorter-lived qualia. And in which case, it is not obviously fundamental, and if it is not, it does us no good here.

So at most we have articulated an argument for the claim that proper temporal parts of persons are fully real. But that proper temporal parts of persons might be fully real is itself a troubling thought, especially in the absence of an argument that persons are fully real. One of the earliest worries about the doctrine of temporal parts seems to be that, on this view, nothing really persists: there are just short-lived temporal parts. (This worry would be somewhat misguided as a response to the weaker versions of the doctrine of temporal parts on which there could be temporally extended objects without proper temporal parts.) Probably one source of this intuition is the thought that composition is inherently a spatial relation in the sense that it always relates things that are themselves spatially related to one another. If you have this thought, it will be hard to see how there could be a composition relation that takes in its domain objects existing at different, non-overlapping, times, and so hard to see how there could be anything temporally extended. But, on this thought, there would also be no way to build time out of time's temporal parts either, and I think this is one reason to reject this possible source of the intuition that on the doctrine of temporal parts, nothing really persists.[34]

But even if an (or even if the) original source of the intuition stems from a false judgment about composition, something like that intuition might be right: perhaps we

---

[32] I owe this suggestion to Jordan Dodd.

[33] An extreme defender of a kind of psychological approach to personal identity could deny that we exist while "in a dreamless slumber." On this view, we are a temporally gappy fusion of psychologically connected temporal parts. See Hudson (2001) for the articulation of this kind of view.

[34] That said, Joshua Spencer has pointed out to me that, since there are many kinds of composition, the intuition that spatial objects must be spatially related in order to stand in *their kind of composition* would not necessarily compromise moments of time from composing *in a different way* longer intervals of time.

have a good reason to think that certain temporal parts are fully real, and perhaps we have a good reason to think that cross-temporal fusions exist, but have not yet produced an argument for the claim that cross-temporal fusions are themselves fully real. Remember that we have some reason to reject the claim that fusions of fully real things are always themselves fully real: the cases of mere aggregates or heaps, mentioned earlier in this chapter, provide compelling counter-examples. We shouldn't immediately assume that fusions of fully real things are never themselves fully real. But in the absence of an argument for the full reality of a given object, perhaps our default assumption should be that it is not. On such a view, the short-lived enjoyers of qualia are fully real, but (perhaps) nothing fully real persists beyond them.

As far as I am aware, those foes of the doctrine of temporal parts who are moved by the worry that on the doctrine of temporal parts nothing really persists are not typically moved to argue that time itself is unreal in the sense that there are only moments of time and no temporally larger object made out of these instances. Why the asymmetry?

There is a plausible picture of the nature of time according to which the fundamental bearer of geometrical properties, broadly construed, is time itself.[35] (Or better: space–time itself.) On this sort of view, parts of time (or space–time) have their properties in virtue of being embedded in time (or space-time). Time (or space-time) enjoys perfectly natural properties, but its proper parts do not. On this view, time itself (or space–time) is a fundamental object, but perhaps its proper parts are not. The view that space and time are metaphysically prior to spaces and times is a fairly traditional view, and one way of explicating this priority is via the thought that space and time are more real than spaces and times.

There are other views concerning persistence besides the doctrine of temporal parts. Perhaps persons fare better if persons endure rather than perdure. There are many ways to characterize endurantism, but here I will characterize it merely negatively: something endures across an interval of time I just in case it occupies some subregions of I that collectively compose I (or it occupies I itself) but not in virtue of there being some other temporally smaller objects that collectively occupy those subregions. Enduring objects do not persist by virtue of anything like temporal parts. And because of this fact, there is no temporal stand-in for the enduring object to be the true bearer of qualia.

However, we shouldn't assume that endurantism is the key proposition that will allow one to move from the perfect naturalness of qualia to the full reality of people. First, one could hold that qualia are not instantiated by persons, enduring or otherwise, but rather by sub-personal proper parts of persons. This is an intriguing possibility, perhaps suggested by so-called split-brain experiments. But set this aside.

---

[35]   This conception of the whole of space and time as prior to their parts appears in Kant even during his critical period. See Kant (1999a: 175, A24–25/B39).

For there are some possibly thorny issues concerning how persons enjoy temporary properties that should be addressed.

One version of endurantism is the so-called relationalist version of endurantism, according to which many of what we took to be properties are really relations to times (or regions of space–time). On this view, when an enduring object transitions from being spherical at t_1 to pyramid-shaped at t_2, it is by way of bearing the *is spherical at* relation to t_1 and the *is pyramid-shaped at relation* to t_2. The same sort of story is true of temporary qualia: when one goes from enjoying chocolatey flavor to feeling queasy, this is in virtue of standing in the *enjoying chocolatey flavor* relation to some times, and standing in the *feeling queasy* relation to other times. Strictly, there are no qualia *properties* but there are qualia *relations*.

Consider now the attempt to move from the fundamentality of qualia to the full reality of persons. Recall the principle that only fully real objects can instantiate perfectly natural properties or relations. So if qualia relations are perfectly natural and a person stands in one to a time, then it follows that the person in question is also fully real. But it also follows that the time is fully real, since it is as much of a relatum of this relation as the person is. This seems a little troubling, since it is surprising that an argument concerning qualia could yield substantive conclusions about the nature of times. But perhaps we should accept that it could. If we think that times are not fundamental items in our ontology, but rather are something like logical constructions out of space–time regions, then we should probably never have said that qualia (or other "temporary intrinsic properties" for that matter) were relations to *times* rather than *space–time regions*.

If we want to avoid this consequence, we need a different version of endurantism. I don't think adverbialism, according to which what is represented by the copula itself is in some way a relation to times (or to space–times?) will do the trick, but to be honest I am not sure. Suppose we adopt a version of endurantism according to which an object is F at a time t in virtue of standing in the is-at-t relation to F. Somehow the time t is incorporated into the fundamental instantiation relation that material objects bear towards their properties. Should we conclude that t is thereby fundamental as well? (Perhaps not, if the various time-relativized instantiation relations are not fundamental. Things are unclear here.) What about a view in which facts, such as the fact that the ball is red, obtain only relative to some times but not others?[36] On this view, a time does not enter into the constitution of temporal facts, but does enter into the constitution of a higher-order fact, namely, the fact concerning the temporal location of the first-order fact. I am also unclear about the consequences of this view, but we should recall that some proponents of facts do not think that the mode of being of a fact must match the mode of being of its constituents.[37]

---

[36] I thank Hao Hong for suggesting this view.   [37] Recall our discussion in section 3.7.

Or consider the version of endurantism defended by Doug Ehring (1997). On Ehring's view, objects enjoy a changing series of temporary intrinsic properties by enjoying a series of short-lived intrinsic tropes. In effect, Ehring proposes endurantism for substances but the doctrine of temporal parts for properties: to be F at t is to just-plain-instantiate an F-trope that is located at t. On this view, the time that the F-trope is located is not a term that I stand in an F-relation towards. (Or at least not a fundamental F-relation; what is primary is the having of a trope.) So far, so good. But in order for the Ehring view to not have the implication that times are fundamental, the relation of *location* that the trope bears to the time cannot be perfectly natural. (Note that non-fundamental things can stand in relations to fundamental things; the restriction we have been operating with is that non-fundamental things can't stand in perfectly natural relations to anything, *period*.) So is this location relation perfectly natural?

The preceding discussion presupposed an eternalist framework about time. But in chapter 3, we discussed alternatives to this framework. One alternative is presentism. If presentism is true, then there are no other times, and to have a property at the present moment is simply to have the property, period. On the presentist's view, one could simply say that some persons flat out instantiate qualia and (given the full reality of qualia) are accordingly themselves fully real. As discussed in section 3.5, I'm no fan of presentism. But presentism is not the only view capable of yielding the desired consequence. In section 3.7, I discussed the Hybrid view, which was a conjunction of PEP—the view that past existence and present existence are modes of being—and the view that things that presently exist just plain have properties whereas things that pastly exist have properties merely relative to times. Given the Hybrid view, presently existing things can also just plain have qualia, and hence can enjoy full reality. (How to handle the enjoying of past properties by past objects, though, is still tricky to navigate and worth contemplating further!)[38]

We haven't settled whether the argument from qualia is successful in establishing the full reality of persons. I doubt we can settle this. What I have hoped to do so far is simply to demonstrate the complexity of the route from the fundamentality of qualia to the full reality of persons. It looks like the best-case scenario for an appeal to qualia is one in which persons persist through enduring and either presentism or PEP is true.

There is one last candidate class of putatively perfectly natural properties that I wish to consider. Unlike qualia, these properties definitely are had permanently by the things that have them, and so issues concerning persistence over time need not concern us. The question we will address here is whether they are fundamental properties. The properties in question are *haecceities*, properties of being *that very thing*. In section 6.7, we will examine more closely the assumption that haecceities are

---

[38] Thanks to Tim Leisz for helpful discussion here.

best thought of as first-order properties. For now, let us assume that they are. Examples of haecceities include *being Kris McDaniel* and *being Shieva Kleinschmidt.*

The case for the fundamentality of haecceities is based on the claim that there is a possible world that is exactly like this one except with respect to whether I exist. In this other possible world, there is a person born when I was born, a child of my actual parents, who grows through life having the same life history, and who dies a qualitatively similar death. But that person is not me. He's merely a qualitative duplicate of me. What motivates this claim? I believe that the source of this intuition is the deeper intuition that any completely "objective" description of reality must leave out something of ultimate importance, namely, whether and where I am to be found in that reality. Facts about subjectivity are not fixed by all the objective facts.

There is an interesting question of whether this intuition and the intuition favoring the non-supervenience of qualia have the same root—or whether the intuition apparently favoring the non-supervenience of qualia really favors the non-supervenience of haecceities. Perhaps the reason that one might feel that an objective description of all of the putatively relevant physical facts does not capture what it's like to experience orange is because it doesn't capture what it's like for *me* to experience orange.[39] If this is correct, we could grant that the fact that there is a particular distribution of orange sensations might be fixed by a particular distribution of physical properties—but this distribution of physical properties nonetheless under-determines the ultimate subjective facts, namely, facts concerning *who* the people who have these orange sensations are. On this way of thinking, even facts about what experiences are like are objective facts that could be determined by other objective facts. But regardless of whether the haecceitistic intuition stems from the same root as the qualia intuition, let us take it at face value for now and see where it leads us.[40]

Suppose the haecceitistic intuition is correct. Consider the following argument. There is a possible world exactly like this world in all other respects except Kris McDaniel does not exist at that world. If there is a possible world like this, then being Kris McDaniel does not supervene on the distribution of all other perfectly natural properties and relations. So far, so good. But we can't simply appeal to the principle used earlier, since that was formulated in terms of qualitative properties. Instead, we'll employ a more general principle: if a property or relation P fails to supervene on all other perfectly natural properties or relations, then P is itself a perfectly natural property or relation. Given this sufficient condition for being

---

[39] Remarks in Nagel (1983: 221–4) suggest that there is an explanatory gap between an objective description of the world and a description that has me explicitly in it. This explanatory gap seems akin to the explanatory gap between a physicalistic description of the world and a description that includes facts about what experiences are like.

[40] This is not to say that the case for fundamental haecceities rests solely on this intuition about subjectivity. Mackie (2006) provides a powerful case for the claim that there are no sufficient conditions for being me, which is an important component of the case for fundamental haecceities.

a perfectly natural property mentioned, being Kris McDaniel is a perfectly natural property. But at least one person has this property. So at least one person is fully real.

As with all the other arguments we have attended to, there are ways to resist. An initial worry one might have is over whether it is illicit to place properties like being Kris McDaniel on the naturalness scale. Arguably, when Lewis first introduced the notion of a perfectly natural property, he had only what one might call "qualitative" properties in mind, and certainly the putative examples of perfectly natural properties suggested by Lewis and those in his school are all "qualitative." That said, I don't think that it is illicit to include "non-qualitative" properties among those ranked with respect to their naturalness. For one thing, we are already ranking modes of being along the naturalness scale, but modes of being do not seem to be "qualitative" properties in the same way that, for example, colors or shapes are. Moreover, I am open to the view that a haecceity just is a mode of being that, as a matter of necessity, is enjoyed by exactly one thing. We'll explore this possibility later in section 6.7, but if this theory of the nature of haecceities is correct, then if we allow any mode of being to be ranked on the naturalness scale, we must allow haecceities thus construed as well.

A second worry is that the more general principle is subject to counter-examples. Consider the property *being the actual inventor of bifocals*. On the face of it, this property does not supervene on the distribution of all other perfectly natural properties and relations, since a duplicate of this world could fail to contain the person who is the actual inventor of bifocals, who we will assume to be Ben Franklin. (That other world contains someone who at that world is the inventor of bifocals, but who is not the actual inventor of bifocals.) But *being the actual inventor of bifocals* is not a perfectly natural property. So the more general principle is subject to counter-example.

Perhaps it is—but it is not clear that this is a counter-example. For *being the actual inventor of bifocals* might have in its supervenience base *being Ben Franklin*, and if the latter is a perfectly natural property—or in turn supervenes on other perfectly natural properties or relations—then we do not have a counter-example to the more general principle.

A third worry is that this argument overgeneralizes. Perhaps other beings besides persons have haecceities that fail to supervene in the same way. Then a parallel argument will yield the conclusion that these beings are fully real as well. I'm not unduly concerned about the existence of a parallel argument for the full reality of conscious beings that do not have sufficient mental acuity to count as persons, since I am inclined to think that any being enjoying conscious states enjoys full reality. But I would be disturbed were the argument generalizable so as to apply to things such as holes. Does it?

Perhaps. Suppose there is a God. Suppose this God were to create two universes that are mirror images of each other (so to speak) but spatiotemporally disconnected from one another. In each universe, there is a donut with a single hole in the middle of it.

These holes, henceforth hole$_1$ and hole$_2$, are not identical with each other. Now God could have created just one of these universes without creating the other, and had God done this, either hole$_1$ or hole$_2$ (but not both) would have existed. And yet, in all other respects, there would still be the same distribution of perfectly natural properties and relations. So the property of being hole$_1$ does not supervene on all other perfectly natural properties and relations, and so the property of being hole$_1$ is itself a perfectly natural property, and so hole$_1$ is fully real, despite being a hole.

Although this argument might seem initially plausible, it's also resistible. Although God could have created the universe that contains hole$_1$, it is not true that being hole$_1$ fails to supervene on all other perfectly natural properties and relations. What is true is that it fails to supervene on all other perfectly natural non-haecceitistic properties and relations. If there are other perfectly natural haecceitistic properties for *being hole$_1$* to supervene upon, the sufficient condition for being a perfectly natural property is not satisfied. And I think that there are. Perhaps the property of being that donut is one of them, but I am more inclined to think that the various haecceities of the fundamental particles that compose the donut are better candidates for being perfectly natural properties. So the thought is this: the haecceity of the hole is constrained by the haecceity of the donut, which is in turn constrained by other haecceitistic properties, which might include those of the particles that compose it.

Good. But now we face a worry. Once we grant that at least some haecceitistic properties supervene on others (and hence we lose the argument for their across-the-board fundamentality), why do we think that ours do not? Perhaps *being Kris McDaniel* fails to supervene on the distribution of qualitative properties but still supervenes on the distribution of the haecceities of my parts. To the extent that we trust the initial motivations for thinking to the contrary, we will have a reason to set this concern aside. But the case for our full reality admittedly feels shaky.

At this point, we've seen how thorny the theoretical arguments for our full reality can be. But perhaps there is another option. Kant (1999a: 112–13, Bxxi–Bxxii) distinguished between two ways of defending metaphysical positions: theoretical arguments and arguments from practical reason. In the next section, we will assess the prospects for an argument from practical reason.

6.6 Practical Arguments for Full Reality

In this section, we will explore several "practical arguments" for our full reality.

The first "warm-up" argument can be stated concisely: a necessary condition of our having the value we take ourselves to have is that we are fully real. We must take ourselves to have the value that we take ourselves to have. So we must take ourselves to be fully real.

The first premise was defended in section 6.2, so I will focus on the second premise. Why *must* we believe that we have a certain sort of metaphysical value? And in what sense *must* we? One possibility is that we simply are psychologically incapable of thinking of ourselves as less than fully real. When I consider that I might be less than fully real, I experience a kind of existential vertigo that induces something akin to nausea. When I look at my children and I look at the heaps my children make, it seems impossible for me to view the ontological status of my children as being more like that of the heaps rather than, for example, a fundamental particle. Perhaps I am nothing in the eyes of God, but my kids damn well better not be!

For better or for worse, though, I doubt that we are psychologically incapable of considering ourselves to be beings by courtesy. Friends of mine have reported to me that they have no problem doing so! Philosophers such as F. H. Bradley (1930: chs. 9–10) argued that selves are not fully real. Moreover, it is one of the central tenets of certain strands of Buddhism that we are nothing more than heaps or collections of mental occurrences—that in some fundamental sense, there are no selves, and we do not exist.[41] Moreover, this metaphysical claim plays a central role in the accompanying ethical and religious components of the system: a necessary condition of achieving enlightenment and thereby breaking free from the wheel of suffering is to recognize one's ontological status as a non-entity (in a fundamental sense). So when constructing practical arguments for our full reality we should also be aware of traditions that offer practical arguments for our lacking full reality!

Let me be clearer about what I mean by a *practical* argument versus a theoretical argument. The terminology I am using has a Kantian ancestry, but as with many terms of this lineage, it is unclear what their originator intended them to mean. A practical argument for *P* has as its premise that the truth of *P* is a necessary condition for an aspect of our normative practice to make sense; its conclusion is that we therefore have a practical reason to believe that *P*. In a similar vein, Robert Adams (1987: 150) says that practical arguments are those that give normative reasons for belief. On this way of thinking, there are at least two kinds of reasons for belief one can have. The first kind of reasons are *evidential reasons*. As the name suggests, these are reasons for belief that stem from evidence, such as perception, memory, rational intuition, testimony, good arguments, and so on. The second kind of reasons are *practical reasons*. Among the practical reasons for belief might be *prudential* reasons; perhaps what Pascal's (1995: 121–7) wager teaches us is that it is in our best interests to believe in God and hence we have a powerful prudential reason to believe in God. Perhaps also among the practical reasons for belief are *moral* reasons for belief; we have such reasons when it is, in a sense, in *morality's* best interest for us to believe accordingly. On this way of thinking, both evidential reasons and practical reasons are genuine reasons, and can be compared with and weighed against each other, and perhaps sometimes practical reasons carry the day, thereby making a belief reasonable in virtue of the practical reasons in its favor despite the paucity of evidence for it, or even despite the existence of evidence against it.

---

[41] See Siderits (2007: ch. 3, 142–4) and Garfield (2015: 102–16) for discussion.

What follows in this section will presuppose that there can be practical reasons for belief; I make this assumption to assess whether the case for our full reality can be supported by practical reasons even granting the possibility of practical reasons for belief.

Kant thought that our moral practices presupposed what he called *postulates of practical reason*. According to Kant, "These postulates are those of *immortality*, of *freedom* considered positively (as the causality of a being insofar as it belongs to the intelligible world), and *of the existence of God*."[42] Our moral practices presuppose that we have genuine freedom. (We will discuss the idea of genuine or transcendental freedom more in a bit.) Moreover, our moral practices make sense only against a background belief in which the universe is fundamentally a just place in which desert and reward ultimately coincide. But for desert and reward to ultimately coincide, there must be a God in charge of the development of the universe and there must be more to our existence than our earthly lives.

Let's consider a practical argument that is based on the idea that taking morality seriously demands taking some moral properties to be fundamental. Here's a snapshot of the kind of argument I am envisioning. Suppose a form of reductive naturalism is true according to which moral properties are identical with non-fundamental properties that can be designated by recognizably non-moral predicates. Since these properties are non-fundamental, our normative vocabulary could very easily have designated other properties without missing a joint in reality: fundamentally speaking, nothing is really right, wrong, good, or bad, and so on. Moreover, our concepts that have these properties as their content are *incorrect* in the sense elucidated in section 6.2. (Presumably the concept of correctness is also incorrect given reductive naturalism, which in itself is somewhat disquieting.) Once we view morality in this way, the importance of morality itself seems greatly diminished. Can our moral practices survive the realization of their fundamental insignificance?

Adams (1987) asks us to consider a scenario in which we learn that the omnipotent and omniscient creator of our universe is indifferent to moral considerations. In this scenario, some acts are right or wrong, some states of affairs have intrinsic value, and so forth, but this entity does not care. Adams suggests that our realization of the indifference of our creator to morality would undercut the felt importance that we attribute to morality even if it did not lead us to change our moral beliefs. I suggest that learning that moral features reduce in the way described above would have a similarly deflating effect. Adams's hypothesis of an indifferent creator merely puts a personal face on the idea that the universe is a fundamentally amoral place. According to this argument, we therefore have a practical reason to think that the universe is not a fundamentally amoral place, and so there are at least some fundamental moral features.

---

[42] See Kant's *Critique of Practical Reason* (1999b: 146, Ak. 5:132).

There is something to this argument even though it is unclear whether it is ultimately successful. But let's set this aside and grant that recognition of the fundamentality of some moral properties is essential to the felt importance of our moral practices. This by itself does not provide the basis of a practical argument for our full reality, since we need further premises to establish that among these fundamental moral properties there must be some that have persons as their bearers. Note that the "cosmic significance" of our moral practices might be secured by anchoring them in a fundamental property of intrinsic value instantiated by states of affairs; this is the kind of meta-ethical position favored by those in the Moorean tradition, for example.[43] In short, the practical reason to believe in fundamental properties provides a practical reason to believe in the full reality of their bearers, but this does not by itself provide a further practical reason to think that those bearers are persons.[44] We would need additional arguments here. This is not to say that none could be made, but to investigate them now would take us deep into the axiological and meta-ethical forests, and we might forget our way back to the territory I wish to discuss!

Let's turn to the second "practical argument" for our full reality. Here is a concise statement. A necessary condition for our moral practices to survive critical examination is our positing that we possess transcendental freedom. Since our moral practices must survive critical examination, we must posit that we possess transcendental freedom. But our possessing transcendental freedom ensures our full reality.

Transcendental freedom is a kind of spontaneous causality that persons in themselves putatively possess. It is also, for Kant, an intrinsic feature—for Kant, a property can be both an intrinsic property and a power.[45] In this context, to say that a feature is spontaneous is to say that its presence and its activities are not determined by anything else. I do not think that Kant simply means that it is not causally determined, but rather that there are no other fundamental features upon which its presence and activities supervene. Rather, it is part of Kant's practical-based metaphysics that our exercises of transcendental freedom appear in the ground-floor account of what gives rise to the phenomenal realm.[46] So, if we have transcendental freedom, we have a feature that fails to supervene on all other perfectly natural properties and relations.[47] By the principle articulated in sections 5.7 and 6.5,

---

[43] See Moore (1993). It is arguably part of the Moorean tradition that other forms of intrinsic value, including those that can be ascribed to persons, are derivative forms of value—and that from which they derive is a kind of impersonal intrinsic value. For an illustration of this claim and a defense of one aspect of it, namely, the reduction of prudential value to the intrinsic value of states of affairs, see McDaniel (2014c).

[44] Rashdall (1924: 206) argues that it is part of our moral psychology that persons are at least as real as any physical thing posited by the sciences; see also Mander (2011: 404) for commentary.

[45] See Kant's first *Critique* (Kant 1999a: 535–46, A538/B566–A558/B586) for a discussion of transcendental freedom. See Pereboom (2006: 544–7) for a discussion of fundamental yet intrinsic causal powers, and for the claim that transcendental freedom would be one of them. Langton (1998: 117) worries whether causal powers can be intrinsic.

[46] See, for example, Kant (1999a: 545, A556/B589).

[47] O'Connor (2014: 30–1) argues that some proponents of "libertarian free will" are committed to a form of emergentism in which "our mental states and capacities" are "ontologically basic." Also of

we should conclude that transcendental freedom is itself a perfectly natural property. But the possession of a perfectly natural property suffices for being fully real. So any practical argument for possessing transcendental freedom would suffice for us to be fully real.

Moreover, the problems concerning persistence over time that we discussed in section 6.5 would not arise here, at least if we accept the Kantian picture in which things in themselves are fundamentally non-spatiotemporal: transcendental freedom must be ascribed to the whole person rather than any sub-personal stages. However, if we abandon the view that persons are fundamentally atemporal beings, the worries about persistence over time threaten us once more, unless it is the case that persons are transcendentally free at each moment that they exist.

How fares the doctrine of transcendental freedom when it is shorn of transcendental idealism? If you are attracted to libertarianism about free will—that is, the doctrine that we have free will even though having free will is incompatible with causal determinism—then the doctrine of transcendental freedom should be seriously considered. The general intuition in favor of incompatibilism is that the existence of factors outside of your control sufficient to *ensure* your choices is also sufficient to ensure that your choices are not free. If we are mere beings by courtesy, then every feature we enjoy, including features related to our choices, supervenes on the distribution of fundamental properties and relations. And the distribution of fundamental properties and relations across a given possible world seems to be as much out of our control, at least if we are not fully real, as facts about the past and the laws of nature.[48] But if we enjoy transcendental freedom, then there is an aspect of us that is not determined by features outside of our control, and this aspect suffices for our full reality as well.

6.7 Individual Modes of Being

Before closing this chapter, let us explore one more intriguing way in which persons might be fundamental. Perhaps persons are fully real not by sharing in a fundamental mode of being but rather by virtue of each person's enjoyment of a unique fundamental mode of being. On this view, there is a fundamental mode of being that I and only I enjoy, and the same is true of each of you. Let us call this view *individualistic fragmentationalism*, or "IF" for short.

If we adopt IF, we face questions. Call my personal mode of being K. Do I enjoy K as a matter of necessity or could I have enjoyed some other mode of being instead of K? And if I could have enjoyed some other mode of being, could something non-identical with me have enjoyed K? There are plausible ontological schemes in which

relevance is Cover and Hawthorne's (1996) compelling case that materialism and agent-causation do not fit nicely together.

[48] See Cover and Hawthorne (1996: 58–60) and O'Connor (2014: 29–30).

entities enjoy some of their modes of being merely contingently. So the answers to these questions are non-obvious.

Let's provisionally assume that, as a matter of necessity, I enjoy K if I enjoy any mode of being at all, and that, as a matter of necessity, anything that enjoys K is identical with me. On these assumptions, enjoying K is a property that necessarily I and only I exemplify. In section 6.5, we discussed haecceities but did not pursue an account of their nature. But given the assumptions just made, a plausible account presents itself: my haecceity just is the property of enjoying my personal mode of being. On this way thinking, a haecceity is not a complex property that somehow has an individual as a constituent. Instead, it is built up purely out of other properties in just the same way as other ways of enjoying modes of being. We are thereby spared the need to consider what manner of composition is in play that constructs haecceities out of individuals and properties.

On this way of thinking, we have a kind of explanation of why haecceitistic facts are brute facts. In general, it is brute which modes of being are fundamental, and it is a brute fact which of these modes of being are enjoyed. If personal modes of being are among the fundamental, there is no metaphysical explanation to be had of why this is the case—and there is also no metaphysical explanation to be had for why those of them that are enjoyed are enjoyed. If I enjoy my own personal mode of being, it is therefore less surprising that whether I exist at a given world is not determined solely by the array of qualitative features present at that world.

Does this mean that whether a person persists over time must be brute as well? Not obviously—it depends on how we understand the relationships between person, world, and time. It might be that the relation between a person and a time is not an existential relation, contrary to what was suggested in section 2.4.1, but rather simply is a relation of occupation. Given this, it might be that, even though whether a person exists in a world at all is a brute fact, whether a person occupies a given time is accounted for by facts about her occupation of previous times, the array of qualities enjoyed by that person across time, and so on.

6.8 Chapter Summary

There are people, but how people exist is unclear. I argued that it is part of our evaluative self-conception that persons are fully real, but declined to take this as proof that we are fully real. Instead, I explored a series of arguments for this conclusion. A common premise of these arguments is that a sufficient condition for being fully real is instantiating a perfectly natural property or relation. Specific arguments appealed to properties such as *what it's like to taste chocolate, being Kris McDaniel*, certain moral properties such as intrinsic value, and freedom. We did not settle the question of whether we fully exist, but I hope that I have demonstrated how complex the issues involved are.

7

Degrees of Being

7.1 Introduction

In chapter 5, we delved into the idea that some things are ontologically superior to others in that they have *a higher degree of being* than others. And, in chapter 6, we focused on what degree of being we enjoy, hoping for the best and fearing for less. In this chapter, the notion of degree of being will take center stage. In previous chapters, we understood this notion in terms of quantification and a notion of naturalness. Here, we will assess whether the notion of a degree of being should have been taken as primitive instead, and if so, what the prospects are for understanding naturalness in terms of it.

As before, let us provisionally assume that everything that there is exists, and that to be, to be real, and to exist are ultimately one and the same: to be something. Still, questions remain. Does everything that there is exist to the same degree? Or do some things exist *more than* others? Are there gradations of being?

Perhaps no view is more despised by analytic metaphysicians than that there are gradations of being. But what if, unbeknownst to them, they have helped themselves to the doctrine that being comes in degrees when formulating various metaphysical theories or conducting metaphysical disputes? What if *degree* or *gradation of being* is already playing a significant role in their theorizing, albeit under a different guise?

In chapter 5, I argued that, given certain plausible assumptions, the notion of degree of being or grade of being can be analyzed in terms of naturalness. Here I will argue that, given certain plausible assumptions, naturalness can be analyzed in terms of the notion that being comes in degrees or grades. There are several reasons why this result is interesting. First, the notions of naturalness, fundamentality, and structure are ones that most contemporary metaphysicians grant are intelligible, whereas the claim that existence, being, or reality might come in degrees is regarded by many metaphysicians as being unintelligible. One way to assist a philosopher in grasping a notion that she regards as unintelligible is to show her how one can use that notion to define ones that she antecedently accepts as intelligible.

Second, it is widely believed by metaphysicians that at least one of the notions of naturalness, fundamentality, structure, or grounding is theoretically fruitful, whereas most contemporary metaphysicians see little use for the thought that existence comes in degrees. For example, metaphysicians such as Lewis (1983a, 1984, 1986) are willing to take the notion of naturalness as a primitive because they recognize that it can be used to define or partially characterize the following philosophically important concepts: *objective similarity, intrinsic properties, laws of nature, materialism, meaning* and *reference*, and so forth. If we can define the notion of naturalness in terms of degrees of being, then metaphysicians will have an equally strong reason to take the notion of degrees of being as primitive, since it can do all of the work that the notion of naturalness can do.

Third, whenever two notions are shown to be in some sense inter-definable (given certain assumptions), interesting questions arise. If, for example, degrees of being and naturalness are, in some sense, inter-definable, have metaphysicians been really committed to there being degrees of being all along? If they are identical metaphysical phenomena, then the answer seems to be yes. I am implicitly committed to fusions of H_2O molecules by being explicitly committed to water: I am committed to certain fusions of H_2O molecules under the guise of water. But suppose they are not identical phenomena despite being inter-definable. Then is one metaphysically prior to the other? Can arguments be given that one *ought* to take the notion of a degree of being as a primitive rather than naturalness or vice versa?

Finally, some philosophers still have doubts concerning metaphysical primitives such as naturalness, grounding, and structure. I suspect that these philosophers would be overjoyed to discover that the notion of naturalness and the notion of degree of being are inter-definable, for then (by their lights) the notion of naturalness would be demonstrably disreputable.[1] And perhaps some philosophers on the fence will be moved one way or the other.

Here is the plan for the rest of the chapter. Section 7.2 will be devoted to articulating the view that being comes in degrees and briefly discussing several variants of this view; I briefly remind the reader of the definition of degrees of being in terms of naturalness. In section 7.3, I provide and motivate a definition of naturalness in terms of degrees of being. In section 7.4, I discuss several questions that one might have about naturalness and show that there are parallel questions one might have about degrees of being. In the context of this discussion, I offer for consideration what I call the *notational variant hypothesis*, according to which theories that differ only in whether they employ the notion of naturalness/structure or the notion of degrees of being are really the same theory, albeit under different guises. One way to resist the notational variant hypothesis would be to promote an argument that, despite their mutual inter-definability, one of the notions of structure or degree of being is in some way prior, and hence there are two distinct phenomena in play rather than two different guises for the same underlying phenomenon. In section 7.5, I develop and then critically evaluate two plausible arguments for taking the notion of naturalness as the primary notion. Although these arguments might seem initially

---

[1] Perhaps they will draw a similar moral about grounding after reading chapter 8.

compelling, ultimately I do not think that they succeed. In section 7.6, I investigate whether there is some reason to prefer taking *degree of being* as the primitive notion. There, I discuss an intriguing argument based on the idea that theories making use of *degree of being* are more ideologically parsimonious. Although this argument is inconclusive, I view it as in better shape than the arguments for taking naturalness/ structure as the prior notion. I thereby endorse a disjunctive conclusion: either the notational variant hypothesis is true—in which case contemporary metaphysicians have been employing degrees of being in their theorizing, albeit not under that guise—or the notion that contemporary metaphysicians have been employing *ought to be further analyzed in terms of degree of being*. If either disjunct is true, then contemporary metaphysicians need to rethink what they've been up to when theorizing in metaphysics, and how their theorizing is oriented towards those long dead who theorized before them. Section 7.7 discusses whether the view defended here faces the objections that Sider (2011: 164–5) raises against what he calls "entity-fundamentality." Finally, section 7.8 briefly discusses an epistemic advantage to taking degrees of being as the prior notion, and indicates some lines of further research worth pursuing.

7.2 Degrees of Being

The view I mean to defend is the view forcefully rejected by McTaggart (1927a: 4–5) in the following passage:

A thing cannot be more or less real than another which is also real. It has been said that reality does admit of degrees. But this can . . . be traced to one of two confusions. . . . Sometimes reality has been confused with power . . . [but] a thing which asserts more power is not more real than one that asserts less. Sometimes . . . the possibility of degrees of reality is based on the possibility of degrees of truth. . . . If, for example, it should be truer to say that the universe was an organism than that it was an aggregate, then it is supposed that we may say that an organic universe is more real than an aggregate-universe. But this is a mistake.

I grant that it would be a mistake to confuse power with reality and a mistake to accept degrees of truth. So let's not make these mistakes. On the view that I am considering, being is not to be conflated with some other feature that comes in degrees. Being itself comes in degrees: to be simpliciter is to be to some degree or other, just as to have mass simpliciter is to have some determinate amount of mass. And just as not everything has the same amount of mass, not everything that is exists to the same degree.[2]

---

[2] Hughes (1989: 26) denies that existence comes in degrees. Miller (2002) defends the claim that some instances of existence are "richer" than others, but since Miller's system seems vastly different from my own, I will not pursue this idea further here.

There are a number of ways to flesh out this view and, depending on what the correct metaphysics of quantities is, different ways will be more attractive. One possibility is that *existence* is a quantitative determinable akin to *mass* and that degrees of being are determinates of this determinable. Another possibility is to take as basic some relation such as *x is at least as real as y*, and hold that something exists iff it bears that relation to something, including to itself. I won't settle the metaphysics of quantity here.[3] For the most part, I will use the locution "degree of being" more out of stylistic convenience than a conviction that being is a determinable such that it makes sense to assign numbers to its determinates.

However, on no option does something hover between being and non-being: everything that there is, exists simpliciter, although some things exist more than others. Perhaps Plato thought that particulars are as much as they are not. This is suggested by the discussion in Plato's *Republic* 479c–e (Plato 1971: 719) of things that lie between existence and "not to be."[4] But this is not my view. Consider the following analogy. Even though something enjoying 1 gram of mass is less massive than something enjoying 1 kilogram of mass, it would not be sensible to describe an object enjoying 1 gram of mass as being as non-massive as it massive (or, worse, more non-massive than it is massive). If we must talk this way, then we should say that everything with mass is more massive than non-massive. Similarly, even the things with the smallest amounts of being have more being than non-being. (This is not to affirm that there is an amount of being that is the smallest!)

On the metaphysics I am attracted to, some things do exist to the highest degree whereas other beings exist to a lesser degree. As noted in section 5.5, I am inclined to take this as a metaphysical axiom. Despite the results of chapter 6, I am still somewhat confident in the maximal existence of myself and other conscious or living beings as well as material objects without parts, but I am less confident that non-living or non-sentient composite material objects enjoy full reality. Nevertheless, as I discussed in chapter 5, the most compelling examples of real but less than fully real entities are almost nothings, such as shadows, holes, cracks, and fissures. That these entities exist but are not fully real is the view of the common person not yet exposed to academic metaphysics. Roy Sorensen (2008: 189) claims that "holes do not sit any more comfortably on the side of being than of nonbeing." But this is to indulge in the (allegedly) Platonic way of talking that it is best to avoid. Instead, it would be better to say that, although holes sit on the side of being, they occupy a lower position than other beings on this side.

---

[3] Some interesting papers on the metaphysics of quantity include Eddon (2013), Hawthorne (2006), and Mundy (1987). For the sake of convenience, I will occasionally talk as if the basic notion is "*x* has *n*-units of being," although this is not the view I would ultimately endorse. A view of being that takes the comparative notion as basic will be discussed in section 7.6.

[4] Dancy (1986: 52–4) suggests that Plato around the time of the *Republic* was committed to this kind of view.

Let's briefly recall how I accounted for degrees of being in earlier chapters. First, I appealed to the notion of a *semantically primitive restricted quantifier*, which is a quantifier that fails to range over everything that there is but is not a semantically complex unit consisting of the unrestricted quantifier and a restricting predicate or operator. I then offered (in chapter 1) the following account of *modes of being*: there are modes of being just in case there are some possible semantically primitive restricted quantifiers that are at least as natural as the unrestricted quantifier. In chapter 5, I defended the following definition of *degree of being*: x exists to degree *n* just in case the most natural possible quantifier that ranges over x is natural to degree *n*. In slogan form: *an object's degree of being is proportionate to the naturalness of its most natural mode of existence*. If something exists and is in the domain of a perfectly natural quantifier, it has the highest degree of being: it *fundamentally* exists. If something exists but is not within the domain of a perfectly natural quantifier, it exists *degenerately*. To exist degenerately is to exist to a less than maximal degree.

Both the notion of a mode of being and the notion of a degree of being can be straightforwardly accounted for in terms of the naturalness of certain quantifiers, and can be used by friend and foe alike. The foe of modes of being could claim that no other quantifier could be as natural as the unrestricted quantifier, thereby ensuring (given the definitions above) that everything has the same fundamental mode of being and exists to the same degree.

Here I propose to temporarily table the question of whether there are modes of being in order to focus on whether being comes in degrees. Modes of being will play a role in one of the arguments discussed in section 7.5, but will mostly fade into the background in this chapter.

7.3 Defining Naturalness in Terms of Degrees of Being

I will now turn to the question of whether one can understand the notion of naturalness in terms of the notion of degrees of being.

First, recall that Sider prefers a nominalistic construal of naturalness or structural facts, to use his preferred locution. According to this nominalistic construal, no entity is needed to "back up" claims about naturalness or structure. Sider regiments talk of naturalness in a putatively nominalistic way via his "S" operator, which can prefix open sentences containing any type of unbound variable and thereby yield a closed sentence stating a fact about structure.

One nice thing about Sider's proposal is that it provides a way to make sense of how other expressions besides predicates can be metaphysically important. But the realist about properties could agree with Sider that other expressions besides predicates can be ranked on the naturalness scale. In fact, the realist view is arguably the more intuitive view: what makes sentences using "S" true are facts about the naturalness of the entities that correspond to the constituents of these sentences. The properties that correspond to sentential operators are properties of propositions, whereas the properties that correspond to quantifiers are properties of properties. On the property-realist construal, some higher-order properties are more natural than others.

A more intriguing form of realism might deny that the ontological correlates of sentence operators are properties but rather belong to a different ontological category altogether; this is the view of Mulligan (2010: 583, fn. 24), for example, who calls the ontological correlates "connectors." Similarly, one might hold that the ontological correlates of quantifiers are not properties but rather are modes of being understood as *sui generis* entities. Provided that this more intriguing form of realism countenances the ranking of such entities on the same naturalness scale, what I say about the less intriguing version of realism holds also for the more intriguing.

Let's provisionally be realists about properties; we'll examine later in this section how much rides on this provisional move. Here is an interesting question: to what extent do non-natural properties exist? Here are two plausible but competing answers. Answer one: all properties, natural or unnatural, exist to the same degree, whatever that degree is. Answer two: more natural properties exist to a higher degree than less natural properties.

I think that the second answer is better than the first, and that some prominent metaphysicians who work on the metaphysics of properties have implicitly committed themselves to this view. One slogan championed by nominalists is that properties are mere shadows cast by predicates. I disagree: perfectly natural properties have a glow of their own. However, less than natural properties are mere shadows, although they are cast by the perfectly natural properties rather than by linguistic entities. Shadows are real, but they are less real than that which is their source.

Let us consider the work of D. M. Armstrong (1997), who is a full-blooded realist about perfectly natural properties, which he identifies with universals. But his attitude towards the less than perfectly natural properties is harder to discern. Consider the following puzzling remarks:

The first-class properties of particulars are the universals they instantiate. The second-class properties of particulars have the following necessary and sufficient condition. They are not universals, but when truly predicated of a particular, the resultant truth is a contingent one.... What is their status? Will it be said that they do not exist? That will be a difficult saying, since it can hardly be denied that innumerable statements in which these property- and relation-words appear are *true*.   [Armstrong 1997: 44]

To this is added the thesis of the ontological free lunch. What supervenes in the strong sense is not something that is ontologically anything more than what it supervenes upon.... The second-class properties are not ontologically additional to the first-class properties.... The second-class properties are not properties additional to the first-class properties. But it is to be emphasized that this does not make the second-class properties unreal. They are real and cannot be talked away.   [Armstrong 1997: 45]

Armstrong correctly notes that we cannot deny that there are second-class properties because there are true propositions about them. For example, it is true that red is a color and that bachelorhood is correlated with loneliness. Armstrong's remarks here should feel familiar and not simply because you just read them. Rather, Armstrong's remarks echo those medieval philosophers, such as Aquinas and Suárez, who said very similar things about a different group of second-rate entities, namely, beings of reason. Recall that, according to Aquinas, there are two proper uses of the word "being": the first use is to signify things that belong to the categories, that is, the entities that enjoy non-degenerate existence. But there must also be a sense of "being" in which entities such as blindness in the eye are beings, since we can form true affirmative propositions about them. However, this sense mustn't be taken to be metaphysically fundamental, for otherwise negations, privations, and the sort would be full-fledged entities in their own right. Things that are said to be beings in the second sense *posit nothing in reality*. They are "an ontological free lunch"; they are "ontologically nothing more" than their foundations.

Both Armstrong and Aquinas feel similar pressure to recognize in some way the reality of second-class entities while still holding that these entities are second-class *qua entity*. I suggest that in response to similar pressures, similar tactics should be employed. Aquinas is in better shape than Armstrong when it comes to responding to the pressure, since he has fundamental modes of being (Aquinas's categories) that first-class entities enjoy and a second-rate sense of "being" that beings in the sense of being-true satisfy.[5] Armstrong needs—and is inchoately flapping towards—a similar distinction.

Consider Armstrong's claim that the less than natural properties (and the states of affairs in which they figure) are "no additions to being." Taken at face value, the claim that something is no addition to being is tantamount to the claim that it does not exist, for if it were to exist, it would have to be *counted* among that which exists and hence would be an *addition* to being. So less than perfectly real properties must be counted among the existents—and recall that Armstrong says that they are real—but how can this fact be reconciled with the intuition that they don't count for much? How could one existent *ontologically* count for less than another *unless the former is less real than the latter*?

Things that can be counted are things that can be numbered. Some philosophers claim that there is a close connection between number and existence.[6] There is some connection: this is shown by the fact that one can represent claims about the number of things via the apparatus of quantification, identity, and negation. For example, one

---

[5] Similarly, the founder of modern philosophy, Descartes, recognizes three (or perhaps four or five) fundamental categories of things: God, finite substances (immaterial or material), and modes of substances (immaterial or material). But he also freely quantifies over privations, lacks, and so forth, although he denies them the status of *things*—they are neither substances nor modes; see, e.g., Descartes (1992: 203–4).

[6] See, for example, van Inwagen (2001b).

can say that there are exactly two Fs by asserting that $\exists x \exists y(Fx \ \& \ Fy \ \& \ {\sim}x = y \ \&$ $(\forall z \ Fz \rightarrow z = x \ \text{or} \ z = y))$. So if there is some sense in which certain things are not to be counted, we should also expect that there is some sense in which certain things are not there at all.

Let us develop such a view. There are at least two possible quantifiers in play: a perfectly natural one, "$\exists_n$," that includes all natural properties but no less than natural ones in its domain, and a less than perfectly natural one, "$\exists_i$," that includes all the properties in its domain. One candidate for being "$\exists_i$" is the unrestricted quantifier of ordinary English. For the sake of a simple example, suppose that there are exactly two perfectly natural properties, P1 and P2, and one less natural property, namely the disjunction of them, P1∨P2. On this view, the following sentences are true:

1. $\forall_n z \ [z$ is a property $\rightarrow (z = \text{P1 or } z = \text{P2})]$
2. $\forall_i z \ [z$ is a property $\rightarrow (z = \text{P1 or } z = \text{P2 or } z = \text{P1}\vee\text{P2})]$

We respect the intuition that P1∨P2 is no addition of being by endorsing 1. Given 1, there is a straightforward and metaphysically important sense of "being" according to which there are exactly two properties. P1∨P2 would be an addition of being if it were a false-maker for 1, for then, fundamentally speaking, *it would have to be counted*. That which is an *ontological* addition to being is that which is to be found in the domain of "$\exists_n$." But we also respect the intuition that P1∨P2 exists by endorsing 2 as well. P1∨P2 must be counted among what there is, but it counts for less in virtue of being less than fully real. The denial of 2 is the difficult saying that Armstrong warns us not to utter, but the denial of 2 must not be confused with the affirmation of 1. By accepting both 1 and 2 we accommodate both intuitions in a clean way. Second-class properties really are second-class—they exist merely degenerately—but they are nonetheless within the range of the unrestricted quantifier of ordinary English and hence are real.

The solution to Armstrong's troubles made use of two possible meanings for the existential quantifier, one of which was more natural than the other. One might wonder how essential to the solution the disparity of naturalness is. Would it suffice if both quantifiers were equally natural, given that one does not include the second-class properties that the other includes? In short, would a solution that appeals to *levels of being* rather than *degrees of being* be equally adequate? (The idea is that perfectly natural properties would enjoy two fundamental modes of being, one of which it shares with the second-class properties, whereas the second-class properties enjoy merely one fundamental mode.)

I think appealing to levels of being here is inapt, and for the same reason that appealing to levels of being in the case of almost nothings proved inapt (in section 5.2). The nature and existence of second-class properties are fixed by the nature and existence of first-class properties. That's a given and unsurprising provided that second-class properties do not fully exist. But it would be very surprising if second-class properties are ontologically on a par with first-class properties. By contrast, it is not surprising that past objects have a nature and existence of their own if minimal Meinongian presentism (discussed in section 3.3) is true, since, on that view, past things do enjoy a fundamental mode of being. The right way to think of second-class properties is to think of them as beings by courtesy.

Appealing to orders of existence is also not likely to be successful. The form of existence of second-class properties doesn't seem more polyadic than the form of existence of first-class properties. Of the three kinds of ontological degeneracy I have distinguished, degree of being seems the most apt for the case at hand.

We have seen how one can distinguish between first-class and second-class properties. But one might wish for more fine-grained distinctions than this. For even among the second-class properties, some appear to be more natural than others. We should consider how to capture this apparent fact.

Lewis (1986: 61) faced a similar question when he developed his theory of natural properties. Should we work with a primitive absolute distinction between the natural and the non-natural, and then *define* relative naturalness in some way? Or should we take as primitive a notion of relative naturalness, and define *x is perfectly natural* as *there is no property more natural than x*? Lewis opted to take the former route, and suggested that relative naturalness amounted to length of definition in terms of the perfectly natural properties in some canonical language.

I doubt that Lewis's strategy will be successful. There are notorious difficulties with specifying the purported canonical language, to begin with.[7] But another reason I am doubtful is that I take seriously the possibility of analogous properties that do not have a focal analogue instance. It is hard to see how to capture the difference between such analogous properties and merely disjunctive properties in the way that Lewis proposes. That said, if Lewis's strategy is promising, it can be mimicked by the proponent of degrees of being. The difference between first and second-class properties—that is, the perfectly natural and the rest—can be cashed out in the way suggested, simply by distinguishing between existing in the best way and second-rate existence, and then providing a more stratified naturalness ranking via definition in a canonical language.[8]

But there is a second possibility for relating degree of naturalness and degree of being: hold that the degrees of being of properties are proportionate to their degrees of naturalness. If this is correct, then a straightforward account of naturalness *in terms of degrees of being* is apparent: "property P is *more natural than* property Q" is defined as "P is more real than Q"; "property P is natural to degree *n*" is defined as "the degree to which P exists is *n*." In short, we can define what it is for a property to

---

[7] Sider (2011: xx) sounds a hopeful note, however.
[8] Note that Aquinas did not argue for degrees of being (in my sense) but rather merely made a distinction between first-class entities—those that are God or fall under one of the categories—and the second-class ones which merely are beings in the sense of being true.

be natural *in terms of the notion of degree of being.* The most natural properties are the most real properties. The hierarchy of naturalness is determined by the relative reality of properties.

One interesting difference between the first and the second ways of relating naturalness to degrees of being is the following. If we wish to follow Lewis on relative naturalness, we need to say that (i) all perfectly natural properties are equally as real as each other and (ii) all less than perfectly natural properties are less real than any perfectly natural property. This is what gives us the initial cut between the perfectly natural properties and the rest. But we needn't say that (iii) the naturalness of a less than perfectly natural property is proportionate to its degree of being. (We are committed to adopting (iii) given the second possible way of relating naturalness and degree of being.) It *might* be that length of definition in a canonical language doesn't neatly correlate with degree of being.

In what follows, I will pursue the second possibility. One of the provisional assumptions employed here is that there are properties, and that talk of naturalness should be regimented by appealing to a naturalness ordering on properties. Although there are ways to regiment talk about comparative naturalness without presupposing that there are properties, and the doctrine that some things exist more than others does not presuppose that there are properties, the analysis of *natural* offered here in terms of degrees of being seems to make ineliminable use of the assumption that there are properties. For this reason, it is worth determining the extent to which it is defensible to believe that there are no properties, and the extent to which the presupposition that there are properties is ineliminable.

Let us distinguish *extreme nominalism* from *moderate nominalism*. Extreme nominalism is the view that properties in no way exist. Moderate nominalism is the view that properties do not fundamentally exist but do degenerately exist.

Extreme nominalism is not a sustainable doctrine. Consider the sentence, "Some anatomical property is had by both whales and wolves." This sentence is literally true; it explicitly quantifies over properties; it is not amendable to paraphrase in terms of some sentence that does not.[9] These facts ensure that properties enjoy some kind of reality. (Similar facts about shadows or holes could be adduced to show that shadows or holes enjoy some kind of reality.) Even if the sense of "some" in the above sentence is not the same sense as in "Some donut is in the next room," it suffices that there is *some* sense of "some" in which the above sentence is true.[10] For this sense of "some"

---

[9] *Pace* Yablo (1998, 2005), I can detect no whiff of make-believe associated with such sentences. But perhaps here is a place where one might attempt to resist the argument; there's a lot to be thought about here. On paraphrase strategies, the classic piece is Quine's "On What There Is," reprinted in Quine (1963), along with Alston's (1958) important rejoinder. Carrara and Varzi (2001) provide a useful discussion of the possibility of paraphrase strategies of various sorts.

[10] For example, Cian Dorr (2008) distinguishes between what he calls a *superficial* sense and a *fundamental* sense of the existential quantifier. That there is a superficial sense suffices to make my point, but it is not necessary: all that is necessary is that some *possible* meaning for the quantifier that ranges over properties is not maximally unnatural.

is either a maximally natural sense of "some" or it is not. If it is a maximally natural sense, then properties exist to the maximal degree. If it is not, then properties exist to at least the extent that this sense of "some" is natural. Either way, properties exist to some degree or other.[11]

Could it be that the quantifier employed in the sentence "something is a property" is *maximally unnatural*? Let's provisionally identify being maximally unnatural with being natural to degree zero, and let's provisionally assume that there might be some properties or relations that are natural to degree zero. An entity that falls *only* within the range of a *maximally* unnatural quantifier is an entity that exists to zero degrees. Perhaps the claim that properties exist to degree zero is a version of extreme nominalism worth considering.

Unfortunately for the extreme nominalist, even if the quantifier in question is *highly* unnatural, it is not *maximally* unnatural. With respect to the naturalness scale, there are possible semantically primitive quantifiers that score far worse. Consider, for example, a semantically primitive quantifier that ranges over everything ranged over by the ordinary English quantifier except for pinky fingers, things with exactly seven proper parts, and the property of being a bachelor. The ordinary English quantifier, which ranges over properties, is doing better on the naturalness scale than that one! So there is at least one quantifier that ranges over properties that is not maximally unnatural, i.e., that is natural to a degree greater than 0. Since there is at least one possible quantifier ranging over properties whose naturalness is greater than 0, properties exist to a greater than 0 degree.

Extreme nominalism cannot be sustained. If the analysis of naturalness in terms of degrees of being ineliminably presupposes that extreme nominalism is false, then so be it. Good analyses are allowed to assume that false theories are false.

Moderate nominalism, on the other hand, is not obviously unsustainable. However, the analysis offered here does *not* presuppose the falsity of moderate nominalism. Recall the analysis of naturalness in terms of degrees of being: property P is *more natural than* property Q = df. P is more real than Q; property P is natural to degree n = df. the degree to which P exists is n. Neither part of the analysis ineliminably presupposes that any property exists to a maximal degree. A perfectly natural property is a property such that no other *property* is more real than it. Maybe there are other entities than properties that are more real than even the perfectly natural properties.

Let *Platonism* be the view that some properties are more real than any individual; let *non-reductive realism* be the view that some individuals and some properties are such that nothing else is more real than they are. Let *otherism* be the view that there are some entities that are more real than any property or individual. Platonism, non-reductive realism, and otherism are the main competitors to moderate nominalism.

---

[11] To be clear, I am not committing myself to the claim that "some" does have these two senses, but rather merely noting that even if it does, this does not help the extreme nominalist.

The analysis of naturalness in terms of degrees of being does not presuppose any of these views or any of their denials.

One interesting question is what to say about uninstantiated properties. I'm going to assume in what follows that there are uninstantiated properties. But one might worry that uninstantiated properties generate a problem for the proposed analysis.[12] Consider two determinates of the same determinable, one of which is instantiated whereas the other is uninstantiated. As noted in section 2.2, I think determinates of the same determinable are equally natural and as natural as the determinable itself. Hence, given the analysis, they all have the same degree of being. However, one might also intuit that the uninstantiated property is less real than the instantiated one.

If need be, I'd be willing to let theory overrule the intuition; it's not obvious that there is an ontological distinction between instantiated and uninstantiated properties.[13] But there also are ways to try to soothe this intuition rather than overrule it. I've distinguished several kinds of ontological superiority, and it might be that the uninstantiated determinate has the same degree of being as the instantiated determinate but in some other way the instantiated determinate is ontologically superior to the uninstantiated one. For example, perhaps uninstantiated properties are analogous to merely possible particulars, and so appealing to something like levels of being in this context might be appropriate. For now, let me set aside the question of uninstantiated properties, but we will address this issue again in section 7.6.

Given plausible assumptions, we can define the notion of degree of being in terms of the notion of naturalness. Given plausible assumptions, we can define the notion of naturalness in terms of degree of being. We now face some puzzling questions. Is a theory that makes use of the notion of naturalness *merely a notational variant* of a theory that makes use of the notion of a degree of being? If one of these notions is in some way prior, which notion *should be* defined in terms of the other?

7.4 Theoretical Claims and Questions

Let the *notational variants hypothesis* (*NVH*) be the hypothesis that two theories that differ only with respect to whether they employ the notion of naturalness or the notion of a degree of being are mere notational variants of each other.

Sometimes, what we think are two different phenomena really are the same phenomenon appearing under two different guises. And sometimes a phenomenon appearing in one theory under a particular guise is the same phenomenon playing the same role in an apparently different theory under a different guise. In either case, we

---

[12] In fact, an anonymous referee did have this worry!

[13] Mundy (1987) and Tooley (1987) both provide a powerful case for at least some uninstantiated properties. However, note that those attracted to the substance-attribute metaphysics described in section 2.4.2 should be suspicious of uninstantiated properties, since they would have the mode of being of an attribute without *being in* an attribute.

have two different ways of talking about the same underlying reality. According to the NVH, *degrees of naturalness* and *degrees of being* are the same phenomenon showing up under different guises.

The NVH is supported by more than the fact that these notions can be defined in terms of each other (given plausible assumptions). First, note that the two primitive notions can be used to partition classes of entities in exactly the same ways. One may apply the notion of naturalness to substances as well as properties. Just as some ways of partitioning classes of entities are more natural than others, some decompositions of an entity are more natural than others. Consider an arbitrary undetached part of Ted Sider. Why does this part deserve to be called arbitrary? It just isn't as natural as Sider himself, or his brain, or one of his cells. The friend of degrees of being may grant that both Sider and this arbitrary undetached part exist, but hold that Sider is more real than his arbitrary parts. Friends of naturalness employ the phrase "carving nature at its joints"—and it is objects that literally have joints to be carved.

Just as there is arbitrary decomposition, there is arbitrary composition: arbitrary fusions of individuals are less natural than the individuals they fuse. The arbitrary sums countenanced by unrestricted mereology have an air of unreality to them—consider the thing made out of Sider, the moon, and a piece of cheese—and the friend of degrees of being may grant that arbitrary fusions are real, albeit less real than that which they fuse.

Just as negative "substances"—shadows and holes—are less real than "positive entities," so too are negative properties less real than positive ones. On my view, P1 is a negation of P2 only if, necessarily, everything has exactly one of them and P1 is less natural than P2.[14] And just as arbitrary sums of substances are less real than what they sum, arbitrary disjunctions of properties are less real than that which they disjoin. (From a logical perspective, the summing function of classical mereology and the disjunction function behave similarly.) Recall that P is a mere disjunction of Q and R only if (i) necessarily, if something has Q or has R it has P, (ii) anything that has P either has Q or has R, and (iii) P is less natural than Q and less natural than R.[15] A friend of degrees of being will accept the first two clauses and substitute for (iii) that P is less real than Q and less real than R.

Some philosophers use "is natural" primarily to predicate something of an attribute, but as the examples above show, there is insufficient reason to claim that "is natural" cannot also be applied to objects.[16] Each of the above claims that employs the notion of naturalness and its analogue that employs the notion of degree of being are equally defensible. If it were to turn out that "is natural" could be predicated only

---

[14]   Compare with Hirsch (1997b: 59–60).

[15]   If properties are individuated intensionally rather than hyperintensionally, these "only ifs" can be replaced with "if and only ifs."

[16]   I thank Alex Skiles and an anonymous referee for helpful discussion here. Note that Hirsch (1997b) discusses a notion of naturalness that applies to objects.

of properties, we could always add a clause to the definition of "is natural" requiring this. The more interesting upshot would be that degrees of being would emerge as the more general notion, which would suggest that it is also the notion that is prior.

That these analyses are equally defensible is predicted by the NVH, since on the NVH each claim is a mere notational variant of its analogue.

Further evidence for the NVH stems from the fact that there are many important questions about naturalness for which there are parallel questions about degree of being.

If we take naturalness as primitive, we can define the notion of a degree of being. But there are hard questions facing anyone who takes the notion of naturalness as primitive. For example, consider the following questions:

1. Is *being natural* natural? How natural is *being natural to degree n*?
2. Is *x is more natural than y* more basic than *x is natural to degree n*?
3. Can things other than properties have degrees of naturalness?

If we take degrees of being as primitive, we can define the notion of naturalness. But there are equally hard questions facing anyone who takes the notion of degrees of being as primitive, such as the following:

4. Does the property of maximally existing maximally exist? To what extent does the property of existing to degree *n* exist?
5. Is *x exists more than y* more basic than *x exists to degree n*?
6. Can things other than properties have degrees of being?

That parallel questions arise in this fashion is *predicted* by the NVH. On the NVH, questions 1–3 are merely notional variants of questions 4–6, and so, given the NVH, it is unsurprising that parallel questions arise about one and same primitive notion.[17]

Before proceeding to further assess the case against NVH, I'll discuss one preliminary objection. In general, necessarily equivalent properties or relations needn't be identical. If we think of properties and relations as closely tied to meanings in natural language or in thought, then we will definitely distinguish some necessarily equivalent properties such as triangularity and trilaterality. Similarly, even if it turns out that naturalness and degrees of being necessarily co-vary, in what sense could they be the same phenomena, given that "naturalness" and "degree of being" clearly differ in meaning and theoretical role?

Two responses. First, it is not obvious to me that "naturalness" and "degree of being" do differ in meaning. The dominant conception of naturalness is a concept of fundamentality, and fundamentality and ontological superiority of some sort seem to me closely tied together. Moreover, given my previous arguments, degree of being

---

[17] Questions 2 and 5 are perhaps less exciting, since they might arise for any degreed notion. This doesn't undercut NVH's prediction that both 2 and 5 will arise, but it does make that prediction less interesting. Thanks to Alex Skiles for discussion here.

can do the jobs that naturalness has been invoked to do, and hence in that respect, they do not differ in their theoretical roles.

Second, let me concede that one legitimate role that properties can play is to serve as meanings. And if we take triangularity and trilaterality to be properties playing this role, they are numerically distinct since their corresponding expressions differ in meaning. But then so too are the properties of being water and being constituted by H_2O molecules. And even if we want to distinguish between these properties, in some sense the phenomena are the same. Moreover, the sense in which the phenomena are the same is not merely that necessarily every token of one is a token of the other and vice versa. Suppose that necessarily everything extended is colored and vice versa; the phenomena of extension and color are nonetheless not identical. I am interested in properties and relations better understood as *referents* of predicates rather than as their *meanings*. It may well be that there are necessarily equivalent yet non-identical properties even when conceived in this way; in fact, I think that there are. On this conception of properties, however, being water and being constituted by H_2O molecules are not merely necessarily coextensive properties, but rather are identical and have been discovered to be so. My view is that we can also discover identities of properties so conceived via philosophical reflection.

However, if I am wrong about this, there is still an interesting question about priority to be settled, and the next two sections attempt to answer this question.

7.5 Is Naturalness the Prior Notion?

I've sketched a case for the NVH. But we shouldn't immediately embrace the NVH, for there might emerge reasons to think that one notion is in some way prior to the other. We can define "grue" and "bleen" in terms of "blue" and "green" (plus some other machinery), but "blue" and "green" can also be defined in terms of "grue" and "bleen" (plus the same machinery). But it doesn't follow from this fact that a theory stated using "green" and "blue" is just a notational variant of a theory stated in terms of "grue" and "bleen." "Green" and "blue" are *metaphysically* prior to "grue" and "bleen," so *ought to be* prior in definition as well. A theory that takes the notion of "grue" as *undefined* is making a *metaphysical* mistake.

Let's examine two arguments for taking the notion of naturalness rather than degrees of being as the *metaphysically* prior notion.

The first argument is the *meta-Euthyphro argument*. Two properties are not metaphysically on a par simply because they mutually supervene on each other. Euthyphro puzzles arise whenever we suspect that one of the properties is more fundamental than the other. Is the fact that it is morally obligatory why God commands that it be done, or does God's commanding that it be done make it the case that it is morally obligatory? The question "which property, *being morally obligatory* or *being commanded by God* is *prior?*" is intelligible, and tough to answer even if we grant that both properties are necessarily coextensive. (The atheist has an easier time with this puzzle.)

A plausible account of the notion of priority explicates it in terms of *intensiveness* and naturalness. Say that property F is at least as *intensive* as G if and only if the set of possible and actual instances of G is a subset of the possible and actual instances of F.

(IV1):   Property P obtains *in virtue of* property Q obtaining = df. P and Q both obtain; P is at least as intensive as Q and Q is more natural than P.[18]

The tricky cases we've discussed are ones in which the relevant properties are at least as intensive as each other, i.e., are necessarily co-extensional. In such cases, IV1 says the sole factor that determines which property is prior is which is more natural. More formally:

1.   If two properties P1 and P2 are necessarily co-extensional and P2 obtains in virtue of P1 obtaining, then P1 is more natural than P2.

The properties that concern us here are *naturalness* and *degrees of being* and we are considering the hypothesis that

2.   *Naturalness* and *degrees of being* are necessarily co-extensional, but one of them obtains in virtue of the other obtaining.[19]

It follows from premise 1 and 2 that

3.   One of *naturalness* and *degrees of being* is more natural than the other.

But which is more natural?

4.   If one of *naturalness* and *degrees of being* is more natural than the other, then *naturalness* is more natural than *degrees of being*.

I don't have much to say in favor of premise 4, but isn't naturalness just intuitively more likely to be natural than any competitor to it?

∴   So *naturalness* is more natural than *degrees of being*.

This argument is interesting. However, it can be resisted. Note that the champion of degrees of being needn't accept IV1. Instead, she should accept:

(IV2):   Property P obtains in virtue of property Q obtaining = df. P and Q both obtain; P is at least as intensive as Q; Q is more real than P.

---

[18]   This is not to say that it is the best account of priority. Perhaps an electron does not have the property being such that there are infinitely many prime numbers in virtue of being negatively charged. We'll have more to say about priority in chapter 8; for now, let this account of priority suffice to illustrate the point here. And so much the worse for the argument that naturalness is prior to degrees of being if this kind of account of priority fails. Thanks to Alex Skiles for discussion here.

[19]   Here I am using both "naturalness" and "degrees of being" to designate the relevant quantitative properties. We could run similar arguments using specific amounts of these quantities as well.

IV2 is no less plausible than IV1. IV2 is part of a nice picture according to which the maximally real serve as the complete supervenience base for the less than maximally real.

A parallel meta-Euthyphro argument using IV2 as a basis can be constructed as follows:

1*.   If two properties P1 and P2 are necessarily co-extensional and P2 obtains in virtue of P1 obtaining, then P1 is more real than P2.

2*.   *Naturalness* and *degrees of being* are necessarily co-extensional, but one of them obtains in virtue of the other obtaining.

3*.   So one of *naturalness* and *degrees of being* is more real than the other.

4*.   If one of *naturalness* and *degrees of being* is more real than the other, then *degrees of being* is more real than *naturalness*.

∴   So *degrees of being* is more real than *naturalness*.

Premise 1* relies on IV2. Premise 2* is numerically identical to premise 2. Premise 3* is a logical consequence of premises 1* and 2*. Premise 4* is no less plausible than premise 4. In my opinion, neither version of the meta-Euthyphro argument is more convincing than the other.

In fact, the NVH provides an explanation of why neither argument is more convincing than the other. First, the friend of the NVH will hold that IV1 and IV2 are notational equivalents of each other. Moreover, on the NVH, the parallel arguments are notational variants of each other, and so both have faulty second premises. Finally, human beings are subject to framing effects: the same phenomenon when presented under different guises can elicit different psychological reactions. When presenting earlier versions of this chapter in various venues, I would occasionally switch the order in which the arguments appeared. According to the reports of some of my audience members, the first argument was always somewhat tempting, regardless of which argument it was. If the NVH is true, it is unsurprising that we might be susceptible to this kind of framing effect.[20]

Let's consider a second argument for the priority of naturalness. This argument is based on some remarks by Sider (2011), whose preferred locutions are "structure" and "is structural" rather than "naturalness" and "is natural." Sider (2011: 141) writes, "The reason for thinking that structure cannot be merely somewhat structural is its first-order heterogeneity—if structure is not perfectly structural then it is disjunctive and therefore highly nonstructural." Sider is concerned with what he calls first-order heterogeneity. The various structural properties don't seem to have anything in common with each other besides their being structural. For example, what else does charge have in common with set-membership? So the only plausible reductive

---

[20]   That said, if the NVH is true, then both premise 2 and premise 2* are necessarily false. If 2 and 2* are both plausible, is it more likely that one of them is true rather than both are false? If so, NVH pays a cost by denying both of them. Thanks to Joshua Spencer for pointing this out.

analysis of structure would be a highly disjunctive analysis: to be structural is to be charge or to be set-membership or to be.... Since no such reductive account is possible, naturalness must itself be perfectly natural.

This is a weak argument. It's based on the assumption that any analysis of naturalness must be in terms of the properties that are natural. But an analysis of naturalness in terms of degrees of being is not an analysis in terms of the properties that are natural or most real.

Let's consider a third argument. This is the argument from *ways of being*. A presupposition of this argument is that, not only do some things have more reality than others, but additionally some things have a different *kind* of reality than others. Making a case for modes of being is one of the central goals of this book. If this case is incompatible with the case for degrees of being, it's hurting time for me. But independently of its consequences for my well-being, this consequence would be philosophically surprising and intriguing, since so far no incompatibility has emerged.

Now if we take naturalness as primitive, we can use it to define the notion of a *way of being* (as in chapters 1 and 2) in addition to the notion of a *degree of being* (chapter 5). But how could we define the notion of a *way* of being in terms of the notion of a *degree* of being? It seems that, if the proposed primitive notion is *x has n units of being*, then we cannot use that primitive to define the notion of a way of being. If there are units of being, then there is a function from the things that have being to the positive real numbers within (0,1]. And if this is the case, then the relation *x has at least as much being as y* will be *comparable*, i.e., for all x and y, either x will have more being than y, or x will have the same amount of being as y, or x will have less being than y. If this relation is comparable, then everything must be real in the same way, even though things might enjoy different amounts of the same kind of reality. Compare: everything is massive in the same way although some things are more massive than another. In none but the thinnest sense is an elephant massive in a different way than a Lego brick. Since taking the notion of naturalness as primitive allows us to define up both *degree of being* and *way of being*, while taking degree of being as primitive does not allow us to define up *way of being*, naturalness is the better choice of a primitive. And so it would be better to take naturalness as metaphysically prior to degree of being.

This argument is tempting, but not good. There is a way to formulate the doctrine that there are modes of being even if *x has at least as much being as y* is comparable.[21] This way mimics the formulation that employs the notion of naturalness. We start with the idea that there are possible alternative meanings for the unrestricted quantifier. These meanings are entities. (Perhaps they are higher-order properties.) Some of these entities are more real than others. There are modes of being just in case

---

[21]   This way was suggested to me by Mark Barber.

there are at least two possible meanings for the unrestricted quantifier that are maximally real.

This response requires that some abstract entities be fully real. A more cautious formulation is one that requires that the modes of being be such that no other entity of their type is more real than them. (So if, for example, modes of being are higher-order properties, there will be no other properties that are more real than them.) Call such modes of being *best modes*.

And note that if we proceed along the above lines, we can still countenance the other kinds of ontological superiority invoked in various places in this book. There are levels of being provided that there are best modes of being such that the domain of one is properly included in the domain of the other. There are orders of being provided that the logical structure of one best mode of being requires an index that is in the domain of a distinct best mode of being. We can take degree of being as our central structuring primitive and nonetheless account for other ontological dimensions in terms of it.

The obvious argument for the incoherence of a system incorporating both modes of being and degrees of being fails. It might not be the only argument though. The final chapter of Shields (1999) is devoted to demonstrating that Aristotle's metaphysics is internally incoherent since it implies both that being is said in many ways and that being comes in degrees. Let's assess both whether Shields's argument generalizes so as to cover not only Aristotle's doctrines but my own as well, and whether Shields's argument is effective against Aristotle's metaphysics (even if it is only effective given the particularities of Aristotle's metaphysics).

Here is Shields's (1999: 261) argument, with my interpretative comments in brackets so that its relevance to my project is evident. These interpretative comments also elucidate Shields's technical expressions.

1. Two *F* things are non-synonymously *F* only if they are incommensurable as *F*s. [Two things are non-synonymously *F* if and only if they are *F*s in different ways.]
2. Beings are always commensurable as beings. [Beings are commensurable as beings if and only if, for any two beings, these two are either equal as beings or one of them is more of a being than the other.]
3. Hence, beings are not non-synonymously beings.
4. The distinction between homonymy and synonymy is exhaustive.
5. Hence, beings are always synonymously beings.
6. If beings are always synonymously beings, then they are univocally beings. [If beings are always synonymously beings, then there are no modes of being.]
7. Therefore, since beings are core-dependent homonyms only if they are non-univocal, beings are not core-dependent homonyms. [Beings are core-dependent homonyms if and only if there is a central way of being in terms of which the other modes of being must be understood.]

In what follows, I will not challenge premises 4 or 6. Since 3 and 5 are interim conclusions that follow validly from their predecessors, the remaining targets are premises 1 and 2. Shields (1999: 261–6) holds that Aristotle is committed to premises 1 and 2. My view is that both premises are false, provided that we understand that what it is for two beings to be non-synonymously beings is for them to have different modes of being.

Let's start with premise 1. To show Aristotle's commitment to premise 1, Shields cites the following passage from *Physics* VII.4, 248b6–11 (Aristotle 1984a: 415):

Non-synonymous things are all incommensurable. Why is [it not possible to say] of what is not commensurable, e.g. a pen, the wine, or the highest note, whether one is sharper [than the others]? The reason is that homonymous things are not commensurable. The highest note in a scale is, however, commensurable with the lead note, since "sharp" signifies the same for both.

Shields also notes putatively other relevant passages: *Categories* 11a5–13 (Aristotle 1984a: 17), *Topics* III.1, 116a1–8 (Aristotle 1984a: 193), and most clearly relevantly, *Politics* I.13, 1259b36–8 (Aristotle 1984b: 1999), in which Aristotle asserts that a difference of more or less never is a difference in kind.

It certainly seems then that Aristotle accepts premise 1. But should he have? First, let's consider the example Shields explicitly cites. A pen, a wine, and a musical note can be said to be "sharp" in some sense. Let's grant that there is a generic sense of "sharp" so that it even makes sense to talk of them each as being sharp, albeit with their own respective modes of sharpness. If there is no generic sense of "sharp," we cannot make the relevant comparative judgments without augmenting our language in some way. The question then would become whether there is a possible generic sense of "sharp" that would permit some kind of comparative judgment.

But is the relation between their respective sharpnesses really like the relation between modes of being, or other interesting cases of analogy in the philosophical sense? (In other words, is the analogy apt?) Not obviously. Perhaps *being sharp* is a mere disjunction. It's true that two of the disjuncts seem to have the following commonality: things that are sharp in one of these ways can be unpleasant when creatures with our constitution are presented with them via the appropriate sensory modality. Sharp pens hurt to touch; I assume sharp wines are painful to drink. Maybe the kinds of painful experiences we have in both cases feel similar to each other, and this is why we find it appropriate to call both of them "sharp." Perhaps there can be also sharp odors emitted by dyspeptic birds. (The "sharpness" of a note is an entirely different phenomenon, and I will set that sense of "sharp" aside in what follows.) But this kind of unity is both extrinsic—it depends on the constitution of our sensory organs—and contingent, since our sensory organs could have been differently constituted. If there is any intrinsic and necessary unity to these modes of being sharp, it merely consists in the respective categorical bases for the dispositions to cause unpleasant sensations of a particular sort in creatures constituted in the manner we actually are. That feels pretty thin to me. Perhaps, though, it is enough to permit a limited amount of comparability: perhaps a mildly sharp pen hurts less to touch than a seriously sharp wine hurts to taste. Is this comparability with respect to sharpness or with respect to painfulness?[22] If *painfulness* is a common aspect to various ways of being sharp, it might be both: there might be a limited kind of comparability between the sharpness of things in virtue of the comparability of their painfulness.

Regardless, what makes *being* analogous rather than merely disjunctive is that there is an intrinsic and necessary unity to the modes of being themselves. The same is true of parthood. When *this* kind of unity is present, it is not obvious that there cannot be comparability. Perhaps part of Shields's motivation here is the thought that being is very thin—it admits no hidden complexities and has no aspects.[23] But the various modes must have "something in common" in order for them to be analogically related. Otherwise *being* would merely be a disjunction of these modes, rather than something that is unified via analogy. Perhaps things can be compared qua beings despite enjoying distinct modes of being in virtue of the common aspects of their respective modes. In my system, it is clear how this could work: one thing is more of a being than another because its most real mode of being is more real than the other's most real mode of being. Because modes of being can be directly compared with respect to how much being they themselves enjoy, an indirect comparison between entities that enjoy those modes is also possible.

Let us turn to premise 2 of Shields's argument. To show that Aristotle accepts premise 2, Shields cites *Metaphysics* XIV.1, 1088a22–5, 29–34 (Aristotle 1984b: 1719), in which Aristotle appears to claim that relations have less being than all other beings, or at least all other beings that fall under a category. The specific quote under contention is "the relative is least of all things."[24]

A bit of caution is in order. Although I alluded to this passage in section 5.5 and claimed that friends of this slogan should consider whether relations are plausibly thought as beings by courtesy, this is not obviously the correct model for understanding Aristotle's metaphysics. *Relation* is a category, and hence by my lights is a fundamental mode of being; Aristotle, recall, treats privations importantly differently than things that fall under the categories, and this suggests that it is a different kind of ontological superiority that Aristotle has in mind via this slogan rather than the kind that I am calling *degree of being*. Perhaps Aristotle has what I have called *order of being* in mind. A relation typically inheres in—exists in—more things than a monadic property. So relations have a worse order of being than those things in the

---

[22] Compare with what Shields (1999: 262–3) says about *choiceworthiness*. Ward's (2008: 126–8) discussion of what Aristotle took to be necessary conditions for commensurability is relevant.

[23] In van Inwagen's (2001a: 4–5) sense, "being" is *thin*. See Berto (2013: 31–3) for discussion and Vallicella (2002, 2004, 2014) for a defense of a *thick* conception of being.

[24] *Metaphysics* XIV.1, 1088a23 (Aristotle 1984b: 1719). Ward (2008: 128) disputes Shields's reading of this passage. She takes Aristotle to be saying of relations that "they possess least the kind of being that substances possess." This reading of Aristotle strikes me as less plausible than Shields's reading, since relations have a different mode of being than substances and hence do not possess *any* of the kind of being that substances enjoy.

other categories: the logical form of the mode of being of a relation is more polyadic than that of the modes of being of the other categories. Hence it is the worst (or "least") of all of them. But because there is comparability between the modes in question, there is also a comparability between entities enjoying these modes: a relation is "less of a being" than an accident in the sense that it has a worse order of being, and this is because of the kind of straightforward comparison made between the adicities of the modes of being these entities enjoy. (These remarks constitute a complaint against premise 1 rather than 2.)

Let's assume though that Aristotle meant what I mean by degree of being rather than order of being. Even so, premise 2 is neither obviously asserted by Aristotle nor obviously true. In the *Metaphysics* passage Shields cites, Aristotle seems to assert that *some* beings, namely relatives, are worse beings than all other beings. But it does not follow from this passage that *all* beings are comparable with respect to how much being they enjoy.

To see this, note that the friend of ways and degrees of being needn't take *x has n units of being* as the basic notion. She might opt instead to take the comparative relation *x has at least as much being as y* as basic. She should say something about the logical properties of this relation: it is intuitive that it is reflexive, transitive, and non-symmetric. But she needn't hold that the relation is *comparable* in the sense that, for any *x* and *y*, either *x* has more being than *y*, or *y* has more being than *x*, or *x* is equal in being to *y*.

Arguably, some relations are comparative without being comparable, although examples are controversial. Consider the relation *x has at least as much intrinsic value as y*. Many states of affairs have intrinsic value, including those in which someone experiences some pleasure and those in which someone knows something. There is at least limited comparability: it is intrinsically better to know whether God exists than it is to experience a very minor pleasure. But it is not obvious that every possible episode of pleasure is less than, greater than, or equal in value to every possible episode of knowledge.[25]

And note that it is not obvious that *x is more natural than y* is comparable. In general, from the fact that a relation is comparative, and hence allows for some true comparative claims, it does not automatically follow that it is comparable.

Moreover, a second way of capturing the idea that there are modes of being is by claiming that *x has at least as much being as y* fails to be comparable. Say that something *x* has a *maximum degree of being* just in case there is no *y* such that *y* has as least as much being as *x* but *x* does not have at least as much being as *y*. On this picture, if there are ways of being—different ways to be real—then there are some things that have a maximum degree of being but are such that none of them has at

---

[25] See Chang (2002) for relevant discussion. Note that Chang introduces another comparative relation into the discussion that she calls "parity." It would be interesting if relative being could induce relations of parity of this sort, but I won't pursue this issue further.

least as much being as the others. An unusual view to be sure—presumably not Aristotle's—but defensible.

Aristotle's claim that some entities (relatives) are lesser beings than all others does not imply premise 2. It is in fact logically independent of premise 2. To see that the claim that relatives are the least of all things is logically independent of the claim that beings are always comparable as beings, consider the following model. Suppose that there is one thing that is less of a being than all others. It is consistent with this claim that no other beings are comparable with respect to how much being they have. On this model, the least being is the bottom point of a structure that branches like a tree. A similar model in which there are many equally low things occupying the bottom point (e.g., all the relatives) suffices for the same conclusion. Conversely, suppose that everything has exactly the same amount of being as everything else. Then beings are always comparable as beings but nothing has the least being of all beings. That relatives are the least of all things is logically independent of the claim that beings are always comparable as beings. Aristotle can consistently reject premise 2.

Suppose we deny that beings are always comparable as beings. Then we can say something like the following. Objects and properties enjoy different ways of being. Both you and your shadow are objects, but you are more real than your shadow. *Having -1 charge* is more real than *being grue*. But since you enjoy a different kind of reality than *having -1 charge*, it is not the case that either one of you has at least as much reality as the other.

What is the proper linguistic guise for *x has at least as much being as y*, if we wish (as I do) to preserve a connection between being and quantification? The idea of a *polyadic quantifier*, which informally we can take to be a single expression capable of binding multiple free variables within an open sentence so as to yield a sentence with no free variables, has been well studied.[26] On the view under consideration, the fundamental existential expression would be a kind of polyadic quantifier. Although this is not the place to develop a formal semantics for such an expression, it might be useful to briefly see how such a device could function. Let's have "$" be the polyadic quantifier that has as its semantic value *x has at least as much being as y*. Informally, a sentence such as "$x,y (Fx,Gy)$" could be used to say that some F has at least as much being as some G, while a sentence like "$x,y (x = a, y = b)$" could be used to say that *a* has at least as much being as *b*. And either of *x* or *y* might be individuals, or properties, or objects of any ontological type.

We have now discussed two arguments for the priority of naturalness over degrees of being: the meta-Euthyphro argument, and the argument from modes of being. Both arguments failed. I know of no other arguments for taking naturalness to be more basic than the notion of a degree of being.

---

[26] See, for example, Peters and Westerståhl (2006).

7.6 Is Degree of Being the Prior Notion?

We have explored arguments against the NVH that tried to establish that naturalness is the prior notion. I think they failed. A second way of undercutting the NVH is to argue that degree of being is the more basic notion. Here I will discuss one plausible argument for this claim, which is an argument from *ideological parsimony*.

The *ideology* of a theory consists in the notions taken as primitive or undefined by the theory. Consider two theories. Perhaps they are theories about the nature of intrinsicality, or causation, or supervenience. Whatever the theories are about, they are extremely similar theories. In fact, these two theories should be exactly alike with respect to the primitives they employ, except that the first theory appeals to the notion of existence but claims that existence comes in amounts, while the second theory appeals to both the notion of existence *and* the notion of naturalness, and claims that naturalness comes in amounts.

By comparing pairs of theories in this way, we can precisely isolate the question of which ideology is simpler. Every interesting philosophical notion defined or partially characterized in terms of the ideology of the second theory that appeals to natural-ness and quantification can be defined or partially characterized in terms of the ideology of comparative reality of the first theory. From the perspective of ideological parsimony, the first theory is simpler. Both theories postulate a primitive that comes in amounts, but the second theory employs an additional primitive notion.

Note that Sider (2011) commits himself both to the structuralness of quantification and the structuralness of structure itself, which suggests that Sider is also dubious about defining up a notion of quantification in terms of structure. In this respect, both being and structure are parts of Sider's ideology. Similar remarks apply to the system of Schaffer (2009: 374), who makes use of a primitive notion of *grounding* rather than structure but who also explicitly denies that *existence* can be defined in terms of grounding.[27] Both philosophers have a primitive notion of quantification or existence, as well as a primitive notion that structures in some way what there is.

Let us explore whether we can do with fewer primitives. For the sake of clarity, let's first consider the view that the fundamental existential notion is comparative: *x has at least as much being as y*.[28] Recall that in the previous section we briefly discussed how the proper linguistic vehicle for a comparative notion of being is a polyadic quantifier that binds two variables at once. With the comparative notion, we can easily define up the "absolute" notion of being: to be is to have at least as much being as oneself. We capture this idea by defining "absolute" or "monadic" existential quantification in terms of the polyadic quantifier as follows: for any formula in which "x" is the only

---

[27] Many philosophers stress the indefinability of "existence." See, e.g., Coffey (1938: 33), Gibson (1998: 1), and Miller (2002: 1).

[28] I am confident that a similar story can be told for other views about the nature of quantities, but focus on this one in order to clearly express the moral of the story.

free variable, "Ex Ψ" is true if and only if "$x,x (Ψ)" is true. And to say that a property F is at least as natural as property G is to say, "$x,y (x = F, y = G)." We have an existential notion, expressed by a polyadic quantifier, and both "absolute" existential quantification and naturalness are defined in terms of it and the notion of identity.

(Perhaps identity is another notion that will be part of the ideology of any viable metaphysical theory. If the friend of naturalness can define away identity *in a way not available* to the friend of degrees of being, we would have to reassess the question of ideological parsimony. I see no route to doing this.)

The question now is whether a theory that makes use only of the notion of naturalness or structure but does not have quantification in its fundamental ideology can nonetheless define up a notion of quantification. To ensure parallel treatment, we focus on the view according to which the fundamental naturalness notion is also comparative: *x is at least as natural as y.* But from this notion it is not at all clear how one can define up either monadic or polyadic quantification in terms of it. If we help ourselves to quantification we can use it plus naturalness to define a comparative notion of being, as was discussed earlier. But in order to establish ideological parity, we need to be able to define either absolute or polyadic quantification in terms of *naturalness alone,* that is, *without the aid of any other quantificational notions.*

The difficulty of this task should not be obscured by the fact that *being* and *naturalness* are both, in a sense, "properties of properties." But perhaps this fact provides a clue to how we can define up being in terms of naturalness. If we embrace the connection between being and quantification, then, to say that there is an F amounts to attributing to F the property of "having an instance." With this in mind, let us consider one way of attempting to account for quantification in terms of naturalness. Suppose we say that there is a P just in case P is at least as natural as P, that is, Ex (x has P) if and only if N(P,P), where "N" is the predicate for comparative naturalness. (In general, say that an open formula is satisfied by something just in case the property or relation that corresponds to it stands in the comparative naturalness relation to itself.) If this is a successful way of defining up being in terms of naturalness, ideological parity will be restored.

This way of defining up being in terms of naturalness presupposes that *every* property and relation is instantiated. Many embrace this presupposition, but it is metaphysically contentious; recall our brief discussion of this question in section 7.3. When we frame the assumption in terms of degrees of being, it is this: a property exists to some extent or other only if some instance of it exists to some extent or other. The friend who takes a comparative notion of being as her primitive notion needn't accept this claim, though she needn't reject it either. But it is not clear to me that one can define up being without this assumption, although, as the kids say, it is hard to prove a negative. Insofar as we are cautious about the existence of uninstantiated properties, we should be cautious about this way to establish ideological parsimony.

But let us provisionally grant this assumption. Then ideological parity will have been restored. In both cases, there is one primitive comparative notion. On this view, the notion of naturalness has straightforward existential implications, and not only in the trivial way in which if something has a property, then it is something. (If a property is natural, it follows that the property is something, just as it follows from the claim that my dog is hungry, that my dog is something.) *An assertion of the naturalness of a property straightforwardly implies the existence of a thing beyond the property itself.* In short, the fundamental notion of naturalness *is an existentially loaded notion.* One ought to conclude that those who speak of naturalness speak of *gradations of being*, albeit under a different guise.

Either the NVH is true or it is false because *naturalness* ought to be understood in terms of *degrees of being*.

7.7 Entity Fundamentalism

The view defended here takes the locus of fundamentality to be entities that enjoy various amounts of reality: relative fundamentality simply is relative amount of being. Sider (2011: 164–5) has argued against views of broadly this sort; here we'll see whether the objections have merit.

Briefly, Sider offers three arguments. The first argument is that taking entities as fundamental requires thinking of abstract objects as the locus of fundamentality, and this is problematic. Reply: it requires thinking of abstract objects as enjoying some degree of fundamentality, i.e., some amount of being, but this is not problematic, for they do enjoy some amount of being. The only remaining question is how much. The approach here does not imply that only abstract objects enjoy some amount of reality; that claim would be absurd. Nor does it imply that abstract objects are as real as concrete objects; some might be, but many will not be.

The second argument is that taking entities as the locus of fundamentality conflates whether an entity is fundamental with whether what that entity represents is fundamental. I deny that this conflation is a consequence of the view. First, neither objects nor properties are representational qua object or property. I represent nothing except only in some very strained sense, but even then, no one should conflate the claim that I enjoy some degree of reality with the claim that whatever I represent enjoys that degree of reality. The property of being blue is also not a representation. Sentences are representational; they also have some degree of reality. That degree of reality needn't be proportional to the degree of reality of that fact that the sentence pictures, and in many cases it won't be. Perhaps propositions are "intrinsically representational" but, as with sentences, one shouldn't run together a claim about how much being a proposition has with a claim about how much being the corresponding state of affairs has, even when that proposition is about the amount of being a given state of affairs enjoys.

Finally, Sider claims that the entity-fundamentalist conflates claims about the fundamentality of an object's existence with claims about the fundamentality of an object's nature. He claims that he can distinguish the question of whether the existence of a chair is fundamental from the question of whether the chair's nature is fundamental. I reply that I can as well. Although I am tempted to think that only fully real entities enjoy perfectly natural properties (recall section 5.7), I am sure that fully real entities can enjoy less than perfectly natural properties as well. So nothing stops me from agreeing in principle with Sider that, for example, a table enjoys as much being as an electron even though none of the properties that the table exemplifies enjoy as much being as the most real properties of that electron.

7.8 Brief Philosophical Diatribe

If my arguments are sound, then contemporary metaphysicians have much more in common with their historical predecessors than they initially thought, and accordingly ought to treat the historical doctrine that there are gradations of being with the respect it is due rather than with the derision it is commonly met with. For those who truck with naturalness either truck with gradations of being under a different guise, or are taking as primitive a notion that demands analysis in terms of gradations of being. Either way, the self-conception of these metaphysicians must change.

There are philosophers who elevate failing to understand the primitive notions of their interlocutors into a form of performance art. When they hear terms like "grounding," or "structure," or "naturalness," they leap up with excitement and emphatically deny their very intelligibility. They claim to have no idea what could possibly be meant by such expressions. But no philosopher can sincerely deny that they understand "being," which is not to say that there aren't interesting philosophical puzzles about being. *Everyone has sufficient grasp of the notion of being to entertain interesting philosophical claims about it.* Those who claim to deny this are merely frothing with words. To these philosophers, I say that you understand my primitive, and you understand the thesis that this primitive stands for a quantitative aspect.[29] Investigate the arguments for this thesis! And to the friends of naturalness who have been frothed upon, note that if my arguments are sound, you have the same response available to you. This is more than sufficient compensation, if any is needed, for embracing degrees of being.

---

[29] *Pace* Daly (2012: 92), talk of degrees of being is *not* quasi-technical talk for which we require a definition to understand. *Pace* Audi (2012: 118) and van Inwagen (2014: 240), that there are degrees of being is perfectly intelligible.

7.9 Chapter Summary

In this chapter, I argued that the naturalness of a property or relation is proportionate to the degree of being of that property or relation, and that once we recognize this proportionality, we see a way to define naturalness in terms of degree of being. Several arguments against this purported reduction of naturalness to degrees of being were discussed and rebutted. A further argument for the reduction, the central premise of which is that theories making use of degrees of being are ideologically simpler than those making use of naturalness and quantification, was tentatively defended.

8

Being and Ground

8.1 Introduction

Anyone familiar with metaphysics as it is done in the analytic tradition at the time proximate to my writing this introduction knows that the theme of grounding is the topic *du jour*. Talk of ground, metaphysical explanation, the in virtue of relation, "because," and so forth, is ubiquitous in contemporary philosophical discourse. Largely this is because of the excellent work of Kit Fine and Jonathan Schaffer, among others, that gave rise to the current debate. Partly this is because philosophers in general are always looking for a new toy to play with. But one cannot deny that such expressions have enjoyed great currency in philosophical theorizing well before the present age, and that the task of understanding them is one that philosophers cannot in good conscience shirk. Especially important are the potential connections between ground and being.[1] For these reasons, I reluctantly contribute this chapter to the ever-growing literature. Admittedly, I want to play with the toys too.

Here are the questions and issues I plan to focus on. Some of them are specifically about ground. Should we be pluralists about grounding? On the assumption that talk of ground is talk of a relation, is there exactly one grounding relation? If there are many grounding relations, how are they related to one another? Is there a generic relation of grounding, and is it a mere disjunction of the specific relations, or is it unified by analogy? In what sense is ground a metaphysical primitive? Is talk of ground really schematic talk best replaced by specific discussions of other relations already well studied, as is suggested by Wilson (2014: 539)? Some of them are about the relation between being and ground. If x is grounded in y, does it follow that y is in some way ontologically superior to x? If so, which way? Can we define, reduce, or in some way understand ground in terms of kinds of ontological superiority? Are relations of ontological superiority *ipso facto* grounding relations? Does the inducement of ontological superiority in some way account for the unity of grounding? Is grounding itself an entity in the ontology, and if so what mode of being does it enjoy?

We have a lot of surface to cover. Here's my plan for proceeding in this chapter. In the remainder of this introduction, I will first discuss the question of whether ground

---

[1] As Silverman (2013: 106) notes, that there is a tight connection between being and ground is as old as Plato.

is in some way primitive. I will then discuss one split between proponents of ground, namely, whether it is a topic-neutral relation or whether it is defined only on facts, propositions, or other such entities with similar structure. One proponent of the former view is Schaffer (2009), who thinks of grounding as a relation that relates entities of any particular ontological category. Section 8.2 will focus on this view of grounding. I will argue that ground on this conception can be reduced to either degree of being or order of being. Accordingly, although talk of grounding in this manner is perfectly acceptable, at the fundamental level, it is dispensable: it isn't needed for saying everything there is to be said about the world in the most fundamental terms. In section 8.3, I will turn to the idea that ground is a relation between facts. It is harder to give a reductive account of this notion of ground; some accounts will be discussed, but perhaps none of them is wholly satisfactory. In section 8.4, I will discuss the question of the unity of ground, which is a question that pluralists about grounding face. Finally, in section 8.5, I will discuss whether grounding monists have a reason to posit a further structuring feature, such as naturalness or degrees of being.

Let's start with the discussion of whether and in which sense or senses ground might be primitive. We'll distinguish ideological primitiveness, methodological primitiveness, and metaphysical primitiveness.

To say that grounding is ideologically primitive is to say that we cannot give a reductive definition or analysis of the notion of grounding.[2] This might be because in principle no such reductive definition or analysis is possible. Or it might be merely because we lack the conceptual or logical resources to state what is in principle definable. I don't want to get too bogged down in what is involved in successful reductions, but a minimum requirement for a reductive account of grounding is that, given such an account, any sentence in which a grounding expression occurs can be replaced with a necessarily equivalent sentence in which no such expression occurs. (Consider for comparison Lewis's reductive account of modality, which provides a recipe for replacing any sentence in which a modal expression occurs with a sentence in which no modal notion occurs.)

To say that grounding is methodologically primitive is to say that it is dialectically permissible to appeal to grounding in one's metaphysical theories without attempting to define or analyze this notion, regardless of whether it is ideologically primitive.[3] The basic idea is that if grounding is methodologically primitive, then proponents of ground do not have the burden of proof with respect to whether the notion of ground is sufficiently intelligible to use in theorizing; rather, it is those who wish to cast doubt

---

[2] Compare with Trogdon (2013b). Schaffer (2009: 364) and Rosen (2010) take grounding to be ideologically primitive.

[3] Vallicella (2002: 43–6) argues that the notion expressed by "in virtue of" is indispensable to metaphysics. I take it that if a notion is indispensable, it is methodologically primitive.

on its intelligibility who have the burden of proof. (One presents a *demand* for a definition when one doubts that the target in question is well understood.)

Ideological and methodological primitiveness are not equivalent. For one thing, whether something is methodologically primitive might be something that is relative to a context; in one kind of metaphysical inquiry, it might be OK to appeal to grounding without defining it, but in a different kind of context, perhaps not. (Perhaps in the metaphysics of ordinary objects or social kinds, it doesn't really matter whether grounding is in any way primitive, but it does in "fundamental" metaphysics.) But even setting aside this difference, there are others. Ground might be methodologically primitive but not ideologically primitive. But if this is so, then one has the dialectical right to theorize in terms of grounding in advance of any attempt to define "ground," even though there is a definition to be had. Ground might be ideologically primitive but not methodologically primitive. But it would be unfortunate if this were so: if it is not methodologically primitive, then one must attempt to define or analyze the notion before employing it, but if it is ideologically primitive, no such attempt will succeed. Perhaps we should refrain from using expressions that suffer from this combination.

Finally, what is it to say that grounding is metaphysically primitive? For me, to say that grounding is metaphysically primitive is just to say that the grounding relation is a perfectly natural relation, i.e., is among those properties and relations that are most real.[4] Perhaps this is to impose an external framework that grounding theorists might be hostile to. I want to avoid begging questions here. For now, it would be good to have alternative characterizations of metaphysical primitiveness that do not have this consequence, even if at the end of the day this characterization is the best one to adopt.

Three alternatives suggest themselves. First, if we think, along with Schaffer, that all entities enter into grounding relations, then we could say that grounding is metaphysically primitive$_1$ if and only if nothing grounds the grounding relation.[5] The other two alternatives assume that grounding is a relation between facts or propositions. Second, we might say that a relation is metaphysically primitive$_2$ just in case there are ungrounded facts that have that relation as a constituent.[6] Third, we

---

[4] Joshua Spencer has suggested to me that if grounding is a perfectly natural relation, there cannot be duplicates whose parts stand in opposing grounding relations. (For example, it is not possible that I am grounded in my parts while my duplicate grounds his parts.) I do not regard this as a cost but rather a benefit of the proposal. This relies on Lewis's (1986: 59–63) idea that duplication should be understood in terms of 1–1 correspondences between parts that preserve perfectly natural properties and relations, which I accept.

[5] In section 8.2, there will be a brief discussion of whether Schaffer now intends to take grounding to be maximally general in this way.

[6] Bennett (2011a) and deRosset (2013) deny that grounding is metaphysically primitive$_2$. Alex Skiles has suggested to me that we should make further distinctions here, corresponding to the different ways in which a property or relation can appear as a constituent in a fact. It might appear as a *predicative constituent* and it might appear as a *subject constituent*. (Note the difference between the fact that *a* grounds *b* and the fact that *grounding* is a relation.) Corresponding to these two ways of appearing in a fact are two finer-grained ways of understanding metaphysical primitiveness. This is an interesting suggestion,

might say that a relation is metaphysically primitive$_3$ just in case there is a fact F such that (i) F has the grounding relation as constituent and (ii) every fact that either grounds F or is among the facts that ground F itself has the grounding relation as a constituent.[7] Perhaps there are other notions of metaphysical primitiveness worth articulating, but these three will suffice for now.

None of these construals of metaphysical primitiveness is equivalent to ideological primitiveness or methodological primitiveness. A feature might fail to be perfectly natural and yet be ideologically primitive. *Being* is probably like this. Similar remarks apply to the second and third construals. DeRosset (2013) thinks that every (atomic) grounding fact is grounded in a non-grounding fact, but maintains that grounding is still ideologically primitive.[8] Conversely, we might have a definition in our language for an expression that *should* be taken as primitive. (Recall the speakers of the Gruesome Tongue from section 1.3, for whom "grue" is a semantically primitive expression from which their expression "green" is defined.) A non-natural feature might also be methodologically primitive. I have my doubts about whether set-membership is perfectly natural since I suspect that sets are beings by courtesy. Yet there is nothing methodologically improper in mathematicians or metaphysicians employing set-theoretical notions in their theories without first defining "set." (As Lewis (1991: 29–31) notes, when mathematicians attempt definitions of "set," the definitions produced are often inapt, unclear, or involve mere picture thinking.)

We've distinguished three kinds of primitiveness. The questions of whether grounding is ideologically or metaphysically primitive will loom large in the sections that follow. So here I will focus on the question of methodological primitivism.

Let's first note that some proponents of grounding embrace *grounding monism*, the view that there is exactly one grounding relation, while others embrace *grounding pluralism*, the view that there is more than one grounding relation. Given grounding pluralism, we must assess the case for the methodological primitiveness of *each* grounding relation. All versions of pluralism generate a similar sort of question. Here, the question is: in virtue of what is a given relation a grounding relation?

One way to try to answer this question is to attempt a *definition* of what it is to be a grounding relation. It might be that no such definition is forthcoming, however. Recall the discussion of compositional pluralism in section 2.3. There are many

---

and worth pursuing. Here, however, I will focus on whether an element is in some way a constituent of an ungrounded fact.

[7] That grounding is metaphysically primitive$_3$ seems to be a consequence of the view defended in Kang (ms). See also Raven (2016). Alex Skiles has suggested to me a weaker requirement: instead of every grounding claim being grounded in a grounding claim, merely require that there is some grounding claim whose only grounds are further grounding claims.

[8] I imagine that, given deRosset's other commitments, he would accept that every grounding fact is grounded in some non-grounding fact. See also Skiles (2015).

parthood relations but I doubt that there is any illuminating definition that will tell us why these parthood relations are all *parthood* relations. The best one can say is that these relations form an analogous relation (in the sense of section 2.3) rather than a mere disjunction. If one of these relations is our paradigmatic parthood relation— such as the relation between hand and human organism—then the aptness of calling the remaining relations "parthood relations" is explained by their analogy with the paradigm. Similarly, even if grounding pluralism is true, there might be nothing more to say about why each grounding relation is *a* grounding relation besides to point out that the generic form of grounding is an analogous relation rather than a mere disjunction.[9] (Whether this is all that can be said will be discussed more in section 8.4.) If this is the case, then the only remaining questions about methodological primitivism concern whether the individual grounding relations are sufficiently intelligible to be utilized in theoretical contexts.

For now, let's focus on grounding monism. Why demand a definition of "ground" prior to its employment in metaphysical theories? Definitions are useful for demonstrating the coherence of notions, but they are not strictly necessary for such demonstrations. Another way to show the coherence of a notion is to use it in one's theories and then show that one doesn't run into logical problems or incoherencies. This is one of the points of Rosen (2010). I take the efforts of Rosen (2010), Fine (2012a), Audi (2012), and others to at least provide a prima facie case that grounding locutions are coherent. In general, one ought to be charitable when faced with an expression in a linguistic community that appears to be consistently used to utter sincerely expressed sentences in contexts in which speakers are attempting to express literal claims. "Ground" seems to meet this condition. Charity certainly does not demand that one forego the quest for analyses or accounts of alien vocabulary, but it does require forfeiting the demand that one's interlocutor present them in one's home vocabulary. I am comfortable with claiming that grounding is methodologically primitive. Methodological primitiveness is the least philosophically interesting form of primitiveness.

A quick clarification: as I understand methodological primitiveness, it is appropriate to appeal to grounding locutions in one's first-order theorizing in advance of providing definitions or analyses of these notions. It is a further question whether it is methodologically appropriate to theorize about grounding per se—as one does when one seeks to determine the "logic" of ground—in advance of definition or analysis. My tentative view is that this is also appropriate, but one must also not take such

---

[9] Cameron (2014: 49) suggests that there is "some prior instance of priority on which the other instances ontologically depend." In the terminology of section 2.2, the suggestion is that grounding might enjoy metaphysical analogy with a focal point. My concern with this suggestion is that, as Cameron (2014: 50) notes, it is unclear what the focal grounding relation is to which all others are to be referred. If there is no plausible candidate, then at best grounding enjoys metaphysical analogy without a focal point. That might be analogy enough, though; recall that in section 2.3, I suggested that parthood enjoys metaphysical analogy without a focal point. And perhaps *being* does as well.

explorations to be definitive in advance of further first-order metaphysical inquiry. This will hopefully become clearer in what follows.

Regardless, it is fair to ask the proponents of grounding to state how they think that the relation works. Fortunately, they have been more than happy to oblige. One split among proponents of ground is over whether talk of grounding is appropriately cashed out in terms of a grounding predicate or rather in terms of a sentence operator. Both ways of proceeding are consistent with denying that there is a relation of grounding. Perhaps not all predicates correspond to properties or relations; Lowe (2004) discusses what he calls "formal ontological relations," which despite the name are not entities in his ontology, and Sider (2009) makes room for metaphysically fundamental locutions to which no entity corresponds. Both ways of proceeding are also consistent with affirming that there is a grounding relation. Of course, a predicate might correspond to an entity; I think they always do unless paradox threatens, though many of these will be mere beings by courtesy. And a sentence operator might have as its semantic value a relation between propositions, although again such a relation might be a mere being by courtesy.[10] (What this discussion already indicates is that an ontological pluralist will care not merely about whether grounding is an entity; she will also care about which way grounding is an entity. More on this in section 8.2.)

Related to the first split is the question of the extent of ground. Some proponents of ground, most notably Schaffer (2009), hold that it is a relation that can relate entities regardless of ontological category. This position seems to demand the use of a grounding predicate rather than an operator; if ground talk is regimented via an operator, then at most grounding is a relation between entities with propositional structure. A pluralist about ground might accept both relations in her ontology. But for now let us consider monistic views on which these are in apparent competition. We'll begin with a discussion of Schaffer in section 8.2, and then turn to a discussion of ground as a more restricted relation in section 8.3. We'll directly compare the two views in section 8.5.

There are other issues that separate proponents of ground. One concerns the "internality" of ground: if x grounds y, does x ground y in every world in which they both exist? Another concerns the "logic" of ground: is it a transitive, asymmetric relation, or does it have a more complex logical structure? Neither of these questions will be extensively discussed in what follows, but when the particular theories that I will focus on imply answers to these questions, I will note this.

---

[10] Two small points. First, many proponents of grounding say that it is a relation between facts rather than propositions per se, although perhaps facts are just true propositions. By way of contrast, in McDaniel (2015), I explore a view in which a kind of grounding, which I call *invirtuation*, is a relation between propositions of all truth-values. (This relation is not identical with what Fine (2012a) calls "non-factive grounding.") Second, recall Mulligan's (2010: 583, fn. 24) view, according to which the correlates of operators are not properties or relations but rather things from a distinct ontological category.

8.2 Entity Grounding

My plan for this section is to present an overview of Schaffer's views, discuss the status of ground as an entity in its own right, and then turn to the question of whether ground as understood by Schaffer is dispensable. With respect to the final question, I'll argue that, given the metaphysical tools already in our possession, there is no need for a metaphysically primitive grounding relation as understood by Schaffer. One possibility is that talk of grounding can be replaced with talk of degrees of being plus other interesting metaphysical relations.

According to Schaffer (2009), the fundamental task of metaphysics is not to determine what kinds of things exist but rather to determine which kinds of things are fundamental, and to determine how the remainder depends upon the fundamental. An entity is *fundamental* just in case nothing grounds it; an entity is *derivative* just in case something grounds it.[11]

On Schaffer's (2009) view, the relation of *grounding* is asymmetric and transitive.[12] Schaffer (2009: 375–6) distinguishes relations of partial and total ground, but holds that they are inter-definable: x is a partial ground of y if and only if x is among those xs that are the total ground of y; xs are a total ground of y if and only if any partial ground of y is among the xs.[13] (The plural variables can take single objects, and hence it is possible for a single object to be a total ground of another object.) In what follows, by "ground" I intend "total ground," unless I explicitly state otherwise. According to Schaffer, grounding is an ideologically primitive relation. (We will discuss shortly whether it is in some sense a metaphysically primitive relation.)

On Schaffer's view, the questions of whether entities such as numbers, meanings, wholes, or holes exist are uninteresting: they obviously do. Schaffer notes that there are many true, affirmative propositions that imply the reality of such entities. (This should ring a bell!) The interesting questions are whether these entities are fundamental entities or derivative entities. As I indicated in sections 5.5 and 5.6, I am inclined to agree.

One of the metaphysical questions driving Schaffer is whether wholes are prior to their parts. On Schaffer's (2010) *monistic* view, the universe, which is the mereological sum of all concrete objects, is an *integrated whole*, where the notion of an integrated whole is defined by him as follows:

x is an integrated whole = df. x grounds each of x's proper parts.

We can contrast the notion of an integrated whole with that of a mere aggregate, which is a whole that is grounded by its proper parts. In what follows, we will try to

---

[11] Schaffer (2009: 373). Compare with Baumgarten (2014: 102). Note that, if we accept that some entities are not even apt for being grounded, we might wish to revise the definition of fundamentality: an entity is *fundamental* if and only if it is apt for grounding and ungrounded. See Dasgupta (2015, forthcoming) for this sort of view, and Schaffer (2009: 373, fn. 32) for an antecedent to it.

[12] Schaffer (2012) abandons transitivity. See Javier-Castellanos (2014) for a critical response.

[13] Compare with Baumgarten (2014: 105–7).

separate Schaffer's views about grounding per se from his applications of that notion in his metaphysical system. This won't always be possible though; in general, it is a mistake to divorce the assessment of questions about the nature of ground from the assessment of other metaphysical questions.

To see why this is, let us turn to the question of whether we should think of grounding as an entity.[14] From my perspective, this is not the best question to pose: rather than ask whether grounding is an entity, i.e., an existent in our ontology, we should ask what sort of mode of being grounding might possess. But for now set this aside and focus on whether grounding is an entity.

If we accept Schaffer's easy ontological ways, isn't the answer "obviously yes"? There are innumerably many true statements in which grounding is apparently referred to—hence we should accept that there is a relation of grounding, unless paradox threatens by our doing so.[15] From a Schafferian perspective, shouldn't we say that the interesting question is whether grounding itself is fundamental or derivative, not whether grounding exists?[16]

But we can't answer this question without also entering into more general metaphysical debates, because we need to know what sort of thing grounding is supposed to be in order to assess whether grounding is grounded. Is grounding a universal? Are universals necessarily instantiated? If a universal is instantiated in some thing or things, is it grounded in those things? Or are universals and things always both grounded in *facts* that consist in things instantiating universals? What grounds facts about grounding? If grounding is not a universal, does "ground" refer to a class of grounding tropes, i.e., particular properties or relations? In general, are tropes grounded in the objects that exemplify them? If tropes are not in general grounded in the objects that exemplify them, should we expect there to be a kind of uniformity to the grounds of grounding tropes?

It might be that all properties, whether universals or tropes, are grounded in some substance or substances. If so, grounding is not metaphysically primitive₁. However, on this view, no property or relation is metaphysically primitive₁. We should infer then that there is a distinction between properties that we have not yet captured. Recall that in section 7.3 I characterized perfectly natural properties and relations as those properties and relations such that no other property or relation is more real than them. This characterization allowed us to say that no property or relation is fully real while still marking an important distinction between properties and relations. Similarly, we should distinguish those properties and relations that are not grounded

---

[14] Schaffer (2009: 373, fn. 32) raises this question.

[15] Does it matter if all the apparently true statements in which grounding is apparently referred to are statements that philosophers make? Shamik Dasgupta has suggested to me that philosophers' talk of grounding is really just a regimentation of an ordinary sense of "because" in natural language. If the ordinary folk trade in talk of grounding, the case for the existence of such a relation appears stronger, but is it a weak case if they do not?

[16] Recall the discussion of easy ontology in section 5.6.

in any other properties and relations from those that are. Call the former properties and relations *ultimate*. Is grounding ultimate regardless of whether it is metaphysically primitive$_1$?

We get different answers depending on whether grounding is a universal or there are tropes of grounding.

Suppose grounding is a universal. Then there are two important questions about how grounding relates to itself. First, there is the question about whether the universal of grounding is itself ultimate. Second, there is the question about the grounds of grounding *facts*. Many proponents of universals include *facts* in their ontology; such entities are conceived as structural complexes whose constituents are universals and particulars.[17] Consider a given physical fact P that grounds a given mental fact M. There is also the fact that P grounds M; call this fact G. What grounds G? Perhaps P alone.[18] Perhaps P and M collectively ground G.[19] Perhaps the essence of M grounds G.[20] (If we are thinking about grounding as a relation between entities, what sort of entity is an essence? Fortunately, that question will be discussed in section 9.4.)

All of these answers have some plausibility, but none of them is clearly relevant to the question of what grounds the grounding relation itself. *If* all relations are grounded in facts in which that relation is a constituent, then it is plausible that what grounds grounding includes what grounds facts about grounding. But if the constituents of facts are not grounded in facts, then one of the answers to the question of what grounds grounding facts might be right, while grounding might nonetheless be an ultimate relation.

Suppose grounding is best treated trope-theoretically. Then strictly speaking there is no single relation of grounding, but rather there are many tropes of grounding. The closest approximation to a single relation of grounding is a maximal class of grounding tropes. And plausibly this maximal class of tropes is grounded in its elements.[21] What about the tropes of grounding themselves? First, note that most

---

[17] Armstrong (1997) is one of the leading proponents of facts construed in this way. See also McDaniel (2009a).

[18] This is the view defended by Bennett (2011a) and deRosset (2013).

[19] Schaffer has suggested to me in personal communication that it is plausible that ground is an internal relation in the Lewisian sense: that is, grounding never differs between duplicate pairs; this suggests that it is not merely P and M that collectively ground G, but rather P and M along with their intrinsic natures. However, as Alex Skiles has pointed out to me, in Schaffer's (2009) system partial grounding is understood as a binary relation that takes single entities rather than pluralities as its relata, and hence we could not say that P and M are collectively partial grounds of G. That said, I take it that Schaffer's statement of the logical form of partial grounding is highly negotiable.

[20] With respect to fact grounding, a version of this view is defended by Dasgupta (2015); see also Rosen (2010), Fine (2012a), and Correia (2013) for discussions of several formulations of this kind of view (for fact grounding).

[21] Many proponents of grounding think that sets are grounded in their elements; see, e.g., Schaffer (2009: 375). For a potentially contrasting view, see Ehring (2011), who holds that tropes get their character from the natural classes of which they are members. This suggests that, for tropes, the class is prior to the member.

proponents of tropes do not accept facts as well into their metaphysics.[22] Let us consider a fact-free trope view. So instead of invoking a physical fact that grounds a mental fact, the proponent of tropes would directly invoke the relevant physical property trope P and the mental property trope M, and the specific grounding trope G that relates them. We can now consider what grounds G, and note that similar answers as earlier are available. Perhaps P alone. Perhaps P and M collectively ground G. Perhaps the essence of M alone grounds G. But note that whichever of these answers we select, there is no further room for grounding tropes to be ultimate.

The upshot is this: the possible range of answers to the question of what grounds grounding depends on whether grounding is a universal or there are tropes of grounding. We can't approach the question of the grounds of grounding in a "metaphysically neutral" way.

There is one final option worth considering. The proceeding discussion assumed that grounding belonged to the same ontological category as other properties or relations. But perhaps this is not so; perhaps grounding belongs to a *sui generis* ontological category. It does seem to be an entity unlike all the others in the ontological system of Schaffer: it is the structuring agent rather than a part of what is structured. It might still be right to call grounding a "relation," but perhaps "relation" is said in many ways. In short, there might be a categorial divide among the properties and relations, just as there is a categorial divide among the entities.[23] Suppose this is right, and that grounding does not share a mode of being with other properties or relations. Then one might say that grounding is not *apt to be grounded* in the following sense: it is a category mistake to self-ascribe grounding. Recall that in section 4.5 we discussed a view in which sets can sensibly be said to have members, even the empty set, but at the fundamental level one can't even express that individuals have members. In the case of ground, entities of other ontological categories can sensibly be said to be grounded or ungrounded; but with respect to the category that ground belongs to, the type restriction rules this out. On this view, what it means to say that grounding is not even "apt to be grounded" is that it is a category mistake to ask whether ground is grounded.[24] (A similar view could also be developed concerning grounding *facts* as well; in section 9.4 we will discuss a view like this concerning facts about strict essence.) This is not a view I favor; insofar as I accept a relation of entity grounding, I view it as a being by courtesy rather than as

---

[22]   That said, there's no inconsistency in doing so and it might be theoretically helpful to do so. And perhaps facts can be identified with suitable constructions constituted by tropes.

[23]   In personal conversation, Schaffer has suggested to me that he finds this picture appealing. In his words, he is interested in exploring the idea that the fundamental categorial divide is between what he calls "entities" and "principles." Then we have fundamental and derivative entities, where fundamental entities are ungrounded entities. But grounding rules are principles and not entities at all. Note that Schaffer wishes to remain neutral on whether categories are best construed as modes of being.

[24]   The importance of the notion of *aptitude* for grounding is stressed in Dasgupta (2015, forthcoming).

enjoying a fundamental mode of being. However, it is a view I recommend to the proponents of grounding to consider.

The notion of grounding and the notion of naturalness perform similar jobs in the respective metaphysics of Schaffer and Sider. Perhaps we can use the notion of an ultimate property to define up a notion of mode of being in a way analogous to how we proceeded in chapter 1, in which naturalness was appealed to. And we should determine whether we can *define up* the notion of grounding from the notion of a degree of being in a similar way as the notion of naturalness was defined in terms of degree of being in chapter 7. We should also investigate whether the other notions of ontological superiority we are already familiar with can be used to understand grounding.

Suppose that grounding is a universal and that universals are not grounded in the facts of which they are constituents. Just as this view makes room for grounding as an ultimate relation, there is room for either existence or modes of existence as ultimate properties. For example, even if every fact that a thing exists is grounded in the thing itself, existence might still be ultimate, and hence a kind of ontological monism would be true. Alternatively, we might tell a similar story about modes of existence if we understand them as ultimate first-order properties of things. A similar story could be offered of modes of being as ultimate second-order properties. But such positions do not seem plausible on a trope-theoretic view of properties for the same reason that grounding as an ultimate relation seemed unfeasible on a trope-theoretic view.

So given suitable—but very contentious!—assumptions, we can understand modes of being in terms of ultimate properties, which in turn are defined in terms of grounding. Let's turn to the question of whether we can define grounding in terms of modes of being. If so, we face a similar situation to that of chapter 7 in which we worried about the possibility that allegedly disparate phenomena, in that case naturalness and degree of being, might at root be the same.

Let's first note that the grounding relation is not identical with the relation *x is at least as real as y*. The latter relation is reflexive and hence not asymmetric. A better candidate for the grounding relation is *x is more real than y*, which is asymmetric.[25] This latter notion can play many of the same roles as grounding. For example, we can use it to define *fundamental* and *derivative* in a way similar to Schaffer:

x is *fundamental* = df. nothing is more real than x.
x is *derivative* = df. something is more real than x.

In this vein, note also that the semi-mereological notions of an *integrated whole* and a *mere aggregate* can be defined in terms of degrees of being: an integrated whole is more real than its proper parts, whereas a mere aggregate is less real than its proper

---

[25] We can define this notion in terms of *x is at least as real as y* as follows: *x is more real than y* = df. x is at least as real as *y* and it is not the case that *y* is at least as real as *x*.

parts.[26] (Intermediate cases are possible: perhaps artifacts are more real than their arbitrary undetached parts but less real than their constituent particles.)

As I mentioned, Schaffer (2009) argues that the fundamental task of metaphysics is to determine which things are fundamental and which things are derivative. I agree with Schaffer that this is one of the fundamental tasks of metaphysics. Schaffer (2009) also argues that this was understood to be the fundamental task of metaphysicians by many of the great figures in the history of metaphysics, such as Plato, Aristotle, Spinoza, Leibniz, and Kant. Perhaps he is correct—but note that each of these figures also believed that some things were ontologically superior to others. That which is prior is that which is ontologically superior. The appeal to traditional metaphysical practice does not obviously support taking grounding as either ideologically or metaphysically primitive.

One might worry that the notion of grounding cannot be analyzed in terms of the notion of *being more real than* since there might be metaphysical systems in which the grounding relation imposes more structure than the being more real than relation. A specific example might be helpful. Consider a metaphysic according to which there are concrete particulars and their modes, which are particularized and dependent attributes. Suppose there are two concrete particulars, one of which enjoys a mode of blueness whilst the other enjoys a mode of redness. Intuitively, the mode of redness is grounded solely by the red substance whereas the mode of blueness is grounded solely by the blue substance. Plausibly, both substances are equally real whereas both modes are equally real, and both substances are more real than both modes. And so information about the *particular* connection between the mode of redness and the red substance is lost if we identify the grounding relation with the *being more real than* relation.

There are a couple of ways to respond to this worry. One obvious response is to account for the particular connection in terms of the instantiation relation itself. The appearance that there is more to the grounding structure arises because there is a further relation in play. A second response is similar to the first, but far more concessive to the objection: instead of directly defining *x grounds y* in terms of *x is more real than y*, identify the grounding relation with the disjunction of conjunctions consisting of *x is more real than y* and the other connective relations one already accepts on the basis of other metaphysical commitments.[27] For example, in an ontology that consists of modes, events, and substances, one might accept the

---

[26]   Peter Finocchiaro has suggested to me that it might be worthwhile to instead treat "integrated whole" as the contradictory of "mere aggregate," and so use "integrated whole" to stand for those wholes that are at least as real as their parts.

[27]   A related strategy has been suggested to me by Alex Skiles: rather than identify the grounding relation with the disjunction of these conjunctions, identify the grounding relation with the relation of instantiating one of these conjunctions. (In short, prefer quantification over the conjunctions rather than disjoining them.) Skiles's strategy is the one that we should use if it is contingent which connecting relations exist; thanks to Joshua Spencer for pointing this out.

following: *x grounds y* if and only if *x* is more real than *y* and either (i) *x* instantiates *y* or (ii) *y* is an event involving *x*. In general, there is never a bare relation of grounding between distinct individuals, but rather there is always a further relation between them. That there is always a further relation between entities related by grounding is part of the basis of Wilson's (2014) argument that grounding does no metaphysical work, a conclusion which I find congenial, at least with respect to entity grounding.[28]

Taking this second strategy is consistent with claiming that grounding is ideologically primitive. The second strategy doesn't try to explain what "grounding" means, but rather tells you what grounding—the entity in the ontology—is. On the second strategy, grounding might be highly disjunctive if there is a sufficiently large number of connecting relations in play, and yet each disjunct will share a common metaphysical core provided by the *more real than* relation. On this strategy, what grounding is cannot be assessed without doing some first-order metaphysics; you won't learn a lot about grounding simply by taking grounding as the sole focus of your metaphysical exploration.

How fares the quest for the "correct logic" of ground on this second strategy? Probably no better or worse than the question for the correct "logic" of parthood or metaphysical necessity. In each case, we bring to metaphysics some notion that permits implementation in a variety of formal systems. Some aspects of these systems will strike us as more reflective of the "core" of the relevant notion. But I would reject a methodology that licensed us to make mereological judgments independently of metaphysical investigations of the kinds of things that there are and how they relate to one another.[29] (A mereology with facts in it might look very different than one without facts, for example.) Similarly, I hesitate to grant a given modal "logic" the status of being that which all modal metaphysics must accommodate.[30] Implementation of a notion in a formal system is an excellent way to clarify the commitments of one's theories that make use of that notion, but it is not a substitute for the theories themselves.[31] Does this mean that grounding is not methodologically primitive? I think not, for one may still develop such formal systems in advance of first-order metaphysics, and some evaluation of them is permissible in advance—such as whether the system in question is internally consistent, for example, or has some other more interesting formal properties. One can note that certain formally stated axioms strike one as intuitively plausible. What one is not permitted to do is to treat questions about grounding as *settled* in advance of first-order metaphysical inquiry.

---

[28] That entity grounding does no metaphysical work over and above degrees of being and the connective relations we already need between objects was the conclusion of the appendix to McDaniel (2013b), which has been revised and incorporated in this section. Wilson's (2014) critique is far more comprehensive, and targets the proponents of grounding as a relation between facts as well. I'll have more to say about Wilson's broadside against grounding in section 8.3.

[29] This is forcefully argued for in Donnelly (2011).   [30] *Pace* Williamson (2013).

[31] Compare with Wilson (2014), who doubts the propriety of asking questions about ground.

What about the question of the ground of grounding? Assume that grounding is a universal. Perhaps one connective relation between properties and relations is the relation of being a constituent. Perhaps since grounding is a disjunction of conjunctions, each of the conjunctions is a constituent of grounding. Each of these conjunctions (which are disjuncts of grounding) is more real than grounding, and bears an appropriate connective relation to ground. On the second strategy, then, it would be plausible to say that each is a ground of grounding. (This would fit the idea that disjunctive properties are grounded in each of their disjuncts.) Perhaps a similar but more complicated story could be told about facts of grounding.[32]

On the second strategy, whatever work the notion of grounding is called to do, the notion of comparative reality can do just as well. We therefore have a choice between two systems, each of which accepts the same plurality of connecting relations. But one of these systems takes the notion *x is at least as real as y* as basic and defines existence simpliciter and grounding in terms of it, while the other system takes both the notion of existence and the notion of grounding as basic. (As I noted in section 7.6, Schaffer (2009: 374) explicitly denies that *existence* can be defined in terms of grounding.) I suggest that the first system scores better with respect to ideological parsimony—we needn't take the notion as primitive once we grasp the recipe for defining it and settle on an adequate systematic metaphysics—and since it can do the same work as the second, it is to be preferred. (Compare the argument given here with that of section 7.6 for the priority of degrees of being over naturalness.)

Suppose we do not accept the second strategy. There is a third strategy available, which is to deny that *x is at least as real as y* is comparable in the sense defined in section 7.5. If *x is at least as real as y* is not comparable, and we want to capture the connection between a thing and its modes wholly in terms of the grounding relation, we can do so. In the case mentioned earlier, one needs to deny that the mode of redness is equally as real as the mode of blueness, and hold that neither mode is more real than the other. On this third strategy, they are not related to each other by the at least as real as relation.[33]

The third strategy is a mirror of the first strategy. According to the first strategy, the grounding relation induces as much structure as comparative reality. It is illusory that grounding is richer. On the third strategy, comparative reality has more structure than we initially thought. On this third strategy, grounding and comparative reality are the same phenomena under two different guises.[34] This suggests that "ground" and "comparative reality" are mere notational variants of each other. This possibility is especially salient in light of the considerations of sections 7.4–7.7,

---

[32] Again, Wilson (2014) is relevant.

[33] On each of these strategies, the grounder is ontologically superior to the grounded. Audi (2012: 102) rejects this. As I see things, my project needn't accommodate everything every grounding theorist says about grounding in order to be successful.

[34] Daly (2012: 94) suggests that talk about grounding and degree of reality might just be the same thing under different names.

in which we addressed whether naturalness and degree of being are the same phenomenon under distinct guises. My inclination in this case is that the guise of comparative reality is the more perspicuous guise, since comparative reality is also the semantic value of a polyadic quantifier.

This discussion so far has operated on the assumption that we are working only with one relation of ontological superiority, namely, that of comparative reality (or degree of being). Dropping this assumption yields a more complicated but also more attractive picture of grounding. One important claim of this book is that there is more than one kind of ontological superiority. The way in which an attribute or mode is grounded in its substantial bearer is not the way in which a shadow is grounded in its host. This is not simply because the connective relations in question differ; they do, but that understates the difference. In the case of a mode and a substance, the connective relationship just is a relationship of ontological superiority: when a mode is instantiated by a substance, that mode *exists in* the substance. (Recall section 2.4.2.) Holes do not exist in their hosts in the way that a mode exists in a substance. (Recall section 5.3.) Simply saying that both holes and modes are grounded in substances covers up a vast difference in the how of it.[35]

That's my deeper reservation about strategy three. But it also points to a need to revise strategy two. Rather than contextually defining grounding as the disjunction of conjunctions of the more real than relation with a suitable connective relation, we should think of grounding as the disjunction of conjunctions of some relation of ontological superiority coupled with a suitable connecting relation (that might in some cases be identical with a relation of ontological superiority). And even this probably is not sophisticated enough; probably it is better to call this disjunctive relation G and then define grounding as the transitive closure of G.[36] The "logic" of ground still might turn out quite messy, or it might be rather streamlined—what it looks like will depend largely on what the correct metaphysics is, which after all is what supplies us with the information about which connecting relations are suitable.

Given this picture of grounding, is it the case that if x grounds y, then x grounds y in every world in which they both exist? The answer is probably "no." I assume that if x is ontologically superior to y, then this is the case in every world in which they are found. (We will reassess this assumption in section 9.7.) But the relevant connecting

---

[35] I think much of the grounding literature is guilty of this kind of covering up. See, e.g., Schaffer (2009: 375–6), who puts holes and singletons on the same "great chain of being." Similarly, Koslicki (2012b: 206–11) distinguishes different relations of what she calls "ontological dependence," but lumps the kind of dependence of a hole on its host under the same umbrella as the kind of dependence a trope has to its bearer. On the other hand, Koslicki (2015: 329–39) defends a kind of lightweight grounding pluralism that is sensitive to differences in how a coarse-grained relation of grounding is implemented.

[36] There's an interesting question about what to say if grounding is a contrastive relation, as is defended by Schaffer (2012). We could posit a contrastive relation of comparative reality, but that feels to me intuitively implausible. That said, I am not convinced by the case Schaffer (2012) presents for "going contrastive"; see Javier-Castellanos (2014) for criticism.

relationship between x and y might fail to obtain. We can't assess this question without examining also what the correct metaphysics is.

The upshot of this section: I accept the acceptability of talking about a relation of grounding between entities of potentially any ontological category. But I view it as metaphysically superficial. The deeper work is done by various kinds of ontological superiority and the connective relations between entities that are independently needed in the correct metaphysical system.

8.3 Fact Grounding

Let us turn now to the idea that grounding is best construed as a kind of relation between facts or propositions specifically rather than entities more generally. Let's first address an initial complaint. Many proponents of "fact grounding" prefer to regiment grounding talk with a sentential operator precisely to avoid ontological commitment to facts, propositions, or other such entities. Nonetheless, I will proceed to talk in terms of a relation between facts, and not merely because it is convenient. It is clear that there are facts and propositions; the interesting ontological question is how these entities exist, not whether they exist in some way or other. (I'll have more to say about how facts exist momentarily.) And proponents of operator-talk grant that, if there are such entities, then there is a straightforward translation of operator-talk into talk of relations between them.

If the task is to articulate a *concept* of grounding that is maximally neutral with respect to any possible metaphysical debate, then I can see why one might want to regiment via a sentence operator. However, that's not my task! I am supposing that proponents of grounding have succeeded in latching on to some aspect of reality, and I want to understand that aspect itself rather than articulate some concept of it, the thinness of which might not reflect the complexity of its object. *Perhaps* grounding is metaphysically primitive in one of the ways articulated earlier; *perhaps* it in some sense lacks internal complexity or aspects that can be teased apart; *perhaps* it is not an entity at all. But *perhaps* none of this is the case. How do we decide which is true independently of doing first-order metaphysics?

Shamik Dasgupta has suggested to me a motivation for casting ground talk in terms of sentence operators even if it is obvious that there are facts and propositions. Even if one is confident that there are such entities, one might be less confident about their nature. And one might be concerned not to let one's theory about the nature of propositions warp one's theory about grounding. For example, if propositions are sets of possible worlds, one could not accept a hyperintensional grounding relation between propositions.

My response is that this purported motivation is an instance of the same tendency that I am pushing back against: the tendency to try to theorize about grounding in as much independence from first-order metaphysics as possible. This tendency should be resisted! Those committed to grounding should make sure that they have an adequate theory of propositions that accords with that commitment.[37]

The strategy for identifying fact grounding is much the same as the strategy for identifying entity grounding discussed in the previous section. First, do first-order metaphysics in order to get an inventory of the various connective relations between facts that are needed for a complete theory. Perhaps this inventory of connective relations will include the relation of *entailment* (in play when one fact obtains in all the worlds in which another fact obtains), *constitution* (in play when the existence of a lump of matter constitutes the existence of a statue or a moral fact is constituted by a physical fact), *determination* (in play when the fact that something is scarlet determines the fact that something is red), *disjunction* (in play when two facts form their disjunction), and many others. We won't know what they are independently of doing first-order metaphysics. Wilson (2014) calls these kind of relations "small-g grounding relations" and suggests that these relations plus some notion of absolute fundamentality suffice to do all the work that fact grounding is supposed to do. Similarly, Silverman (2013: 105) worries that grounding does no work at all, since Fine himself accepts three specific kinds of grounding and thinks of generic grounding as something like a disjunction of them (this will be discussed more in section 8.4), and, according to Silverman, these three more specific grounding relations in turn are replaceable by even more specific relations of the kinds that Silverman calls reductive, emergent, and supervenience relations.

I find much of what Wilson and Silverman say very congenial. In what follows, I'll focus on Wilson's discussion, since it is far more extensive.

Wilson employs a notion of absolute fundamentality. I accept such a notion; in fact, I accept many such notions. One of them was the focus of chapters 5 and 7: the absolutely fundamental as the fully real. And similarly, for me, "relative fundamentality" talk is best cashed out in terms of some kind of ontological superiority. In this case, the relevant kind of ontological superiority seems to be degree of being.

Let's see whether degree of being is the right kind of ontological superiority to appeal to in this context. Suppose that some facts have more being than others. (We needn't suppose that any fact has the highest degree of being.) Provided that we have arrived at a suitable list of connecting relations between facts, we could identify grounding (the phenomenon!) with the transitive closure of the disjunction of the conjunctions of connecting relations plus *being more real than*.[38]

Will such an identification succeed? I assume once again that there are no "bare relations of grounding." That is, it is never the case that two facts are related by the grounding relation without there being other relations obtaining between them that

---

[37] One might consider a theory of propositions that individuates them in terms of grounding; this is more or less the theory I explore in McDaniel (2015).

[38] If we wish to accommodate the possibility of many-one grounding, then some of these connecting relations must also take plural arguments. I foresee no special difficulty with this.

are intuitively the implementation of the grounding relation. In general, small-g grounding relations induce big-G grounding, and this is why there is systematicity to the array of grounding. To put it in slogan form, no small-g grounding between facts without big-G grounding but no big G-grounding without some small-g grounding as well. More carefully put, whenever big-G grounding is instantiated by some facts, the transitive closure of the disjunction of the small-g grounding relations is also instantiated.

Here is one potentially important difference between Wilson (2014) and me. In a way, I have understressed the importance of "relative fundamentality" so far. In addition to playing a direct role in the "real definition" of grounding, it plays an indirect role in the characterization of what it is to be a small-g or suitable connecting relation.[39] For me, what makes a given relation a small-g relation is that it is uniformly correlated with a difference in the relative fundamentality of its relata, i.e., R is a small-g relation if and only if necessarily, for all x and y, if Rxy, then x is in some way ontologically superior to y.[40] Accordingly, unlike Wilson (2014: 539), I do not think of parthood as a small-g grounding relation, since some wholes are ontologically superior to their parts and some parts are ontologically superior to their wholes.[41] And certainly then numerical identity fails to be a small-g relation, again *pace* Wilson (2014: 570–5).[42]

What should we say about situations in which x bears one small-g grounding relation to y while y bears a distinct small-g grounding relation to x? Perhaps we should say that they are impossible.[43] That such situations are impossible is

---

[39] Wilson (2014: 569) does suggest that whether a relation is a small-g relation will "typically depend" on other facts, including which things are fundamental.

[40] Alex Skiles has suggested to me that this criterion will count many gerrymandered relations as small-g relations. For example, if set-membership is a small-g relation, then so too is *x is a member of y and x is such that 2 + 2 = 4*. We could address this example by adding an additional necessary condition: R is a small-g relation only if there is no other R* such that (i) R* is more natural than R and (ii) R* induces the same pattern of ontological superiority as R. But probably the easier route is to accept that not all small-g relations are of much interest to metaphysicians: only those that are sufficiently natural are. A related route is to demand that a small-g relation be highly natural (but perhaps not perfectly natural!). "Highly natural" is vague, and hence it might be vague what grounding is. I suspect that it is vague, and hence am not too troubled by this consequence. For a contrary proposal to what I defend here, see Bennett (forthcoming), who argues that patterns of relative fundamentality are a consequence of the distribution of what she calls "building relations"; I hope to discuss Bennett's intriguing view in future work.

[41] For the same reason, I do not think that parthood is properly thought of as a "building" relation in the distinctive sense that Bennett (2011b) gives to that expression.

[42] It is also an open question whether I should accept that *determination* is a small-g grounding relation. In section 2.2, I indicated that I thought that determinates of a property are equally natural as the determinable of which they are determinates. In light of the results of chapter 7, I would now say that determinates are as real as determinables. So being scarlet is as real as being red. But perhaps nonetheless the fact that x is scarlet is more real than the fact that x is red. And if so, I could maintain that determination is a small-g grounding relation. (Given that Wilson (2012) has similar views about the nature of determinates and determinables, I am curious about whether she ought to think that determination is a small-g relation as well.) Thanks to Paek Chae-Young for discussion here.

[43] In McDaniel (2009a), in the context of attempting to understand Armstrong's (1997) version of compositional pluralism, I distinguished between mereological composition and s-composition, the latter

potentially a weakness with the proposal. Alex Skiles has suggested to me in personal communication a more moderate response. He writes,

Let's suppose that there were such small-g grounding relations, R and R*. A reasonable expectation is that facts about relative fundamentality will systematically track the distribution of R and R*: in cases where *exactly one* is instantiated, relative fundamentality will always run in the same direction; in cases where *both* are instantiated, one of the two will inevitably "trump" the other insofar as the direction of relative fundamentality is concerned. So, even if there were such relations as R and R*, it remains a reasonable expectation that a sort of systematicity would be retained—a systematicity that (our judgments of) the facts about big-G grounding would still track. One would then have to tweak other bits of your view a bit: in particular, (*i*) what it takes for something to be a small-g grounding relation and (*ii*) which relation "built up" from small-g grounding relations we should take big-G grounding to be necessarily coextensive with. Regarding (*i*), the tweak could be to think of small-g grounding relations as only *indirectly* inducing differences in relative fundamentality rather than doing so directly. Here's one implementation of that thought. For any arbitrary x and y, let's call a *complete small-g profile with respect to* $R_1, R_2, \ldots$ any conjunctive property the conjuncts of which specify, for each $i = 1, 2, \ldots$ whether or not x bears R_i to y and vice versa. Someone could just take these to *be* the small-g grounding relations, rather than $R_1, R_2, \ldots$; I'm not sure what much would be at stake if one instead insisted on taking $R_1, R_2, \ldots$ to be them instead. Perhaps one worry would be that this would undermine the ideological parsimony of your proposal, since if we can't analyze what it is to be a small-g grounding relation in terms of its ability to *directly* induce differences in relative fundamentality, what else could this be analyzed in terms of instead? Perhaps though one could narrow down the class of complete small-g profiles to just those that uniformly induce differences in relative fundamentality, and then take the small-g grounding relations to be whatever relations these complete small-g profiles are "built up" from. Regarding (*ii*), and continuing with the proposal above, we could then take big-G grounding to be necessarily coextensive with the disjunction of complete small-g profiles rather than the disjunction of conjunctions of relations like constitution, determination, set membership, etc.

I find Skiles's suggestion here very intriguing and definitely worth keeping in mind when assessing the tenability of the overall picture I am proposing.

Let us return to the discussion of Wilson (2014). I suspect that Wilson believes that we antecedently think of what Wilson calls "small-g grounding relations" as inducing metaphysical explanations, that is, they are the kind of relations one can appeal to when giving a non-causal and non-teleological explanation of why something is the case. For example, the fact that a statue has 100 kg of mass is explained by the fact that a lump that has 100 kg of mass constitutes that statue. I also suspect she is probably right about this, but since the notion of a metaphysical explanation and the

---

of which generates facts from universals and particulars and structural universals from unstructured universals. If both such relations are small-g grounding relations, then we cannot say that small-g grounding relations always induce relations of relative fundamentality. All the more reason then to deny that mereological composition is a small-g grounding relation.

notion of ground are closely tied together in the minds of grounding theorists, I'd prefer not to appeal to the notion of explanation when characterizing what it is to be a small-g relation.[44] There does not seem to be a common core to the various small-g relations besides their inducement of relations of relative fundamentality.[45] (This doesn't mean that each small-g relation is itself definable in terms of relative fundamentality plus some other relation; I doubt this is the case.)

Wilson (2014: 568, 576) suggests that extant grounding claims in the non-grounding literature are largely schematic or general over the small-g ones. That is, to say that x grounds y is just to say that there is some relation R between x and y that is relevant to explaining why y exists or obtains given the existence or obtainment of x. That might be the case; we'd have to ask specific authors who have made such claims what they had in mind. Perhaps this is all those who employ the word "ground" in contemporary discussions of the philosophy of mind intend; for example, a physicalist might wish to say that there is some way in which the physical grounds the mental without being very confident about what that way is.

I doubt, however, that as we go deeper into the history of philosophy, we will find that grounding talk is merely schematic. One can characterize much of the grounding literature (indeed much of contemporary metaphysics) as pre-critical in the Kantian sense. And in this case, this characterization is not ungrounded. Consider, for example, the important pre-critical metaphysician Baumgarten (2014), whose *Metaphysica* served as Kant's textbook for the majority of his academic career.[46] For some illustrative examples, note that Baumgarten closely links grounding and metaphysical explanation in section 14 and immediately defines a notion of dependency in terms of ground; in section 21, he distinguishes sufficient from partial grounding; and, in section 25, he defends the transitivity of grounding. What Baumgarten does looks a lot like what Schaffer does. Baumgarten appears to be a fan of entity grounding, and spends some time discussing it before invoking it in other contexts. There is little reason to think that Baumgarten is merely making schematic claims. Similar remarks apply to the important post-Kantian philosopher, Bolzano, whose philosophical depth is fortunately becoming increasingly well known. Bolzano (2014b: 243–80) provides an extensive discussion of fact grounding, carefully distinguishes it from other notions in the neighborhood with which it might be conflated, describing a rudimentary logic of ground, introduces various technical notions that might be defined in terms of ground, and so forth. Bolzano (2014b: 252–3) also states that his notion of grounding is ideologically primitive. I do not see evidence that talk of grounding is merely schematic in Bolzano.

---

[44] For example, Dasgupta (2015) simply identifies grounding with metaphysical explanation.

[45] As Wilson (2014: 568–70) points out, there are many formal differences between the various small-g grounding relations she discusses. Cameron (2014: 50) suggests that one advantage of accepting that grounding "is said in many ways" is that we accommodate these formal differences while preserving some degree of unity.

[46] See Watkins (2009: 85–6) for a discussion of Kant's use of Baumgarten's *Metaphysica* as a textbook.

Another possibility is that (some of) the contemporary authors Wilson alludes to are not implicitly quantifying over specific relations, but rather are asserting the presence of a *generic* relation of ground, and these authors are not taking a stand on whether such a relation is in some way primitive or fundamental. The latter possibility strikes me as more probable. But I have not surveyed the authors in question.[47]

Let's consider the following objection. Suppose that there is no small-g grounding relation instantiated by some facts without those facts also instantiating the big-G grounding relation, and that the big G-grounding relation is instantiated by some facts only if the transitive closure of the disjunction of the small-g grounding relations is also instantiated by those facts. Then grounding is necessarily coextensive with the transitive closure of the disjunction of the small-g grounding relations. But it doesn't follow that they are identical. Why think that we have identified what grounding *is* as opposed to merely what grounding is coextensive with?

This is a fair question, but recall the discussion of a similar question in section 7.4. Perhaps the wrong conception of properties for considering cases of philosophical reduction or identification is one that closely ties properties to *meanings* rather than *referents*. But suppose we deny the numerical identity of grounding and the transitive closure of the disjunction of the small-g grounding relations. The more interesting question then is which is in some way prior. Given their necessary equivalence, I think the grounding theorist should not say that grounding is metaphysically prior. Consider any given grounding fact, such as the fact that F grounds G. Why does F ground G? Perhaps F constitutes G. Or perhaps G is a disjunction of which F is a disjunct. Or perhaps F constitutes some fact that is a disjunct of G. Any of these possibilities would suffice to explain why F grounds G. Given the hypothesis of necessary covariance, one of these possibilities does obtain and hence does suffice to explain why F grounds G. Strictly, we needn't say that, whenever grounding is instantiated, its instantiation is grounded by the instantiation of the transitive closure of the disjunction of the small-g grounding relations. But it also does not seem plausible that any given instantiation of grounding grounds an instantiation of the transitive closure of the disjunction of the small-g grounding relations. Rather, both such facts would have a common ground, and this common ground is a fact in which big-G grounding is not a constituent.

The notion of ground might be ideologically or methodologically primitive. But I am unconvinced that it is metaphysically primitive, at least if we are thinking of grounding as a relation instantiated solely by facts, and we are thinking that metaphysical primitiveness should itself be understood in terms of grounding. On Schaffer's picture, for all I have said here, grounding might still be an ultimate relation, though perhaps it too is grounded by each of the small-g grounding relations. And on the

---

[47] Shamik Dasgupta in personal communication has informed me that his attitude towards grounding is more or less this: there is a relation of grounding (provided that grounding talk is best regimented via a predicate rather than an operator), it is highly general, it might be fundamental, but it also might not be.

picture of fundamentality I prefer, grounding itself might still be a highly natural relation. But given the role that degree of being/naturalness plays in characterizing what it is to be a small-g grounding relation, and given the connection between small-g and big-G grounding assumed so far, I would not think that grounding has more being than degree of being.

I have assumed in what preceded that there is no unmediated instantiation of big-G grounding: every instantiation of big-G grounding is accompanied by an instantiation of some small-g grounding relation, or some connecting chain of them. The proposal falls apart if this assumption is false.[48] Let me grant that though I think the assumption is plausible, it also isn't obviously true. Suppose, for example, that there is a God as classically conceived, and that each fact of the form *x is intrinsically good* is grounded in a corresponding fact of the form *x is intrinsically desired by God*. It isn't obvious that there is a further small-g grounding relation between these two kinds of facts that undergirds the pattern of grounding. Perhaps one fact *constitutes* the other, and this relation of constitution is the small-g relation in play, but this isn't obviously correct. So one can think of situations in which the assumption is false.[49] And to the extent that we have a reason to think one of these situations obtains, we should be nervous about the assumption. But conversely it would be unwise to reject the assumption if all one can do is describe situations that one does not take to be metaphysically possible. My recommendations are to seriously consider the assumption but neither decisively accept nor reject it independently of doing other first-order metaphysical explorations.[50]

Given this picture of grounding, is it the case that if *x* grounds *y*, then *x* grounds *y* in every world in which they both exist? I am unsure (recall section 8.2). If it emerges, however, that facts always have their connecting relations to each other as a matter of necessity, then the answer is "yes," given that relations of ontological superiority never merely accidentally obtain. (Some connecting relations, such as the relation of a disjunction to its disjuncts, are never exemplified merely accidentally.)

Before moving on, it might be worth considering other attempts to give "reductive" accounts of grounding that do not explicitly rely on the assumption that there is no unmediated instantiation of big-G grounding. We'll look at a proposal that attempts to understand ground in terms of (strict) essence. (Questions about strict essence and being will be the focus of chapter 9.)

Fine (1994a, 1995b), Lowe (2008), and others have argued that there is an important non-modal notion of essence; that which it purportedly is a notion of

---

[48] Wilson's (2014) and Silverman's (2013) criticisms also lose much of their teeth if this assumption is false.

[49] For a less theologically loaded example, consider Dasgupta's (2014: 2) claim that facts about how many kilograms of mass an object has are (plurally) grounded in scale-independent facts about comparative mass relations between objects. If Dasgupta (2014) is correct, there is no clear small-g grounding relation to serve as the intermediary.

[50] Thanks to Tim O'Connor for discussion here.

will henceforth be called *strict essence*.[51] Fine's now stock example is this: Socrates and Socrates's singleton exist in all the same possible worlds. It is part of the strict essence of Socrates's singleton that Socrates exists (and is a member of it). It is not part of Socrates's strict essence that his singleton exists. So we cannot understand strict essence straightforwardly in terms of modality. Fine (1994a) distinguishes between what he calls *constitutive* essence and *consequential* essence.[52] Roughly, the constitutive essence of a thing is what is "directly" definitional of that thing, whereas the consequential essence of a thing is what is a consequence of the constitutive essence of the thing. In what sense of consequence? Four options present themselves: logical consequence, analytic consequence, modal consequence, and what the constitutive essence grounds. The logically consequential essence of x consists of the constitutive essence of x plus all that logically follows from that essence.[53] The analytic consequential essence of x consists in the constituent essence of x plus all that analytically follows from that essence. (So the analytic consequential essence of x will always include that which is included in the logical consequential essence of x, but the converse will typically not be the case.) The modal consequential essence of x consists of the constituent essence of x plus all that is entailed by that essence. (And so the modal consequential essence of x will always include what is included in the analytic consequential essence of x, but the converse will typically not be the case.) Finally, the grounding consequence of x consists in the constituent essence of x plus all that is grounded in that essence. (The question of how the grounding consequential essence of x overlaps with the other consequential essences of x is tricky, and will be set aside for now, although the modal consequential essence of x will include what is included in the grounding consequential essence of x given that grounding induces entailment.)[54] I see no reason to think that one of these notions of consequential essence is *the* correct notion of consequential essence with which to theorize, though in some contexts some will be more useful than others.[55]

We proceed now to the next stage of the reduction: reducing ground to strict essence. As a warm-up, consider the proposal defended by Dasgupta (2015) that what grounds the truth that B is grounded in A is that B has the strict essence it has.[56] In support of this claim, Dasgupta asks us to consider the claim that the fact that

---

[51] Proponents of strict essence do not take themselves to be calling attention to a newly discovered phenomenon but rather rediscovering or at least calling our attention to a phenomenon that once was of great interest. See, e.g., Charles (2000: 18–19).

[52] Pasnau and Shields (2004: 66) discuss *propria*, which are "necessary accidents," that is, those features that are had as a consequence of having a certain (strict, constitutive) essence but are not included in it.

[53] This seems to be Correia's (2013) preferred way of understanding "consequential essence."

[54] Whether grounding induces entailment is contentious in the grounding literature. See Trogdon (2013) and Skiles (2015) for discussion.

[55] Koslicki (2012) critiques various ways of drawing a distinction between consequential and constitutive essence and suggests an Aristotelian notion of demonstration as the way to do it, which is developed in pp. 196–201.

[56] As noted earlier, Rosen (2010) and Fine (2012a) also discuss this view but do not endorse it.

various people have acted in a certain way grounds the fact that there is a conference. When pressed to what grounds this grounding fact, it is natural to say that it is of the essence of the fact that there is a conference that whenever there are people behaving in the relevant ways, then there is a conference. In short, B's having the strict essence that it has grounds the fact that A grounds B.[57]

Now given a reductive account of strict essence, we can give a reductive account of what grounds grounding facts. This is great, but insufficient for our purposes. For our purposes, we need a reductive *definition* of *grounding* itself. But here is a suggestion for how to achieve this reduction. The first step is to forbid any unanalyzed grounding claim in a statement of the constitutive essence of a thing but allow other kinds of determination claims, such as claims about entailment, to enter in this statement.[58] So, for example, do not say that it is part of the constitutive essence of the fact that there is a conference that, whenever there are people behaving in certain ways, then there is a conference that is grounded in that behavior.[59] But do say that it is part of the constitutive essence of the fact that there is a conference that, necessarily, whenever there are people behaving in certain ways, there is a conference where those people are behaving.

One might worry that this restriction is unmotivated.[60] Consider, for example, disjunctive facts. Don't we have strong intuitions that it is part of the constitutive essence of a disjunctive fact that it is grounded in its disjuncts? My proposal requires distinguishing between:

(1) It is part of the constitutive essence of P or Q that P or Q is entailed by P
and
(2) It is part of the constitutive essence of P or Q that P or Q is grounded in P.
And it also requires that we accept only (1).

---

[57] Strictly speaking, things are more complicated than this: if we assume that grounds necessitate that which they ground, we must also say that A is a partial ground of the fact that A grounds B. Let E = the proposition that states B's essence; let's follow Rosen (2010) and use brackets to convert sentences into terms that denote facts. If E is total ground for [A grounds B], then any world in which E obtains is a world in which [A grounds B] obtains. [A grounds B] obtains only if A obtains. But there is a world in which E obtains but A doesn't. (A conference could have existed and had the essence that it actually has, even if some of the people that actually constitute the conference did not attend.) Thanks to Shamik Dasgupta and Alex Skiles for discussion here.

[58] I am not certain that this is strictly required; it is easier to see how a reduction of ground could be possible if no essentialist statement appeals to ground. But perhaps it is not impossible even if one does.

[59] Contra Rosen (2010), who endorses essentialist claims that include information about grounding within the scope of the essentialist operator.

[60] Alex Skiles has suggested to me that this restriction is unneeded, and in which case, it might well be unmotivated. His thought is that all that is required is that the relevant entailment fact belong to the constitutive essence; it is OK if in addition further facts about grounding are also part of the constitutive essence. His point seems to me to be technically correct. However, I have the following concern: if both the facts about entailment and the facts about grounding belong to the constitutive essence of, e.g., a given disjunction, then the constitutive essence is in a way redundant *since the grounding facts entail the entailment facts*. But maybe that's OK?

But I think this is OK. It might be that disjunctions are always grounded in their disjuncts, and in fact the full analysis of grounding we will consider will have this consequence given (1). But insofar as I have intuitions about the constitutive essences of disjunctive facts, these intuitions are tied closely to what I think of as the "definition" of disjunction, which in turn is tied to disjunction's logical/inferential/semantic roles, such as, for example its implicit "definition" via its truth-table. I grasp what it is to be a disjunctive fact when I grasp its real definition (if such facts have real definitions!), which is that it is that fact which is entailed by its disjuncts. Other facts are also entailed by these disjuncts—any necessary truth is, for example—but it is not of the constitutive essence of these facts that they are so entailed. Considerations of this sort lead me to think that, insofar as I've glommed onto the idea of constitutive essences as objective definitions of non-linguistic entities, the essence of a disjunctive fact is captured by something like (1) rather than (2). (We'll discuss shortly a second response to this concern.)

With this restriction in place, we can now explore whether we can define *grounding* in terms of essence. Correia (2013) suggests one possible analysis: the fact that B is grounded in the fact that A just in case (i) the proposition that A is true, (ii) the proposition that A entails the proposition that B, and (iii) it is part of the constitutive essence of the proposition that B that the proposition that A entails the proposition that B.[61] Note that, if we want to ensure that grounding is an asymmetric relation, we can add a fourth clause: (iv) it is neither part of the constitutive essence of the proposition that A that it entails the proposition that B nor is it part of the constitutive essence of that proposition that A that the proposition that B entails it.[62]

One nice thing about this analysis is that it allows us to capture much of the intuition that it is part of the strict essence of a disjunctive proposition that it be grounded in its disjuncts. On my construal of Correia's (2013) proposal, it is not part of the constitutive essence of a disjunction that it be grounded in its disjuncts—but it is part of its analytic consequential essence. Perhaps one is rightly confident that it is part of the strict essence of a disjunctive fact that it be grounded in its disjuncts—but I doubt that one is rightly confident that it is part of its constitutive essence rather than part of one of its consequential essences.

This purported reduction of ground to strict essence seems to presuppose that all facts have strict essences. But this isn't obviously correct. We'll see in section 9.2 challenges to the claim that everything has a strict essence. Less than fully real facts might not have essences, and in which case the purported reduction also seems dubious.

Our explorations so far have been pretty speculative. That's to be expected; at this level of abstraction, one can do little more than speculate, albeit in a disciplined and

---

[61] This is not the only analysis suggested by Correia, but it is the one that I will pursue here.
[62] See Jenkins (2011) and Wilson (2014) for discussion of whether grounding is asymmetric or merely non-symmetric.

orderly way. And questions about the nature and status of ground cannot be arrived at without further first-order metaphysical speculation as well. My primary interest is in the connection between ground and being, and which of these two aspects of reality is in some way primary. I won't be unsettled if ground turns out to be metaphysically primitive in some way, but neither will I rejoice. But I will happily make use of the notion even if it can only be taken as metaphysically primitive if it is to be taken at all, and in chapter 9 I will avail myself of talk of ground.

One further question is whether the friend of ground has a reason to take on board some further structuring metaphysical notion, such as naturalness or degree of being. I think the answer is "yes," provided that one is also a pluralist about grounding. Let's turn to this further question next.

8.4 Ground: Unity, Plurality, Analogy

I'll argue that if one is a pluralist about grounding, then one should also accept a further structuring feature, such as degrees of being. This argument won't rely on whether some feature like degree of being is needed to characterize what it is to be a small-g grounding relation, and it won't rely on any identification of grounding with some construction out of degrees of being plus suitable connecting relations. The central premise of the argument is that the proponent of grounding pluralism needs to have some way of accounting for the unity of the generic relation of grounding, since it is not plausible that the generic relation of grounding is simply a mere disjunction of the more specific relations of grounding.[63] In order to assess the argument, though, we need to get clearer on what it is to be a pluralist rather than a monist about grounding. To do this, we'll discuss two different ways of being a pluralist about grounding, which I'll call *thin* and *thick* pluralism respectively.

The monist about grounding believes that there is exactly one distinctive relation of grounding. If it is a relation between entities in general, it applies to entities regardless of ontological category, save for perhaps the category to which grounding itself belongs; if it is a relation between facts only, it nonetheless can relate facts concerning any subject matter, save for perhaps the subject matter of grounding itself. (Recall the discussion of the grounds of grounding in section 8.2, which accounts for the hedging here.) Call this relation, whatever its relata might be, *generic grounding*.[64] The pluralist thinks that there is more than one distinctive relation of grounding. The kind of pluralist that I will focus on is one who believes in both

---

[63] As Cameron (2014) notes, opponents of grounding have held that at best grounding is a merely disjunctive relation, while proponents of grounding have often been monists.

[64] This is not to say that grounding is a *genus* in the Aristotelian sense. Just as in chapter 1, where I distinguished between a generic mode of being and specific modes of being, and stated that the generic mode of being is merely that mode of being that any being enjoys whenever it enjoys some mode of being or other. Similarly, generic grounding is that relation that relates pairs whenever they are related by any other specific relations of grounding (provided that there are such relations).

generic grounding and also many other grounding relations such that each of them is more specific than generic grounding in the sense that they relate fewer kinds of entities or facts than generic grounding. (My paradigmatic pluralist about grounding holds analogous views to a paradigmatic ontological pluralist.) The pluralist holds that these specific relations are at least as fundamental (in whatever sense of "fundamental" is apt in this case) as generic grounding; the paradigmatic pluralist holds that they are *more* fundamental than generic grounding.

Thin pluralism is the view that each of the specific relations of grounding cannot be identified with the small-g relations we might antecedently recognize, but rather each must be taken on its own terms. Fine (2012a: 39–40) appears to be a thin pluralist in this sense; he distinguishes between what he calls *metaphysical, nomological*, and *normative* grounding but proffers no analyses or identifications of these relations.[65] Thick pluralism is the view that each specific relation of grounding just is one of the small-g relations, such as constitution or determination, that we antecedently recognized. Perhaps Wilson (2014) could be thought of as a thick pluralist. Interim positions are possible as well.

All pluralists must face the question of how the many relate to the one. Compositional pluralists believe in a plurality of specific composition relations as well as a generic relation of composition. Ontological pluralists believe in a plurality of modes of being as well as being itself. Grounding pluralists believe in specific relations of grounding as well as generic grounding. In each case, it is fair to ask: what if anything unifies the specific properties or relations? Is the generic property or relation a mere disjunction? Is the generic property or relation a determinable of which the specific properties or relations are its determinates? Is the generic property or relation an analogous property or relation? If it is an analogous property or relation, is it one with or without a focal specification?[66]

Fine (2012a: 38–40) says that generic grounding is something like a disjunction of the specifics. Notice that he does not say that it is a *mere* disjunction. *That* position is extremely implausible. Metaphysical, nomological, and normative grounding have more unity than metaphysical grounding, nomological grounding, and the *is 5 feet from* relation. That's more like a mere disjunction! So in what does the unity consist? And can that unity be explained without appeal to a notion like naturalness or degree of being?

Perhaps their unity consists in the fact that each of the specific relations plays similar roles in their respective field of application and satisfies similar formal principles. The extant specification of those roles is not particularly illuminating though: in each case, the role is to be an explanatory relation for why something is the case. And satisfying a set of formal principles doesn't generate that much unity; there

---

[65] Mulligan (2006a: 38) also distinguishes between an essentialist and a normative sense of "because."

[66] As noted earlier, Cameron (2014) discusses the hypothesis that grounding is an analogous relation with a focal specification.

are innumerably many relations that satisfy the same formal principles as those grounding is purported to satisfy but are not relations of grounding.[67] Conversely, if the generic grounding relation is either systematically variably polyadic or systematically variably axiomatic (recall section 2.3), then the case for grounding pluralism (rather than monism) is quite strong.[68] The case for grounding pluralism (rather than monism) is weaker the more similar the specific relations are to one another.[69]

Moreover, it's not clear to me that the thick pluralist can even say that the various small-g grounding relations play similar roles, and it is clear that many of the purportedly small-g grounding relations are formally dissimilar in many respects. Both the thick and thin pluralists could say that each grounding relation induces a relation of ontological superiority on its relata, and that this is what accounts for their unity. I welcome this response—perhaps the grounder has a higher degree of being than the grounded, or the grounded *exists in* the grounder, and so forth. (This is more or less roughly what I believe.) But since we are exploring considerations independent of those of the previous sections, set this possibility aside.

Can the grounding pluralist simply take as ideologically primitive the relations of determinate to determinable, of analogue instance to analogous property, and of mere disjuncts to mere disjunction? And once they have taken these relations as ideologically primitive, simply say that it is a brute fact the specific grounding relation stand in one of the first two of these relations (rather than the third) to the generic grounding relation?[70] It might make sense for a thin pluralist to say that the specifics are determinates of the generic, whereas the thick pluralist should probably say that they are analogue instances of the generic.[71]

Frankly, I did little better than take these specification relations as ideologically primitive in chapter 2, but I did do a little better! There, I said that in each case, if some object or objects instantiate some specification of the generic, then it or they instantiate the generic as well, and if some object or objects instantiate the generic, then there is some specification such that this same object or these same objects instantiate it too. But I also said that what distinguishes these three relations of specification is that determinates and determinables are always equally natural,

[67] Wilson (2014: 569–70) notes this, but also worries that there is not much formal unity to the various small-g relations she discusses.

[68] In a similar vein, if some putative grounding relations induce modal ties between their relata, whereas others do not, the case for pluralism is strengthened. In this context, consider that deRosset (2010), Fine (2012a), and Rosen (2010) all endorse the claim that if *x* grounds *y*, then in any world in which *x* exists, *x* grounds *y*, while Schaffer (2010b) denies this claim.

[69] Contra Cameron (2014: 52), even if all grounding relations had the same formal features, this would not seal the deal against grounding pluralism. Fine's (2012a: 39–40) case for pluralism is based on an intuition about a single case in which one kind of grounding allegedly is absent, rather than via an appeal to differences in formal features. I do not know how widely this intuition is shared.

[70] Do not assimilate determinables to disjunctions of their determinates, for that is a bad theory of determinables. See Wilson (2012).

[71] Bliss and Trogdon (2014) explore whether grounding is a determinable. Cameron (2014) explores whether grounding is analogous.

whereas mere disjunctions are far less natural than their disjuncts, and while analogous features are less natural than their analogue instances, the degree to which they
depart from the naturalness of their analogue instances is far less than the degree to
which mere disjunctions depart from the naturalness of their disjuncts. And for me
naturalness just is one kind of ontological superiority—degree of being—as it is
defined on the field of properties. So for me the distinction between these three
kinds of specification is theoretically important, and I am willing to appeal to them in
absence of fully satisfactory accounts of them, but with the background belief that
their pattern of instantiation is fixed by patterns of entailment and naturalness.

The question then is whether the proponent of ground can make sense of the
phenomenon of analogy in terms of ground alone. I don't want to say that it can't be
done, but merely indicate that there is an explanatory challenge here.[72] The prima
facie problem is that with respect to each kind of specification, the grounding
structure looks exactly the same: the instantiation of a determinate grounds the
instantiation of its determinable, the instantiation of an analogue instance grounds
the instantiation of the analogous feature, and the instantiation of the disjunct
grounds the instantiation of the mere disjunction. How do we get the more fine-
grained distinctions? One might try to appeal to higher-order features, but which
ones? The higher-order relations that structure determinates of quantitative determinables might not even have analogues in the domain of qualitative determinables,
for example. And with respect to some analogue instances of a common analogous
feature, it is hard to produce a robust list of common higher-order features. Consider,
for example, the various forms of composition, and compare also the various modes
of being. Is there any commonality to the higher-order features of analogue instances
of parthood and *being* that make these generic features analogous rather than
determinables or mere disjunctions?

I don't see the problem of accounting for analogous properties or relations as
uniquely a problem for grounding pluralism. It is *acutely* a problem for them,
especially if they take the generic relation of grounding to be analogous. But the
grounding monist who is a pluralist about some other feature, such as composition,
faces the same issue. Since I believe in a variety of pluralisms, regardless of whether
grounding monism or pluralism is true, I am very uneasy about operating solely with
grounding as my sole primitive notion for inducing structure on what there is.

8.5 Grounding Monism and Degrees of Being

In the previous section, we assessed whether the grounding pluralist had a reason to
believe in something like naturalness or degrees of being. Here we will assess whether
the monist does as well.

---

[72] Compare with Cameron (2014: 49–53).

In sections 8.2 and 8.3, we looked at two apparently competing views about the nature of grounding, one by Schaffer and Baumgarten and one by Fine and Bolzano. But what if they are only *apparently* in competition? One way to avoid competition would be to embrace grounding pluralism, and hold that both figures have focused on distinct but important relations of grounding.[73] Neither Fine nor Schaffer has offered definitions or analyses of their respective notions, and they seem to differ in many important respects. What ensures that they are talking about the same phenomenon in the world rather than two different relations?[74]

A second way to avoid competition is for one of the parties to the debate to provide a reductive account of their opponent's relation, either in terms of their preferred relation of grounding or in terms of some other relations or features. For an example of the latter attempt, consider whether the proponent of fact grounding could understand entity grounding in terms of what Fine (1995a) calls "ontological dependence," a notion that is in turn understood in terms of strict essence.[75] Note that when Schaffer (2009: 375) claims that pure sets are grounded in the empty set, he cites as a precedent Fine (1994a). But in that piece, no claim about the grounding of sets is defended; rather, what is defended are claims about the essences of sets. This suggests that Schaffer is really talking about something like Fine's (1995a) notion of ontological dependence.[76]

That said, I'll focus here on whether two apparently distinct relations are in fact inter-definable in the sense that the entity-grounder can understand fact grounding in terms of entity grounding and vice versa. Surprisingly, in both cases, it is by viewing the allegedly distinct relation as a mere restriction on the more general relation.

This is easier to see in the case of entity grounding. The entity-grounder thinks that grounding relates entities of any ontological category. Facts are entities. So grounding can relate facts to other facts. The entity-grounder can then take the fact-grounder to be focusing on a categorially restricted relation of which Schaffer's entity grounding is the more general case.[77] From the perspective of the entity-

---

[73] Mulligan (2009: 51) notes that Meinong initially thought that grounding related only objectives but later came to think that it could relate objectives to non-objectives as well. This suggests that he switched views, and hence there are two views to switch between.

[74] Daly (2012: 98) suggests that talk of grounding is entirely a philosopher's invention. If this is so, neither Fine nor Schaffer can appeal to ordinary usage of grounding locutions to settle their debate or to help fix what phenomenon in the world is the target of theorizing. Sider (2011: 163) floats the possibility of recognizing both entity grounding and fact grounding within one's system. See also Sider (2011: 161–4) for arguments against entity grounding.

[75] Thanks to Shamik Dasgupta for discussion here.

[76] Conversely, Schaffer (2012: 124) suggests that Fine might be talking about an explanation relation grounded in but distinct from grounding.

[77] In personal communication, Schaffer has communicated to me that he is open to understanding Fine's notion of grounding as a restriction on entity grounding. Sider (2011: 162) worries about understanding Fine in this way on the assumption that the relata of grounding are propositions; but as

grounder, focusing solely on relations between facts yields an impoverished view of ground.

Conversely, the fact-grounder can understand entity grounding within her own system. The friend of fact grounding can view the proponent of entity grounding as holding an unduly narrow view of which facts stand in the grounding relation. Let's make a safe-in-this-dialectical-context assumption that there are infinitely many facts and that the cardinality of these facts is at least as great as the cardinality of those entities that are not facts. Given this assumption, there is a function that will take us from ordered pairs of entities related by the entity-grounding relation to ordered pairs of facts that are suitably related to those entities. So whenever an entity-grounder claims that an entity x grounds another entity y, the fact-grounder can understand that grounding claim in terms of a relation between facts suitably related to x and y. One obvious translation scheme is the following: x entity-grounds y = df. the fact that x exists fact-grounds the fact that y exists. (That there are many such schemes might be of little concern to the fact-grounder: it is enough that there is one way to understand entity grounding in terms of fact grounding.)

There is an initial worry that this "translation" of entity grounding into fact grounding will conflate grounding claims the entity-grounder wishes to distinguish. For example, the entity-grounder might think it is an open question whether facts ground individual constituents of those facts or vice versa. Initially, it seems like the proposal under discussion cannot distinguish these possibilities, but this is not so. Under the considered translation, if an entity-grounder says that an individual constituent C grounds fact F, the fact-grounder understands her to be saying that the existence of C grounds the existence of F. And when an entity-grounder instead says that F grounds C, the friend of fact grounding understands her to be saying that the existence of F grounds the existence of C. More generally, in order to avoid conflating or collapsing entity-grounding claims, the fan of fact grounding can uniformly translate all such claims into claims about the fact-grounding relations between existential facts. And this is why the fact-grounder will thereby view the entity-grounder as having an unduly restrictive view of what the grounding relation relates. From the perspective of the fact-grounder, the entity-grounder thinks that the grounding relation relates only facts of a certain type, namely, existential facts.[78]

Given that the entity-grounder and the fact-grounder can recognize each other's relation of grounding by holding that it is a restriction on their own preferred notion, is there any sense in which one of them has gotten the nature of ground correct? By each of their lights, their own respective notion of grounding might be ideologically primitive and the competing notion unduly restrictive. However, whether in

---

Sider (2011: 163) notes, a different option is to take them to be facts (understood not merely as true propositions).

[78] Thanks to Jonathan Schaffer for discussion here. Note that he does not agree with the lesson I draw. Compare with Sider (2011: 163).

some sense one of them is a metaphysical primitive is a different story. Neither proponent of their relation of ground might take their relation to be metaphysically primitive, but also neither proponent will take their opponent's relation as metaphysically primitive.

At this point, an analogy with quantifier variance (discussed in section 1.4) seems apt. Recall that quantifier variance was supposedly motivated by the apparent intertranslatability of ontological systems. The compositional universalist thinks that whenever there are some *x*s, there is some object composed of those *x*s. The compositional nihilist thinks that whenever there are some *x*s, there are only those *x*s and nothing further. According to the quantifier variantist, the compositional universalist can understand the existential quantifier of the compositional nihilist as being a restriction of the universalist's quantifier. (In much the same way as the entity-grounder can understand the relation of fact grounding as a restriction on entity grounding.) And the compositional nihilist can understand the universalist quantifier in a variety of ways, such as via an "according to the fiction that composition occurs" operator. (In much the same way as the fact-grounder has a plurality of ways of understanding entity grounding in fact-grounding terms.)

Once we see the analogy with quantifier variance, we also see that the potential problem for the monist is more general. Consider, for example, entity grounding. For every pair of entities related by grounding, there is a pair of their singletons related by a different relation, grounding*. That grounding* could be the content of an ideologically primitive predicate is far-fetched, but not impossible, and no more far-fetched than that the property of being grue might be the content of such a predicate. But regardless of whether such an ideologically primitive predicate is possible, it is clear that there is something goofy about grounding*, which suggests that grounding is doing better than grounding* on some metaphysically important scale. The question then is whether the grounding monist can account for that scale wholly in terms of grounding, or whether she instead should embrace another structuring primitive, such as degrees of being.

One way a foe of quantifier variance can respond to that view is by employing a notion like naturalness or degrees of being and holding that one of the quantifiers under discussion is more natural than the other and hence better suited for use in metaphysical enquiry. How should the proponent of grounding reject quantifier variantism, if she is so inclined? If she can account for ultimate properties (discussed in section 8.2), maybe these could be appealed to. Perhaps *being* or its modes of being are ultimate properties. But if she can't, she'll need some other structuring notion such as naturalness or degrees of being.

Similarly, the proponent of either entity grounding or fact grounding could say that one of these grounding relations is more natural than the other and hence better suited for use in metaphysical inquiry. The scale I prefer is the scale of being: grounding has more being than grounding*, regardless of whether grounding is perfectly natural. In general, grounding must be more natural than any putatively more gruesome variant of it. Proponents of ground seem largely content to take the notion of ground as an ideological primitive while remaining officially neutral on the question of whether and in what sense it might be metaphysically primitive. What these reflections suggest is that the grounding theorist, regardless of whether she is a monist or a pluralist, has a reason either to take grounding as a metaphysical primitive or to enrich her metaphysics with further notions such as naturalness, structure, or degrees of being. I suggest the latter course of action.

8.6 Chapter Summary

In this chapter, I focused on grounding. In what sense, if any, is grounding a primitive relation? Perhaps conceptually or methodologically, but not in any way metaphysically. Several ways of defining up a relation of grounding in terms of some kind of ontological superiority plus other connecting relations were explored. We also explored whether the proponent of grounding should help herself to some relation of ontological superiority as well. I argued that both the grounding pluralist—a person who believes in many different metaphysically important grounding relations—and the grounding monist both have reasons to believe in an additional relation of ontological superiority. The pluralist does because she needs to account for the unity of the generic relation of ground; it is not plausible that it is a mere disjunction, and so it is either a determinable or an analogous property. But these distinctions were accounted for in terms of naturalness, which I argued is a kind of ontological superiority. The monist about grounding needs some way to defuse grounding variantism, a view analogous to quantifier variantism, and here again appealing to naturalness does the job.

9

Being and Essence

9.1 Introduction

The point of this chapter is to explore what sort of interesting connections there might be between being and essence. Let me emphasize that rather than presenting a linear chain of argumentation, this chapter will be speculative and open-ended. The notions of a mode and degree of being, essence, and ground all have an intertwined historical lineage. I will continue the tradition of exploring possible connections.

I will explore two different notions of essence, one of which is understood in terms of modality: the *modal essence* of an entity just is the collection of properties (broadly construed) such that, necessarily, if that object exists in some way or other, then each of these properties is instantiated by that entity. It's a consequence of understanding modal essence in this way that every entity's modal essence overlaps with every other entity's modal essence, since the property of being such that $2 + 2 = 4$ is among the modal essence of every object. For this reason, one might search for a less encompassing notion of essence. This is what the second notion of essence is supposed to be.

The second notion of essence is one that has been recently articulated and defended by Kit Fine (1994a), E. J. Lowe (2013: 201), David Oderberg (2007), and many others. In section 8.3, we called it *strict essence*. The strict essence of an entity is supposed to be that which captures the real definition of that entity. In slogan form, the strict essence of an entity tells us "what it is to be that entity." The strict essence of an entity can also be construed as a collection of properties, and it is common to assume that the strict essence of an entity is a sub-collection of the modal essence of that entity.[1] For reasons that will become clearer later, I don't want to build into the notion of strict essence that the strict essences of entities are always sub-collections of the corresponding modal essences—and I don't want to build into the definition of strict essence that an entity has its strict essence modally essentially. (The latter is not strictly a consequence of the former—it might be that, in every possible world, an object's strict essence is a sub-collection of its modal essence, but *which* subclass it is changes from world to world.) Admittedly, it is plausible that objects have their strict

---

[1] Here is an example: Spinoza (2002: 244), in his *Ethics* part II, definition 2, says that, necessarily, when what pertains to the essence of a thing is annulled, the thing itself is annulled. Galluzzo (2013: 6) says that strictly essential properties are *de re* essential properties that explain the other de re essential properties.

essences modally essentially. Moreover, this claim is plausibly a consequence of the attempt to reduce modal necessity to that which follows (in some non-modal sense) from the strict essences of all things. But for now I want to be cautious about the connection between modal essence and strict essence.[2]

As noted in section 8.3, Fine (1994a) distinguishes between what he calls *constitutive* essence and *consequential* essence. Recall that the constitutive essence of a thing is what is "directly" definitional of that thing, whereas the consequential essence of a thing is that which is a consequence of the constitutive essence of that thing. In section 8.3, we also discussed several kinds of consequential essence. In what follows, I will focus on constitutive essence.

There are six questions concerning the connection between being and essence that I want to discuss. First, in section 9.2, even if all things have a modal essence, does everything have a strict essence? Second, in section 9.3, do truths about the essence of a thing entail that the thing itself exists in some manner? Third, in section 9.4, are essences entities, and if so, what manner of being do essences enjoy? Fourth, in section 9.5, are there some things such that their strict essence is exhausted by the fact that they have the mode of being that they have, or must objects always have a richer strict essence than this? Fifth, in section 9.6, does strict essence reduce in some way to modes of being? Finally, in section 9.7, is it part of the modal or strict essence of things that they have the mode of being that they have?

It's hard to answer any one of these questions without answering at least some of the others. Consequently, the web of speculation to be spun will be both intricate and delicate.

9.2 Do All Things Have a Strict Essence?

Few contemporary proponents of strict essence deny that the notion of strict essence is perfectly general.[3] Moreover, the examples in the extant literature of things that purportedly have essences—sets, people, conferences, events, propositions—also suggest that most proponents implicitly believe that every entity has a strict essence. Some proponents are even explicit: Oderberg (2007: x, 19, 47, 54, 87, 152) holds that *every* entity has a real essence.[4]

---

[2] Note that the connection between strict essence and *de re* modal essence might be historically more contentious than we might have thought. For example, Brower (2014: 288–91) argues that Aquinas's theory of the Incarnation requires him to deny that if something is essentially F, then it is non-contingently F.

[3] Cameron (2010: 263) does not think that all entities have strict essences but rather only the real ones have them. As we'll see, this is the position I favor.

[4] Oderberg's (2007: 105) discussion of privations and other beings of reason suggests a bit of wiggle room, since he says such entities are not real beings. Were they within the range of his putatively universal quantifier? Similarly, Dasgupta (2016) holds that anything that belongs to an ontological category has an essence; but perhaps he does not think that holes belong to an ontological category. (On the account of ontological categories developed in section 4.3, they do not.) Similarly, according to Pini (2005: 81–2), Scotus held that only things that belong to an ontological category have a real essence.

However, this isn't obvious—one can believe that there are non-modal essences while denying that everything has one. Historically, this has been the popular position, and insofar as the contemporary proponent intends to be recapturing this ancient notion, the view that not everything has a strict essence needs to be on the table.

For example, Aquinas (1965: ch. 1) holds that, of those creatures that fall under the categories, only substances can straightforwardly be said to have strict essences. But entities in the other categories of being have essences only in a secondary manner, which is fitting given that they do not enjoy the same mode of being as substances.[5] That substances and accidents do not enjoy essences in the same manner seems to be a doctrine that goes back to at least Aristotle.[6]

Second, in *Metaphysics* VII.4, 1030a11, Aristotle (1984b: 1626) appears to deny that accidental unities, such as pale Socrates, have essences.[7] According to Aquinas, privations, such as blindness in an eye, holes, or shadows, have no essence at all.[8] Suárez also agrees that these entities—which he and Aquinas thought of as beings of reason—lack essences.[9] I agree that there are such entities, which I identified with beings by courtesy. However, although there are such entities, and although there are *de re* necessary truths about them, they lack essences in the strict sense.[10]

We've discussed the historical precedents for the claim that some entities lack strict essences.[11] Let's now discuss two arguments that some things lack strict essences. The things in question are beings by courtesy. Interestingly, there are two routes to the conclusion that beings by courtesy lack strict essences. The first route assumes that the notion of strict essences is metaphysically fundamental. The second route is via a particular reductive account of strict essence.

Suppose that strict essence is a metaphysically ground-floor notion. In section 5.7, we examined the principle that only fully real entities can enjoy fundamental

---

[5] See Galluzzo (2013: 258–69). Amerini (2014: 337–8) notes that Alexander of Alessandria also held that accidents have essences only in a secondary manner, provided that they have essences at all. By way of contrast, the contemporary essentialist Oderberg (2007: 152) says that accidents have essences, since everything has an essence. He does not distinguish there between primary and secondary ways of having an essence.

[6] See, for example, *Metaphysics* VII.4, 1030a27–b13; (Aristotle 1984b: 1626–7), where Aristotle appears to assert that nothing which is not a species of a genus has an essence. Tahko (2013: 52) claims that, for Aristotle, only species have essences. Cohen (2009: 203) disagrees, holding that Aristotle probably does not intend in this passage to deny that members of species have essences as well.

[7] See Cohen (2009: 203–5) for discussion.

[8] See chapter 1 of Aquinas's (1965) *Being and Essence*. In his commentary, Kenny (2005a: 4) notes that only first-class beings have essences, whereas privations do not, and accidents have essences at best only in a secondary way (Kenny 2005a: 7). See also Brower (2014: 25, 200) and Wippel (1982: 132).

[9] See Suárez, Disputation 54, section 1, subsection 10 (Suárez 2005: 65–6).

[10] Interestingly, Ryle (1971: 91, 107) also seems skeptical about the universality of essences. He holds that we can speak of the nature or essence of triangles or bicycles, or the nature or essence of this thing *qua* bicycle, but we cannot speak of the nature or essence of a particular that is a bicycle.

[11] See also Robinson (1950: 149–52) for further discussion of historical figures who believed in "real definitions." Interestingly, one of Robinson's (1950: 154) complaints about the notion of essence is that, according to some proponents of this notion, not everything has an essence.

properties or stand in fundamental relations. A natural generalization of this principle is that metaphysically ground-floor notions apply only to entities that are fully
real.[12] Holes, shadows, and other beings by courtesy are not fully real. So the notion
of strict essence does not apply to them. Therefore, they lack strict essences, just as
the historical tradition suggests.

Perhaps strict essence is not metaphysically basic. Many think that Fine (1994a)
has successfully shown that strict essence does not straightforwardly reduce to
modality. But there might nonetheless be a reductive account that is not as straightforward. There are two reductive accounts that do not straightforwardly imply that
beings by courtesy lack strict essences. One of them, defended by Brogaard and
Salerno (2013), analyzes strict essence in terms of counter-possible conditionals.[13]
The other, defended by Dunn (1990), provides an account of essence in terms of
necessary relevant predication. Brogaard and Salerno's account plausibly implies that
everything has a strict essence, but I won't explore this here. Similarly for Dunn's
account, but I am somewhat less sure about this. But there is also an account
defended by Wildman (2013), according to which an object has a property strictly
essentially if and only if it has that property modally essentially and that property is a
perfectly natural property.[14] Wildman's view, in conjunction with the principle
(articulated in section 5.7) that only fully real entities enjoy perfectly natural properties and relations, straightforwardly implies that beings by courtesy lack strict
essences. This strikes me as a feature rather than a bug of Wildman's account,
since the account fits in quite nicely with the traditional view.

Suppose beings by courtesy lack strict essences. This fact is not without consequence. First, it generates a problem for one answer to the question of what grounds
facts about grounding. Second, it might generate a similar problem for a particular
view about truth-making. Third, as hinted at it in section 4.8, this fact raises troubles
for one way of understanding the putative discipline of formal ontology. Before
moving on, let's briefly discuss these.

In section 8.2, we discussed the question of what grounds facts about grounding.
Recall that Bennett (2011a) and deRosset (2013) hold that when G grounds H, it is
G that also grounds the fact that G grounds H. We contrasted this view with one
defended by Dasgupta (2015), according to which it is the strict essence of H, or one
of H's constituents, that grounds the fact that G grounds H.[15] Here is one of
Dasgupta's (2015; forthcoming) examples: the fact that a bunch of individuals are
interacting in certain ways grounds the fact that those individuals constitute a
conference. And what grounds this grounding fact is the essence of conferences:

---

[12] This principle is similar to Sider's (2011) purity principle.

[13] See Steward (2015) for trenchant criticisms of Brogaard and Salerno's proposal.

[14] See also Cowling (2013a). Relatedly, Gorman (2014b: 123–4) argues that Fine's counter-examples to
the modal view of essence don't work since it should be restricted to "real" properties.

[15] For the reasons footnoted in section 8.3, Dasgupta should also add G among the grounds to get the
total ground of the grounding fact.

"what it is to be" a conference just is for a bunch of individuals to interact in certain ways.

This approach sounds initially plausible. However, conferences are mere aggregates of persons, and hence are beings by courtesy, and the properties of being a conference and constituting a conference are also second-rate properties. Facts about conferences are thereby also mere beings by courtesy. Hence, none of them has a strict essence. Therefore, facts about the strict essences of conferences cannot explain the particular grounding facts at issue here, since no such strict essences exist. In general, if not everything has a strict essence, it is unlikely that this approach to explaining grounding facts will succeed.

Similarly, Audi (2012: 108) asserts that grounding relates two facts in virtue of the essences of the properties involved in those facts. But many properties are beings by courtesy, and if such properties lack strict essences, then there will be far fewer grounding facts than one might have thought.

The same sort of worry faces Lowe's (2006: 203; 2009: 209, 212) attempt to explain the relation of truth-making in terms of strict essence. It is well known that, unless everything is a truth-maker for every necessary truth, we can't simply say that x is a truth-maker for a proposition P if and only if P is true in every possible world in which x exists. Lowe proposes that we appeal to the idea that x is a truth-maker for P only if it is part of the strict essence of P that x's existence ensures P's truth. However, if propositions are mere beings by courtesy—an open possibility but certainly not one that we've established here!—then Lowe's attempted analysis of truth-making fails.[16]

And, as noted in section 4.6, certain ways of understanding formal ontology are predicated on the idea that *being an object* has a strict essence that can be revealed by phenomenological investigation. But if *being an object* just is *being something*, and *being something* is not terribly natural, then *being an object* lacks a strict essence.

In general, the project of formal ontology, at least as initially developed by Husserl, was based on the idea that we have intuitions of the essences of philosophically interesting, topic-neutral notions such as *being an object, identity, part and whole, dependence, ground*, and many others.[17] I take philosophers in the recent school initiated by Kit Fine to be engaged in a similar project. Recall the questions that concerned us in section 8.2: to what extent can we definitively settle the logical or structural features of relations like *parthood* and *grounding* independently of first-order metaphysical theorizing about their relata? If *parthood* and *grounding* have essences for us to intuit, then our intuitions of these essences are the decisive data that tell us the logical or structural features of these relations in advance of other

---

[16] Mulligan (2009: 50) suggests a reading of Pfänder according to which the judgment that every truth has a ground is grounded in the essence of truth and judgment. If judgments are propositions rather than mental acts, the same possible problem Lowe faces also arises for Pfänder's theory. And if truth is a non-fundamental property, as deflationalists about truth hold, a similar problem arises. See Pfänder (2009: 249–60) for relevant discussion.

[17] See McDaniel (2014b) for further discussion of Husserl and intuitions of essences.

metaphysical theorizing. However, if *parthood* and *grounding* are not perfectly natural properties or relations, then they might not have strict essences for us to intuit.

I'll close this section with the following methodological remarks. It is certainly not obvious that everything has a strict essence, even if some entities do. Far more caution in attributing strict essences to entities is warranted. Consider, for example, that the very kind of entity Fine appeals to in the context of arguing that we need a notion of strict essence might itself be ontologically dubious, namely classes or sets. Fine (1994a) argues that we need the notion of strict essence in order to distinguish Socrates from Socrates's singleton, both of which are to be found at all the same possible worlds. Fine notes that it is no part of Socrates's essence that he is a member of his singleton, but that it is a part of Socrates's singleton's essence that Socrates is its sole member.[18] But sets themselves *might* be ontologically equivalent to heaps or aggregates, and hence mere beings by courtesy. In which case, they lack strict essences, and hence it is not part of the strict essence of Socrates's singleton that it has Socrates as its sole member.[19]

9.3 Do Truths about the Strict Essences of Things Entail the Existence of Those Things?

Here we will pursue the question of what is entailed by strict essentialist claims about an object independently of any concerns about the possible grounds for such claims. This question is tied with the historically important question of whether and in what sense essence precedes existence.[20]

Consider the conjunction of all true essentialist claims about y. This proposition is the *total propositional essence* of y.[21] We will now distinguish three views about total propositional essences.

First, *the Cartesian view*. On the Cartesian view, an essentialist claim about x can be true even if x does not actually exist, but that claim does imply that possibly x exists. My choice of name indicates my belief that Descartes accepts this view.[22]

[18] See also Koslicki (2012a: 188), who approvingly makes use of the same argument. Oderberg (2007: 8) is a fan of real essence but is skeptical about this argument.

[19] Another worry worth briefly mentioning: it is unclear how Fine's (1994a) suggested reduction of metaphysically necessary truths to truths of strict essence will fare if not everything has an essence. We'll revisit Fine's suggested reduction in section 9.7.

[20] Aristotle wrestles with this question in the *Posterior Analytics* II.8, 93a16–24 (Aristotle 1984a: 153).

[21] Perhaps it could also be called "the real definition of y." As Koslicki (2013: 171) notes, real definitions can be thought of as propositions that state the essences of things.

[22] In Descartes' (1991a: 45) *Fifth Meditation*, we are told that even if there are no triangles, there are still determinate essences of triangles. In his *Replies to the First Set of Objections* (Descartes 1991a: 83), we are told that what we clearly and distinctly perceive is possible. We can clearly and distinctly perceive essences; hence, the things that have those essences must be possible. And we are told in his *Replies to the Fifth Set of Objections* (1991a: 263) that the idea of a triangle (which corresponds to a genuine essence) contains the idea of possible existence, unlike the idea of a chimera (which does not correspond to a genuine essence).

Perhaps Avicenna held this view as well.[23] I am also inclined to attribute the view to Leibniz circa the period in which he accepted the complete concept theory of substance, according to which what it is to be a substance is just to have a concept so complete that all truths about this substance are contained in this concept.[24] During this period, Leibniz happily distinguishes the actual Adam, whose complete concept is actually exemplified, from merely possible Adams, each of whom has distinct complete concepts, none of which is actually exemplified.[25] Leibniz does not, however, appear to traffic in complete concepts of impossible objects. Complete concepts are, for Leibniz, good candidates for being the essences of substances.[26] And there are several places in Leibniz's work where the connection between real definition and possibility is explicitly asserted.[27]

I distinguish the Cartesian view (about strict essence) from the distinct epistemological claim that, in principle, we can know some strict essentialist claims about x prior to knowing whether x in fact exists.[28] That said, the Cartesian view about strict

---

Descartes (1991a: 354) tells us that knowing the essence of something doesn't entail that the thing exists. See also Descartes (1991b: 343; 1992: 197). See also Curley (1978: 147–50) and Secada (2000: 59–60), who also attribute the Cartesian view to Descartes. For a recent proponent of something like this view, see Tahko (2013: 53), who claims that only possible existents have strict essences, and that even merely non-existent possible entities (2013: 56) have essences too. Correia (2006: 764) holds that essential truths are necessary truths, which suggests that he rejects the existentialist view discussed below; but it is not clear which of the other views discussed here he might favor. Trogdon (2013: 467) also accepts that essential truths are necessary truths.

[23] For discussion of Avicenna, see Wisnovsky (2003: 10–11, 158–60; 2005: 105–13) and Druart (2005: 337–8). Miller (2002: 14) claims that Avicenna holds that an essence that could possibly be exemplified can be contemplated by a mind even if no individual has that essence, and hence existence is "detachable" from essence; he also claims that Avicenna recognizes a mode of being particular to essences, *esse essentiae*. Kenny (2005a: 45–6) suggests something similar, but note that Kenny (2005a: 88) also suggests that Avicenna believes in merely possible individuals, which suggests that he attributes the possibilist view to Avicenna as well.

[24] This is defended in his *Discourse on Metaphysics*, included in Leibniz (1989).

[25] See Leibniz (1989: 72–3). Leibniz endorsed a kind of possibilism prior to the *Discourse on Metaphysics* in which there are possible things that do not exist that nonetheless have "definitions," but in order to discern the reason why an object exists we must go beyond its "definition"; see Leibniz (1989: 19–20). In a later work, Leibniz (1989: 114–15) says that the essences of created things are eternal even though the created things are not, and that these essences depend on God's understanding but not his will.

[26] Adams (1994: 14) sounds a note of caution; he suggests that even in the *Discourse on Metaphysics*, in which Leibniz appears to identify complete concepts with essences, it might be better to think of the essence of a substance as that which in conjunction with the essences of all other substances generates the complete concept of that substance; see also Adams (1994: 58). That said, even on this interpretation, a merely possible Adam has a complete concept, and so must have an essence.

[27] See, for example, his *Primary Truths*, in which Leibniz (1989: 26) asserts that a real definition of a thing provides a proof of the possibility of that thing; Leibniz (1989: 273) asserts that the essences of things are co-eternal with God but their existences are not. See also Adams (1994: 136–9) for relevant discussion. The Cartesian view is also endorsed by Leibniz's successors, such as Christian Wolff, who holds both that the essence of a thing is necessary and immutable, but also that having an essence implies being a possible existent. See Watkins (2009: 13–14) for the relevant passages from Wolff.

[28] Descartes (1991a: 78) tells us that, according to the true logic, we must never ask of the existence of a thing without first knowing its essence. Tahko (2013: 60–3) presents the search for the Higgs boson as a case in which an essence is known prior to the existence of the thing. (My inclination is to deny that we have grasped an essence in that case, but merely have grasped a theoretical role that an entity could play. In

essence might support the epistemological view and vice versa. Recall that Descartes claims to discover the essence of extended substance prior to determining whether there actually are extended substances, and he makes this claim partly because of his view about strict essence.[29]

Spinoza seems to reject the Cartesian view, since he appears to accept that there are things that cannot exist and yet have essences.[30] So the Cartesian view was not uniformly accepted among the early moderns. Among later thinkers, Meinong is also a candidate for rejecting the Cartesian view. His impossible objects have *Soseins* that distinguish them from each other, though none of them can exist. Their *Soseins* are plausibly properly thought of as their real definitions, i.e., their essences.[31]

Second, *the possibilist view*. The possibilist view endorses the Cartesian view along with the additional claim that those things that possibly exist have a distinctive mode of being, *possible existence*, that differs from actual existence. Whether Descartes endorsed the possibilist view in addition to the Cartesian view is less clear.[32] In general, the question of whether there can be truths of essence about what are in some sense possible beings without there also being, in some way, possible beings, is historically vexed. A clearer case seems to be Giles of Rome (1953: 61–7), who thinks that possible beings are beings with essences that can exist; it is their essences that make them possible beings, and acts of existence that make some of them actual.[33]

---

general, I am very suspicious of any claim to know the strict essences of fundamental physical entities.) Lowe (2008: 40) says that essence precedes existence, because (i) the essence of a thing can't preclude its existence, (ii) we can't know something exists without knowing what it is, and (iii) we can know the essence of a thing prior to knowing that it exists. Note that Aristotle (1984a: 153) seems to reject this epistemological principle in the *Posterior Analytics* II.8, 93a16–24.

[29] The priority of our knowledge of essence over existence in Descartes is the central theme of the excellent book by Secada (2000). (Note that Secada (2000: 8–9) characterizes both the theses that he calls "essentialism" and "existentialism" as theses about the priority of either knowledge of essence or knowledge of existence over the other; here, I use these expressions as theses primarily in metaphysics.)

[30] See Spinoza (2002: 183), in which Spinoza tells us that the reason that a chimera cannot exist is that its essence is contradictory. Similar remarks are made at 2002: 15 and 2002: 178. Note though that at p. 178, Spinoza denies that chimeras are beings, so it is not fully clear what Spinoza's position is. See Curley (1978: 149–54) for discussion of why Descartes rejected attributing essences to impossible objects.

[31] Findlay (1933: 49) explicitly says that, for Meinong, "what an object is" and its "real essence" consist in its determinations of *Sosein*. Note that both Fine (1994a) and Dasgupta (2016) seriously consider whether impossible entities such as round squares have essences. Charles (2000: 50) briefly discusses whether Aristotle thought that non-entities can have strict essences.

[32] See Brown (2011) and Cunning (2014) for a discussion of Descartes and the reality of the possibles. Nolan (2015) suggests that, although Descartes does distinguish between *necessary existence* and *possible existence*, what he means by the latter is *dependent* or *contingent* existence, rather than a kind of existence that contrasts with *actual* existence.

[33] Trentman (2000: 826–7) claims that, for Suárez, fictional characters do not have real being of any sort, but there is a genuine kind of being that merely possible things have: possible things have objective possible being. Wippel (2000: 403) notes that, for Henry of Ghent, there can be meaningful knowledge of merely possible beings but not of imaginary entities, and hence possible entities enjoy a mode of being had by neither actual entities nor fictional entities. This mode of being might be existence in the mind of God.

Finally, *the existentialist view.* On the existentialist view, true essentialist claims about x entail that x has some form of actual existence.[34] We can distinguish the existentialist view from the possibilist view only if we can distinguish actual and possible forms of existence.[35]

It might seem that the existentialist view is supported by the view that propositions are structured entities that have "what they are about" as constituents. One might think that a proposition exists in a world only if its constituents exist in that world. My total propositional essence is about me, and hence, in some manner, contains me as a constituent. Hence, on this line of thought, my total propositional essence exists in a world only if I do. Further, my total propositional essence is true at a world only if it exists at that world. Hence, the existentialist view is true.[36]

Even if we grant that propositions are structured entities, there are a couple of ways to resist this line of thought.[37] First, there is the distinction between a proposition's being true *at* a world versus its being true *in* a world.[38] In addition, one could argue that it is the former rather than the latter that is relevant here. Second, even if we grant the premises of this argument, it is not clear that they support the conclusion. All that this argument supports is that there is some mode of being that objects enjoy in worlds in which propositions about them are true; it does not support the claim that this mode of being is a form of actual existence. In fact, it does not even support the claim that this mode is a fundamental mode. Only when we supplement the argument with considerations from section 9.2, specifically the claim that only fundamental things can have essences, are we entitled to conclude that the constituents of true propositional essences must exist in some fundamental way.[39] But need this be a kind of *actual* existence?

---

[34] Wippel (2000: 401) says that, for Godfrey of Fontaines, an essence cannot be understood as actual unless its corresponding existence is also actual, and hence the possessor of the essence exists. He also notes that Godfrey defends the real identity of essence and existence in creatures. Marrone (1988: 42) suggests that Scotus was attracted to the view that essence requires existence. Gassendi, in his *Fifth Set of Objections* to Descartes' *Meditations* also suggests that something has an essence only if it actually exists; see Descartes (1991a: 225). Wilson's (2003: 162) discussion of Descartes' *Fifth Meditation* suggests some sympathy with existentialism. Frost (2010) argues that Aquinas allows for an essentialist claim to be true at a time in which its object does not exist, but also holds that the object must exist at some time or other in order for that essentialist claim to be true; see Frost (2010: 213, fn. 27). This suggests that Aquinas is also an existentialist. Remarks by Pereira (2007: 121–4, 132) also suggest that Suárez is an existentialist, though in light of the fact that Suárez also recognizes merely possible beings, it is also tempting to attribute the possibilist view to him.

[35] Shamik Dasgupta has suggested to me a weaker version of the existentialist view, according to which only actual objects have strict essences, and yet there can be truths about their strict essences in possible worlds in which they do not exist.

[36] Miller (2002: 86–95) discusses and rejects the claim that a proposition about Socrates can exist either temporally prior to or modally independent of Socrates himself.

[37] As Jeff Brower has pointed out to me, many of the long-dead proponents of strict essences that I have discussed would eschew this view of propositions.

[38] See Adams (1981).

[39] It would be interesting to contrast the view described here with the view of Williamson (2013), according to which everything necessarily exists, but some of these necessary existents are only contingently concrete.

In the next section, we will discuss whether essences are entities. We'll see there that the nature of essences has implications for whether true essentialist claims about an object entail the existence of this object.

9.4 Are Strict Essences Entities?

In section 9.1, I blithely construed strict essences as collections of properties. Now I'll be more careful about their nature and their ontological status. Should we construe strict essences as entities, and if so, what kinds of entities are they? Are they identical with the things that they are essences of? (Is Socrates identical with the essence of Socrates?) Are they classes of properties or conjunctive properties? Are essences of objects formal constituents of those objects? Are they *sui generis* entities? If they are entities, do they have a distinctive mode of being? Are they fully real or only beings by courtesy?

These questions arise if we take talk of strict essences to be talk about entities. But contemporary proponents of strict essentialism have by and large opted to state their essentialist claims using an operator such as *it is of the essence of x that Φ*.[40] On the face of it, the use of an operator of this sort ontologically commits one to no more than the *x* to which one is antecedently ontologically committed. Therefore, it seems that on this preferred way of expressing essentialist doctrines, talk of essences as entities is pointless.[41]

Perhaps use of an essentialist operator avoids ontological commitment, at least in the sense that ascriptions of essences to things do not simply, as a matter of their semantics, imply that essences are entities. But ontological commitment to essences might sneak in the back door via two questions about essentialist statements that employ this operator. We'll illustrate this with a specific example. Suppose it is of the essence of David Lewis that he is a person. What is the truth-maker for this claim? What is the ground for its truth? Suppose that this claim has a truth-maker. Whatever it is, it might be reasonable to call it an essence of David Lewis. Suppose the ground for the essentialist claim is the fact that *y* exists. In which case, it might be reasonable to call *y* the essence of David Lewis. Only if we both formulate our essentialist claims using a suitable essentialist operator and reject these two questions can we dodge the question of the ontological status of essences.

---

[40] Fine (1994a and 1995b) contain the classic discussion on how essentialist talk can and should be regimented. Lowe (2013: 203) says that an essence is either identical with its bearer or it is no entity at all. Tahko (2013: 55) says that it is better to think of essence-talk as fundamental ideology rather than as corresponding to entities.

[41] Perhaps even worse than pointless? Tahko (2013: 56) claims that all entities have essences, and hence if essences were themselves entities, they themselves would have essences, and hence there would be an infinite regress. But no regress looms if each essence is its own essence, which is a view Lowe (2013: 203–5) considers, noting explicitly that such a view would not be susceptible to a regress; see also Charles (2000: 277).

What is the relation between truth-making and grounding? Unclear! (Though as we saw in section 9.2, some believe that the notion of ground must be appealed to when explaining the notion of truth-making.) Let's stipulate that for x to be a truth-maker of P is for the proposition that x exists to entail the truth of P. Let's provisionally assume that grounding is a relation between propositions, and that when P grounds Q, it follows that P entails Q. Let us say that x is an *ontic ground* for P if and only if the proposition that x exists grounds P. On these assumptions, if x is an ontic ground for P, then x is a truth-maker for P. In what follows, I am going to set aside the question of truth-making and focus on the question of grounding.

In light of what was said earlier, if x is an ontic ground of the total propositional essence of y, then let us say that x is (one of) y's *ontic essence(s)*. Since, in general, a fact can have multiple grounds, it might be that there are multiple entities that are the ontic grounds of a given essentialist fact, and this definition leaves this open. It will be nice also to have a more discriminating notion of ontic essence to work with. Let's say that x is y's *final ontic essence* just in case either x is the unique ontic essence of y or any other ontic essence of y is such that its existence is grounded in the existence of x. And let us say that x is y's *ultimate ontic essence* just in case (i) necessarily, if x exists, then x is the final ontic essence of y, and (ii) necessarily, if y has an ontic essence, then x is the final ontic essence of y.

In what follows, we will focus on putative candidates for being ultimate ontic essences. Each choice of a candidate raises interesting metaphysical questions. However, there are two general metaphysical issues about the connection between essence and ground raised by any choice, which I will discuss before turning to the specific questions about specific candidates.

Here is the first issue. Recall the proposal discussed in section 9.2 that grounding facts are grounded in facts about essences. Suppose that A grounds B. On the view under consideration, the total propositional essence of B grounds the fact that A grounds B. This view, in conjunction with the demand for ontic grounds for essentialist claims, generates an interesting infinite series. (I hesitate to use the word "regress.") Call the total propositional essence of B "C." C grounds the fact that A grounds B. But, if C has an ontic ground, then there is a proposition D that expresses the existence of this ontic ground and that grounds C. What grounds the fact that D grounds C? The total propositional essence of C. And so on. Perhaps this series is not a vicious regress, but we should be cognizant of its existence. One way out is to abandon the view that facts about grounding are grounded in facts about essences. If grounding facts must be grounded, there are other views on the table, such as the view defended by Bennett and deRosset. Another way out is to deny that there are ontic grounds for essentialist claims.

But another possibility is to deny that facts about essences have a ground at all—and this takes us to the second general metaphysical issue that we should address. One position worth considering, recently defended by Dasgupta (2016), is that facts about essences are not merely ungrounded, but are not even *apt* to be grounded.

Although I am intrigued by Dasgupta's proposal, I find his notion of being apt to be grounded obscure. Well, most metaphysics is obscure; it is what it is. But still, I'd like to have a better understanding of what Dasgupta means by "aptitude." Dasgupta draws an analogy between causation and grounding to help us grok the idea of aptitude for grounding. Here's one example of the kind of analogy he uses: the initial state of the physical universe is uncaused but apt to be caused, whereas the causal laws that govern the universe are neither caused nor even apt to be caused. Similarly, there could be facts that are ungrounded but apt to be grounded—perhaps the fundamental physical facts are like this—while there are other facts that are ungrounded and not even apt to be grounded.

I'm a little uncomfortable with taking the notion of aptitude to be grounded as primitive. So let's see whether we can give a theory of it. We'll begin by exploring further the analogy Dasgupta employs between grounding and causation. Let's set aside whether the causal laws that govern the universe are apt to be caused: perhaps they could, in principle, be caused by a god? Let's focus on the initial state. Here are some reasons to think that the initial state of the universe is apt to be caused even if in fact uncaused. First, the initial state of the universe is one of the relata of the causal relation, and one might think that if one is apt to cause, then one is apt to be caused. (In general, however, one can't always assume that being a relatum in a dyadic relation makes one apt to be in either slot of a dyadic relation.) Second, there is a possible world in which either it or a duplicate of the initial state in fact has a cause. So the initial state of the universe is possibly caused, or something just like it is. Third, the initial state of the universe is apt to be caused because it is an instance of a kind of thing that has possible instances that are caused. (What is the relevant kind of thing? I suppose it is events involving physical properties.)

Let's see whether we can develop a heuristic for determining when facts are not apt to be grounding. To that end, let's consider parallel claims. The first parallel claim is that any fact that is a relatum in a grounding relation is apt to be grounded. Dasgupta definitely cannot accept this claim. Facts about essences are relata of the grounding relation. Suppose it is of the essence of x that F. This fact grounds the fact that either it is of the essence of x that F or P, for any P. [42] (Disjunctions, I suppose, are always grounded in their disjuncts.)

The second parallel claim is that an ungrounded but apt to be grounded fact has a duplicate that is grounded, or is itself possibly grounded. This is harder to assess. Perhaps the ungrounded is necessarily ungrounded. (Though, in general, a grounded fact can have different grounds in different possible worlds. Why then must a grounded fact be necessarily grounded or an ungrounded fact necessarily ungrounded?) If something ungrounded is necessarily ungrounded, then the only way in which ungrounded physical facts can be apt to be grounded (given the second parallel

---

[42] Dasgupta (2016) distinguishes between mediated and non-mediated essence claims, and argues that the former are not autonomous.

claim) is if they have possible duplicates that are grounded. But here is an argument for the claim that all duplicates of ungrounded physical facts are ungrounded. That a fact is ungrounded is not itself a brute fact, but rather is itself grounded in the nature of that fact. But which aspect of the nature is relevant? Consider an ungrounded physical fact Fa. That the fact has a as a component rather than, for example, b is irrelevant—this fact is ungrounded because the property of being F is a fundamental property. It is the qualitative aspect of the fact that is responsible for its being ungrounded. And so it is necessary that all facts of the form Fx are ungrounded if any of them are ungrounded. Any duplicate of the fact that Fa will contain a constituent that is a duplicate of F and a constituent that is a duplicate of a. But any possible duplicate of F is itself numerically identical with F.[43] So any duplicate of Fa will be a fact of the form Fx, and hence will be ungrounded as well. So if the second parallel claim is true, ungrounded physical facts are *not* apt to be grounded.

Finally, let's consider a third parallel claim: ungrounded facts that are apt to be grounded are instances of the same kind of fact that has possible instances that are grounded. Here we run in to a kind of generality problem—an ungrounded fact is an instance of many kinds, but what is the relevant kind that makes it apt to be grounded rather than inapt to be grounded? My intuitions on this score are very weak, even with purportedly easier cases. Suppose that the fact that the singleton of Socrates exists is grounded in the fact that Socrates exists. Is the fact that the empty set exists grounded or ungrounded?

I guess it is ungrounded. Fine (2012a: 48) says that it is grounded, but grounded in nothing! (Truly, the nothing has nothed here.) Is the fact that the empty set exists apt to be grounded though, because it is of the kind *facts about sets*, and this kind has many actual (and hence possible) instances that are grounded? Maybe that's OK to say. It is also a member of the kind *facts about abstract objects*, which in turn all facts about essences are members of. But many facts about essences are not apt to be grounded on Dasgupta's proposal. It's not clear how to solve this generality problem. I think Dasgupta should reject the third parallel claim.

Let me close the discussion of aptitude for grounding by suggesting one route that Dasgupta doesn't employ. This route also suggests an interesting connection between being and essence. Suppose that "x is inapt for grounding" amounts to "it is a category mistake to claim that x is grounded or ungrounded." Recall that in section 4.5 category mistakes are linked to modes of being. So one way to make sense of Dasgupta's proposal is to hold that there are two kinds of facts—facts about essences and the other facts—and these two kinds of facts do not exist in the same way. In a more metaphysically perspicuous language, the grounding predicate of that language is type-restricted: the result of attaching it to an expression referring to an

---

[43]   Unless some version of trope theory is correct!

essentialist fact is syntactic garbage. (We discussed a similar view about grounding facts as well in section 8.2.)

In general, there seems to be patterns to facts about essences. The existence of Socrates's singleton is grounded in the existence of Socrates; the existence of Kit Fine's singleton is grounded in the existence of Kit Fine; the existence of my singleton is grounded in the existence of me. The pattern is obvious, and it demands a metaphysical explanation, one that seemingly cannot be met if essence facts are inapt to be grounded.[44]

So let's explore putative candidates for being the ontic grounds of essential facts. To make things more concrete, let's consider David Lewis and his total propositional essence. Here I explore five candidates for his ultimate ontic essence. The first candidate is David Lewis himself. The second is a proper constituent of David Lewis; on one traditional metaphysic, David Lewis is a hylomorphic compound of matter and form, and, in my terminology, his substantial form is the ontic ground for his total propositional essence.[45] The third candidate to be explored here is the set of properties attributed to David Lewis by his total propositional essence. The fourth candidate is a traditional theistic answer that essences are ideas in the mind of God. In my terminology, the ontic ground of David Lewis's total propositional essence is an idea in the mind of God. Finally, a fifth candidate is that David Lewis's total propositional essence is a *sui generis* entity. This isn't even an exhaustive list; for example, a sixth candidate, which will be explored in section 9.6 but not here, is David Lewis's mode of being.[46]

Has anyone held the view that David Lewis is the ultimate ontic ground for his total propositional essence? That David Lewis might be an ontic essence for himself is suggested by some remarks by Aristotle in his *Metaphysics* VII.4, 1029b1–3, 13–6 (Aristotle 1984b: 1625–26):

Since at the start we distinguished the various marks by which we determine substance, and one of these was thought to be the essence, we must investigate this. And first let us say something about it in the abstract. The essence of each thing is what it is said to be in virtue of

---

[44] Dasgupta (2016) recognizes that there is a pattern here, but attempts to account for it in terms of the logical consequences of various essentialist claims rather than by providing a grounding-based explanation. Fine (2012b: 11) claims that there is a set of fundamental essential truths that when conjoined with non-essential truths yield all the essential truths; this also suggests a metaphysical explanation for this kind of pattern.

[45] There are other proper constituents worth considering. Perhaps Lewis's matter and form are *collectively* the ontic ground. This is suggested by Oderberg (2007: 65), but I think his considered view is that things are their essences; see Oderberg (2007: 121). But perhaps their forms are their ultimate essences; see Oderberg (2007: 247). Pasnau (2011: 121, 551) notes that, for Aquinas and other medievals, common matter is also part of the essences of created corporeal things. Brower (2014: 112–13, 200–3) holds that, for Aquinas, both matter and substantial form determine the essences of hylomorphic compounds; see also Galluzzo (2014: 231–4). Another candidate for being the ontic essence of David Lewis is his proper parts considered collectively; such a view is neutral on whether David Lewis is a hylomorphic compound. However, I have only so much space and I imagine that my readers have only so much patience.

[46] Provided that we reify modes of being. In section 9.6, we will pursue the question of whether facts about modes of being ground facts about essence independently of whether modes of being are entities.

itself. For being you is not being musical; for you are not musical in virtue of yourself. What, then, you are in virtue of yourself is your essence.

However, it is not clear that the phrase "in virtue of yourself" should be understood as "in virtue of the fact that you exist."[47] Moreover, even if David Lewis is an ontic essence for himself, it is not clear that David Lewis is his *ultimate* ontic essence. I am inclined to think that, from an Aristotelian perspective, David Lewis's substantial form has at least as much right to be considered *an* ontic essence, and perhaps is the ultimate essence of David Lewis.[48]

A better candidate for a historical proponent of this view is Descartes circa *The Principles of Philosophy*.[49] In this work, Descartes defends the view that each substance has one principle attribute, which constitutes its "essence."[50] A given substance cannot have more than one principle attribute, for if it did, it would have more than one nature or essence, and this is impossible.[51] For this reason, it is plausible to attribute to Descartes the view that the principle attribute of a substance is that which grounds the essence of that substance. For corporeal substances, the principle attribute is extension, and for incorporeal substances, the principle attribute is thought.[52] Strictly, each substance has its own numerically distinct principle attribute: there is no common universal that all corporeal substances participate in, for example.[53] But interestingly, Descartes also suggests that each substance is numerically identical with its principle attribute.[54] It would follow then that each substance is a ground of its total propositional essence. Descartes rejects substantial forms, and it is dubious that Descartes took the parts of an extended substance to also be

---

[47] Koslicki (2012a: 191) suggests that essentialist truths are grounded in identities of the objects of the essences, which is in the neighborhood of the view under discussion.

[48] Cohen (2009: 204–6) says that definable things, such as universals, are their own essences, but that Socrates is not his own essence, and that the essence of a thing is its form. Tahko (2013: 55) identifies form and essence in Aristotle, citing *Metaphysics* VII.7, 1032b1–2 (Aristotle 1984b: 1630); we'll have more to say about this putative identification soon. But Tahko (2013: 55) also says that essences are primitive for Aristotle and not grounded in anything else.

[49] Descartes is not the only plausible historical candidate. According to Normore (2012: 90, 95), Ockham identified himself with both his existence and essence. Matsen (1974: 103) claims that Alessandro Achillini defends the "essential" identity of essence and existence in creatures. See also Gilson (1952: 1012). Kok (2014: 523–4) argues that Buridan identifies a thing with its essence. Conti (2014b: 559–62) says that Paul of Venice claims that there is merely a formal difference or difference in reason between a creature and its essence. Bakker (2014: 607–8) claims that Albert the Great identified a thing with its essence. Galluzzo (2014: 250) notes that Aquinas appears to identify "separated substances" with their own essences. In this context, one also must wonder what Locke (1979: 417) meant when he said that essence is the very being of the thing whereby it is what it is.

[50] See *Principles* I.53 (Descartes 1992: 210).

[51] See Descartes (1992: 298).

[52] In *The World*, Descartes (1992: 92) asserts that extension is the "true form and essence" of material bodies; in the *Discourse on the Method*, Descartes (1992: 127) asserts that he is a thing whose essence is thinking.

[53] See Secada (2000: 205–6) for a discussion of individual essences in Descartes.

[54] See *Principles* I.62–3 (Descartes 1992: 214–15). What is suggested is that, in reality, a substance and its principle attribute are the same.

additional ontic grounds for Descartes' essence. This suggests to me that, by Descartes' lights, Descartes himself is his own ultimate ontic essence.[55]

There are two related complications with this interpretation, however. First, Descartes presents a version of the ontological argument that seems to turn on identifying God's existence and essence, but also appears to overgeneralize if, in created substances, there is not a real distinction between essence and existence.[56] (We'll discuss this argument in section 9.5, and whether it overgeneralizes, as well as how relevant the identity of God's essence with God's existence is for the success of the ontological argument.). It is hard to make sense of a real distinction between existence and essence in created substances if each created substance is its own ontic essence. And there are places where Descartes suggests that the relation between essence and existence in creatures is different from that in God; e.g., in the *First Set of Replies* Descartes (1991a: 83) says that "we fail to notice how closely existence belongs to essence in the case of God as compared with that of other things." On the other hand, there are passages in which Descartes (1991b: 280) denies that the essence and existence of created things are distinct outside of thought.[57]

Second, Descartes also seems to accept that truths about the essences of created substances are necessary, even though the existences of created substances are contingent. Given the definition of "ultimate ontic essence," the claim that the propositional essence of Descartes is necessary although the existence of Descartes is contingent is consistent with the claim that Descartes is his own ultimate ontic essence.[58] However, if this is the case, then in those worlds in which Descartes does not exist, Descartes' total propositional essence must lack an ontic ground. And in this case, it is unclear what, if anything, would ground x's propositional essence in those worlds. Can an actually grounded fact be only contingently grounded?

Let us now explore the second candidate. Suppose that David Lewis is a hylomorphic compound of some sort, and that one of his constituents is a *substantial form*. I'll assume that substantial forms are particulars rather than universals, and that they are not transferable: necessarily, if x has S as its substantial form, then, necessarily, any y that has S as its substantial form is identical with x. The second candidate is substantial form construed in this way.[59]

---

[55] Note that Secada (2000: 190, 193–4) calls Cartesian substances "determinable essences."

[56] See Nolan (2015) for a related worry about how Descartes' views on existence and essence compromise his ontological argument.

[57] See Secada (2000: ch. 8) for a lengthy and informative discussion of Descartes' view of existence and essence in creatures.

[58] Provided that singular propositions about objects can exist in worlds in which those objects do not exist. We discussed this issue in section 9.3.

[59] Wisnovsky (2003: 11) says that both "perfection and essence can each be understood as referring to a thing's substantial form." Gilson (1952: 74) says that form can be taken as essence when it is the proper object of intelligible definition. Knuuttila (2012: 63) says that, for Aquinas, form determines essence. Pasnau (2011: 551) notes that many philosophers took the substantial form of a thing to in some way account for or determine the essence of that thing. (He also notes that this is not the sole role that substantial forms are invoked to play.) Adams (1994: 100) says that, for Leibniz, essence is to be either

Note that it does not follow from these assumptions that the substantial form of x exists only in worlds in which x exists. If forms can be detached in this way, then the ontic ground of the total propositional essence of x can exist even when x does not. And in which case, that total propositional essence of x is true in these worlds. If forms are detachable in this way, are they necessary beings? In which case, true essentialist claims are necessarily true.

Defenders of substantial forms have historically been divided into two camps: those who believe that a given object has one substantial form versus those who believe that it has a plurality of substantial forms.[60] Why believe in a plurality of substantial forms? Consider a human person. She is not merely a lump of matter, but rather she is an organized corporeal entity with many capacities. Her rational substantial form is what makes her a human person, which, let us say, is what she strictly essentially is. But were she to suffer a terrible accident and lose her rationality, something might still remain, e.g., a living animal, which in turn is a hylomorphic compound. Since some informed material thing persisted, there must have been an animal (or sensitive) substantial form all along.[61]

Suppose an object has multiple substantial forms. Is each form an ontic essence for that object? Are any of its forms a good candidate for being the ultimate ontic essence of the object? I believe the answer to the first question is "no," which is also why the answer to the second question is "yes."[62]

My impression is that the proponents of multiple forms believe that they are hierarchically ordered. Consider a human being with three substantial forms, one of which is her rational substantial form, another of which is her animal/sensitive substantial form, and, finally, one of which is her material/corporeal substantial form.[63] Her possession of a rational substantial form ensures her possession of an animal form, which in turn ensures the possession of her material substantial form. But it's not the case that each form is an ontic ground for her essence. Rather, there are two possibilities. The first possibility is that the ontic ground for her essence is solely the rational form, which grounds her possession of the other two forms as well.

---

identified with substantial form or is at least "fully expressed" by substantial form. Galluzzo (2013: 6) says that, for Averroes, "the essence of material substances is exhausted by their form alone."

[60] See chapters 24 and 25 of Pasnau (2011) for a riveting discussion of the debate over whether created things have one substantial form or many. See also Kok (2014: 534–5).

[61] See Pasnau (2011: 580–8) for more on the twists and turns of this kind of argument.

[62] De Raeymaeker (1957: 162) appears to claim that substantial forms are the grounds of essences; he also addresses in footnote 9 a worry about what to say if things have more than one substantial form— which form is then the ground of essence? The worry about multiple substantial forms seems analogous to a worry Descartes has about principle attributes. Descartes (1992: 210–11), *Principles* I.53, tells us that the principle attribute of a thing is its "principle property which constitutes its nature and essence, and to which all its other properties are referred." Descartes (1992: 398) later claims in *Comments on a Certain Broadsheet* that, if something had more than one principle attribute, it would have more than one essence, which is impossible. See Hoffman (2011) for further discussion.

[63] This is the sort of view defended by Ockham, according to Pasnau (2011: 577).

The second possibility is that none of the forms individually is the ontic ground of her essences, but collectively they all are.[64] Both are worth exploring.

If the substantial form of an object is the ultimate ontic essence of that object, does the substantial form in turn have a distinct ultimate ontic essence? Probably the Aristotelian will say "no." Every substantial form is its own ultimate ontic essence. Hence, one thing can be the ontic ground of two (or more) distinct essences, if forms are universal.

Let us consider the third candidate, according to which the ontic ground of the total propositional essence of David Lewis just is the set of properties that propositional essence attributes to David Lewis. On the face of it, this candidate is not promising: this set of properties corresponds to the total propositional essence of David Lewis *because* this total propositional essence is true and *not because* this set is its ontic ground. (Similar remarks apply to the idea that the properties collectively are the ontic essence of David Lewis.) Nonetheless, let us note that if properties in general are necessary beings and sets of properties in general are the ontic grounds of true essentialist claims, then true essentialist claims are necessarily true.[65] If there are some creatures that both contingently exist but have strict essences, then the total propositional essence of x can sometimes be true even when x does not exist.[66]

We turn next to a discussion of the fourth candidate: the ontic ground of David Lewis's propositional essence is an idea in the mind of God.[67] This view also has traditional defenders who think that the mode of being of essences is "existing objectively in the mind of God" rather than a distinctive and more independent mode. This might be the view of Henry of Ghent, but it is arguably Leibniz's view as well.[68] On this view, essences either just are ideas in the mind of God or they are entities that are ontologically parasitic on ideas in the mind of God.

This view is plausible only if there is a God, but let's go with the flow, since views about the nature of God have interesting consequences worth drawing out. Suppose that God is absolutely simple: not only does God lack proper parts, but also there is no genuine distinction between God's (intrinsic) features and God.[69] On this view,

---

[64] Pasnau (2011: 577) suggests a view on which a substantial form is posited for "each essential attribute," which suggests the second sort of view here. Frost (2010: 202) claims that defenders of a plurality of substantial forms in a single creature hold that the "composition" of these forms is the ground of what I call the total propositional essence of that creature.

[65] Assuming that if x grounds y, then necessarily, if x obtains, y obtains.

[66] A related possibility, one that might be attractive for certain fans of truth-making theories, is that the ultimate ontic ground for a propositional essence is the fact that the object has that propositional essence. Thanks to Hao Hong for suggesting this candidate.

[67] Gilson (1952: 84–5) suggests that Scotus holds this.

[68] Wippel (2000: 403–4) suggests that, for Henry of Ghent, the being of essences consists in being objects of God's knowledge. Frost (2010) explains why Aquinas rejects this view. Recall that I suggested that, for Leibniz, complete concepts are good candidates for being ontic essences. Complete concepts are ideas in the mind of God.

[69] This view was attributed to Aquinas in the introduction to this book. It is also the view of Descartes (1992: 128–9). Cunning (2014) notes some problems for Descartes' modal metaphysics that stem from

we can in some sense distinguish different ideas in the mind of God but the distinctions we draw are mere distinctions of reason, and the ideas thereby distinguished are mere beings of reason. (Or, to use the terminology of chapter 6, mere beings by courtesy.) One might think that if the ontic grounds of true essentialist claims are mere beings of reason, then strict essence is not a metaphysically ground-floor notion: what undergirds strict essences are entities that exist only in a non-fundamental sense. The general principle I am appealing to is this. Suppose that any proposition containing a constituent β necessarily has an ontic ground for its truth. Suppose also that, necessarily, the ultimate ontic grounds for the truth of any proposition containing a constituent β do not fundamentally exist. Then β is not metaphysically fundamental.

One could resist the conclusion of this argument, however, by denying that ideas in the mind of God are the *ultimate* ontic essences of things. Instead, God is the ultimate ontic essence of things. And so there is no threat to the metaphysical fundamentality of strict essence. If God is the ultimate ontic essence of all things that have a strict essence, then, unless all things that have strict essences exist necessarily, the truth of a given propositional essence of a thing needn't imply the existence of that thing.

Alternatively, one could accept an alternative conception of God that embraces mereological simplicity without embracing complete metaphysical simplicity. Though God has no proper parts, nonetheless God has many genuinely non-identical features. Among these features are various numerically distinct divine ideas, each of which could serve as the ontic ground of a true essentialist claim without compromising the metaphysical fundamentality of strict essence, provided that these features enjoy a perfectly natural mode of existence. It is unclear whether ideas in the mind of God must be necessary beings, and hence it is unclear whether one's essence is modally more robust than one's existence.

Finally, let us turn to a discussion of the view that essences are *sui generis* entities. Perhaps little positively favors this view—this is the view to embrace when other alternatives fail. And because essences are *sui generis* entities, we are more in the dark about whether they in some way depend on those things of which they are essences. What it is for essences to be a *sui generis* entities is for them to form their own ontological category, which, as defended in section 4.4, is for them to share a distinctive mode of being. Perhaps this view can be motivated by the concerns about the grounds of essential facts we discussed earlier. Perhaps those sympathetic to the idea that facts about essences are not apt to be grounded should seriously consider instead taking essences themselves to be *sui generis* entities.

Descartes' identification of God's will with God's understanding. See also Kaufman (2003) for a discussion of both Aquinas's and Descartes' theories of divine simplicity, as well as how Descartes' views on divine simplicity connect up with his doctrine that God freely creates "the eternal truths."

Earlier, I suggested that *form* is a traditional candidate for an ontic essence. But interestingly some advocates of substantial forms also seem to think of essences as a distinct kind of entity. First, let us consider Aquinas on created incorporeal agents, such as angels. These entities are not hylomorphic compounds, since they have no matter. Instead, they are forms. However, they are nonetheless not absolutely simple—even angels have some metaphysical complexity, since in them there is a *real* distinction between existence and essence.[70] For Aquinas, to say that there is a real distinction between essence and existence is not obviously to say that the entity that is the essence of a thing could exist without the thing existing, but it is still to treat essences as some sort of entity.[71] Treating essences as entities seems to be the position of Giles of Rome, who distinguishes both matter and form and existence and essence, but holds that there are many distinctions between these pairs.[72] He also appeals to a real distinction between essence and existence in order to explain the possibility of creation.[73] Even more than in Aquinas, Giles of Rome does seem to treat essences as entities of some sort.[74] However, these essences cannot be (modally) separated from that which they are essences of.[75]

So it seems that neither Aquinas's nor Giles of Rome's position provides the basis for an argument that truths of essence are modally independent of truths of existence. Perhaps the appropriate basis of such an argument is the view of Avicenna, which many interpret as the claim that existence is a superadded accident of essence.[76]

---

[70] MacDonald (2002: 150–1) notes that, for Aquinas, even in separated substances, there is a real distinction between essence and existence, and so separated substances are not absolutely simple. See also Kenny (2005a: 33) and Nolan (2015). Trentman (2000: 882) claims that Suárez interprets Aquinas as holding that essences are entities.

[71] For a contrary view, see Wippel (2000: 395), who says that Aquinas does not think of essence and existence as things but rather as "ontological principles." Brower (2014: 17–18, 196) claims that Aquinas does not think of essences as entities but rather talk of a real distinction between essence and existence serves to emphasize the ontological dependence of creatures on God. Kenny (2005a: 35) suggests an even more deflationary view: the doctrine of the real distinction between *esse* and essence amounts to the claim that I can grasp a concept without knowing whether it is instantiated.

[72] Giles of Rome (1953: 38–41). Matsen (1974: 77) credits Giles of Rome with being the first to formulate the view that there is a real distinction between essence and existence in creatures, and this is a distinction between two *things*.

[73] In Giles of Rome (1953: 36), we are told that creation takes place when God "impresses" an existence on an essence, and at (1953: 100) he explicitly asserts that without the distinction between existence and essence, a thing would be eternal and unable to be created. See Cunningham (1970: 62–3) and Wippel (1982: 134–41; 2000: 396–7).

[74] But see Wippel (2000: 396–8) for discussion that suggests that this aspect of Giles of Rome's thought should be downplayed.

[75] Some attribute the view that essences are *sui generis* entities with their own mode of being to Henry of Ghent as well. See, e.g., Coffey (1938: 87), Gilson (1952: 76), and Wielockx (2006: 297–9).

[76] Averroes (1987: 236) claims that Avicenna thinks of the existence of a thing as an "attribute additional to its essence." See also Wippel (2000: 393), Miller (2002: 16), and Donati (2006: 267), the latter of whom suggests that Giles of Rome's position is quite close to Avicenna's. For criticism of this interpretation of Avicenna, see Morewedge (1972). See also Galluzzo (2014: 239–42) and Shehadi (1982: 75–7). Gilson (1952: 91) says that Anthony of Brindisi also thought that existence is an accident of essence, and that perhaps Wolff thought so as well (1949: 118).

On this view, there is a distinction between essence and existence in creatures, and a creature's existence seems to be contingently predicated of the essence of that creature. On this view, it seems that the essence of a thing could exist even when the existence of that thing (and hence the thing itself!) does not exist.[77] In which case, there would be true propositional essences grounded in the existence of these *sui generis* ontic essences even in worlds in which the objects of those essences are not to be found.

From my perspective, something like the (allegedly) Avicennian view is attractive. For me, a mode of existence of an entity is a higher-order property or relation; it is not a feature of that entity per se but rather of some other entity intimately related to it. Perhaps that other entity is a property necessarily uniquely had only by that object. Perhaps a *sui generis* essence is nonetheless appropriately thought of (in a suitably analogous way) as a property, and hence is also a candidate for that to which existence is attributed. If so, then I could happily say that modes of being are properties of *sui generis* essences. And, if these properties were exemplified contingently, it would seem fitting to say that modes of existence are accidents of essence.

9.5 Are There Things Whose Strict Essence is Exhausted by their Mode of Being?

Traditional metaphysics distinguished two questions one can ask about a putative entity. The first question is the question of existence: is there such an entity? The second question is the question of essence: what is the essence or nature of that entity? These questions seem to be distinct questions, at least if there are no modes of existence. However, we are in a context in which we are distinguishing different manners in which things exist, and in which we are allowing that things belonging to different ontological categories have different modes of being. (In section 4.4, we explored whether ontological categories just are fundamental modes of being.) In which case, facts about whether an object is and what its ultimate nature is might not be distinct after all.

The notion of a strict essence is subject to few conceptual constraints. As far as I can detect, there is no immediate conceptual incoherence in positing that there is an entity E and mode of being B such that the total propositional essence of E consists in E's enjoying the mode of being B. There might be theoretical reasons to reject putative total propositional essences that include information about existence in them, and we will explore one of them later in this section.

But first let's examine two candidates for being an entity whose essence includes its existence.

---

[77] Gilson (1952: 75–8) holds that Avicenna thought essences had a kind of being in themselves, as well as being in things and being in minds, and this is why they can exist independently of things or cognitions. See also Kenny (2005a: 45–6) and Perszyk (1993: 69–70).

Heidegger (1962: 67) claimed that "The 'essence' of Dasein lies in its existence." Heidegger interpretation is always dangerous, but let us be brave once more.[78] My inclination is to interpret this claim as saying that there is nothing more to the essence of Daseins, which are what we are, i.e., roughly, finite embodied persons, than the fundamental mode of being that we enjoy. Heidegger calls this mode of being *Existenz*, and offers a painstaking account of the various aspects of this manner of being. The attempt to give a painstaking account of the manner of being of Dasein is called "the existential analytic of Dasein."[79] So we should not think that the claim that the essence of Dasein lies in its existence is one in which things like us have, in a sense, a very thin essence.[80] But we should also be careful about how we state what is involved in offering an existential analytic of Dasein or, for that matter, any account of the manner of being of entity.

Among what we learn from Heidegger's existential analytic is that things that enjoy *Existenz* are necessarily finite, embodied, social individuals embedded in a network of norms that govern them and the objects that they manipulate in their environment. This suggests that we learn from an existential analytic that the strict essence of Dasein contains a rich variety of properties. But then what sense does it make to say that the strict essence of Dasein merely consists in its manner of being? (Note that by "essence," Heidegger cannot mean mere modal essence, since Dasein is modally essentially such as to not be the number 2, and so on.)

Let "E" be the special quantifier that designates the mode of being *Existenz*. (If we wish to be cute, we can call it the "Existenzial quantifier.") E is a semantically primitive restricted quantifier, and so is not to be understood as being defined in terms of an unrestricted quantifier conjoined with restricting predicates. But any sentence in which the Existenzial quantifier appears is intensionally equivalent to a sentence in which it is systematically replaced by the unrestricted quantifier and suitable restricting predicates. Let's assume that the suitable predicates in this case are F, G, and H. (What is suitability? More on this is in a minute.) Then "$Ey\ (x = y)$" is intentionally equivalent to "$Fx\&Gx\&Hx$." (Note that, we are looking for first-order predicates intensionally equivalent to *enjoying* a mode of being.) But don't forget that we are trafficking here in hyperintensional metaphysics twice over! First, two expressions might be intensionally equivalent and yet one expression might be,

---

[78] One reason the interpretation of Heidegger's remarks here is dangerous is that he puts the German equivalent of scare quotes around the word "essence," which suggests that he might not be talking about strict essence. My suspicion is that the scare quotes serve a different function. I am inclined to attribute to Heidegger the following view: just as Dasein does not exist in the way in which other things exist, Dasein does not have an essence in the way in which other things do, and accordingly just as there are modes of being, there are modes of essence. Hence, when talking about the essence of Dasein, some way of marking how Dasein's mode of essence differs from that of, e.g., merely present-at-hand entities, is important. The German equivalent of scare quotes might serve this purpose.

[79] See Heidegger (1962: 67–77).

[80] A converse view seems suggested by Philipse (1998: 17), according to which the essential structures of Dasein—the facts about Dasein's essence—constitute Dasein's mode of being.

from the metaphysician's perspective, the better expression to employ because it is the more metaphysically natural expression. The notion of metaphysical naturalness employed here is hyperintensional. (For example, plausibly, every natural predicate is intensionally equivalent to some gruesome disjunction of non-natural predicates.) On the view under consideration, "E" is a fundamental mode of being, and this mode of being is prior to whatever properties are articulated in the existential analytic of Dasein. Second, the notion of strict essence is hyper-intensional as well. We cannot assume that just because two properties F and G are necessarily coextensive, that F will be among the strict essence of a thing if and only if G is.

But why then does the existential analytic yield the specific set of properties that it does rather than any other any set of properties the conjunction of which would be intensionally equivalent to the conjunction of the former? (In short, what makes a set of predicates or properties "suitable"?) If modes of being were (for Heidegger) first-order properties of individuals, and these properties were mereologically complex, and there were facts about which sets of intensionally equivalent properties were its parts, then the set of properties that are "suitable" would be just the set of properties that are parts of the mode of being in question. The analytic of Dasein's mode of being really would be *analysis*, that is, an articulation of the mode into its constituent parts. A view along these lines is ably defended by Joshua Tepley (2014). But since I take modes of being to be represented by quantifiers rather than (first-order) predicates, I can't take this straightforward route and must say something more subtle. (Or perhaps "more desperate" is more apt.)

Here's my attempt to do this. First, some assumptions that are not at all obvious. Assumption one: for any fundamental mode of being, there are many conjunctions of first-order properties such that each conjunction is intensionally equivalent to enjoying that mode of being. Assumption two: among these conjunctive properties, one of them is the most metaphysically natural. (It might also be as natural as the mode of being, but it is definitely not more natural.) Assumption three: an *articulation* of a mode of being consists in giving an account of each of the conjuncts of this most natural property. If we like, we can distinguish between the *fundamental essence* of Dasein, which consists simply in having *Existenz*, and the *derived essence* of Dasein, which consists in this conjunctive property. (The distinction between fundamental and derived essence is not the same as the distinction between constitutive and consequential essence.) But as always, what is primary is the enjoying of the mode of being.

Here is an interesting consequence of this way of understanding Heidegger's claim that the essence of Dasein lies in its existence. Suppose there is more than one Dasein, but each Dasein enjoys the same mode of being. So each Dasein has exactly the same strict essence. Say that a strict essence F is an *individual essence* of x just in case, necessarily, if any y has F then y = x. No Dasein has an individual essence. If what it is to be an *individual* in the metaphysical sense is to have an individual essence, then Daseins are merely non-identical with one another but are not individuals.

Alternatively, we could take this observation as motivating Haugeland's (2013) interpretation of Heidegger, according to which there is one Dasein, which each of us is a case of. We are not Daseins on this view, but rather are something like instances or cases of Dasein, in much the same way as an individual ailment can be a case of smallpox.

Suppose that everything has an individual essence. It follows from this supposition that an entity's essence consists in its mode of existence only if it is necessary that it and only it has that mode of being (if it has any mode of being at all). In one strand of scholastic metaphysics, exactly one being meets this description: God. The manner of being enjoyed by God is not shared by created beings; their mode of being is only in some way analogous to the mode of being of God. In God, there is no distinction to be drawn between existence and essence, unlike in created beings: God's essence simply consists in God's existence.[81] (Fine (1994a: 2) does note that in traditional metaphysics only one being enjoys existence as His essence—but doesn't note that the kind of existence He has is also enjoyed only by Him.)

On this tradition, there is a special mode of being enjoyed only by God. (Perhaps this mode of being is even identical with God, as a more radical version of the doctrine of divine simplicity would hold.) There might nonetheless be a privileged way of articulating this mode of being. Let "D" stand for the mode of being enjoyed by God, and let "C" denote the most natural conjunction of properties such that, necessarily, Dx ($x = y$) if and only if Cy. Perhaps C will decompose into a traditional list of divine attributes. God's goodness will be among C, but God's being such that $2 + 2 = 4$ will not—and perhaps this would give proponents of this tradition a reason to say things like "God is God's goodness" but not "God is God's being such that $2 + 2 = 4$," since the former statement more accurately corresponds to a fact about God's essence than the latter.

For traditionalists, it is of God's essence to be good. But it is merely necessarily the case that God is such that $2 + 2 = 4$. However, for traditionalists, God's essence just is His existence. So how to make this contrast? My thought here is that *goodness* will be part of the articulation of God's mode of being in a way that being such that $2 + 2 = 4$ will not, and hence the former is rightfully thought of as part of God's derivative essence whereas the latter is not.[82]

Suppose God's essence is God's existence.[83] How fares the fabled ontological argument? Let's get a version of that argument on the table. Here's a Cartesian

---

[81] See Aquinas's (1948: 17) *Summa Theologica* part 1, question 3, article 4.

[82] We've seen how this sort of story plays out for God and Dasein. Perhaps a similar story could be told that would allow the less than fully real entities to have strict essences as well, if that is desired. If such an entity has a most natural mode of being, then this will also have an articulation, which is what generates the list of strictly essential features of the entity.

[83] Recall our discussion of divine simplicity in section 1.5.3. If God is His existence as well, then God is the semantic value of the fundamental quantifier that appears in the statement of God's total propositional essence, as well as the ontic ground of that total propositional essence.

version of that argument, based on remarks in Descartes' *Fifth Meditation*.[84] Premise 1: I have a clear and distinct idea of God. Premise 2: having a clear and distinct idea of x just is grasping the essence of x, i.e., knowing the total propositional essence of x.[85] Interim conclusion: so I know the total propositional essence of God. Premise 3: any total propositional essence is necessarily true, independently of whether the possessor of that essence exists; this is where the Cartesian view of essence, discussed in section 9.3, comes into play. Premise 4: the total propositional essence of God is that God exists (in the manner in which God exists). Conclusion: so God necessarily exists (in the manner in which God exists).

There are many ways to resist this argument. One could embrace what I called "existentialism" in section 9.3 and thereby deny premise 3. Fittingly, this is a plausible move to make with respect to a parallel argument for the necessary existence of Dasein. If truths of essence are not necessary but rather contingent on truths of existence, then things can have their modes of being essentially without necessarily existing. (Conversely, if one accepts the possibilist view described in section 9.3, one might happily accept that there is a mode of being that as a matter of necessity everything enjoys.)

But with respect to this ontological argument, the more cutting responses might be to reject premise 1 or premise 2.[86] This might be even clearer if we consider a second version of the ontological argument.

Here is a second Cartesian ontological argument. Premise 1: I have a clear and distinct idea of God. Premise 2: having a clear and distinct idea of x just is grasping the essence of x, i.e., knowing the total propositional essence of x. Interim conclusion: so I know the total propositional essence of God. Premise 3*: for any total propositional essence of something, it is possible that this something exists. (Essences correspond to possible existents.) Premise 4*: the total propositional essence of

---

[84] Descartes (1991a: 44–9) contains the *Fifth Meditation*. There are some similarities between the reconstruction I offer here and Curley's (1978: 141–69); the most important similarities are that there can be truths about the natures or essences of things regardless of whether they exist, and that our clear and distinct perceptions of these essences are veridical. Interestingly, Doney (1993) argues that, "in a sense and with qualifications," there are two different versions of the ontological argument to be found there; he calls these two arguments "argument A" and "argument B." The argument I discuss here is not formulated in the same way as either Doney's argument A or B, but it is much closer to his A than his B. Schmaltz (2014: 216–17) responds to Doney (1993).

[85] Gewirth (1998: 97, fn. 72) notes that a crucial part of Descartes' ontological argument in the *Fifth Meditation* is that our idea of God represents a real essence. In Descartes' (1991a: 83) response to Caterus, he reaffirms that he takes us to have a grasp of the essence of God. See Doney (1993: 81–2) for a discussion of Descartes' response to Caterus. Schmaltz (2014) provides a general overview to Descartes' ontological argument; see also Koistinen (2014: 230–6). Secada (2000: 163) says that our idea of God is an idea of God's essence.

[86] Aquinas is committed to rejecting either premise 1 or premise 2 of this argument because he holds that we do not have a grasp of God's essence, not because His essence does not imply existence. See Aquinas's (1948: 11–12) *Summa Theologica* part 1, question 2, first article and Aquinas's (1991: 82) *Summa Contra Gentiles* book I, chapter 11, section 5, and finally Aquinas (1994: 69–70). See also Pasnau and Shields (2004: 64).

God implies that God necessarily exists if he possibly exists. Conclusion: so God necessarily exists.

If premise 3 of the first Cartesian argument was our sole target, then premise 3* of the second Cartesian argument will probably also be our sole target. But premise 3* is plausible, perhaps more plausible than premise 3, unless we countenance essences of impossible objects. This suggests that the common premises 1 or 2 are likely targets.

In light of these remarks, one might wonder about the relevance of God's identity with His essence for the success of the ontological argument. In my terminology, the fact that an object is identical with its ultimate ontic essence is not sufficient for the success of an ontological proof of the existence of that object. In fact, the question of whether an object is identical with its ultimate ontic essence turns out to be pretty much irrelevant.[87] What matters isn't the ontic ground of the total propositional essence of an object, but instead is whether (i) that propositional essence includes the proposition that the object exists (in some specific way or just in general), and (ii) propositional essences are necessarily true. So, for example, Descartes might be his own ultimate ontic essence, but since the total propositional essence of Descartes consists merely in that he is thinking but does not include that he exists, no ontological proof of the actual existence of Descartes will succeed.[88]

A second observation of the ontological argument is that the versions presented here do not require that existence in any sense be a property.[89] Both versions merely require that statements of the form "$\exists x\ x = y$" (or similarly statements about modes of being) can appear in statements of y's total propositional essence.

I've claimed that there is no conceptual incoherence in holding that the essence of an entity includes its existence, and I've shown that the route from this claim to an ontological proof for the existence of an entity in question is not at all straightforward. This relieves some of the pressure against a blanket ban on allowing the existence of an entity to enter into that entity's essence.

That said, certain metaphysical systems might require a blanket ban. Consider a kind of Meinongianism on which every object, whether existent or not, has a strict essence, and this essence consists in all the properties that characterize the object in question. So, for example, the round square's strict essence includes that it is round and square. It is hard to see how the Meinongian can deny that the total propositional essences of objects are necessarily true: what is contingent is which objects have or

[87] Oderberg (2007: 128) suggests that having one's existence included in one's essence suffices for one's being a necessary being. Vallicella (2002: 71) claims that if one's essence and existence are identical, then one is a necessary being. The reflections of this section show that at a minimum more premises are needed before either conclusion can be reached.

[88] In light of these remarks, it is worth once again re-examining other classical arguments for the existence of God. For example, Dasgupta (2016) argues that the Principle of Sufficient Reason implies that there is some thing (or things) whose essence includes their existence, although he denies that these must be a God.

[89] *Pace* Geach (2006: 122).

fail to have being, not what each object essentially is.[90] If a property characterizes an object only if it instantiates that property, then we must disallow existence as one of the properties that can appear in the essences of objects.[91] (Otherwise the existent round square would exist, necessarily!) So in this framework, a distinction between extra-nuclear and nuclear properties might be motivated.[92]

9.6 Can Strict Essence Be Reduced in Some Way to Being?

The notion of reduction is a particularly slippery one, and I certainly don't intend here to spend a lot of time trying to clarify the different things that philosophers have or could mean by "reduction." One notion of reduction is very strong: to successfully reduce, e.g., strict essence to something else is to provide a recipe for systematically replacing any sentence in which any essentialist notion, such as "it is part of x's strict essence that P," occurs with a necessarily equivalent sentence in which no such essentialist notion occurs. The latter sentences must be antecedently better understood than the former sentences in order for the reduction to result in clarification of the notion of strict essence. And if one is motivated by a worry that the notion of strict essence is in some way metaphysically suspicious, then the latter sentences must also not invoke any notions that are at least equally as metaphysically suspicious as the notion of strict essence. However, one might find the notion of strict essence to be neither unclear nor metaphysically suspicious, and yet be interested in whether there is a reduction in this sense simply because one's theory would be tidier if there were.

In the previous section, we examined the question of whether the essence of a being could consist simply in its mode of being. Here's an interesting connection between that question and the question we are considering now. If the essence of *every* being were simply its mode of being, there'd really be no need to have a separate notion of essence in addition to the notion of a mode of being, since the former would be straightforwardly reducible to the latter.[93] In fact, rather than say that the strict essence of a thing is its mode of existence, we could define the constitutive essence of a thing as the articulation of its mode of being. Those who are inclined to

---

[90] See Perszyk (1993: 98–100) for discussion of how Meinong might make sense of an object's seemingly possessing properties merely contingently.

[91] See Berto (2013: 14–16, 116–19) for discussion. Many Meinongians deny that the round square *instantiates* roundness, but hold rather that it stands in some other relation to roundness. Zalta (1983), for example, claims that the round square encodes but does not instantiate roundness; see also Berto (2013: 128–32).

[92] See Parsons (1980) for a development of a theory making use of this distinction.

[93] Perhaps we can also allow a being by courtesy to have an essence, provided that the most natural mode of being it enjoys has a privileged *articulation* in the sense of section 9.5.

hold that the distinction between essence and existence in things is a merely conceptual distinction should consider this view seriously.

But if in most (if not all) cases, the strict essence of a thing is richer in content than its mode of being, if there is a way to reduce the notion of an essence to talk of modes (or degrees) of being, the reduction is not straightforward. Suppose, for the sake of an example, that sets have strict essences. Consider, for example, the singleton of Socrates, which is strict-essentially such that Socrates is its element. The strict essence of Singleton Socrates is an individual essence in the sense articulated earlier. The essence of the singleton of Socrates is not the same as the essence of singleton of Plato, yet these singletons belong to the same ontological category, and hence share the same mode of being.

A substantially weaker notion of reduction makes use of the notion of grounding: to reduce essence in this sense is to show that all facts about essences are grounded in facts not about essences.[94] A successful determination of the grounds of a set of facts does not by itself provide any sort of conceptual clarification about the notions needed to express these facts. Maybe no such clarification is needed—and yet insofar as we believe there are facts about strict essences, it is worth investigating whether such facts must be grounded and, if so, what are the natures of their grounds.

Consider a traditional metaphysics of substance and attribute, according to which (i) attributes are essentially such that they are instantiated by some substance or other, but (ii) substances are not such that they essentially instantiate some attribute or other.[95] Are these facts about the strict essences of the entities ungrounded facts? My inclination is to say that they are grounded in the respective modes of being of the entities in question. As discussed in chapter 2, substances enjoy an absolute form of existence—their mode of being is a monadic mode. Attributes on the other hand enjoy a polyadic form of existence—classically called *being-in*: what it is for an attribute to exist is for it to exist *in* a substance. Here the difference in essence is directly reflected in the difference in how the objects exist.

Question: would it be better to say that these differences in essences are grounded in facts about the difference of modes of being enjoyed? Or would it be better to say that these essences are different because the relevant modes of being are among the essences in question? In the former case, the essences are different because their grounds are different; in the latter case, the essences are different because a complete statement of these essences will include the modes of being of the entities in question. Are these alternatives exclusive? That is, can the grounds of a strict essence be in

---

[94] Miller (2002: 135, fn. 9) suggests that an entity's existence is that in virtue of which it belongs to its species and has certain properties. Were Miller to restrict these properties to those that are strictly essential—rather than *all* of that entity's properties (Miller 2002: 167)—his view would be in line with the views discussed here.

[95] Galluzzo (2013: 340) says that Albert the Great held that accidents depend on substances (strictly) essentially.

some sense among that strict essence? If the strict essence of an object is its existence, can its existence also ground its strict essence?

Just to illustrate the complexities involved, consider an entity k whose mode of being is represented by "E" and whose strict essence is exhausted by having that mode of being. Consider now the following propositions P and Q:

$$P = k\text{'s strict essence wholly consists in } Ex \; x = k.$$
$$Q = Ex \; x = k.$$

Can we say that Q is the ground of P? I assume that Q grounds P only if Q entails P. Even if it can be contingent what mode of being a thing has and contingent what strict essence a thing has, we might think that this entailment still holds. So at least one necessary condition for Q's grounding P is met. Does P entail Q? If we assume that (i) necessarily, facts about k's essence obtain only if k exists in some way or other, and (ii) necessarily, k exists only if k enjoys $Ex \; x = k$, then we do get that P entails Q as well. But symmetric entailment does not rule out asymmetric grounding![96]

What I've just sketched is a modest and local attempt at grounding some essences in modes of being. Let's now consider a very ambitious attempt to partially ground all essential facts in facts about the modes of being of various entities. Let's restrict our focus to the essences of sets, since people's intuitions about their essences seem reasonably (or unreasonably) firm. In general, it is part of the essence of a set that it has the elements that it has. Is this general fact about the essences of sets collectively grounded in the particular facts about specific sets or does the general fact partially ground each particular fact? Neither choice is mandatory, but my inclination is to take the general fact as prior to its instances—perhaps much like how causal laws seem to have a kind of priority over the patterns they induce. That is, this general fact has the character of a general law.

The fact that the general law is necessarily true, while in many cases it is contingent which sets exist since it is contingent which members of these sets exist, doesn't settle this question. It does settle that the general law can't be a full ground for the specific essentialist facts, since the general law doesn't entail the specific essentialist facts, at least on the assumption that the specific essentialist facts are true only if the relevant sets exist. (Recall our discussion in sections 9.3 and 9.4 of this issue.)

---

[96] One might also wonder whether what mode of being an entity enjoys is grounded in its strict essence. Mulligan (2006a: 37–8) proposes this view. Mulligan has also directed my attention towards this passage written by the important phenomenologist Max Scheler in which this position is defended: "I am of the view . . . that modes of being can be distinguished from essence (*in mente*, not *in re*) but that essence (for example the essence of the person, the essence of life etc.) also determines (*bestimmt*) the mode of being." (This is Mulligan's translation of Scheler's *Gesammelte Werke, vol. 9, Späte Schriften*, p. 285). I thank Kevin Mulligan heartily for discussion on this issue and directing me towards Scheler's remarks. I won't pursue this question further here, as we have already too many questions on our plate as it is. However, it definitely needs further thought; I would think one attracted to the Cartesian view discussed in section 9.3 would find the position that essences ground modes of being especially attractive.

Here is a hypothesis: specific facts about the essences of specific individuals are never brute but are always partially grounded in a more general covering law that specifies the essence of a kind of thing. I have no idea how to prove this, so I offer it for you as an intriguing hypothesis.[97] Suppose this hypothesis is true. Suppose also that there are maximally general laws of strict essences, that is, laws that govern the strict essences of all and only the members of a given ontological category. What, if anything, grounds these most general laws of strict essence? Second hypothesis: these general laws of strict essence are in turn grounded in the existence of the relevant ontological categories, which (recall section 4.3) simply are modes of being. The general law that the strict essence of a set is to have the members that it has is grounded in how sets exist.

Now we must be careful. In what does a fact about the existence of an ontological category consist? Let "B" be a quantifier that corresponds to a mode of being M. Suppose that the fact that M exists simply is the fact that $Bx\, x = x$. But if so, is this fact itself grounded in further facts of the form $Bx\, x = y$? And if so, have we snuck in particular facts as partial grounders of general principles through the back door? To make this worry more concrete, let M be the mode of being that all sets share. Let S be a particular set. Is $Bx\, x = S$ grounded in something more basic, such as $S = S$? Here my inclination is to say no. Remember that "B" is a restricted quantifier, and hence the move from Φy to $Bx\, \Phi x$ is not guaranteed to preserve truth. So there is room to take S's enjoying a fundamental mode (i.e., $Bx\, x = S$) as an ungrounded fact.

So far we have a story of the partial grounding of all essential facts about sets. To get the full ground of, for example, the fact that the essence of singleton Socrates is to have Socrates as a member we simply conjoin this general law of the essences of sets with the particular fact that Socrates is a member of singleton Socrates. I assume that if a fact F fully grounds G, then necessarily, if F obtains, G obtains. And so the general law of the essence of sets is not sufficient to fully ground the essence of the singleton of Socrates, since the former obtains necessarily, while the latter obtains only if Socrates exists. However, if we think that, in general, the fact that the essence of x is to be F is metaphysically independent of the existence of x, then there is room to say that the general law of essence fully rather than partially grounds each fact about the essences of specific sets.

This is one way in which modes of being could serve as grounds of essence. Let's consider a second alternative way. Perhaps the mode of being sets enjoy is a partial ground of each particular essentialist fact about sets. On this second alternative, what grounds the fact that the essence of Socrates' singleton is to have Socrates as a member is the conjunction of the mode of being of this set along with the particular claim that Socrates is the sole member of this set. All claims about the particular

---

[97] Kit Fine has communicated to me that he finds this hypothesis attractive as well. Recall that Fine (2012b: 11) claims that there is a set of fundamental essential truths that coupled with the non-essential truths yields all the essential truths. Dasgupta (2016: section 4) discusses this hypothesis too.

essences of sets are grounded in a similar way. In turn, the generalization that all sets essentially have their members is fully grounded in the conjunction of the particular essential claims. Like the first alternative, the second alternative appeals to modes of being to ground facts about essences, but in other respects the grounding structure is inverted.

9.7 Is It Always Part of the Modal Essence of Things That They Have Their Mode of Being (or Modes of Being)?

Suppose the strict essence of a thing is always a proper subset of the modal essence of a thing. If there are some entities that either could have had a different mode of being or could have existed in a different way, then these entities have neither their mode of being nor their degree of being as a matter of strict essence. And perhaps it is never the case that the mode or degree of being of a thing is encapsulated in its strict essence even if it is modally essential to that thing. For these reasons, I will focus here on the question of whether all entities are such that it is modally essential to them that they have either the mode of being or degree of being that they have.

It is impossible to satisfactorily answer this question without having settled some first-order ontological questions and questions in the metaphysics of modality. But it's probably fair to say that our initial inclination is to answer negatively. How could something change its mode of being, which is tantamount to changing ontological category?

One of the most fascinating metaphysical doctrines discussed in Robert Pasnau's recent book, *Metaphysical Themes*, is the doctrine that God has the power to change the mode of being of a mere "inhering accident"—something that in its current manner of being can exist only in something else—to a mode of being such that this very same entity can then exist as a free-standing being existing in its own right.[98] Pasnau finds the idea that objects could undergo a change of their manner of existing to be incredible, and suggests that there is no good precedent or analogy for this view. Briefly, the main motivation for this view is the problem of the Eucharist—and you might think that if we need to appeal to a miracle to justify something incredible, so much the worse for the alleged possibility.[99]

However, there are less divinely motivated metaphysical schemes on which change of mode of being is more plausible. Consider a version of *possibilism* according to which the difference between the actual and the possible is a difference in mode of

---

[98] See Pasnau (2011: 188–90). See also Pini (2005: 70–1).

[99] Jeff Brower has suggested another interpretation of how the medievals understood the Eucharist: rather than attributing to them the view that an entity enjoys a change of mode of being, it attributes to them the view that accidents never had *being-in* to begin with, but instead were merely disposed to be instantiated by substances.

being: the possible and the actual both exist, but in different ways. Any merely possible thing could have been actual, and many actual things could have been merely possible. It's built into this ontological framework that things could have had a different mode of being than the mode they actually have. Relatedly, if Meinongianism is your thing, it's not crazier to think that the mode of being of the things that exist, which is not enjoyed by those entities that are merely objects, can be gained or lost.

Next, consider a version of the A-theory of time according to which merely past or merely future objects have a different mode of being than present ones. A particularly intriguing version is one in which only presently existing things enjoy an absolute form of existence—they just plain exist—whereas merely past and merely future things enjoy a relative kind of existence—they always exist *at* some time or other. (We discussed this view in section 3.7.) This view implies that a change of mode of being literally happens all the time. Moreover, it's a change from a kind of polyadic mode—existing at—to a kind of absolute existence—existence simpliciter—which, in this respect, mirrors the change of being that a mode can undergo in putative miracles: the mode ceases to enjoy existence-in and comes to enjoy existence, full stop.

Finally, let's consider a radical view about intrinsic change over time defended by Elizabeth Barnes (ms-a). On this view, apparent intrinsic qualitative change—enjoying one property and then another—is best understood as change of mode of being. On the view Barnes suggests, every monadic intrinsic predicate corresponds to a mode of being. One putative advantage of Barnes's system is that we can provide truth-makers for intrinsic predications without adding properties or facts to our ontology. Barnes suggests, for example, that the truth-maker for the proposition that the rose is red is just the rose *existing redly*. (Recall our discussion of truth-making in section 3.5 for a similar proposal about truths about the past.)

Suppose we accept one of these ontologies and so in turn accept that what mode of being a thing has is sometimes a matter of contingency. In the previous section, we discussed an attempt to provide partial grounds for particular claims about the essences of objects. Is this attempt compromised if what mode of being a thing can have is contingent?

There are three reasons this is unclear. First, it might be that the mode of being a thing enjoys differs across worlds while its strict essence does not, but nonetheless in each world the essence of the thing is (partially) grounded in that world in the mode of being the thing enjoys at that world. (Compare: a disjunction might be true in many worlds, but grounded in a different disjunct in each world.)

Second, even if all general laws of essence are ultimately grounded in some modes of being, it doesn't follow that all modes of being ground general laws of strict essence. Perhaps if things change some of their modes of being as time passes or when they undergo qualitative change, these particular changing modes are irrelevant to their essences. Perhaps only if a mode is possessed necessarily and eternally is it a potential grounder of a strict essence. For example, if God really can change the mode of an attribute from a polyadic mode to a monadic mode, then it doesn't seem to be part of the strict essence of that attribute that it has either mode of being.[100] But maybe this is OK, since many medieval thinkers think that, with the exception of God, it is never part of the strict essence of a thing that it enjoys any mode of being.

Third, one could deny that strict essences are modally essential to the things that have them. This is probably the most radical of the proposals, but is more defensible than one might think.

A property is modally essential to a thing just in case that thing has that property in every world in which it exists. This is an interesting notion of a kind of essence but it isn't the only one. Let's spot for a moment that metaphysical necessity is perfectly natural. Still, the generic mode of being that everything enjoys is not. Enjoying a fundamental mode of being is prior to enjoying the generic kind of being. So if we wish to speak "more deeply" in the metaphysically perfect language, we will formulate different and more selective notions of modal essence. Suppose there are two fundamental modes of being b and c which are represented by two quantifiers, "**B**" and "**C**." Corresponding to these two quantifiers are two metaphysically better notions of modal essence:

x is b-essentially F = df. $\Box[\mathbf{B}y\,(x = y) \rightarrow Fx]$
x is c-essentially F = df. $\Box[\mathbf{C}y\,(x = y) \rightarrow Fx]$

These notions of modal essence are defined solely in terms of perfectly natural notions (again on the assumption that "$\Box$" is perfectly natural). And it might be that an object that actually enjoys b-existence has its strict essence b-essentially, even though it could have c-existed, and would not have had its actual strict essence c-essentially had it c-existed, but would rather have had some different strict essence altogether. In general, I feel the need to ensure that the strict essence of a thing is also had in some modally robust way, but this way of proceeding seems to meet this need adequately enough.

This third proposal might not give every fan of strict essence everything they want. It is not obvious how to carry out the reduction of modality to essence proposed both by Fine (1994a) and Lowe (2013: 202–3) on this third proposal.[101] (I assumed momentarily for the sake of illustration the fundamentality of modality just now. But this feels to me to be inessential to the spirit of the third proposal.) But if we are existentialists in the sense of section 9.3, we will hold that many truths of strict essence are contingent on the existence of objects, and hence will be suspicious of a purported reduction of modality to strict essence. (A related question: if existentialism (discussed in section 9.3) is true, can modality reduce to strict essence?)

---

[100] Donati (2014: 155–6) notes that Aquinas denies that the mode of being of a finite thing is included in its essence.
[101] Thanks to Joshua Schechter for discussion of this point.

Before closing this chapter, one last fun question: is the degree of being of a thing modally essential to it?[102] (We've focused so far only on whether modes of being are essential.) It is difficult to come up with plausible metaphysics in which the degree of being of an entity changes across worlds, but let me sketch a putative system. First, suppose counterpart theory about *de re* modality is true, and that the modal essence of an entity is a function of how similar it is to other entities in other possible worlds. Suppose that, unlike Lewis (1986), we take counterpart theory in full generality and hence are counterpart theorists about the *de re* modal properties of properties and relations.[103] Finally, let us say that what determines the counterpart relation between properties is similarity of pattern of instantiation across worlds. It seems to me then that there could be two properties that are counterparts of each other, but such that one property is perfectly natural whilst the other is determined by more natural properties in the world it is in. (Consider, for example, a possible world in which the pattern of instantiation of every actual intrinsic property and relation is filled with distinct intrinsic properties and relations, and moreover, there is a further set of properties and relations among which those supervene.) Since on my view natural-ness just is degree of being as defined on properties, if such a metaphysics were true, there would be entities that could have been more or less real than they actually are.

9.8 Chapter Summary

The focus of this chapter was on the connections between being and essence, where "essence" was primarily understood as *strict essence*. We discussed whether every entity has a strict essence; I argued that plausibly not. We discussed whether truths about essence implied truths about existence; I plumped for a positive answer to this question, but discussed several alternative views. We discussed whether essences should be understood as entities, and if so, what kind of entity they might be. We also discussed whether truths about essences are grounded not in entities in general but rather in the ways in which entities exist. Finally, we assessed whether the properties an object strictly essentially has are had as a matter of modal necessity.

---

[102] Hirsch (1997b: 49) answers affirmatively.   [103] Heller (1998) has such a view.

Concluding Unsystematic Postscript

We've nearly reached the end of this long book, which I hope has not worn out its welcome. It's time to take stock and call it a day.

I have not demonstrated beyond a reasonable doubt that there are modes of being or various forms of ontological superiority. Such things cannot be demonstrated beyond a reasonable doubt. Metaphysics is and always will be a highly speculative endeavor, and its conclusions subject to rational reappraisal. That we speculate in a disciplined yet humble way should be our aim in metaphysics. Certainty is neither to be sought nor hoped for.

So what was accomplished?

One important goal of this book was to stress the importance of separately evaluating the metaphysical question of whether being fragments and the semantic question of whether ontological expressions are polysemous. I believe that I have shown why distinguishing these questions is both important and fruitful. And I have done this while still maintaining that there are interesting connections between quantification and being. Quantifiers are the apt linguistic home for modes of being rather than predicates, which are the apt linguistic homes for properties.

I have taken old ideas and put them in new clothing, but I have also provided new applications to these old ideas and connected them up with contemporary problems in metaphysics. One of these ideas is that the notion of analogy is critically important to several topics in ontology. Along the way, I hope to have indirectly shown the relevance for contemporary metaphysics of the history of philosophy.

I believe that I have demonstrated the fecundity of the idea that there are modes of being and various forms of ontological superiority. There are many varieties of ontological pluralism corresponding to the many applications of the doctrine to extant philosophical problems and disputes. In not every case is an instance of ontological pluralism the best solution available, but in many cases I think it will be, and I have produced many applications for your evaluation.

But I have also taken these applications on a case-by-case basis and have not attempted to provide a unified, single version of ontological pluralism to handle all of the problematic phenomena I have discussed, which included substance, time, categorial differences, possibility and necessity, presence and absence, persons and value, ground and consequence, and essence and accident. A more philosophically satisfying defense of ontological pluralism would include a statement and defense of the best version of ontological pluralism that does systematically account for these phenomena. I would have preferred to do this, but given that it has taken me many pages and many years to write this book, this task is for the future. I believe that the explorations here will at least be of use to any future persons who take it up.

Thank you for reading this book.

Bibliography

Adams, Robert. 1981. "Actualism and Thisness," *Synthese* 49: 3–41.

Adams, Robert. 1987. *The Virtue of Faith and Other Essays in Philosophical Theology*, Oxford University Press.

Adams, Robert. 1994. *Leibniz: Determinist, Theist, Idealist*, Oxford University Press.

Adams, Robert. 1997. "Things in Themselves," *Philosophy and Phenomenological Research* 57.4: 801–25.

Adamson, Peter and Richard Taylor (eds.). 2005. *The Cambridge Companion to Arabic Philosophy*, Cambridge University Press.

Albertazzi, Liliana, Dale Jacquette, and Roberto Poli (eds.). 2001. *The School of Alexius Meinong*, Ashgate Publishing.

Alexander of Aphrodisias. 1992. *On Aristotle's Metaphysics 2 & 3*, trans. William E. Dooley and Arthur Madigan, Cornell University Press.

Alison, Henry. 1973. *The Kant-Eberhard Controversy*, Johns Hopkins University Press.

Alison, Henry. 2004. *Kant's Transcendental Idealism: an Interpretation and Defense (rev. and enl. edn)*, Yale University Press.

Alston, William. 1958. "Ontological Commitments," *Philosophical Studies* 9: 8–17.

Alston, William. 1993. "Aquinas on Theological Predication: a Look Backward and a Look Forward," in Stump (1993).

Ameriks, Karl. 2000. *Kant's Theory of Mind*, Oxford University Press.

Ameriks, Karl. 2003. *Interpreting Kant's Critiques*, Oxford University Press.

Amerini, Fabrizo. 2014. "Alexander of Alessandria's Commentary on the *Metaphysics*," in Amerini and Galluzzo (2014a).

Amerini, Fabrizo and Gabriele Galluzzo (eds.). 2014a. *A Companion to the Latin Medieval Commentaries on Aristotle's Metaphysics*, Brill Publishing.

Amerini, Fabrizo and Gabriele Galluzzo. 2014b. "Introduction," in Amerini and Galluzzo (2014a).

Anagnostopoulos, Georgios (ed.). 2009. *A Companion to Aristotle*, Wiley-Blackwell.

Aquinas, Thomas. 1948. *Summa Theologica vol. I*, trans. the Fathers of the English Dominican Province, Benziger Brothers.

Aquinas, Thomas. 1961. *Commentary on the Metaphysics of Aristotle, vol. I*, trans. John Rowan, Henry Regnery Company.

Aquinas, Thomas. 1965. *Aquinas on Being and Essence: a Translation and an Interpretation*, ed. Joseph Bobik, University of Notre Dame Press.

Aquinas, Thomas. 1991. *Summa Contra Gentiles, book I: God*, University of Notre Dame Press.

Aquinas, Thomas. 1993. *Selected Philosophical Writings*, trans. Timothy McDermott, Oxford University Press.

Aquinas, Thomas. 1994. *Truth vol. II*, trans. James McGlynn, Hackett Publishing Company.

Aristotle. 1924. *Aristotle's Metaphysics: a Revised Text with Introduction and Commentary, vol. I*, ed. W.D. Ross, Oxford University Press.

Aristotle. 1984a. *The Complete Works of Aristotle vol. I*, ed. Jonathan Barnes, Princeton University Press.

Aristotle. 1984b. *The Complete Works of Aristotle vol. II*, ed. Jonathan Barnes, Princeton University Press.

Armstrong, D. M. 1978. *Universals and Scientific Realism*, Cambridge University Press.

Armstrong, D. M. 1982. "Metaphysics and Supervenience," *Critica* 14: 3–18.

Armstrong, D. M. 1989. *Universals: an Opinionated Introduction*, Cambridge University Press.

Armstrong, D. M. 1997. *A World of States of Affairs*, Cambridge University Press.

Armstrong, D. M. 2004. *Truth and Truthmaking*, Cambridge University Press.

Ashworth, E. J. 1995. "Suarez on the Analogy of Being: Some Historical Background," *Vivarium* 33.1: 50–75.

Ashworth, E. J. 2005. "Logic and Language," in McGrade (2005).

Ashworth, E. J. 2013a. "Medieval Theories of Analogy," in *Stanford Encyclopedia of Philosophy*, https://plato.stanford.edu/entries/analogy–medieval/.

Ashworth, E. J. 2013b. "Analogy and Metaphor from Thomas Aquinas to Duns Scotus and Walter Burley," in Bolyard and Keele (2013).

Audi, Paul. 2012. "A Clarification and Defense of the Notion of Grounding," in Correia and Schneider (2012).

Augustine. 1961. *Confessions*, trans. with an introduction by R. S. Pine-Coffin, Penguin Books.

Averroes. 1984. *Ibn Rushd's Metaphysics: a Translation with Introduction of Ibn Rushd's Commentary of Aristotle's Metaphysics, Book Lām*, trans. Charles Genequand, Brill Publishing.

Averroes. 1987. *The Incoherence of the Incoherence vols I & II*, trans. Simon Van Den Bergh, Gibb Memorial Press.

Avicenna. 2005. *The Metaphysics of the Healing*, trans. Michael Marmura, Brigham Young University Press.

Ayer, A. J. 1952. *Language, Truth, and Logic 2nd ed.*, Dover Publications.

Baker, Lynne Rudder. 1999. "Unity without Identity: A New Look at Material Constitution," *Midwest Studies in Philosophy* 23: 144–65.

Baker, Lynne Rudder. 2000. *Persons and Bodies*, Cambridge University Press.

Baker, Lynne Rudder. 2002. "On Making Things Up: Constitution and Its Critics," *Philosophical Topics: Identity and Individuation* 30: 31–52.

Bakker, Paul. 2014. "Fifteenth-Century Parisian Commentaries on Aristotle's *Metaphysics*," in Amerini and Galluzzo (2014a).

Balashov, Yuri and Michel Janssen. 2003. "Presentism and Relativity," *British Journal for the Philosophy of Science* 54.2: 327–46.

Barcan Marcus, Ruth. 1995. *Modalities: Philosophical Essays*, Oxford University Press.

Barnes, Elizabeth. MS-a. "Ways of Truth-Making."

Barnes, Elizabeth. MS-b. "Symmetric Dependence."

Barnes, Jonathan. 1972. *The Ontological Argument*, St. Martin's Press.

Barnes, Jonathan. 1995a. *The Cambridge Companion to Aristotle*, Cambridge University Press.

Barnes, Jonathan. 1995b. "Metaphysics," in Barnes (1995a).

Baumgarten, Alexander. 2014. *Metaphysics: a Critical Translation with Kant's Elucidations, Selected Notes, and Related Materials*, trans. and ed. Courtney D. Fugate and John Hymers, Bloomsbury Publishing.

Baxter, Donald. 1988. "Identity in the Loose and Popular Sense," *Mind* 97: 575–82.

Bealer, George. 1998. "Propositions," *Mind*, vol. 107.425: 1–32.

Bell, David. 1999. *Husserl: the Arguments of the Philosophers*, Routledge.

Bennett, Jonathan. 1966. *Kant's Analytic*, Cambridge University Press.

Bennett, Jonathan. 1974. *Kant's Dialectic*, Cambridge University Press.

Bennett, Karen. 2004. "Spatio–Temporal Coincidence and the Grounding Problem," *Philosophical Studies* 118.3: 339–71.

Bennett, Karen. 2011a. "By Our Bootstraps," *Philosophical Perspectives* 25: 27–41.

Bennett, Karen. 2011b. "Construction Area (No Hard Hat Required)," *Philosophical Studies* 154.1: 79–104.

Bennett, Karen. Forthcoming. *Making Things Up*, Oxford University Press.

Berti, Enrico. 2001. "Multiplicity and Unity of Being in Aristotle," *Proceedings of the Aristotelian Society*, 101: 185–207.

Berto, Francesco. 2013. *Existence as a Real Property: The Ontology of Meinongianism*, Springer Publishing.

Beyssade, Jean-Marie. 1992. "The Idea of God and Proofs of His Existence," in *The Cambridge Companion to Descartes*, Cambridge University Press, 174–99.

Bigelow, John. 1996. "Presentism and Properties," *Philosophical Perspectives* 10: 35–52.

Bird, Alexander. 2005. "Explanation and Metaphysics," *Synthese* 143: 89–107.

Bird, Graham. 2000. "Review of *Kantian Humility: Our Ignorance of Things in Themselves* by Rae Langton," *Philosophical Quarterly* 50.198: 105–8.

Blanchette, Oliva. 1999. "Suárez and the Latent Essentialism of Heidegger's Fundamental Ontology," *Review of Metaphysics* 53.1: 3–19.

Bliss, Ricki. 2013. "Viciousness and the Structure of Reality," *Philosophical Studies* 166.2: 399–418.

Bliss, Ricki. 2014. "Viciousness and Circles of Ground," *Metaphilosophy* 45.2: 245–56.

Bliss, Ricki and Kelly Trogdon. 2014. "Metaphysical Grounding," in *Stanford Encyclopedia of Philosophy* (winter 2014 ed.), https://plato.stanford.edu/archives/win2014/entries/grounding/.

Bobik, Joseph. 1965. "Introduction to Aquinas on Being and Essence," in Aquinas (1965).

Bolyard, Charles. 2013. "Accidents in Scotus's *Metaphysics* Commentary," in Bolyard and Keele (2013).

Bolyard, Charles and Rondo Keele (eds.). 2013. *Later Medieval Metaphysics: Ontology, Language, and Logic*, Fordham University Press.

Bolzano, Bernard. 2014a. *Theory of Science, vol. I*, trans. Paul Rusnock and Rolf George, Oxford University Press.

Bolzano, Bernard. 2014b. *Theory of Science, vol. II*, trans. Paul Rusnock and Rolf George, Oxford University Press.

Bolzano, Bernard. 2014c. *Theory of Science, vol. III*, trans. Paul Rusnock and Rolf George, Oxford University Press.

Bolzano, Bernard. 2014d. *Theory of Science, vol. IV*, trans. Paul Rusnock and Rolf George, Oxford University Press.

Boolos, George. 1984. "To Be Is To Be a Value of a Variable (or to Be Some Values of Some Variables)," *Journal of Philosophy* 81: 430–50.

Boolos, George. 1985. "Nominalist Platonism," *Philosophical Review* 94: 327–44.

Bosanquet, Bernard. 1897. "In What Sense, if Any, Do Past and Future Times Exist?" *Mind* 6.22: 228–31.

Bosanquet, Bernard, A. S. Pringle–Pattison, G. F. Stout, and Lord Haldane. 1917–18. "Symposium: Do Finite Individuals Possess a Substantive or an Adjectival Mode of Being?" *Proceedings of the Aristotelian Society New Series* 18: 479–581.

Bourne, Craig. 2002. "When Am I? A Tense Time for Some Tense Theorists?" *Australasian Journal of Philosophy* 80.3: 359–71.

Braddon-Mitchell, David. 2004. "How Do We Know It is Now Now?" *Analysis* 64.3:199–203.

Bradley, F. H. 1914. *Essays on Truth and Reality*, Clarendon Press.

Bradley, F. H. 1930. *Appearance and Reality (9th ed.)*, Oxford University Press.

Brentano, Franz. 1966. *The True and the Evident*, Routledge & Kegan Paul.

Brentano, Franz. 1969. *The Origin of Our Knowledge of Right and Wrong*, Routledge & Kegan Paul.

Brentano, Franz. 1973. *The Foundation and Construction of Ethics*, Routledge & Kegan Paul.

Brentano, Franz. 1978. *Aristotle and His World View*, University of California Press.

Brentano, Franz. 1981a. *On the Several Senses of Being in Aristotle*, University of California Press.

Brentano, Franz. 1981b. *The Theory of Categories*, Martinus Nijhoff Publishers.

Brentano, Franz. 1988. *Philosophical Investigations on Space, Time and the Continuum*, trans. Barry Smith, Routledge & Kegan Paul.

Bricker, Phillip. 2001. "Island Universes and the Analysis of Modality," in Gerhard Preyer and Frank Siebelt, eds., *Reality and Humean Supervenience: Essays on the Philosophy of David Lewis*, Rowman & Littlefield, 27–55.

Bricker, Phillip. 2006. "Absolute Actuality and the Plurality of Worlds," *Philosophical Perspectives* 20: 41–76.

Brogaard, Berit and Joe Salerno. 2013. "Remarks on Counterpossibles," *Synthese* 190: 639–60.

Brough, John. 1975. "Husserl on Memory," *The Monist* 59.1: 40–62.

Broughton, Janet and John Carriero. 2011. *A Companion to Descartes*, Blackwell.

Brower, Jeffrey. 2005. "Medieval Theories of Relations," in *Stanford Encyclopedia of Philosophy*, https://plato.stanford.edu/entries/relations-medieval/.

Brower, Jeffrey. 2008. "Making Sense of Divine Simplicity," *Faith and Philosophy* 25: 3–30.

Brower, Jeffrey. 2009. "Simplicity and Aseity," in *The Oxford Handbook of Philosophical Theology*, ed. Michael Rea and Thomas Flint, Oxford University Press.

Brower, Jeffrey. 2014. *Aquinas's Ontology of the Material World: Change, Hylomorphism, and Material Objects*, Oxford University Press.

Brown, Deborah. 2011. "Descartes on True and False Ideas," in Broughton and Carriero (2011).

Brueckner, Anthony. 1998. "Conceptual Relativism," *Pacific Philosophical Quarterly* 79.4: 295–301.

Burger, Ronna. 1987. "Is Each Thing the Same as Its Essence?: On 'Metaphysics' Z.6-11," *Review of Metaphysics* 41.1: 53–76.

Burrell, David. 1973. *Analogy and Philosophical Language*, Yale University Press.

Burton, David. 1999. *Emptiness Appraised: a Critical Study of Nāgārjuna's Philosophy*, Curzon Press.

Calkins, Mary Whiton. 1927. *The Persistent Problems of Philosophy: an Introduction to Metaphysics through the Study of Modern Systems (5th ed.)*, Macmillan Company.

Cameron, Margaret. 2014. "Is Grounding Said-in-Many-Ways?," *Studia Philosophica Estonica* 7.2: 29–55.

Cameron, Ross. 2008. "Truthmakers and Ontological Commitment: or How to Deal with Complex Objects and Mathematical Ontology without Getting into Trouble," *Philosophical Studies* 140.1: 1–18.

Cameron, Ross. 2010. "How to Have a Radically Minimal Ontology," *Philosophical Studies* 51: 249–64

Cameron, Ross. 2011. "Truthmaking for Presentists," *Oxford Studies in Metaphysics* 6: 55–100.

Cameron, Ross. 2015. *The Moving Spotlight*, Oxford University Press.

Caplan, Ben. 2007. "Millian Descriptivism," *Philosophical Studies* 133.2: 181–98.

Caplan, Ben. 2011. "Ontological Superpluralism," *Philosophical Perspectives* 25.1: 79–114.

Caputo, John. 1982. *Heidegger and Aquinas: an Essay on Overcoming Metaphysics*, Fordham University Press.

Carman, Taylor. 2003. *Heidegger's Analytic*, Cambridge University Press.

Carman, Taylor. 2013. "The Question of Being," in Wrathall (2013).

Canteñs, Bernard. 2003. "Suárez on Beings of Reason: What Kind of Being (*entia*) are Beings of Reason, and What Kind of Being (*esse*) Do they Have?," *American Catholic Philosophical Quarterly* 77: 171–87.

Carnap, Rudolph. 1956. "Empiricism, Semantics, and Ontology," in *Meaning and Necessity: A Study in Semantics and Modal Logic*. University of Chicago Press.

Carrara, Massimiliano and Achille Varzi. 2001. "Ontological Commitment and Reconstructivism," *Erkenntnis* 55.1: 33–50.

Casati, Roberto and Achille Varzi. 1994. *Holes and other Superficialities*, MIT Press.

Casati, Roberto and Achille Varzi. 2004. "Counting the Holes," *Australasian Journal of Philosophy*, 82.1: 23–7.

Chalmers, David. 1997. *The Conscious Mind: In Search of a Fundamental Theory*, Oxford University Press.

Chalmers, David, David Manley, and Ryan Wasserman (eds.). 2009. *Metametaphysics: New Essays on the Foundations of Ontology*, Oxford University Press.

Chang, Ruth. 2002. "The Possibility of Parity," *Ethics* 112: 659–88.

Chappell, Vere. 2011. "Descartes on Substance," in Broughton and Carriero (2011).

Charles, David. 2000. *Aristotle on Meaning and Essence*, Oxford University Press.

Chisholm, Roderick. 1960. *Realism and the Background of Phenomenology*, Free Press.

Chisholm, Roderick. 1996. *A Realistic Theory of Categories: An Essay on Ontology*, Cambridge University Press.

Cocchiarella, Nino. 1969. "Existence Entailing Attributes, Modes of Copulation, and Modes of Being in Second Order Logic," *Noûs* 3.1: 33–48.

Cockburn, David. 1997. *Other Times*, Cambridge University Press.

Coffey, Peter. 1938. *Ontology or the Theory of Being: An Introduction to General Metaphysics*, Peter Smith.

Cohen, S. Marc. 2009. "Substances," in Anagnostopoulos (2009).

Conti, Allessandro. 2014a. "Giles of Rome's Questions on the *Metaphysics*," in Amerini and Galluzzo (2014a).

Conti, Allessandro. 2014b. "Paul of Venice's Commentary on the *Metaphysics*," in Amerini and Galluzzo (2014a).

Coombs, Jeffrey. 1993. "The Possibility of Created Entities in Seventeenth-Century Scotism," *Philosophical Quarterly* 43.173: 447–59.

Corkum, Phillip. 2009. "Aristotle on Nonsubstantial Individuals," *Ancient Philosophy* 29: 289–310.

Correia, Fabrice. 2006. "Generic Essence, Objectual Essence, and Modality," *Noûs* 40.4: 753–67.

Correia, Fabrice. 2013. "Metaphysical Grounds and Essence," in *Varieties of Dependence: Ontological Dependence, Grounding, Supervenience, Response-Dependence*, ed. M. Hoeltje, B. Schniederm, and A. Steinberg, Philosophia Verlag.

Correia, Fabrice and Benjamin Schneider (eds.). 2012. *Metaphysical Grounding: Understanding the Structure of Reality*, Cambridge University Press.

Cover, J. A. and John Hawthorne. 1996. "Free Agency and Materialism," in *Faith, Freedom, and Rationality: Philosophy of Religion Today*, ed. Jeff Jordan and Daniel Howard-Snyder, Rowman & Littlefield.

Cowling, Sam. 2013a. "The Modal View of Essence," *Canadian Journal of Philosophy* 43: 248–66.

Cowling, Sam. 2013b. "Ideological Parsimony," *Synthese* 190: 889–908.

Crisp, Thomas. 2007. "Presentism and the Grounding Objection," *Noûs* 41:1 90–109.

Cross, Richard. 1999. *Duns Scotus*, Oxford University Press.

Cunning, David (ed.). 2014a. *The Cambridge Companion to Descartes' Meditations*, Cambridge University Press.

Cunning, David. 2014b. "Descartes' Modal Metaphysics," in *Stanford Encyclopedia of Philosophy*, https://plato.stanford.edu/entries/descartes–modal/.

Cunningham, F. A. 1970. "Richard of Middleton, O.F.M. On Esse and Essence," *Franciscan Studies* 30: 49–76.

Curley, E. M. 1978. *Descartes Against the Skeptics*, Harvard University Press.

Daly, Chris. 2012. "Skepticism about Grounding." In Correia, F. and B. Schnieder (2012).

Dancy, Russell. 1986. "Aristotle and Existence," in Knuuttila and Hintikka (1986).

Dasgupta, Shamik. 2014. "On the Plurality of Grounds," *Philosophers' Imprint* 14.20: 1–28.

Dasgupta, Shamik. 2015. "The Possibility of Physicalism," *Journal of Philosophy* 111.9: 557–92.

Dasgupta, Shamik. 2016. "Metaphysical Rationalism," *Noûs* 50:2: 379–418.

Davies, Brian (ed.). 2002. *Thomas Aquinas: Contemporary Philosophical Perspectives*, Oxford University Press.

Davies, Brian (ed.). 2006a. *Aquinas's Summa Theologiae: Critical Essays,* Rowman & Littlefield.

Davies, Brian. 2006b. "Aquinas on What God Is Not," in Davies (2006a).

Della Rocca, Michael. 2012. "Violations of the Principle of Sufficient Reason (in Leibniz and Spinoza)," in Correia and Schneider (2012).

Denise, Theodore C. 1964. "Review of Ways of Being: Elements of Analytic Ontology by Herbert W. Schneider," *Philosophical Review* 73: 122–4.

De Raeymaeker, Louis. 1957. *The Philosophy of Being: a Synthesis of Metaphysics*, trans. Edmund Ziegelmeyer, B. Herder Book Co.

deRosset, Louis. 2010. "Getting Priority Straight," *Philosophical Studies*, 149: 73–97.

deRosset, Louis. 2013. "Grounding Explanations," *Philosophers' Imprint*, 13: 1–26.

Descartes, Rene. 1991a. *The Philosophical Writings of Descartes vol. II*, trans. John Cottingham, Robert Stoothoff, and Reginald Murdoch, Cambridge University Press.

Descartes, Rene. 1991b. *The Philosophical Writings of Descartes vol. III: the Correspondence*, trans. John Cottingham, Robert Stoothoff, Dugald Murdoch, and Anthony Kenny, Cambridge University Press.

Descartes, Rene. 1992. *The Philosophical Writings of Descartes vol. I*, trans. John Cottingham, Robert Stoothoff, and Reginald Murdoch, Cambridge University Press.

Doepke, Fred. 1982. "Spatially Coinciding Objects," *Ratio* 24: 45–60.

Donati, Silvia. 2006. "Giles of Rome," in Gracia and Noone (2006).

Donati, Silvia. 2014. "English Commentaries Before Scotus: a Case Study: the Discussion on the Unity of Being," in Amerini and Galluzzo (2014a).

Doney, Willis. 1993. "Did Caterus Misunderstand Descartes's Ontological Proof?" in *Essays on The Philosophy and Science of Rene Descartes*, ed. Stephen Voss, Oxford University Press.

Donnelly, Maureen. 2011. "Using Mereological Principles to Support Metaphysics," *Philosophical Quarterly* 61.243: 225–46.

Dorr, Cian. 2008. "There are No Abstract Objects," in *Contemporary Debates in Metaphysics*, ed. John Hawthorne, Theodore Sider, and Dean Zimmerman, Blackwell.

Doyle, John. 2005. "Introduction to Suarez's *On Beings of Reason: Metaphysical Disputation LIV*," in Suarez (2005).

Doyle, John. 1967. "Suarez on the Reality of the Possibles," *Modern Schoolman* 44: 29–48.

Dreyfus, Hubert. 1994. *Being-in-the-World: A Commentary on Heidegger's Being and Time, Division I*, MIT Press.

Druart, Thérèse-Anne. 2005. "Metaphysics," in Adamson and Taylor (2005).

Dummett, Michael. 1991. *Frege: Philosophy of Mathematics*, Harvard University Press.

Dunn, J. Michael. 1990. "Relevant Predication 3: Essential Properties," in *Truth or Consequences*, ed. J. Michael Dunn and Anil Gupta, Kluwer Academic Publishers.

Eddon, Maya. 2013. "Fundamental Properties of Fundamental Properties," *Oxford Studies in Metaphysics* 8: 78–104.

Ehring, Doug. 1997. "Lewis, Temporary Intrinsics, and Momentary Tropes," *Analysis* 57: 254–8.

Ehring, Doug. 2011. *Tropes: Properties, Objects, and Mental Causation*, Oxford University Press.

Eklund, Matti. 2006. "Metaontology," *Philosophy Compass*, 1.3: 317–34.

El-Bizri, Nader. 2001. "Avicenna and Essentialism," *Review of Metaphysics* 54.4: 753–78.

Ellis, Brian. 2002. *The Philosophy of Nature: a Guide to the New Essentialism*, McGill-Queen's University Press.

Embry, Brian. 2015. "Truth and Truthmakers in Early Modern Scholasticism," *Journal of the American Philosophical Association* 1.2: 196–216.

Evnine, Simon. 2009. "Constitution and Qua Objects in the Ontology of Music," *British Journal of Aesthetics* 49.3: 203–17.

Falkenstein, Lorne. 1995. *Kant's Intuitionism: a Commentary on the Transcendental Aesthetic*, University of Toronto Press.

Fenner, Peter. 1990. *The Ontology of the Middle Way*, Kluwer Academic Publishers.

Feser, Edward (ed.). 2013. *Aristotle on Method and Metaphysics*, Palgrave Macmillan.

Field, Hartry. 1973. "Theory Change and The Indeterminacy of Reference," *Journal of Philosophy* 70. 14: 462–81.

Findlay, J. N. 1933. *Meinong's Theory of Objects and Values*, Oxford University Press.

Fine, Kit. 1994a. "Essence and Modality," *Philosophical Perspectives* 8: 1–16.

Fine, Kit. 1994b. "Compounds and Aggregates," *Noûs* 28: 137–58.

Fine, Kit. 1995a. "Ontological Dependence," *Proceedings of the Aristotelian Society* 95: 269–90.

Fine, Kit. 1995b. "Senses of Essence," in *Modality, Morality, and Belief: Essays in Honor of Ruth Barcan Marcus*, ed. Walter Sinnott-Armstrong, Diana Raffman, and Nicholas Asher, Cambridge University Press.

Fine, Kit. 2000. "A Counter–Example to Locke's Thesis," *The Monist* 83: 357–61.

Fine, Kit. 2001. "The Question of Realism," *Philosophers Imprint* 1.1: 1–31, http://hdl.handle.net/2027/spo.3521354.0001.002.

Fine, Kit. 2006. "The Reality of Tense," *Synthese* 150: 399–414.

Fine, Kit. 2012a. "Guide to Ground," in Correia and Schneider (2012).

Fine, Kit. 2012b. "What is Metaphysics" in Tahko (2012).

Forrest, Peter. 2001. "Counting the Cost of Modal Realism," in Preyer and Siebelt (2001).

Forrest, Peter. 2004. "The Real But Dead Past: a Reply to Braddon–Mitchell," *Analysis* 64: 358–62.

Frede, Dorothy. 1993. "The Question of Being: Heidegger's Project," in Guignon (1993).

Frede, Michael. 1987. *Essays in Ancient Philosophy*, Oxford University Press.

Frege, Gottlob. 1979. *Posthumous Writings*, Blackwell.

Frege, Gottlob. 1980a. *The Foundations of Arithmetic*, trans. J. L. Austin, Blackwell.

Frege, Gottlob. 1980b. *Translations from the Philosophical Writings of Gottlob Frege*, 3rd ed., trans. Peter Geach and Max Black, Rowman & Littlefield.

Friedman, Russell L. 2014. "Peter Auriol," *Stanford Encyclopedia of Philosophy* (spring 2014 ed.), https://plato.stanford.edu/archives/spr2014/entries/auriol/.

Friedman, Russell L. 2015. "Act, Species, and Appearance: Peter Auriol on Intellectual Cognition and Consciousness," in *Intentionality, Cognition, and Mental Representation in Medieval Philosophy*, ed. Gyula Klima, Fordham University Press: 141–65.

Frost, Gloria. 2007. "Thomas Aquinas on Truths about Nonbeings," *Proceedings of the American Catholic Philosophical Association* 80: 101–13.

Frost, Gloria. 2010. "Thomas Aquinas on the Perpetual Truth of Essential Propositions," *History of Philosophy Quarterly* 27.3: 197–213.

Gajendragadkar, Veena. 1988. *Kanāda's Doctrine of the Padārthas, i.e., the Categories*, Sri Satguru Publications.

Gallois, André. 2004. "Comments on Ted Sider: Four Dimensionalism," *Philosophy and Phenomenological Research* 68.3: 648–57.

Galluzzo, Gabriele. 2013. *The Medieval Reception of Book Zeta of Aristotle's Metaphysics vol. I*, Brill Publishing.

Galluzzo, Gabriele. 2014. "Aquinas's Commentary on the Metaphysics," in Amerini and Galluzzo (2014a).

Garfield, Jay. 2002. *Empty Words: Buddhist Philosophy and Cross-Cultural Interpretation*, Oxford University Press.

Garfield, Jay. 2015. *Engaging Buddhism: Why It Matters to Philosophy*, Oxford University Press.

Geach, Peter. 1969. *God and the Soul*, London: Routledge & Kegan Paul.

Geach, Peter. 1980. *Logic Matters*, University of California Press.

Geach, Peter. 2006. "Form and Existence," in Davies (2006a).

Gewirth, Alan. 1998. "Clearness and Distinctness in Descartes," in *Descartes*, ed. John Cottingham, Oxford University Press.

Gibson, Quentin. 1998. *The Existence Principle*, Springer.

Giles of Rome. 1953. *Theorems on Existence and Essence*, trans. Michael Murray, Marquette University Press.

Gilmore, Cody. 2007. "Time Travel, Coinciding Objects, and Persistence," *Oxford Studies in Metaphysics* 3: 177–200.

Gilson, Etienne. 1952. *Being and Some Philosophers, 2nd ed.*, Pontifical Institute of Mediaeval Studies.

Goodman, Nelson. 1955. *Fact, Fiction, Forecast*, Harvard University Press.

Gorman, Michael. 1993. "Ontological Priority and John Duns Scotus," *Philosophical Quarterly* 43: 460–71.

Gorman, Michael. 2005. "The Essential and the Accidental," *Ratio* 18: 276–89.

Gorman, Michael. 2014a. "Two Types of Features: An Aristotelian Approach," *Ratio* 27: 140–54.

Gorman, Michael. 2014b. "Essentiality as Foundationality," in Novotný and Novák (2014).

Gracia, Jorge and Timothy Noone. 2006. *A Companion to Philosophy in the Middle Ages*, Blackwell.

Gracia, Jorge and Daniel Novotný. 2012. "Fundamentals in Suarez's Metaphysics: Transcendentals and Categories," in Schwartz (2012a).

Gronding, Jean. 2005. "Why Awaken the Question of Being?" in Polt (2005).

Grossman, Reinhardt. 1973. *Ontological Reduction*, Indiana University Press.

Guignon, Charles. 1997. "Heidegger, Martin," in Kim and Sosa (1997).

Guigon, Charles. 1993. *The Cambridge Companion to Heidegger*, Cambridge University Press.

Guyer, Paul. 1987. *Kant and the Claims of Knowledge*, Cambridge University Press.

Haack, Susan. 1978. *Philosophy of Logics*, Cambridge University Press.

Haaparanta, Leila and Heikki Koskinen (eds.). 2012. *Categories of Being: Essays on Metaphysics and Logic*, Oxford University Press.

Haldane, John. 2007. "Privative Causality," *Analysis* 67.295: 180–6.

Hankinson, R. J. 2009. "Causes," in Anagnostopoulos (2009).

Haslanger, Sally. 1989. "Endurance and Temporary Intrinsics," *Analysis* 49: 119–25.

Haslanger, Sally. 2003. "Persistence through Time," in *The Oxford Handbook of Metaphysics*, ed. Michael Loux and Dean Zimmerman, Oxford University Press.

Haugeland, John. 2000. "Truth and Finitude: Heidegger's Transcendental Existentialism," in Wrathall and Malpas (2000a).

Haugeland, John. 2013. *Dasein Disclosed: John Haugeland's Heidegger*, ed. Joseph Rouse, Harvard University Press.

Hawthorne, John. 2006. "Quantity in Lewisian Metaphysics," in *Metaphysical Essays*, Oxford University Press.

Hawthorne, John and Theodore Sider. 2002. "Locations," *Philosophical Topics* 30: 53–76.

Heathwood, Chris. 2005. "The Real Price of the Dead Past," *Analysis* 65.3: 249–51.

Heathwood, Chris. 2011. "The Relevance of Kant's Objection to Anselm's Ontological Argument," *Religious Studies* 47: 345–57.

Heidegger, Martin. 1962. *Being and Time*, trans. John Macquarrie and Edward Robinson, Harper & Row.

Heidegger, Martin. 1984. *The Metaphysical Foundations of Logic*, trans. Michael Heim, Indiana University Press.

Heidegger, Martin. 1988. *Basic Problems of Phenomenology*, trans. Albert Hofsadter, Indiana University Press.

Heidegger, Martin. 1992. *History of the Concept of Time, Prolegomena*, trans. Theodore Kisel, Indiana University Press.

Heidegger, Martin. 1993. *Basic Writings, rev. and expanded edn*, ed. David Farell Krell, HarperCollins Publishers.

Heller, Mark. 1998. "Property Counterparts in Ersatz Worlds," *Journal of Philosophy* 95.6: 293–316.

Hinchliff, Mark. 1988. *A Defense of Presentism*, dissertation, Princeton University.

Hinchliff, Mark. 1996. "The Puzzle of Change," *Philosophical Perspectives* 10: 119–36.

Hintikka, Jaakko. 1986. "The Varieties of Being in Aristotle," in Knuuttila and Hintikka (1986).

Hirsch, Eli. 1997a. "Basic Objects: a Reply to Xu," *Mind and Language* 12.3–4: 406–12.

Hirsch, Eli. 1997b. "Complex Kinds," *Philosophical Papers* 26.1: 47–70.

Hirsch, Eli. 2002a. "Quantifier Variance and Realism," *Philosophical Issues* 12: 51–73.

Hirsch, Eli. 2002b. "Against Revisionary Ontology," *Philosophical Topics* 30: 103–27.

Hirsch, Eli. 2005. "Physical-Object Ontology, Verbal Disputes, and Common Sense," *Philosophy and Phenomenological Research* 70.1: 67–97.

Hochschild, Joshua. 2010. *The Semantics of Analogy: Reading Cajetan's De Nominum Analogia*, University of Notre Dame Press.

Hoffman, Joshua. 2012. "Neo–Aristotelianism and Substance," in Tahko (2012).

Hoffman, Paul. 2011. "The Union of the Mind and Body," in Broughton and Carriero (2011).

Hofweber, Thomas. 2009. "Ambitious, Yet Modest, Metaphysics," in Chalmers, Manley, and Wasserman (2009).

Holden, Thomas. 2007. *The Architecture of Matter: Galileo to Kant*, Oxford University Press.

Home, Henry/Lord Kames. 2000. *Essays on the Principles of Morality and Natural Religion*, in *Early Responses to Hume's Metaphysics and Epistemology*, vol. I, ed. James Fieser, Thoemmes Press.

Hudson, Hud. 2001. *A Materialist Metaphysics of the Human Person*, Cornell University Press.

Hudson, Hud. 2005. *The Metaphysics of Hyperspace*, Oxford University Press.

Hughes, Christopher. 1989. *On a Complex Theory of a Simple God*, Cornell University Press.

Hull, David. 1999. "On the Plurality of Species: Questioning the Party Line," in Wilson (1999).

Hume, David. 1958. *A Treatise on Human Nature*, ed. L. A. Selby-Bigge, Oxford University Press.

Husserl, Edmund. 1969. *Formal and Transcendental Logic*, trans. Dorion Cairns, Martinus Nijhoff Publishers.

Husserl, Edmund. 1973. *Experience and Judgment*, trans. James S. Churchill and Karl Ameriks, Northwestern University Press.

Husserl, Edmund. 1983. *Ideas pertaining to a Pure Phenomenology and to a Phenomenological Philosophy: First Book*, trans. F. Kersten, Martinus Nijhoff Publishers.

Husserl, Edmund. 1991. *On the Phenomenology of the Consciousness of Internal Time (1893-1917)*, trans. John Barnett Brough, Kluwer Academic Publishing.

Husserl, Edmund. 2005a. *Logical Investigations, vol. I*, trans. J. N. Findlay, Routledge Publishing.

Husserl, Edmund. 2005b. *Logical Investigations, vol. II*, trans. J. N. Findlay, Routledge Publishing.

Ibn Rushd (Averroes). 1984. *Ibn Rushd's Metaphysics: a Translation with Introduction of the Commentary on Aristotle's Metaphysics Book Lām*, trans. Charles Genequand, Brill Publishing.

Inwood, Michael. 1999. *A Heidegger Dictionary*, Blackwell.

Jacobs, Jonathan. 2015. "The Ineffable, Inconceivable, and Incomprehensible God: Fundamentality and Apophatic Theology," in *Oxford Studies in Philosophy of Religion*, Oxford University Press.

Jacquette, Dale. 2001. "*Aussersein* of the Pure Object," in Albertazzi, Liliana, Dale Jacquette, and Roberto Poli (2001).

Javier-Castellanos, Amir Arturo. 2014. "Some Challenges to a Contrastive Treatment of Grounding," *Thought: A Journal of Philosophy* 3.3: 184–92.

Jenkins, Carrie. 2011. "Is Metaphysical Grounding Irreflexive?" *The Monist* 94.2: 267–76.

Kahn, Charles. 1986. "Retrospect on the Verb 'To Be' and the Concept of Being," in Knuuttila and Hintikka (1986).

Kant, Immanuel. 1999a. *Critique of Pure Reason*, trans. Paul Guyer and Allen W. Wood, Cambridge University Press.

Kant, Immanuel. 1999b. *Practical Philosophy*, trans. and ed. Mary J. Gregor, Cambridge University Press.

Kant, Immanuel. 2001. *Lectures on Metaphysics*, Cambridge University Press.

Kaufman, Dan. 2003. "Divine Simplicity and the Eternal Truths in Descartes," *British Journal for the History of Philosophy* 11.4: 553–79.

Keil, Frank. 1979. *Semantic and Conceptual Development: an Ontological Perspective*, Harvard University Press.

Keller, Simon. 2004. "Presentism and Truthmaking," *Oxford Studies in Metaphysics* 1: 83–104.

Kenny, Anthony. 1969. *Aquinas: a Collection of Critical Essays*, Macmillan Company.

Kenny, Anthony. 1995. *Frege: an Introduction to the Founder of Modern Analytic Philosophy*, Penguin Books.

Kenny, Anthony. 2005a. *Aquinas on Being*, Oxford University Press.

Kenny, Anthony. 2005b. *Medieval Philosophy, a New History of Western Philosophy*, vol. II, Oxford University Press.

Kim, Jaegwon and Ernest Sosa. 1997. *A Companion to Metaphysics*, Blackwell.

King, Peter. 2001. "Duns Scotus on Possibilities, Powers, and the Possible," in *Potentialität und Possibilität: Modalaussagen in der Geschichte der Metaphysik*, ed. Thomas Buchheim, Corneille Henri Kneepkens, and Kuno Lorenz, Frommann-Holzboog Verlag: 175–99.

Kisiel, Theodore. 1993. *The Genesis of Heidegger's Being and Time*, University of California Press.

Kleinschmidt, Shieva. 2007. "Some Things about Stuff," *Philosophical Studies* 135.3: 407–23.

Klima, Gyula. 1993. "The Changing Role of Entia Rationis in Mediaeval Semantics and Ontology," *Synthese* 96.1: 25–59.

Klima, Gyula. 2013. "Being, Unity, and Identity in the Fregean and Aristotelian Traditions," in Feser (2013).

Klima, Gyula. 2014. "Being and Cognition," in Novotný and Novák (2014).

Klubertanz, George P. 1957. "The Problem of the Analogy of Being," *Review of Metaphysics*, 10.4: 553–79.

Knuuttila, Simo. 2012. "The Metaphysics of the Categories in John Duns Scotus," in Haaparanta and Koskinen (2012).

Knuuttila, Simo and Jaakko Hintikka (eds.). 1986. *The Logic of Being: Historical Studies*, D. Reidel.

Koistinen, Olli. 2014. "The Fifth Meditation: Externality and True and Immutable Natures," in Cunning (2014).

Kok, Femke. 2014. "John Buridan's Commentary on the *Metaphysics*," in Amerini and Galluzzo (2014a).

Korman, Daniel. 2015. "Fundamental Quantification and the Language of the Ontology Room," *Noûs* 49.2: 298–321.

Koslicki, Kathrin. 2012a. "Essence, Necessity, and Explanation," in Tahko (2012).

Koslicki, Kathrin. 2012b. "Varieties of Ontological Dependence," in Correia and Schneider (2012).

Koslicki, Kathrin. 2013. "Substance, Independence, and Unity," in Feser (2013).

Koslicki, Kathrin. 2015. "The Coarse-Grainedness of Grounding," *Oxford Studies in Metaphysics* 9: 306–44.

Kretzmann, Norman, Anthony Kenny, and Jan Pinborg (eds.). 2000. *The Cambridge History of Later Medieval Philosophy*, Cambridge University Press.

Kukkonen, Taneli. 2012. "Dividing Being Before and After Avicenna," in Haaparanta and Koskinen (2012).

Langer, Susanne. 1930. *The Practice of Philosophy*, Henry Holt and Company.

Langer, Susanne. 1933. "Facts: the Logical Perspectives of the World," *Journal of Philosophy* 30.7: 178–87.

Langton, Rae. 1998. *Kantian Humility: Our Ignorance of Things in Themselves*, Oxford University Press.

Laumakis, Stephen. 2008. *An Introduction to Buddhist Philosophy*, Cambridge University Press.

Laycock, Henry. 2006. *Words without Objects*, Oxford University Press.

Leibniz, Gottfried. 1989. *Philosophical Essays*, ed. Roger Ariew and Daniel Garber, Hackett Publishing Company.

Lewis, David. 1983a. "New Work for a Theory of Universals," *Australasian Journal of Philosophy* 61: 343–77; reprinted in Lewis (1999).

Lewis, David. 1983b. *Philosophical Papers vol. I*, Oxford University Press.

Lewis, David. 1984. "Putnam's Paradox," *Australasian Journal of Philosophy* 62: 221–36; reprinted in Lewis (1999).

Lewis, David. 1986. *On the Plurality of Worlds*, Blackwell.

Lewis, David. 1991. *Parts of Classes*, Blackwell.

Lewis, David. 1999. *Papers in Metaphysics and Epistemology*, Cambridge University Press.

Lewis, David. 2001. "Truthmaking and Difference–Making," *Noûs* 35: 602–15.

Lewis, David. 2004. "Tensed Quantifiers," *Oxford Studies in Metaphysics* 1: 3–14.

Lewis, David and Stephanie Lewis. 1970. "Holes," *Australasian Journal of Philosophy* 48: 206–12; reprinted in Lewis (1983).

Lewis, David and Stephanie Lewis. 1996. "Casati and Varzi on Holes," *Philosophical Review* 105: 77–9; reprinted in Lewis (1999).

Locke, John. 1979. *An Essay Concerning Human Understanding*, Oxford University Press.

Lotze, Hermann. 1884. *Lotze's System of Philosophy Part I: Logic*, trans. Bernard Bosanquet, Clarendon Press.

Lotze, Hermann. 1887. *Lotze's System of Philosophy Part II: Metaphysic, vol. I*, trans. Bernard Bosanquet, Clarendon Press.

Loux, Michael. 2012. "Being, Categories, and Universal Reference in Aristotle," in Haaparanta and Koskinen (2012).

Lowe, E. J. 2004. "Some Formal Ontological Relations," *Dialectica* 58.3: 297–316.

Lowe, E. J. 2006. *The Four-Category Ontology: A Metaphysical Foundation for Natural Science*, Oxford University Press.

Lowe, E. J. 2008. "Two Notions of Being: Entity and Essence," *Being: Developments of Contemporary Metaphysics, Royal Institute of Philosophy Supplement*, ed. Robin Le Poidevin 62: 23–48.

Lowe, E. J. 2009. "An Essentialist Approach to Truth–Making," in Lowe and Rami (2009).

Lowe, E. J. 2013. "Neo-Aristotelian Metaphysics: a Brief Exposition and Defense," in Feser (2013).

Lowe, E. J. and A. Rami (eds.). 2009. *Truth and Truth-Making*, McGill-Queen's University Press.

Lukasiewicz, Jan. 1967. "On Determinism," in *Polish Logic 1920–1939*, ed. Storrs McCall, Oxford University Press.

Lycan, William. 1994. *Modality and Meaning*, Kluwer Academic Publishers.

MacBride, Fraser. 1999. "Could Armstrong have been a Universal?" *Mind* 108: 471–501.

McCabe, Herbert. 1969. "Categories," in Kenny (1969).

McDaniel, Kris. 2003. "Against MaxCon Simples," *Australasian Journal of Philosophy* 81.2: 265–75.

McDaniel, Kris. 2004. "Modal Realism with Overlap," in *Lewisian Themes*, ed. Frank Jackson and Graham Priest, Oxford University Press.

McDaniel, Kris. 2006a. "Gunky Objects in a Simple World," *Philo* 9.1: 47–54.

McDaniel, Kris. 2006b. "Modal Realisms," *Philosophical Perspectives* 20: 303–31.

McDaniel, Kris. 2007. "Extended Simples," *Philosophical Studies* 133.1: 131–41.

McDaniel, Kris. 2008. "Against Composition as Identity," *Analysis* 68.2: 128–33.

McDaniel, Kris. 2009a. "Structure-Making," *Australasian Journal of Philosophy* 87.2: 251–74.

McDaniel, Kris. 2009b. "Ways of Being," in Chalmers, Manley, and Wasserman (2009).

McDaniel, Kris. 2009c. "Extended Simples and Qualitative Heterogeneity," *Philosophical Quarterly* 59.235: 325–31.

McDaniel, Kris. 2009d. "John M. E. McTaggart," in *Stanford Encyclopedia of Philosophy* (spring 2015 ed.), https://plato.stanford.edu/archives/spr2015/entries/mctaggart/.

McDaniel, Kris. 2010a. "A Return to the Analogy of Being," *Philosophy and Phenomenological Research* 81.3: 688–717.

McDaniel, Kris. 2010b. "Being and Almost Nothingness," *Noûs* 44.4: 628–49.

McDaniel, Kris. 2010c. "Parts and Wholes," *Philosophy Compass* 5.5: 412–25.

McDaniel, Kris. 2013a. "Existence and Number," *Analytic Philosophy* 54.2: 209–28.

McDaniel, Kris. 2013b. "Degrees of Being," *Philosophers' Imprint* 13.19: 1–18.

McDaniel, Kris. 2013c. "Heidegger's Metaphysics of Material Beings," *Philosophy and Phenomenological Research* 86.1: 332–57.

McDaniel, Kris. 2013d. "Ontological Pluralism, the Gradation of Being, and the Question 'Why Is There Something Rather than Nothing?'" in *The Puzzle of Existence: Why Is There Something Rather Than Nothing?* ed. Tyron Goldschmidt, Routledge.

McDaniel, Kris. 2014a. "Compositional Pluralism and Composition as Identity," in *Composition as Identity*, ed. A. J. Cotnoir and Donald Baxter, Oxford University Press.

McDaniel, Kris. 2014b. "Metaphysics, History, Phenomenology," *Res Philosophica* 91.3: 339–65.

McDaniel, Kris. 2014c. "A Moorean View of the Value of Lives," *Pacific Philosophical Quarterly* 95: 23–46.

McDaniel, Kris. 2015. "Propositions: Individuation and Invirtuation," *Australasian Journal of Philosophy* 93.4: 757–68.

McDaniel, Kris. Forthcoming-a. "A Philosophical Model of the Relation between Things-in-Themselves and Appearances," *Noûs*.

McDaniel, Kris. Forthcoming-b. "Heidegger and the 'There Is' of Being," *Philosophy and Phenomenological Research*.

McDaniel, Kris. Forthcoming-c: "The Idealism of Mary Whiton Calkins," in *Idealism: New Essays in Metaphysics*, ed. Tyron Goldschmidt and Kenny Pearce, Oxford University Press.

McDaniel, Kris. ms-1. "Kantian Ignorance."

McDaniel, Kris. ms-2. "Ontology and Philosophical Methodology in the Early Susanne Langer."

McDermott, A. C. Senape. 1969. *An Eleventh-Century Buddhist Logic of "Exists": Ratnakīrti's Kṣaṇabhaṅgasiddhiḥ Vyatirekātmikā*, D. Reidel.

MacDonald, Scott. 2002. "The *Esse/Essentia* Argument in Aquinas's *De Ente et Essentia*," in Davies (2002).

McGinn, Colin. 2000. *Logical Properties: Identity, Existence, Predication, Necessity, Truth*, Clarendon Press.

McGrade, A. S. 2005. *The Cambridge Companion to Medieval Philosophy*, Cambridge University Press.

McInerney, Peter K. 1991. *Time and Experience*, Temple University Press.

McInerny, Ralph. 1961. *The Logic of Analogy: an Interpretation of St. Thomas*, Martinus Nijhoff Publishers.

McInerny, Ralph. 1996. *Aquinas and Analogy*, Catholic University of America Press.

McKay, Thomas. 2006. *Plural Predication*, Oxford University Press.

McManus, Denis. 2013. "Ontological Pluralism and the *Being and Time* Project," *Journal of the History of Philosophy* 51.4: 651–73.

McTaggart, J. M. E. 1927a. *The Nature of Existence*, vol. I, Cambridge University Press.

McTaggart, J. M. E. 1927b. *The Nature of Existence*, vol. II, Cambridge University Press.

McTaggart, J. M. E. 1996. *Philosophical Studies*, St. Augustine's Press.

Mackie, Penelope. 2006. *How Things Might Have Been: Individuals, Kinds, and Essential Properties*, Oxford University Press.

Magee, William. 1999. *The Nature of Things: Emptiness and Essence in the Geluk World*, Snow Lion Publications.

Magidor, Ofra. 2013. *Category Mistakes*, Oxford University Press.

Mander, W. J. 2011. *British Idealism: a History*, Oxford University Press.

Mares, Edwin. 2004. *Relevant Logic: a Philosophical Introduction*, Cambridge University Press.

Markosian, Ned. 1998. "Simples," *Australasian Journal of Philosophy* 76: 213–26.

Markosian, Ned. 2002. "Time," in *Stanford Encyclopedia of Philosophy*, https://plato.stanford.edu/entries/time/.

Markosian, Ned. 2004a. "Simples, Stuff, and Simple People," *The Monist* 87: 405–28.

Markosian, Ned. 2004b. "A Defense of Presentism," *Oxford Studies in Metaphysics* 1: 47–82.

Marrone, Steven P. 1988. "Henry of Ghent and Duns Scotus on the Knowledge of Being," *Speculum* 63.1: 22–57.

Marvin, Walter. 1912. *A First Book in Metaphysics*, Macmillan Company.

Marx, Werner. 1977. *Introduction to Aristotle's Theory of Being as Being*, Martinus Nijhoff Publishers.

Matilal, Bimal Krishna. 1982. "Ontological Problems in Nyāya, Buddhism, and Jainism: A Comparative Analysis," in Morewedge (1982).

Matsen, Herbert Stanley. 1974. *Alessandro Achillini (1463–1512) and His Doctrine of "Universals" and "Transcendentals": a Study in Renaissance Ockhamism*, Bucknell University Press.

Matthews, Gareth. 1971. "Dualism and Solecism," *Philosophical Review* 80.1: 85–95.

Matthews, Gareth. 1972. "Senses and Kinds," *Journal of Philosophy* 69: 149–57.

Matthews, Gareth. 1982. "Accidental Unities." In *Language and Logos*, ed. M. Schofield and M. Nussbaum, Cambridge University Press.

Matthews, Gareth. 1992. "On Knowing How to Take Aristotle's Kooky Objects Seriously," presented at the Pacific Division Meeting of the APA, Portland.

Matthews, Gareth. 2009. "Aristotelian Categories," in Anagnostopoulos (2009).

Maurin, Anna-Sofia. 2013. "Exemplification as Explanation," *Axiomathes* 23: 401–17.

Meinong, Alexius. 1904. "On the Theory of Objects," in Chisholm (1960).

Meinong, Alexius. 1983. *On Assumptions*, University of California Press.

Mellor, D. H. 1981. *Real Time*, Cambridge University Press.

Mellor, D. H. 1995. *The Facts of Causation*, Routledge.

Mellor, D. H. 1998. *Real Time II*, Routledge.

Mellor, D. H. 2003. "Replies," in *Real Metaphysics*, ed. Hallvard Lillehammer and Gonzalo Rodriguez-Pereyra, Routledge.

Menn, Stephen. 2005. "God and Being," in McGrade (2005).

Merleau-Ponty, Maurice. 2000. *Phenomenology of Perception*, trans. Colin Smith, Routledge.

Merricks, Trenton. 2003. *Objects and Persons*, Oxford University Press.

Merricks, Trenton. 2006. "Good–Bye Growing Block," *Oxford Studies in Metaphysics* 2: 103–10.

Merricks, Trenton. 2007. *Truth and Ontology*, Oxford University Press.

Merrill, G. H. 1980. "The Model-Theoretic Argument against Realism," *Philosophy of Science* 47.1: 69–81.

Midtgarden, Torjus. 2012. "Charles S. Peirce: Pragmatism, Logic, and Metaphysics," in Haaparanta and Koskinen (2012).

Mill, J. S. 1936. *A System of Logic*, Longmans, Green and Co.

Miller, Barry. 2002. *The Fullness of Being*, University of Notre Dame Press.

Mohanty, J. N. and W. McKenna (eds.). 1989. *Husserl's Phenomenology: a Textbook*, University Press of America.

Moore, A. W. 2012. *The Evolution of Modern Metaphysics: Making Sense of Things*, Cambridge University Press.

Moore, G. E. 1969. *Some Main Problems of Philosophy*, 5th edn, George Allen & Unwin.

Moore, G. E. 1993. *Principia Ethica*, rev. edn, ed. Thomas Baldwin, Cambridge University Press.

Moore, Jared Sparks. 1927. *Rifts of the Universe: A Study of the Historic Dichotomies and Modalities of Being*, Yale University Press.

Morewedge, Parviz. 1972. "Philosophical Analysis and Ibn Sīnā's 'Essence-Existence' Distinction," *Journal of the American Oriental Society* 92.3: 425–35.

Morewedge, Parviz (ed.). 1982. *Philosophies of Existence: Ancient and Medieval*, Fordham University Press.

Mou, Bo. 2013. "On Daoist Approach to the Issue of Being In Engaging Quinean and Heideggerian Approaches," in Mao and Tieszen (2013).

Mou, Bo and Richard Tieszen (eds.). 2013. *Constructive Engagement of Analytic and Continental Approaches in Philosophy: From the Vantage Point of Comparative Philosophy*, Brill Publishing.

Mulhall, Stephen. 1996. *Heidegger and Being in Time*, Routledge Publishing.

Mulligan, Kevin. 2006a. "Ascent, Propositions, and other Formal Objects," *Grazer Philosophische Studien* 72: 29–48.

Mulligan, Kevin. 2006b. "Facts, Formal Objects and Ontology," in *Modes of Existence. Papers in Ontology and Philosophical Logic* ed. A. Bottani and R. Davies, Ontos Verlag.

Mulligan, Kevin. 2009. "Truth and the Truth–Maker Principle in 1921," in Lowe and Rami (2009).

Mulligan, Kevin. 2010. "The Truth Predicate vs. the Truth Connective: On Taking Connectives Seriously," *Dialectica* 64.4: 565–84.

Mundy, Brent. 1987. "The Metaphysics of Quantity," *Philosophical Studies* 51: 29–54.

Nāgārjuna. 2010. *The Dispeller of Disputes*, trans. with commentary Jan Westerhoff, Oxford University Press.

Nāgārjuna. 2013. *Nāgārjuna's Midddle Way*, trans. with commentary Mark Siderits and Shōryū Katsura, Wisdom Publications.

Nagel, Thomas. 1983. "The Objective Self," in *Knowledge and Mind*, ed. Carl Ginet and Sidney Shoemaker, Oxford University Press.

Nakhnikian, George and Wesley C. Salmon. 1957. "'Exists' as a Predicate," *Philosophical Review* 66.4: 535–42.

Napper, Elizabeth. 1989. *Dependent-Arising and Emptiness*, Wisdom Press.

Nolan, Daniel. 1996. "Recombination Unbound," *Philosophical Studies* 84.2–3: 239–62.

Nolan, Daniel. 1997. "Impossible Worlds: a Modest Approach," *Notre Dame Journal of Formal Logic* 38: 535–72.

Nolan, Daniel. 2007. "Contemporary Metaphysicians and Their Traditions," *Philosophical Topics* 35:1 & 2: 1–18.

Nolan, Daniel. 2011. "Categories and Ontological Dependence," *The Monist* 94.2: 277–301.

Nolan, Daniel. 2013. "Impossible worlds. Philosophy," *Philosophy Compass* 8: 360–72.

Nolan, Lawrence. 2015. "Descartes' Ontological Argument," in *Stanford Encyclopedia of Philosophy*, https://plato.stanford.edu/entries/descartes-ontological/.

Nolt, John. 2014. "Free Logic," in *Stanford Encyclopedia of Philosophy*, https://plato.stanford.edu/entries/logic-free/.

Normore, Calvin. 2012. "Ockham on Being," in Haaparanta and Koskinen (2012).

Norton, Bryan. 1977. *Linguistic Frameworks and Ontology: a Re-Examination of Carnap's Metaphilosophy*, Mouton Publishers.

Novotný, Daniel D. and Lukáš Novák (eds.). 2014. *Neo-Aristotelian Perspectives in Metaphysics*, Routledge Publishing.

O'Connor, Timothy. 2000. *Persons and Causes: the Metaphysics of Free Will*, Oxford University Press.

O'Connor, Timothy. 2014. "Free Will and Metaphysics," in *Libertarian Free Will: Contemporary Debates*, ed. David Palmer, Oxford University Press.

Oderberg, David. 2007. *Real Essentialism*, Routledge Publishing.

Oderberg, David. 2014. "Is Form Structure?" in Novotný and Novák (2014).

Okrent, Mark. 1988. *Heidegger's Pragmatism*, Cornell University Press.

Owen, G. E. L. 1986. *Logic, Science, and Dialectic: Collected Papers in Greek Philosophy*, ed. Martha Nussbaum, Cornell University Press.

Parsons, Josh. 2007. "Theories of Location," *Oxford Studies in Metaphysics* 3: 201–32.

Parsons, Terence. 1980. *Nonexistent Objects*, Yale University Press.

Pascal, Blaise. 1995. *Pensées*, trans. A.J. Krailsheimer, Penguin Books.

Pasnau, Robert. 2011. *Metaphysical Themes: 1274–1672*, Oxford University Press.

Pasnau, Robert and Christopher Shields. 2004. *The Philosophy of Aquinas*, Westview Press.

Paul, L. A. 2010a. "A New Role for Experimental Work in Metaphysics," *European Review on Philosophy and Psychology* 1.3: 461–76.

Paul, L. A. 2010b. "Temporal Experience," *Journal of Philosophy* 107.7: 333–59.

Paul, L. A. 2012. "Metaphysics as Modeling: the Handmaiden's Tale," *Philosophical Studies* 160.1: 1–29.

Paul, L. A. 2013. "Categorical Priority and Categorical Collapse," *Aristotelian Society Supplementary Volume* 87.1: 89–113.

Paul, L. A. 2017. "A One Category Ontology," in *Being, Freedom, and Method: Themes from the Philosophy of Peter van Inwagen*, ed. John Keller, Oxford University Press.

Peramatzis, Michail. 2011. *Priority in Aristotle's Metaphysics*, Oxford University Press.

Pereboom, Derk. 1991. "Is Kant"s Transcendental Philosophy Inconsistent?" *History of Philosophy Quarterly* 8: 357–72.

Pereboom, Derk. 2006. "Kant on Transcendental Freedom," *Philosophy and Phenomenological Research* 73: 537–67.

Pereboom, Derk. 2011. *Consciousness and the Prospects of Physicalism*, Oxford University Press.

Pereira, José. 2007. *Suárez: Between Scholasticism & Modernity*, Marquette University Press.

Perszyk, Kenneth. 1993. *Nonexistent Objects: Meinong and Contemporary Philosophy*, Kluwer Academic Publishers.

Peters, Stanley and Dag Westerståhl. 2006. *Quantifiers in Logic and Language*, Oxford University Press.

Pfänder, Alexander. 2009. *Logic*, trans. Donald Ferrari, Ontos Verlag.

Philipse, Herman. 1998. *Heidegger's Philosophy of Being*, Princeton University Press.

Pini, Giorgio. 2005. "Scotus's Realist Conception of the Categories: His Legacy to Late Medieval Debates," *Vivarium* 43.1: 63–110.

Plato. 1978. *Plato: The Collected Dialogues*, ed. Edith Hamilton and Huntington Cairns, Princeton University Press.

Poli, Roberto. 1993. "Husserl's Conception of Formal Ontology," *History and Philosophy of Logic* 14.1: 1–14.

Polt, Richard. 1999. *Heidegger: an Introduction*, Cornell University Press.

Polt, Richard (ed.). 2005. *Heidegger's Being and Time: Critical Essays*, Rowman & Littlefield.

Potter, Karl (ed.). 1977. *Indian Metaphysics and Epistemology: the Tradition of Nyāya-Vaiśesika up to Gaṅgeśa*, Princeton University Press.

Preyer, Gerhard and Frank Siebelt (eds.). 2001. *Reality and Humean Supervenience: Essays on the Philosophy of David Lewis*, Rowman & Littlefield.

Priest, Graham. 2004a. "What's So Bad about Contradictions?" in Priest et al. (2004).

Priest, Graham. 2004b. "Paraconsistent Logic," in *Stanford Encyclopedia of Philosophy*, https://plato.stanford.edu/entries/logic-paraconsistent/.

Priest, Graham. 2006. *In Contradiction, 2nd ed.*, Oxford University Press.

Priest, Graham, J.C. Beall, and Bradley Armour-Garb (eds.). 2004. *The Law of Non-Contradiction: New Philosophical Essays*, Oxford University Press.

Priest, Graham and Richard Routley. 1989a. "First Historical Introduction: A Preliminary History of Paraconsistent and Dialethic Approaches," in Priest, Routley, and Norman (1989).

Priest, Graham and Richard Routley. 1989b. "The Philosophical Significance and Inevitability of Paraconsistency," in Priest, Routley, and Norman (1989).

Priest, Graham, Richard Routley, and Jean Norman (eds.). 1989. *Paraconsistent Logic: Essays on the Inconsistent*, Philosophia Verlag.

Prior, A. N. 1970. "The Notion of the Present," *Studium Generale* 23: 245–8.

Puntel, Lorenz. 2002. "The Concept of Ontological Category: a New Approach," in *The Blackwell Guide to Metaphysics*, ed. Richard Gale, Blackwell Publishing.

Putnam, Hilary. 1987. *The Many Faces of Realism: the Paul Carus Lectures*. La Salle, Illinois: Open Court Publishing Company.

Quine, W. V. O. 1951. "Ontology and Ideology," *Philosophical Studies* 2: 11–15.

Quine, W. V. O. 1963. "On What There Is," in *From a Logical Point of View: Nine Logico-Philosophical Essays*, Harper & Row.

Quine, W. V. O. 1969a. "Speaking of Objects," in *Ontological Relativity and Other Essays*, Columbia University Press.

Quine, W. V. O. 1969b. "Existence and Quantification," in *Ontological Relativity and Other Essays*, Columbia University Press.

Quine, W. V. O. 1970. *Philosophy of Logic*, Prentice-Hall Publishing.

Quine, W. V. O. 1976. *Word and Object*, MIT Press.

Rashdall, Hastings. 1902. "Personality, Human and Divine," in *Personal Idealism: Philosophical Essays by Eight Members of the University of Oxford*, ed. Henry Sturt, Macmillan Company.

Rashdall, Hastings. 1924. *The Theory of Good and Evil, vol. II*, 2nd ed., Oxford University Press.

Raven, Michael. 2012. "In Defence of Ground," *Australasian Journal of Philosophy* 90.4: 687–701.

Raven, Michael. 2016. "Fundamentality without Foundations," *Philosophy and Phenomenological Research* 93.3: 607–26.

Rayo, Agustin and Gabriel Uzquiano. 2007. *Absolute Generality*, Oxford University Press.

Reinach, Adolf. 1982. "On the Theory of Negative Judgment," in Smith (1982).

Rescher, Nicholas. 2014. "Non-Existence and Non-Existents" in Novotný and Novák (2014).

Robinson, Richard. 1950. *Definition*, Oxford University Press.

Rosen, Gideon. 2010. "Metaphysical Dependence: Grounding and Reduction," in *Modality: Metaphysics, Logic, and Epistemology*, ed. Ben Hale and Aviv Hoffman, Oxford University Press.

Rosen, Gideon and Cian Dorr. 2003. "Composition as a Fiction," in *The Blackwell Companion to Metaphysics*, ed. Richard Gale, Blackwell.

Rosenkrantz, Gary. 2012. "Ontological Categories," in Tahko (2012).

Ross, W. D. 1924. "Commentary on Aristotle's *Metaphysics*," in Aristotle (1924).

Russell, Bertrand. 1915. "On the Experience of Time," *The Monist* 25: 212–33.

Russell, Bertrand. 1964. *Principles of Mathematics*, W. W. Norton and Company.

Russell, Bertrand. 1971. *Logic and Knowledge: Essays 1901–1950*, Capricorn Books.

Russell, Bertrand. 1973. *Essays in Analysis*, George Braziller.

Russell, Bertrand. 1997. *The Problems of Philosophy*, Oxford University Press.

Ryle, Gilbert. 1945. *Philosophical Arguments*, Oxford University Press.

Ryle, Gilbert. 1949. *The Concept of Mind*, University of Chicago Press.

Ryle, Gilbert. 1971. *Collected Essays: Collected Papers vol. II 1929–1968*, Barnes & Noble.

Safranski, Rüdiger. 1998. *Martin Heidegger, Between Good and Evil*, Harvard University Press.

Salmon, Nathan. 2005. *Metaphysics, Mathematics, and Meaning*, Oxford University Press.

Saucedo, Raul. 2011. "Parthood and Location," *Oxford Studies in Metaphysics* 6.

Schaffer, Jonathan. 2007a. "From Nihilism to Monism," *Australasian Journal of Philosophy* 85: 175–91.

Schaffer, Jonathan. 2007b. "Monism," in *Stanford Encyclopedia of Philosophy*, https://plato.stanford.edu/entries/monism.

Schaffer, Jonathan. 2009. "On What Grounds What," in *Metametaphysics: New Essays on the Foundations of Ontology*, ed. David Chalmers, David Manley, and Ryan Wasserman, Oxford University Press.

Schaffer, Jonathan. 2010a. "Monism: the Priority of the Whole," *Philosophical Review* 119.1: 31–76.

Schaffer, Jonathan. 2010b. "The Least Discerning and Most Promiscuous Truth Maker," *Philosophical Quarterly* 60: 307–24.

Schaffer, Jonathan. 2012. "Grounding, Transitivity, and Constrastivity," in *Metaphysical Grounding: Understanding the Structure of Reality*, ed. Fabrice Correia and Benjamin Schneider, Cambridge University Press.

Schiffer, Stephen. 2003. *The Things We Mean*, Oxford University Press.

Schmaltz, Tad. 2014. "The Fifth Meditation: Descartes' Doctrine of True and Immutable Natures," in Cunning (2014).

Schwartz, Daniel (ed.). 2012a. *Interpreting Suarez*, Cambridge University Press.

Schwartz, Daniel. 2012b. "Introduction," in Schwartz (2012a).

Scotus, John Duns. 1962. *Philosophical Writings*, trans. Allan Wolter, Library of Liberal Arts.

Secada, Jorge. 2000. *Cartesian Metaphysics*, Cambridge University Press.

Shalkowski, Scott. 2008. "Essence and Being," *Being: Developments in Contemporary Metaphysics, the Royal Institute of Philosophy Supplement*, ed. Robin Le Poidevin 62: 49–63.

Shehadi, Fadlou. 1982. *Metaphysics in Islamic Philosophy*, Caravan Books.

Shields, Christopher. 1999. *Order in Multiplicity: Homonymy in the Philosophy of Aristotle*, Oxford University Press.

Shimony, Abner. 1948. "The Status and Nature of Essences," *Review of Metaphysics* 1.3: 38–79.

Sider, Theodore. 1996. "All the World's a Stage," *Australasian Journal of Philosophy* 74: 433–53.

Sider, Theodore. 1999. "Presentism and Ontological Commitment," *Journal of Philosophy* 96: 325–47.

Sider, Theodore. 2001. *Four-Dimensionalism: an Ontology of Persistence and Time*, Clarendon Press.

Sider, Theodore. 2004. "Replies to Gallois, Hirsch, and Markosian," *Philosophy and Phenomenological Research* 68: 674–87.

Sider, Theodore. 2006. "Quantifiers and Temporal Ontology," *Mind* 115: 75–97.

Sider, Theodore. 2007. "Parthood," *Philosophical Review* 116: 51–91.

Sider, Theodore. 2009. "Ontological Realism," in Chalmers, Manley, and Wasserman (2009).

Sider, Theodore. 2011. *Writing the Book of the World*, Oxford University Press.

Siderits, Mark. 2007. *Buddhism as Philosophy: an Introduction*, Hackett Publishing Company.

Sidgwick, Henry. 1894. "A Dialogue on Time and Common Sense," *Mind* 3.12: 441–8.

Silverman, Allan. 2013. "Grounding, Analogy, and Aristotle's Critique of Plato's Idea of the Good," in Tahko (2013).

Simons, Peter. 1987. *Parts: an Essay in Ontology*, Oxford University Press.

Simons, Peter. 2012a. "To Be and/or Not to Be: the Objects of Meinong and Husserl," in Haaparanta and Koskinen (2012).

Simons, Peter. 2012b. "Four Categories – and More" in Tahko (2012).

Skiles, Alexander. 2015. "Against Grounding Necessitarianism" *Erkenntnis* 80: 717–51.

Skiles, Alexander and Akiko Frischhut. 2013. "Time, Modality, and the Unbearable Lightness of Being," *Thought: a Journal of Philosophy* 2: 264–73.

Skow, Bradford. 2009. "Relativity and the Moving Spotlight," *Journal of Philosophy* 106: 666–78.

Skow, Bradford. 2010. "The Dynamics of Non-Being," *Philosophers' Imprint* 10.1: 1–14.

Skyrms, Brian. 1976. "Possible Worlds, Physics and Metaphysics," *Philosophical Studies* 30.5: 323–32.

Sleigh, Robert. 1990. *Leibniz and Arnaul: a Commentary on Their Correspondence*, Yale University Press.

Smith, Barry (ed.). 1982. *Parts and Moments: Studies in Logic and Formal Ontology*, Philosophia Verlag.

Smith, Barry. 1989. "Logic and Formal Ontology," in Mohanty and McKenna (1989).

Smith, Barry. 1998. "Basic Concepts of Formal Ontology" in *Formal Ontology in Information Systems*, ed. N. Guarino, IOS Press.

Smith, Barry and David Woodruff Smith (eds.). 1995a. *The Cambridge Companion to Husserl*, Cambridge University Press.

Smith, Barry and David Woodruff Smith. 1995b. "Introduction" in Smith and Smith (1995a).

Smith, David Woodruff. 1995. "Mind and Body," in Smith and Smith (1995a).

Smith, David Woodruff. 2004. *Mind World: Essays in Phenomenology and Ontology*, Cambridge University Press.

Smith, Quentin. 2002. "Time and Degrees of Existence: a Theory of 'Degrees Presentism,'" in *Time, Reality, and Experience* ed. Craig Callender, Cambridge University Press.

Solomyak, Olla. 2013. "Actuality and the Amodal Perspective," *Philosophical Studies* 164: 15–40.

Sommers, Fred. 1963. "Types and Ontology," *Philosophical Review* 72: 327–63.

Sommers, Fred. 1965. "Predictability," in *Philosophy in America*, ed. Max Black, Cornell University Press.

Sorensen, Roy. 2008. *Seeing Dark Things: the Philosophy of Shadows*, Oxford University Press.

Sosa, Ernest. 1993. "Putnam's Pragmatic Realism," *Journal of Philosophy* 90: 605–26.

Sosa, Ernest. 1998. "Addendum to 'Putnam's Pragmatic Realism'," in van Inwagen and Zimmerman (1998).

Spencer, Joshua. 2012. "Ways of Being," *Philosophy Compass* 7.12: 910–18.

Spinoza, Baruch. 2002. *The Complete Works*, trans. Samuel Shirley and ed. Michael Morgan, Hackett Publishing Company.

Sprigge, Timothy. 1992. "The Unreality of Time," *Proceedings of the Aristotelian Society* 92: 1–19.

Stang, Nicholas. 2013. "Freedom, Knowledge and Affection: Reply to Hogan," *Kantian Review* 18.01: 99–106.

Stang, Nicholas. 2014. "The Non-Identity of Appearances and Things in Themselves," *Noûs* 48:1: 106–36.

Stebbing, L. Susan. 1917. "The Philosophical Importance of the Verb 'To Be'," *Proceedings of the Aristotelian Society* 18: 582–9.

Stein, Edith. 2002. *Finite and Eternal Being*, trans. Kurt F. Reinhardt, ICS Publications.

Stein, Edith. 2009. *Potency and Act*, trans. Walter Redmond, ICS Publications.

Steward, Steve. 2015. "Ya Shouldn'ta Couldn'ta Wouldn'ta," *Synthese* 192.6: 1909–21.

Stump, Eleonore. 1993. *Reasoned Faith: Essays in Philosophical Theology in Honor of Norman Kretzmann*, Cornell University Press.

Stump, Eleonore. 1999. "Simplicity," in *A Companion to Philosophy of Religion*, ed. Phillip Quinn and Charles Taliaferro, Blackwell.

Suarez, Francisco. 2004. *A Commentary on Aristotle's Metaphysics*, trans. John P. Doyle, Marquette University Press.

Suarez, Francisco. 2005. *On Beings of Reason: Metaphysical Disputation LIV*, trans. John P. Doyle, Marquette University Press.

Szabó, Zoltán Gendler. 2003. "Nominalism," in *The Oxford Handbook of Metaphysics*, ed. M. J. Loux and Dean Zimmerman, Oxford University Press.

Szabó, Zoltán Gendler. 2011. "Bare Quantifiers," *Philosophical Review* 120. 2: 247–83.

Tahko, Tuomas (ed.). 2012. *Contemporary Aristotelian Metaphysics*, Cambridge University Press.

Tahko, Tuomas. 2013. "Metaphysics as the First Philosophy," in Feser (2013).

Tepley, Joshua. 2014. "Properties of Being in Heidegger's Being and Time," *International Journal of Philosophical Studies* 22.3: 461–81.

Thomasson, Amie. 2004. "Categories," in *Stanford Encyclopedia of Philosophy*, https://plato.stanford.edu/entries/categories/.

Thomasson, Amie. 2007. *Ordinary Objects*, Oxford University Press.

Thomasson, Amie. 2015. *Ontology made Easy*, Oxford University Press.

Thomasson, Amie. 2016. "Easy Ontology and its Consequences," in *Meanings and Other Things*, ed. by Gary Ostertag, Oxford University Press.

Tooley, Michael. 1987. *Causation*, Oxford University Press.

Tooley, Michael. 1997. *Time, Tense, and Causation*, Clarendon Press.

Trentman, John A. 2000. "Scholasticism in the Seventeenth Century," in Kretzmann, Kenny, and Pinborg (2000).

Trogdon, Kelly. 2013a. "Grounding: Necessary or Contingent?" *Pacific Philosophical Quarterly* 94: 465–85.

Trogdon, Kelly. 2013b. "An Introduction to Grounding" in *Varieties of Dependence*, ed. M. Hoeltje, B. Schnieder, and A. Steinberg, Philosophia Verlag.

Turner, Jason. 2010. "Ontological Pluralism," *Journal of Philosophy* 107.1: 5–34.

Turner, Jason. 2011. "Ontological Nihilism," *Oxford Studies in Metaphysics* 6: 3–54.

Turner, Jason. 2012. "Logic and Ontological Pluralism," *Journal of Philosophical Logic* 41.2: 419–48.

Turner, Jason. 2014. "Donald Baxter's Composition as Identity," in *Composition as Identity* ed. Aaron J. Cotnoir and Donald M. Baxter, Oxford University Press.

Vallicella, William. 2002. *A Paradigm Theory of Existence: Onto-Theology Vindicated*, Kluwer Academic Press.

Vallicella, William. 2004. "The Moreland-Willard-Lotze Thesis on Being," *Philosophia Christi* 6.1: 27–58.

Vallicella, William. 2014. "Existence: Two Dogmas of Analysis," in Novotný and Novák (2014).

Van Cleve, James. 1999. *Problems from Kant*, Oxford University Press.

van Inwagen, Peter. 1981. "The Doctrine of Arbitrary Undetached Parts," *Pacific Philosophical Quarterly* 62: 123–37.

van Inwagen, Peter. 1990. *Material Beings*, Cornell University Press.

van Inwagen, Peter. 1994. "Composition as Identity," *Philosophical Perspectives* 8: 207–20.

van Inwagen, Peter. 2001a. *Ontology, Identity, and Modality: Essays in Metaphysics*, Cambridge University Press.

van Inwagen, Peter. 2001b. "Meta-Ontology," in *Ontology, Identity, and Modality: Essays in Metaphysics*, Cambridge University Press.

van Inwagen, Peter. 2006. "McGinn on Existence," in *Modes of Existence: Papers in Ontology and Philosophical Logic*, ed. Andrea Bottani and Richard Davies, Ontos Verlag.

van Inwagen, Peter. 2014. *Existence: Essays in Ontology*, Cambridge University Press.

van Inwagen, Peter and Dean Zimmerman (eds.). 1998. *Metaphysics: the Big Questions*, Blackwell.

Varzi, Achille. 2010. "On the Boundary between Material and Formal Ontology Department of Philosophy," *Ontology* 3: 3–8.

von Solodkoff, Tatjana and Richard Woodward. 2013. "Noneism, Ontology, and Fundamentality," *Philosophy and Phenomenological Research* 87.3: 558–83.

Ward, Julie. 2008. *Aristotle on Homonymy: Dialectic and Science*, Cambridge University Press.

Wasserman, Ryan. 2002. "The Standard Objection to the Standard Account," *Philosophical Studies* 111: 197–216.

Wasserman, Ryan. 2003. "The Argument from Temporary Intrinsics," *Australasian Journal of Philosophy* 81: 413–19.

Watkins, Eric (ed. and trans.). 2009. *Kant's Critique of Pure Reason: Background Source Materials*, Cambridge University Press.

Wedin, Michael. 2009. "The Science and Axioms of Being," in Anagnostopoulos (2009).

Weidemann, Hermann. 2002. "The Logic of Being in Thomas Aquinas," in Davies (2002).

Welker, David. 1970. "Existential Statements," *Journal of Philosophy* 67.11: 376–88.

Westerhoff, Jan. 2002. "Defining 'Ontological Category'," *Proceedings of the Aristotelian Society* 102: 337–43.

Westerhoff, Jan. 2003. "The Underdetermination of Typings," *Erkenntnis* 58(3): 379–414.

Westerhoff, Jan. 2004. "The Construction of Ontological Categories," *Australasian Journal of Philosophy* 82(4): 595–620.

Westerhoff, Jan. 2005. *Ontological Categories: Their Nature and Significance*, Oxford University Press.

Westerhoff, Jan. 2009. *Nāgārjuna's Madhyamaka: a Philosophical Introduction*, Oxford University Press.

Westerståhl, Dag. 2011. "Generalized Quantifiers," in *Stanford Encyclopedia of Philosophy*, https://plato.stanford.edu/entries/generalized-quantifiers/.

Wieland, Jan and Erik Weber. 2010. "Metaphysical Explanatory Asymmetries," *Logique & Analyse* 211: 345–65.

Wielockx, R. 2006. "Henry of Ghent," in Gracia and Noone (2006).

Wildman, Nathan. 2013. "Modality, Sparsity, and Essence," *Philosophical Quarterly* 63: 760–82.

Williams, C. J. F. 1981. *What is Existence?*, Oxford University Press.

Williams, C. J. F. 1992. *Being, Identity, and Truth*, Oxford University Press.

Williams, D. C. 1962. "Dispensing with Existence," *Journal of Philosophy* 59.23: 748–62.

Williams, Stephen and David Charles. 2013. "Essence, Modality, and the Master Craftsman," in Feser (2013).

Williamson, Timothy. 1998. "Bare Possibilia," *Erkenntnis* 48: 257–73.

Williamson, Timothy. 1999. "Existence and Contingency," *Proceedings of the Aristotelian Society*, supplemental vol. 73: 181–203.

Williamson, Timothy. 2000. "The Necessary Framework of Objects," *Topoi* 19: 201–8.

Williamson, Timothy. 2001. *Knowledge and Its Limits*, Oxford University Press.

Williamson, Timothy. 2002. "Necessary Existents," in *Logic, Thought and Language*, ed. Anthony O'Hear, Cambridge University Press.

Williamson, Timothy. 2013. *Modal Logic as Metaphysics*, Oxford University Press.

Wilson, Catherine. 2003. *Descartes's Meditations: an Introduction*, Cambridge University Press.

Wilson, Jessica. 2012. "Fundamental Determinables," *Philosophers' Imprint* 12.4: 1–17.

Wilson, Jessica. 2014. "No Work for a Theory of Grounding," *Inquiry* 57.5–6: 535–79.

Wilson, Robert. 1999. *Species: New Interdisciplinary Essays*, MIT Press.

Wippel, John. 1982. "The Relationship between Essence and Existence in Late Thirteenth-Century Thought: Giles of Rome, Henry of Ghent, Godfrey of Fontaines, and James of Viterbo," in Morewedge (1982).

Wippel, John. 2000. "Essence and Existence," in Kretzmann, Kenny, and Pinborg (2000).

Wisnovsky, Robert. 2003. *Avicenna's Metaphysics in Context*, Cornell University Press.

Wisnovsky, Robert. 2005. "Avicenna and the Avicennian Tradition," in Adamson and Taylor (2005).

Witherspoon, Edward. 2002. "Logic and the Inexpressible in Frege and Heidegger," *Journal of the History of Philosophy* 40.1: 89–113.

Witt, Charlotte. 1989. *Substance and Essence in Aristotle: an Interpretation of Metaphysics VII–IX*, Cornell University Press.

Witt, Charlotte. 2003. *Ways of Being: Potentiality and Actuality in Aristotle's Metaphysics*, Cornell University Press.

Wittgenstein, Ludwig. 1966. *Tractatus Logico-Philosophicus*, trans. D.F. Pears and B.F. McGuiness, Routldege and Kegan Paul.

Wrathall, Mark. 2013. *The Cambridge Companion to Heidegger's Being and Time*, Cambridge University Press.

Yablo, Stephen. 1998. "Does Ontology Rest On a Mistake?" *Aristotelian Society Supplementary Vol.* 72.1: 229–83.

Yablo, Stephen. 2002. "Go Figure: A Path Through Fictionalism," *Midwest Studies in Philosophy* 25.1: 72–102.

Yablo, Stephen. 2005. "The Myth of the Seven," in *Fictionalism in Metaphysics*, ed. Mark Kalderon, Oxford University Press.

Yagisawa, Takashi. 1988. "Beyond Possible Worlds," *Philosophical Studies* 53: 175–204.

Yourgrau, Palle. 1993. "The Dead," in *The Metaphysics of Death*, ed. John Martin Fischer, Stanford University Press.

Zalta, Edward N. 1983. *Abstract Objects: An Introduction to Axiomatic Metaphysics*, D. Reidel.

Zangwill, Nick. 2012. "Constitution and Causation," *Metaphysica* 13.1: 1–6.

Zimmerman, Dean. 1997. "Coincident Objects: Could a "Stuff Ontology" Help?" *Analysis* 57: 19–27.

Zimmerman, Dean. 2008. "The Privileged Present: Defending an 'A–theory' of Time," in *Contemporary Debates in Metaphysics*, ed. Theodore Sider, John Hawthorne, and Dean Zimmerman, Blackwell.

Index